Column headers (diagonal): PRESIDENT, SecNav, CHIEF, Na..., CHIEF, Bu..., CHM, AE...

Left-side hierarchy (presidents / officials): TRUMAN — EISENHOWER; MATTHEWS, SHERMAN, CLARK; KIMBALL, FECHTELER, WALLIN, DEAN; ANDERSON, CARNEY, LEGGETT, STRAUSS

Aug	Rickover given responsibility for all AEC zirconium procurement.
8 Aug	Truman authorizes nuclear ship for 1952 ship program, Jan. '55 sea date.
15 Aug	CNO asks BuShips to explore aircraft carrier plant.
Aug	The *Nautilus* prototype (STR Mk I) construction starts.
Jul **1951**	Rickover passed over first time for admiral.
Aug	BuShips signs contracts w/Electric Boat and Westinghouse for *Nautilus*.
Aug	AEC asks Westinghouse to study aircraft carrier plant.
Sep	Rickover starts interviewing line officers for the *Nautilus* crew.
22 Oct	CNO asks BuShips to develop design criteria for high-speed sub.
5 Nov	35 firms invited to bid on zirc. production; no responsive bid received.
13 May **1952**	Carborundum Co. contracts to deliver 200,000lb/yr of zirconium.
14 Jun	Truman lays keel plate for the *Nautilus*.
Jul	Rickover gets Navy medal. SecNav: Most important development.
Jul	Rickover passed over second time for admiral.
Jul	Nuclear aircraft carrier project announced.
Dec	Cadmium control rods fail tests; Rickover picks hafnium.
Dec	BuShips: Don't build aircraft carrier until subs and prototype operate.
12 Dec	Accident at Canada's NRX reactor. Rickover sends teams to help.
Mar **1953**	RADM Wallin testifies to Congress against Rickover promotion.
30 Mar	STR Mk I (*Nautilus* prototype) achieves initial criticality.
31 Mar	AEC (Strauss): Kill nuclear-powered airplane and aircraft carrier projects.
22 Apr	SecDef (Kyes) postpones carrier. Eisenhower says make it civilian.
25 Jun	STR Mk I reaches full power; starts "transatlantic run."
9 Jul	AEC assigns Shippingport civilian power project to Rickover.
27 Jul	**Korean War ends.**
Jul	Rickover made rear admiral.
12 Aug	**USSR tests H-bomb.**
9 Sep	AEC approves Submarine Fleet Reactor (SFR) project.
15 Sep	The *Seawolf* keel laid, to contain GE's sodium-cooled reactor plant.
30 Sep	Navy includes Submarine Fleet Reactor in 1955 shipbuilding program.
9 Oct	Westinghouse contracts with AEC for Shippingport Project.
21 Jan **1954**	The *Nautilus* launched by Mamie Eisenhower.
12 Mar	Ship Design Committee: "Too much emphasis on nuclear power."
18 Mar	Effective date of Duquesne contract as utility for Shippingport plant.
23 Jul	Eisenhower reinstates Large Ship Reactor project.
6 Sep	Eisenhower initiates construction at Shippingport site.
30 Sep	The *Nautilus* commissioned.

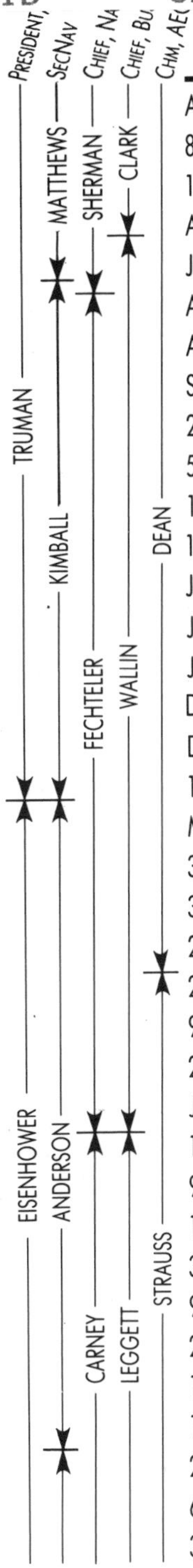

DATE DUE

DATE DUE

The Rickover Effect

THE
RICKOVER EFFECT

How One Man Made a Difference

Theodore Rockwell

NAVAL INSTITUTE PRESS
Annapolis, Maryland

Library of Congress Cataloging-in-Publication Data

Rockwell, Theodore.
    The Rickover effect : how one man made a difference / Theodore
Rockwell.
        p.   cm.
    Includes index.
    ISBN 1-55750-702-3
    1. Rickover, Hyman George.   2. Nuclear submarines—United
    States—History.   3. Admirals—United States—
    Biography.   4. United States.
    Navy—Biography.   I. Title.
    V63.R54R63   1992
    359.3'2574'092—dc20
    [B]   92-3909
                                                                  CIP

Printed in the United States of America on acid-free paper ∞
9   8   7   6   5   4

For Eleonore Rickover, widow of the Admiral. It was she who launched the nuclear attack submarine USS H. G. Rickover with Milton's words: "They also serve who only stand and wait." To her, to his first wife Ruth and their son Robert, and to the spouses and children of all who worked so long and so hard on the Naval Reactors program, I dedicate this book.

Contents

The development of naval nuclear propulsion plants is a good example of how one goes about getting a job done. It is a good subject to study for methods . . . It has involved the establishment of procedures and ways of doing government business for which there was no precedent, and which I believe will be necessary in the future for similar large projects.

H. G. Rickover, address to the
Naval Postgraduate School, 16 March 1954

Preface

THIS IS THE STORY of a man who changed the world. He did most of it in about ten years, by the sheer force of his will and his wit. He did it in the 1950s, when many people would have you believe nobody was doing anything. And he did it as a low-level government bureaucrat, with little power and authority other than what he had created himself.

In 1947 then-Captain Hyman G. Rickover was in Oak Ridge, Tennessee, the home of the atomic bomb, learning the new science and technology that made the release of atomic energy possible, and there he assigned himself the task of building an atomic submarine. By the fall of 1947 he had returned to Washington, where the small group he assembled was broken up and the responsibility for "nuclear matters"—which then meant primarily defense against atomic bombs—was assigned to someone else. But by the end of 1949 he had created a role for himself in the Navy's Bureau of Ships and cognizance within the new Atomic Energy Commission for the development of a nuclear power plant capable of powering a submarine. No such submarine was authorized, and no other nuclear power plants existed, or were even under serious study. The world had not yet felt his impact, but he now had a platform to work from. Then, early in the next decade, he was passed over for promotion and was apparently headed for forced retirement.

During the 1950s Rickover finally prevailed. He was made a three-star admiral and became internationally recognized as the most influential figure in nuclear power. The first atomic submarine, the *Nautilus*, startled the world by running submerged from Pearl Harbor, Hawaii, to England, by way of the North Pole. The *Skate* and her sister ships demonstrated the ability to operate year-round under the polar ice cap and to surface almost at will by breaking through the ice. A new class of high-speed attack submarines headed by the *Skipjack* demonstrated unprecedented military capabilities. The first of a fleet of ballistic missile submarines was commissioned, and the two-reactor submarine *Triton* was about to circle the globe submerged. A series of nuclear-powered surface ships was started, led by the aircraft carrier *Enterprise* and the cruisers *Long Beach* and *Bainbridge*.

More important than the hardware was the broad and deep technological base created by Rickover and his people. No other nuclear power program had made any significant progress, despite a number of "reactor experiments" that generally led nowhere, so Rickover was given the job of building the world's first civilian nuclear power station. He was determined to do this not as an isolated demonstration but with a profusion of unclassified codes and standards, procedures and criteria, handbooks and textbooks, which would form the base of a worldwide enterprise. Whole new industries were set up to produce tonnage lots of zirconium, hafnium, uranium oxide, and other exotic materials previously known only as laboratory curiosities. Totally new types of valves, pumps, heat exchangers, and control systems were developed, which quickly found application in fields as diverse as biomedical research and water treatment plants. New meaning was given to industrial quality control and technical training of personnel. Ultimately, ten thousand officers and sixty thousand enlisted personnel were recruited and trained in Rickover's program, and literally hundreds of thousands of persons in industry felt his personal impact at one time or another.

Providing humanity with a basic new source of energy is an event of overwhelming importance. Energy has always been a key to lifting human life from an endless survival struggle that is "nasty, brutish, and short." The Golden Age of Greece was made possible by a horde of faceless slaves who enabled a handful of intellectuals to create a priceless heritage. Only a few times in our long history has a fundamentally new energy source been given us. The fossil fuels—coal, oil, and gas—made it possible to do without slaves, but these fuels are a finite and polluting resource. Wind, sunlight, and waterpower are renewable but dilute, scattered, and unreliable. The power of the atom, which is the same power that lights the stars and created the planets, is essentially limitless.

Whether one looks approvingly or fearfully at nuclear power, one cannot help but marvel at the impact this man had on the world—the very real world of politics, industry, and technology. Today, when many of us feel helpless and impotent in the face of obstacles that seem to block any significant achievement, we can learn and be inspired by this story.

Americans are quick to give credit to a person who comes up with a new idea. But we are less apt to recognize the importance of the difficult process of implementing an idea, of making it a reality in the world. There is a crucial difference between *ideas* and *accomplishments*, between *science* and *engineering*. The understanding of natural phenomena developed by science enables engineers to envision and create concrete realities. Admiral Rickover did not invent or discover nuclear power, but he made it a reality. It was as an engineer that he was uniquely effective.

Influential figures in history have always inspired books by reporters, professional writers, and historians. But seldom do we get a picture of such persons written "from the inside." In this book I have tried to do just that. It is more a memoir than a history. It presents Admiral Rickover as I saw him close up and continuously, during the program's early fifteen years at his Naval Reactors headquarters, and less frequently during the subsequent twenty-two years until his death—a story that seemed even at the time to be unfolding on some unseen stage. The character of Rickover and the events I describe are presented as accurately as I can recall them, although some of the incidents are compressed to fit the confines of the story. The conversations I relate are not based on tape recordings or even on contemporaneous notes. (Note-taking for this purpose was far from my mind at the time.) But I believe that the basic substance and flavor of the stories are correct. As far as possible, I have checked my account of the incidents with persons involved.

The amount of attention I give various individuals in the book does not represent the importance of that person to the program. I have written primarily about what I saw and experienced—that is, the people I worked with in Rickover's Naval Reactors organization. Yet 90 percent of them are not even mentioned by name, and I am sorry about that. I have given short shrift to the good people of Westinghouse, General Electric, Combustion Engineering, and the shipyards and manufacturers, those who actually carried out the design, fabrication, and installation of this equipment. And I do not do justice to the people of the

Argonne and Oak Ridge laboratories, or to many other heroes unsung whose contributions were vital.

Two groups in particular were crucial: the Supply Corps officers, particularly Vincent A. Lascara, Kenneth L. Woodfin, Mel C. Greer, and Thomas L. "Tim" Foster, whose work behind the scenes arranging money and contractural matters made all the rest of it possible; and the Civil Engineer Corps, who labored at the prototypes and who somehow got it all built. They, and those who followed them, deserve a book of their own, but I am not the one who can write it. In addition, there were a few CEC officers who served with distinction at Naval Reactors headquarters, notably Joseph H. Barker, Jr., who was project officer for the difficult early days of the Shippingport Atomic Power Station.

As I left Naval Reactors, I moved the spotlight of my attention with me, and the reader might thus get the impression that little of importance happened at NR after that. This is, of course, wholly untrue; the program grew ever larger, and new problems, political as well as technical, continued to challenge the best they had. This is an important story, but it is not my story. In fact, I do not even have room to mention many important events and developments that went on while I was there. For a complete and documented history, I refer readers to the official U.S. Atomic Energy Commission histories *Nuclear Navy: 1946–1962* by historians Richard G. Hewlett and Francis Duncan, and *Rickover and the Nuclear Navy* by Duncan, from which I borrowed freely.

The story shows how the general thrust of Rickover's program changed as time went on. Initially, the aim was to build a decisive weapon. Then, as it became clear that this program was to be the means by which nuclear power "for the homes, farms, and factories" was to become a reality, the program emphasized harnessing this basic new source of energy. Later, as industry was brought in to accomplish these goals, it became evident that the program would have to focus on upgrading the quality of American industry. And finally, as the deficiencies of industry were seen to be rooted in basic weaknesses in education and motivation, Rickover found himself on the national bully-pulpit he had created, proclaiming the importance of excellence.

Foreword

THERE HAVE BEEN a number of books written about Admiral Rickover, his accomplishments, his life, his contributions to our society. There are also a number of books in the form of biographies or memoirs wherein authors have described their encounters with him—some not so pleasant. So it is refreshing that Ted Rockwell, who was a key member of the Rickover team during its first fifteen turbulent years, now comes forward to give us an insider's closeup of this very complex individual. His book is not a history. Rather, it is a series of small snapshots taken over a fifteen-year period when the Admiral took an improbable idea and turned it into a reality. The resultant mosaic is as I remember Rickover.

My first encounter with the Admiral was in 1959 when I was selected to enter his nuclear training program for submarine officers. I really did not work closely with him, however, until 1961 upon my return to Washington, where I reported directly to him in his headquarters office and remained in that capacity for nearly four years. The first eighteen-month tryout with him was sheer hell. But then I made the team. How did I know this? . . . Ah, another story in itself. At any rate, the remainder of the tour was productive, action-packed, and educational as Rickover sparked a strengthened sense of professionalism in me to strive to be all that I could be. That association, from 1961 until his death in 1986, grew and developed into a personal as well as a professional relationship. During those twenty-five "autumn years" of his life, I was as close to him as anyone outside his family. To be categorized as "close" to Rickover needs explanation. It means that he would continue to treat me as his pupil, one still worthy of placing demands on his time and energy to help improve me professionally. This never-ending process of educating and training prospective leaders for the Navy was a driving passion in Rickover's life.

But it was during life's closing years that, while he still continued to work seemingly endless hours to ensure the success and betterment of his nuclear programs, he devoted more and more of his energies to addressing broader issues—issues that he had always pursued but that, for a number of reasons, continued to fall on deaf ears nationwide. Remember, he had already achieved his mark in history as the father of the nuclear Navy, Congress had awarded him a gold medal, and he had proved the viability of civilian nuclear power. So with renewed vigor and credentials established, he attacked the educational system in America; he openly criticized the emptiness of government contracting practices while at the same time questioning the basic motives of large government contractors; he cajoled the Navy into rediscovering in its officer corps the value of engineering knowledge to effective warfighting at sea; he hammered away at trying to improve the standards of ethical behavior of professionals—lawyers, doctors, engineers, and others. He continued to champion a hard but nonhysterical approach to protecting the environment and our natural resources, long before the thought even occurred to the public at large. Yet in all his criticisms, he invariably offered constructive remedial approaches to deficient management practices. When he did so, he often projected assured failures should his warnings not be heeded. I seldom found his vision blurred. Take the case of his prediction to me in 1962 that an accident like Three Mile Island would occur within twenty years and the reasons therefor. It occurred seventeen years later, and for the exact reasons he had cited to me.

Did Rickover succeed in all of his teaching endeavors? No, but like all good teachers, he tried hard and left us a good legacy as a result. Thousands of people in America today think differently because they brushed the coattails of this one man. Each of them, because of this man, was pushed a little bit harder; made to think a little bit deeper; forced to develop a little bit better sense of personal responsibility to improve society as a whole.

The cadre of people so affected still range all the way from a lonely seaman to a president of the United States, including their wives, husbands, and children. They continue to affect how this country feels, acts, and thinks. This is the Rickover Effect that Ted Rockwell has so ably brought out in this book.

Few achieve greatness without having their detractors. Rickover had his. Accomplishing his task to build a nuclear fleet required him to move not only in a highly bureaucratic environment but to change the thinking of an organization steeped in tradition, unwilling to accept dramatic changes in the conduct of naval warfare. A number of these individuals with whom Rickover had to deal, most of whom were his seniors at the time, later wrote reminiscences of their encounters with this "irascible old gentleman." While history continues to prove these critics to have been on the wrong side of the professional tracks, the detractors found great joy in highlighting certain trivial, perhaps even socially distasteful, faults as representative of the man. In my opinion, these critics have diminished their own stature and added to that of the Admiral. In spite of them, Rickover and his accomplishments will be remembered long after the passing of his detractors, most of whom won't even make a footnote to history.

Of course, Rickover was a human being just like the rest of us. He made mistakes just as we all do. And what that should tell us is that even while we aren't perfect, we can sure strive to be better, work harder, and achieve some useful purpose in life. That's what he did. That's what most of his students continue to do. And that's what the Rickover Effect is all about.

So I urge you to read this book if you want the real perspective on one of the great American giants of the twentieth century.

James D. Watkins
Admiral, U.S. Navy (Ret.)

Acknowledgments

TO ENSURE THAT the chronology of those busy and complex days is not erroneously portrayed, I have borrowed freely from the histories by Duncan and Hewlett cited in the preface. Dr. Duncan has been kind enough to assist me in checking some of the information, but of course I take full responsibility for the final text. I also referred to Clay Blair, Jr.'s *The Atomic Submarine and Admiral Rickover*, and various articles written at the time, such as Edwin E. Kintner's papers in *Atlantic Monthly* (Jan. 1959) and *American Society of Naval Engineers Journal* (Feb. 1960), and John W. Crawford's paper in the Naval Institute *Proceedings* (Oct. 1987), to help me recall the tone and feeling of those early, long-gone, days. I also found it helpful to review Patrick Tyler's *Running Critical*, and *Nautilus 90 North, Surface at the Pole, Seadragon,* and *Around the World Submerged*, by submarine captains William R. Anderson, James F. Calvert, George P. Steele, and Edward L. Beach, respectively. And, of course, I read *Naval Renaissance* by Frederick Hartmann, *On Watch* by Elmo Zumwalt, and *Command of the Seas* by John Lehman.

Particular thanks to my editor, Mary Yates, and to Connie Buchanan of *Red October* fame for special assistance, and to the good people at the Naval Institute Press, who are proving that all the terrible things authors say about publishers don't *have* to be true.

The following people were sent drafts, or partial drafts, of this book, and many helpful suggestions were incorporated as a result. I am grateful for their assistance. However, since the text changed as a result of each review, none of these people saw the final draft, and I take full responsibility for the text as you see it.

CAPT William R. Anderson, USN (ret.)
CAPT Edward J. Bauser, USN (ret.)
CAPT Edward L. "Ned" Beach, USN (ret.)
VADM James F. Calvert, USN (ret.)
The Honorable Jimmy Carter
Dr. Douglas M. Chapin
CAPT John W. Crawford, Jr., USN (ret.)
CAPT Richard Dobbins, MC, USN (ret.)
Dr. Francis Duncan
CAPT James M. Dunford, USN (ret.)
CDR John C. Dyer, USN (ret.)
CAPT John H. Ebersole, MC, USN (ret.)
Mr. Thomas L. "Tim" Foster
Mr. Donald E. Fry
Mr. Jack C. Grigg
CAPT Edwin E. Kintner, USN (ret.)
CAPT Robert V. Laney, USN (ret.)
CDR David T. Leighton, USNR (ret.)

Mr. I. Harry Mandil
Mr. Howard K. Marks
CDR John Metcalf, USN (ret.)
Mr. Richard Metcalf
CDR Eleonore B. Rickover, USN (ret.)
Ms. Mary C. Rockwell
Robert, Teed, Larry, and Juanita Rockwell
CAPT Louis H. Roddis, Jr., USN (ret.)
Mr. William R. Schmidt
Mr. Carl H. Schmitt
Dr. Glenn T. Seaborg
Mr. Milton Shaw
Frederick, David, and Diana Stork
ADM James D. Watkins, USN (ret.)
CDR William Wegner, USNR (ret.)
Mr. Robert M. Weiner
VADM E. P. "Dennis" Wilkinson,
     USN (ret.)

It is said that a wise man who stands firm is a statesman,
and a foolish man who stands firm is a catastrophe.

H.G.R.

Prologue
The Public Rickover

ON THE STATIONERY of the Joint Congressional Committee on Atomic Energy was a letter inviting me to a ceremony on 15 April 1959, to present a Congressional Gold Medal to Vice Admiral Hyman G. Rickover, USN, "in recognition of his achievements in successfully directing the development and construction of the world's first nuclear powered ships and the first large-scale nuclear power reactor devoted exclusively to production of electricity."

The award was fitting and well deserved. Admiral Rickover was responsible, more than any other person, for bringing nuclear power to the world. Yes, there were Einstein and Fermi and other brilliant scientists who set the stage, but to bring it all to fruition was the accomplishment of Rickover and the engineering team he created—officer and civilian staff at headquarters and at laboratories and shipyards around the world, industrial facilities, research laboratories, training schools, and, in time, several hundred power plants operating flawlessly beneath the Arctic ice, and in the Arabian Sea, and at the world's first civilian atomic power station, which he built at Shippingport, Pennsylvania.

The beautiful new auditorium in the New Senate Office Building was being used for the first time for this occasion. The special facilities for filming and recording activities in this room had not yet been activated, so crude temporary stands were set up for the hordes of photographers and television cameramen who were covering the story. The

1

assemblage of dignitaries was impressive. The entire membership of the prestigious Joint Committee was there, as were Lyndon Johnson, Senate majority leader; Everett Dirksen, minority leader; and other key congressmen including Clarence Cannon, the venerable chairman of the Appropriations Committee. The chairman of the Atomic Energy Commission, the secretary of the Navy, the chief of naval operations, and other naval notables were introduced. Vice President Richard Nixon sent a message congratulating the Admiral, as did Speaker of the House Sam Rayburn, New York Governor Nelson Rockefeller, and others. And there was a private reception in the Old Supreme Court Room of the U.S. Capitol Building after the medal ceremony.

It looked as if the event was being met with universal elation, but I knew better, and so did many others in the room. The timing gave a clue. On 12 August 1958 the first nuclear submarine, the *Nautilus*, astonished the world by surfacing off Portland, England, after sailing submerged from Pearl Harbor via the North Pole. President Dwight Eisenhower invited the ship's captain and a host of dignitaries to the White House to celebrate the event, but the Navy's list of invitees did not include Admiral Rickover. In fact, the Navy had tried more than once to force the Admiral into retirement.

The public uproar over this slight to Admiral Rickover had several consequences. Two days later, on 14 August, twenty-one senators sponsored a bill to award Admiral Rickover a Congressional Gold Medal, and the bill was passed unanimously four days later. On 25 August Admiral Rickover, as official representative of President Eisenhower, welcomed the crew of the *Nautilus* to a traditional New York ticker-tape parade. Meanwhile, a second nuclear submarine, the *Skate*, had surfaced through the ice at the North Pole and radioed her position. By the time Rickover's award ceremony took place, the Navy had yielded to public pressure and promoted him to the rank of vice admiral.

Who was this guy Rickover? With the president, the Congress, the press, and the public idolizing him, why should responsible officials in the Navy want to get rid of him?

A clue to this paradox is revealed in the "Rickover stories" that seem to spring up whenever his name is mentioned. Since ten thousand officers, sixty thousand enlisted personnel, and scores of thousands of government and industrial engineers and officials have been associated with him at one time or another, it is not surprising that such stories are heard frequently, in a wide variety of gatherings. Most people's knowledge of Rickover is based solely on input of this ilk. And a confusing and contradictory input it is. Let me give you a sampling.

Bob Panoff, his submarine project officer, who began working for him in 1942 before he even started the nuclear program, tells this one: "He got a call late one night from one of the submarine skippers. His ship was about to head out on a long, important voyage, and a tiny set screw had fallen down inside the turbine. They had fished for it long and hard but hadn't found it. And time was running out. The next step would be to disassemble the turbine, which was a mammoth job and would delay the voyage. What to do?

"The skipper decided to call Rickover. Design of turbines was not even under Rickover's cognizance. But the skipper knew better than to try to get help on something like this from the head of the turbine section. And, as he had hoped, Rickover had a simple answer: 'At the bottom of the turbine casing you'll find a small inspection plate,' he said. 'It was put there for just such an emergency. Take it off, and you'll find the screw sitting on it. I'll wait,' he said. They did, and it was."

And I could add a Rickover story of my own. He got a letter from some southern military school asking him to provide an inspirational slogan to be engraved onto the silver sword of that year's student battalion commander. The school had them from Douglas MacArthur, Dwight Eisenhower, and everybody back to George Washington, practically. He flung the letter at me to draft a reply and said, "Just make it 'Over the hill, you sons of bitches. I'm bucking for first looey.' " I told him I didn't think that was the sort of inspirational message they had in mind, and he growled, "Well, put it in Latin!"

I didn't know how to say "S.O.B." in Latin, so I went to a good Latin student and we came up with "*Via non trita zaginiis traditionis suffocata est; non timere secare*" ("The untrodden path is choked by the weeds of tradition. Be not afraid to cut through"). He just sent the Latin and left the translation as an exercise for the student.

Jim Dunford, a survivor from the first group of three officers who started with Rickover in 1947 studying nuclear technology in Oak Ridge, Tennessee, says, "I think it's the interviews that most people remember. There are more wild stories about Rickover interviews than about any other aspect of the man. He is determined to get through the glib, rehearsed answers and look at the person underneath. He wants to know how they'll act under stress. He has a lot of creative ways of doing that, in the limited time he has for each interview. One of the commonest stories is that he makes you sit in a chair with the front legs sawed off an inch or two shorter. You don't notice anything consciously, but you keep sort of sliding forward and you're just uncomfortable and off-balance all the time. So you can't concentrate or think straight, and you end up making a complete ass of yourself."

I've seen the famous chair, although I don't recall ever seeing it used in an interview. I remember one reporter stating authoritatively that it had *six inches* sawed off the front legs! That just shows how wild the Rickover stories got. You couldn't begin to sit in a chair with six inches sawed off the front!

Bill Wegner, who used to handle many of Admiral Rickover's personnel matters, says that his favorite interview story is the one about the young officer who was asked, "What do you think is wrong with the Navy?" He answered, "Too much paperwork," and the Admiral asked for a f'rinstance. He explained that his duty was to file reports each month on the use of the base's motorboats: who used them, how often, how much gasoline was used, and so on. "Nobody reads them," said the officer, "but the regs say I have to file them." "What would happen if you just quit turning in the reports?" asked Rickover, and the kid said that the boss's secretary kept a tickler file, and he'd be put on report if he didn't turn one in. So there was nothing he could do.

"Sure there is," said Rickover. "Just pull your tickler card out of the file. It's Friday night. I want to hear first thing Monday morning that you've done that. Just send me a message: TICKLE COMPLETE." It was done, and the officer joined the program.

One we all remember goes like this: Warren Haussler, being interviewed for employment by then-Captain Rickover back in 1953, was led into talking about mountains he had climbed, and Rickover asked him if he could climb Goat Mountain. He said he'd never heard of Goat Mountain, and when the Captain told him it was right nearby, he said he was sure he could climb it. So Rickover said, "If you bring me proof tomorrow morning that you've climbed it, I'll hire you." So Haussler roars out of the office without a word, finds out that Goat Mountain is the concrete mountain peak in the mountain goat cage at the zoo; and he rents a Polaroid camera. He gets to the zoo just before closing time, talks a Japanese tourist into taking his picture, climbs over the fence and up the mountain, and is waiting for the Old Man with his picture-proof at 7:00 A.M. And he's hired!

One of my favorite memories is going with him to visit a new chief of naval operations to pay our respects. That is supposed to be a ritual involving obsequious obeisance and promises of undying fealty, as they say in tales of knighthood. But one time Rickover just asked, "Will you back me?" The Top Admiral, sitting there in all his gold and medals, looked a little startled and said, "I'll back you when you're right, Rick." To which Rickover said, without so much as a smile, "Hell, when I'm right, I don't need your backing."

Jack Grigg, Rickover's instrumentation and controls expert, who also worked for him in his prenuclear days, on hearing this story said, "That's typical of his knack for quick, on-the-spot comebacks. I was with him one time in Scranton, Pennsylvania, when we ran into William Scranton, the former governor, congressman, ambassador, and presidential commissioner, for whose family the city is named. He recognized Rickover and asked, 'What are you doing here?' Without a moment's hesitation the Old Man replied, 'Slumming.' "

Dave Leighton notes that this same blunt Rickover managed to charm Lord Mountbatten and Princess Sofia of Greece. In October 1958, when Leighton was Rickover's project officer for the submarine *Triton* and the cruiser *Bainbridge*, Mountbatten ignored protocol and dropped in to see Rickover, as he usually did when he was in Washington. Rickover addressed his lordship, the earl of Burma, as follows: "While you are here, your hosts will use up your time by sending you to banquets. I'm sure you get enough to eat in England. Why don't you break away for a few hours and let me show you something really interesting?" Without waiting for an answer, Rickover turned to Leighton and asked him to arrange a plane to fly the three of them to the land prototype plant for the *Triton*, and then to the Electric Boat Company shipyard to see nuclear submarines under construction and walk through a full-scale wooden submarine mock-up. Mountbatten was delighted.

The story about Princess Sofia is equally revealing. The princess wanted to see Shippingport (the first commercial atomic power plant, which Rickover had built), and Rickover had arranged for a two-passenger helicopter to take him and the princess on a quick sightseeing flight over Pittsburgh and then on to the plant site. But the princess's aide, a bemedaled Greek general, pulled Rickover aside and explained that Sofia was deathly afraid of flying. "You must tell her that the helicopter is out of order, and we can then drive to the plant."

But Rickover didn't go along. He turned to the princess and said with great seriousness, pointing to the general, "He wants me to lie to you. But I wouldn't lie to a princess. He thinks you are afraid to fly with me. But I know you would never show fear, especially in public. To show fear might jeopardize the whole concept of a female head of state. Since the end of the fifth century, Salic Law has required that monarchs be persons who could lead troops into battle, and only recently have some women been made monarchs. You wouldn't want to set back that great advance." And then he picked her up by the waist, plunked her down in the helicopter seat, jumped into the other seat, pulled one seatbelt across the two of them, and signaled the pilot to take off. He kept her so busy with commentary about the sights that she completely forgot about being afraid.

Some days later we were at the Quincy shipyard outside Boston, when the Admiral remembered that the princess was giving a speech in Boston. He wanted to catch the end of it, and they let us stand backstage in the wings. As she finished her speech, she turned and spotted him standing there. She called him out onto the stage and said to the crowd, "I want you to meet Admiral Rickover, the man who taught the princess not to be afraid."

Jack Crawford, one of the first officers to take the postgraduate course in nuclear engineering that Rickover had initiated at MIT, recalls an early interaction with Rickover. "It wasn't the *first* interview that made such an impression on me," said Crawford. "The one I remember most clearly came right after I had turned in my first trip report. He handed it back to me in the corridor, covered with caustic comments about my writing style. 'How the hell did you ever pass plebe English?' he asked.

"I had won two English awards at the Naval Academy, and I wasn't going to take that lying down. I said something like, 'Captain, writing a report for you is not like writing an essay on Milton.' 'What do you know about Milton?' he asked. 'Can you recall anything he wrote?'

"Now I figured I was on home turf. After all, he was a technocrat, I figured, and I was not. Confidently I started to recite Milton's sonnet on his blindness:

When I consider how my light is spent
Ere half my days in this dark world and wide . . .

I was going great until near the end, but I just couldn't recall the last few lines. Anyway, I figured I had made my point. Rickover just looked at me and picked up where I had left off:

> His state
> Is kingly: thousands at his bidding speed,
> And post o'er land and ocean without rest;
> They also serve who only stand and wait.

I know it all now, but I had gone blank at the time. But Rickover wasn't through. 'I'm going to give you another chance,' he said. 'Pick any poet in the English language and try again.' He had picked up a few spectators in the hall by this time and was thoroughly enjoying himself.

"*Well, he may have lucked out once,* I thought. *But I'll get him this time.* I started the Wordsworth sonnet:

> The world is too much with us late and soon
> Getting and spending, we lay waste our powers . . .

But again I blanked out, just before the end. Rickover looked as me as I mumbled the last line I could remember, slammed his fist into his other hand, and fairly shouted the lines:

> GREAT GOD, I'd rather be
> A pagan suckled in a creed outworn . . .

and finished it off with verve and polish. He then turned and started down the hall, stopped, spun around, and pointed a finger at me: 'That's the trouble with you young guys; you don't think I know anything.'

"I resolved right there never to underestimate him again. But he continued to surprise and infuriate me. He told me once that everybody agreed he had accomplished a miracle, that probably no one else could have done it, yet people complained about how he did it. He asked me, 'Is that reasonable? Should I revise my methods to satisfy the people who admit they couldn't have accomplished what I did?' I had to admit he had a point there. Besides, he did a great many things that showed he was a much more complex and sympathetic character than the public Rickover stories would have you believe. Not many people really know what he was like."

Who was this man, Rickover, and what was he really like? How did he get so much power? Did he earn it? Did he use it wisely? Was he only a "character," or was there a real human being under all the wisecracks and showmanship? What does his story tell us about leadership in today's world?

That's what this book is all about.

Part I

Getting Ready
(1939–1947)

I.

*What it takes to do a job will not be learned from
management courses. It is principally a matter of experience,
the proper attitude, and common sense—none of which can
be taught in a classroom . . . Human experience shows that
people, not organizations or management systems, get things
done.*

H.G.R.

Getting Ready
1939–1947

IT WAS CHRISTMAS vacation, 1943, and I couldn't sleep. I was going
to Oak Ridge, Tennessee, the next morning, to interview for a job as
an engineer. The company representative who had interviewed me at
Princeton had refused to say what the job would entail, or even what
product the company made. It was a highly important war project—
that was all I'd been told. Of course, I took that as a challenge. My
father had business contacts; he'd tell me what it was all about. But my
father came up empty-handed; he had talked with lots of people who
had sold vast quantities of valves, steel, electrical gear, and other equipment of every description to be shipped to Oak Ridge, but nobody had
been able to piece together a picture of what came out of there. It must
be an awfully dinky little town, we figured; it wasn't even on the maps.

FRONTIER LIFE AMONG THE ATOM SPLITTERS

The flight to Knoxville was uneventful. But upon arrival I got my first
indication of the crazy world of Oak Ridge when I and the other job
applicants were escorted to a contraption straight out of the comics: a
'39 Chevy sedan that had been sawed in half and given a metal-and-
plywood insert, resulting in a dachshund-like vehicle that looked as if
it had suddenly applied rear brakes only. Old Fords, Packard Clippers,

and a fairly new '42 Buick had also been maimed this way, and I reluctantly conceded that the result, though awkward, was practical. But the lines of the vehicle were buried in reddish brown mud. Mud covered the entire exterior, dripped from the fenders, clotted under the running boards, and smeared heavy, opaque layers over the windows.

The next hour seemed like preflight training for shooting Niagara Falls in a rotating barrel, as the crazed vehicle lurched blindly over the crater-pocked back roads from Knoxville to Oak Ridge. Suddenly the car slammed to a stop, and the door was opened by an unshaven farmer wearing a khaki uniform marked Auxiliary Military Police. He was armed to the teeth, as were the other three who suddenly appeared and removed the baggage. They searched through it diligently while the first guard scrutinized the driver's papers and the passes of all the passengers. And as suddenly as it had begun, the search was over, and the car lurched forward again. We were now inside the area fence, and we strained to catch a glimpse of the Secret City. But it remained safely hidden behind the mud-coated windows.

Another abrupt stop, and the driver announced, "Person–*nay*ull. All out." A burly armed guard confronted us as we emerged from the vehicle. He had the same insignia as the guard at the gate, but his uniform was slate blue rather than khaki. He scrupulously examined the well-thumbed passes, and when all had been examined, we were escorted into a temporary-looking structure where we were told we would be "cleared" and "processed."

The next two days were a blur of signing papers, being jabbed with hypodermic needles, signing papers, reading the Espionage Act, signing papers, being x-rayed, signing papers, reading papers . . . all in triplicate . . . quadruplicate . . . four different colors . . . three signatures required . . . third door on your right . . . take this to Captain So-and-so, Wing 3 North, second floor . . . just wait here a moment . . . All the people fell into two classes: those already employed, who gave orders, and those being hired, who were confused. Among the former were some locals who were trying to mimic their bureaucratic bosses, but most of them celebrated their heritage, as illustrated by the voice over the loudspeaker asking saucily, "Which one of yew jughaids is next?"

One of the papers I signed allotted me a dormitory room in West Village, a new town springing up about three miles west of Townsite, where I had been processed. My new ID badge had my picture on it and said I was now CEW-TEC 500-8403, address WV-33-154. WV-33 was the thirty-third dormitory in West Village, and 154 was my room number in that dormitory. I could figure that much out.

The trip to West Village introduced me to another unique vehicle, a huge trailer bus. The cab was a typical truck unit, but the trailer was unlike anything I had ever seen, an olive-drab cattle-car sort of structure, with wooden benches and two tiny windows: one up front, looking into the back window of the cab, and one in the single door on the side. There was a cord that was supposed to ring a buzzer in the cab telling the driver to stop at the next stop. I wondered why the flimsy fiber-board inner door panel had been kicked through, but I soon found out. After a mile or two I could see through the little window a cluster of shacks that looked like platform tents, creating the appearance of a Klondike gold miners' camp. A husky fellow passenger with an armful of welding gear pulled the stop cord, got up off the bench, and went over to the door. But the bus didn't even slow down. Clearly, the buzzer wasn't working.

One of the passengers jerked again and again on the cord, while another pounded on the front window to get the driver's attention. The driver looked back, saw the commotion, and slammed on his brakes, threatening to pile all the passengers off the bench and onto the forward wall of the trailer. The welder tried to open the door but it was stuck, and he began kicking it. The driver, convinced that he had now allowed enough time, started up again with a jolt, and the pounding on the door and on the front window intensified. Finally, the door flew open, the welder jumped out of the accelerating trailer, someone pulled the door shut, and the trip to West Village resumed.

There was one more abrupt stop, after which the bus turned, pro-ceeded a short distance, backed up, and turned the other way. Excavation for a new building had apparently begun in the middle of the roadway, and the driver was trying to improvise a new path through the muddy fields. Finally, the bus stopped, and the passengers assured me that this was West Village. A year later I would come to admire the pleasant ambiance created by the graceful curved walks, grass, badminton courts, midget dance pavilions and canteens, and rustic wooden bridges. But now all I could see was an apparently aimless array of wooden buildings, dwarfed by the Gargantuan chunks of red and yellow clay pushed up by bulldozers and front-end loaders.

The mud and dust were an experience all by themselves. I had never before seen a place where you could sink slowly into the albuminous red muck while choking in a thick cloud of heavy yellow dust. I learned that it was standard Oak Ridge etiquette to remove one's shoes before entering a house, and the dormitories usually had a line of people in front of the janitor's sink waiting to wash their shoes under the faucet. Mud was an accepted part of life, and the well-dressed man wore a conservative, well-pressed suit with a heavy layer of mud on the cuffs. The ladies, bless 'em, seemed to float above such earthly contamination, and their eternal spotlessness was one of the inspirations that pulled us sodden males through that first dismal spring.

For two weeks I had been in Oak Ridge and had not seen a work area. There were brightly colored "demountables": red, yellow, and green slices of houses that arrived daily on trucks. There were modernistic "efficiency apartments," which looked like postcard pictures of the boulevard apartments of Rio. There were "A houses" and "B houses," all the way up to "F houses," six different styles of family houses built of two-by-fours and cement-and-asbestos sheeting, with red brick fireplaces. But there was no sign of a factory. I saw buses labeled Y-12, K-25, and X-10, but I was not allowed to board them. I spent my time on The Hill, as the Oak Ridge headquarters area was called, awaiting military clearance. I heard lectures on first aid, plant safety, and Tennessee driving laws and folklore, and saw an occasional archaic Felix or Mickey Mouse cartoon. The roll was called before every class, and a few lucky persons whose clearance was complete were released for work. Then one day I heard my own name called, and a new phase of my life began.

Starting Work in the Secret City

The town and residential areas sparkled with the many-colored ID badges representing the scores of companies that worked on the site. But at Y-12 there was only one. This badge did not admit one to the work area; for that purpose I turned in my plastic badge and was issued a blue cardboard tag with my name, number, and some capital block letters on it. Later I was issued a plastic picture badge with a Roman numeral (showing what level of classified information I was entitled to receive), an Arabic numeral (showing what work phase I was involved with), and several capital letters (showing what fenced-in work areas I could enter). Coupled with my payroll number (which told when I was hired), the badge gave a pretty complete picture of a person's place in the scheme of things, but this badge was worn only inside the additionally secured work zones and was turned in for the "town badge" when one left the plant for the relative freedom of the fenced-in residential area.

The first people to greet me at the plant were the formidable security team of Larry Riordan, as red-headed and Irish as his name, quiet, competent Gene Connor, and smiling Bill Singleton. (I can still see the three of them sitting at their respective posts at the plant entrance, an image startlingly reinforced when I went back about twenty years later and saw all three of them, scarcely touched by the years, in just about the same positions, although at a different and fancier plant entry building.)

Inside the plant site I was taken to the training school, where a remarkable and interesting program unfolded. First, it was clear that they were not going to tell any of us what was being produced at the plant; the product was merely referred to as a "catalyst," and even the point at which it was produced was left vague. Second, all parts of the equipment were given code names or letters.

In addition, as in any plant, slang terms were dreamed up by the workers for everything and anything, and these names were standardized and encouraged. They formed an admirable code system that was painless to learn and to use but extremely difficult for an outsider to figure out. For example, a wedge-shaped piece of carbon was used to "scrape" the stream of uranium-235 ions from the heavier uranium-238 ions in the plasma, and these units were dubbed "shavers." A gang of them, mounted in an assembly, formed a "barbershop." Each design version was required by custom to have a proper name to distinguish it from later models, and the first barbershop design was naturally called Figaro, after the premier Barber of Seville.

The product and the residue were called, respectively, P and Q, which we were told stood informally for "pweshus" and "quap." This allowed the supervisors to warn employees to watch their Ps and Qs, which did in fact refer to the meters reporting the rate at which these two materials were being accumulated. But when the receptacle for the product became known as the "P pot," they changed the code letter to R.

The environment created by high-level classification was also new to me. My thesis work for the National Research Defense Council had been stamped "Restricted," but the paperwork associated with that level of classification was completely trivial. At Oak Ridge I found double envelopes, sealing wax, receipts in triplicate, special couriers, red waste-baskets for scratch paper (emptied by armed guards each night and burned in the presence of military security guards), and all the accoutrements of a special secret project in wartime. Signs warned, "ENEMY EARS ARE NEAR YOUR BEERS." Yet the atmosphere was more like a university. Many professors were on loan here, and special courses, seminars, and workshops were in session at all times, on topics ranging from quantum mechanics to the electron theory of metals. There was a "student shop," where experienced machinists taught young scientists how to turn out emergency or special parts. Distribution lists on reports had more Ph.D.'s than misters. And the presence of so many bright, dedicated young scientists was a constant inspiration to work even harder.

The job continually presented me with new experiences. The one thousand huge magnets that bent the glowing beam of ionized uranium atoms into a curved path, permitting the isotopes to be separated, had a field so strong that when I walked the wooden catwalk above them it tugged at the nails in my shoes, giving a feeling of walking through light glue. Nonmagnetic tools had to be used, and occasionally a worker would carelessly get too close with an ordinary wrench or hammer, and it would fly out of his hand to crash against the tank wall. Watchmakers in Oak Ridge got used to workers bringing in watches whose innards were smashed but whose cases had never been opened. (Watchmakers in other cities couldn't believe it.)

I will never forget the day I was looking through the heavy lead glass inspection window at the beautiful blue glow of the uranium plasma, when an electron oscillation started up. Copper fins had been designed into the equipment to prevent such oscillations, but it was found that they quickly burned through. The next step was to install refractory tungsten and tantalum inserts to stand up under the high temperatures that sometimes built up. This usually worked, but not always, and as I watched, the tungsten suddenly glowed white-hot and then melted and ran in rivulets down the copper. Copper and silver solder vaporized in a flash, the whole system was incandescent, and the unit shut down, all within a few seconds.

Perhaps the most bewildering phenomenon was the operators of these powerful devices. Many, if not most, were young women who had not graduated from high school and had been trained for the job with a wholly false story as to what was going on. To the young physicists from Brooklyn, these "hillbilly girls" with their Daisy Mae accents and casual personalities seemed totally incapable of carrying out the awesome responsibility entailed in operating these sophisticated machines. As I looked up from the molten chaos unleashed by the sudden electron oscillation to the vacant, gum-chewing face of the operator, I couldn't escape a feeling that the powers that had bent to the minds brilliant enough to conceive of these devices might yet rebel at being asked to submit to the will of someone totally unaware of the forces involved. And yet I had seen these operators develop an intuitive sensitivity to the equipment, like the stereotypical country boy and his flivver, and had seen them get a unit purring again after a Ph.D. scientist had botched an effort to improve performance. These women personified their units and complained bitterly if they were forced for personnel reasons to operate a different unit (one that any scientist would tell you was identical). When one of the production buildings was shut down after the war, the operators wrote sentimental notes and farewell poems with lipstick on their instrument panels, and shed tears of real sorrow at the forced separation from the esoteric devices with which they had developed such a strange and productive relationship.

I Meet Captain Rickover

By war's end I had begun to feel like an old-timer. I enjoyed regaling the newcomers with stories about how Oak Ridge had been when I arrived on the scene. But occasionally I ran into someone who had been there five months before I had, when there was only one building and the operating companies had not even begun to arrive. In those days the workers were brought in by station wagons and driven out to the nearest town for lunch. There was not yet any water piped into the area, and a water jug was passed around the office from time to time for the workers. These people would end their stories by smiling tolerantly and remarking sweetly that you were lucky to have arrived after the mud had been tamed and civilization had been installed. I would protest mildly at this but wish fervently that I too had been in on the *very* beginning.

The Y-12 electromagnetic process for enriching uranium was being replaced by the cheaper K-25 gaseous diffusion process, and twenty thousand people were being laid off. It seemed to me a good time to transfer to the Oak Ridge National Laboratory, as the X-10 site was now called. This was where nuclear reactors were being developed, and this, I decided, was where the action was going to be. A chemistry professor named Farrington Daniels from the University of Wisconsin had an idea for a type of reactor that might someday be used to produce useful power, and the laboratory had invited technical representatives from industry to come down and learn about this new source of energy and how it could be used in civilian life.

The possibility of harnessing the atom for peaceful purposes had caught the fancy of the public and officials alike. Since the war's end a great deal of concern had been focused on ensuring that this new force would be explored for public use, and not solely for secret military purposes. In that context, the handful of "students" sent to Oak Ridge from various industrial and research organizations was a modest beginning indeed for the loudly trumpeted Atomic Age. But a special curriculum was quickly set up for the new students, and senior scientists already at the lab were allowed to monitor a few courses they felt would help them in their work. I decided to sit in on the quantum mechanics course. I had already taken three semesters of the subject from three different instructors as part of my earlier training, so I expected to have little trouble with it. But I felt the subject was so fundamentally important that I could use another go at it.

The lecturer was Dr. Frederick Seitz, an eminent physics professor who later became head of the National Academy of Sciences and president of Rockefeller University. Obviously a man worth listening to when it comes to physics, I figured. That's when I found out that the Navy had also sent a few officers down for this training. They didn't wear uniforms, but there was this one silver-haired guy who kept asking simple, basic questions, making himself look pretty stupid and getting a lot of knowing chuckles from the wiseacres. I found out he was Captain Hyman G. Rickover, an engineering duty officer with an electrical engineering background. The course was pretty tough, even for me, and when one student asked timidly, "Please, Professor, could you tell us, at what level will this course be given?" the prof answered genially, "Let us say at a popular, postdoctoral level."

At this point the silver-haired Captain said, "I'm not getting this. Would you please go over it again?" The prof waltzed through it again, with about the same words as before, and the Captain said, "I still don't get it." The rest of the class was getting a little restless and wondering why the Navy would send somebody down who was incapable of getting the material. The prof then asked condescendingly, "Would you perhaps like to have us provide you with some tutoring in the evenings?"

Not taking this as a put-down, the Captain said merely, "I would appreciate that very much, sir." So the tutoring class was in fact set up, despite the chuckles, and I decided I could probably get some good out of it myself. When I got to the tutoring class, a little late, I was surprised to see not only the Captain but a dozen or more of his classmates, including some of the chucklers, all busily taking notes. Noting my startled look, the Captain said, "I guess I'm not the only dummy in the class. Just the only one with the guts to admit it."

It was my first meeting with the iconoclastic Captain. In the years ahead, I would get to know him better.

RICKOVER REVEALED

> To practice a profession one must have acquired mastery of an academic discipline as well as a technique for applying this special knowledge to the problems of everyday life. A profession is therefore intellectual in content, practical in application.
>
> H.G.R.

It wasn't until Rickover became famous—and notorious—that we began to find out a little about his background. He was a very private person, and he seldom talked about his private life, or even his professional life prior to nuclear power. But when his unorthodox ways caused conflict within the Navy, he became a public figure. He appeared on the cover of *Time*, and cover stories in *Look*, the *Saturday Evening Post*, the *New York Times Magazine*, and even *National Geographic* described the spectacular feats of the growing nuclear fleet, and they inevitably devoted some space to the controversial figure behind them. Bit by bit, the story came out.

Coming to America and Getting Started

Hyman George Rickover was born on 27 January 1900. So it was always easy to tell, in any given year, how old he was: he was as old as the twentieth century. When he was only six his father made the type of bold decision for which his son would later become famous. Facing squarely the fact that life for Jews in Makow, Poland, then under Russian rule, was intolerable, he decided to take his family to America. Years later, in a speech after his retirement, the Admiral described those early days as follows:

I was born in Poland, then a part of Russia. I was not allowed to attend public schools because of my Jewish faith. However, starting at the age of four, I attended a religious school where the only learning was from the Old Testament, in Hebrew. School hours were from sunrise to sunset, six days a week. On the seventh day, we attended the synagogue a good part of the day . . .

I remember the first time I ate an orange. Each year, just before the holy days, the Jewish settlers in Palestine, nearly all of whom had come from Russia or Poland, shipped boxes of oranges to the Jews in Russian and Polish towns. It was the duty of each family to buy at least one orange to help the settlers. So my mother bought an orange and shared it with my sister and me.

My father immigrated to the United States shortly before 1900, and saved enough money from his work to send tickets for my mother, my sister and me. My mother packed as much of our possessions as she could carry in a sheet. This included bedding and 10 days' supply of kosher food . . . The second-class passengers from the deck above occasionally threw us children an apple or orange, as we looked up at them from between decks.

The night before the ship reached New York harbor, the ship's purser gathered all the immigrants and told them they should send a telegram to their next of kin to assure being met at Ellis Island. My mother gave him all that was left of the money my father had sent for the voyage. But, apparently, the purser kept the money and did not send the telegram, because my father was not at Ellis Island to meet us. In fact, he did not greet us until day 10, the last day our family could remain at Ellis Island before the steamship company was required to return us to the port of departure.

It so happened that a man who knew my father and mother in Poland came to Ellis Island to meet his wife, who had just arrived. He saw my mother sitting in a large hall with her bundle of possessions and reported this to my father. He came just in time to retrieve us. During my naval career, many contractors have probably cursed the man who reported my arrival and thus prevented my being shipped back to Poland.

First in New York and then in Chicago, the father was able to support them by working six long days a week as a tailor, which he did until he died at the age of eighty-six. Young Rickover was determined to contribute to the family income, and during high school he worked weekends, and from 3:00 P.M. to midnight weekdays, as a Western Union delivery boy. In 1916 the Republican National Convention was held in Chicago, and Rickover, knowing where the big tips were apt to be, managed to get himself on the convention beat for Western Union. He proudly kept to the end a yellowed news clipping from the *Chicago American* with a photo of himself at the age of sixteen, delivering a telegram to Warren G. Harding at the podium.

Stubborn ambition was the norm in the neighborhood where Rickover grew up. "Irish mothers all wanted their boys to grow up to be priests; Jewish mothers wanted doctors and lawyers," he recalled. He was stubborn enough (he tells the story that his father once had to break away his front teeth to force-feed him some medicine he didn't like!), but his direction was not yet fixed anywhere but upward and out. So when Congressman Adolph Sabath, who knew his uncle, offered him an appointment to the Naval Academy, he jumped at the chance. "I haven't experienced real elation many times in my life," he once confided. "But I recall two such times clearly. Once was when I learned that I might go to the Naval Academy and receive a college education, a dream that had previously appeared out of reach. The other time was when I first saw the turning of the propeller shaft of the *Nautilus* prototype, and I knew we had finally proved for the first time that the atom could do a significant amount of useful work."

The Naval Academy Years

Upon graduating from high school, Rickover put nearly all of his savings into tuition for a prep school near Annapolis, to cram for the Naval Academy entrance exams. He was only a third alternate for a coveted plebe appointment, and he wanted to do well. But he quit after only two weeks at the prep school, deciding that the school curriculum was not up to the task. So he forfeited the tuition and studied on his own, night and day. He passed the exam, but immediately after entering, he and several other midshipmen were quarantined as possible diphtheria carriers and were kept out of class for several weeks. When he finally joined his classmates, he found himself hopelessly behind. In his efforts to catch up, he ran into the first of the academy's arbitrary rules: no one is allowed to study after taps. This archaic rule was apparently created in a misguided spirit of fairness, to prevent some midshipmen from getting ahead of others by working long hours. Rickover did so anyway, as a matter of survival, and thus incurred the wrath of his classmates, who considered this behavior unsportsmanlike.

Class standing at the Naval Academy is not a trivial matter. Selection for promotion and for special assignments is based, first of all, on class standing. This applies throughout an officer's entire career. When he is in the eligible zone for promotion, he is said to be "passed over" if a person in the zone, but ranked below him in class standing, is selected. This is the first step toward involuntary retirement, although class standing tends to be less and less decisive as an officer accumulates more experience. To ensure that intellectual capacity and hard work are not the only considerations in career advancement, the academy has a number of safeguards. First, the practice just mentioned of requiring lights out at an early hour and prohibiting studying beyond that point. But most important, the ranking includes not just academic performance but also such subjective attributes as military adeptness and bearing, leadership abilities, and personality. Rickover found that his class standing was dragged down by his minimal participation in athletics and perceived deficiencies in leadership potential, and by his poor grades in military bearing and performance on the drill field.

Engineering Duty on the *La Vallette* and *Nevada*

However, Rickover did graduate, and he ranked 107th out of 540 in the class of 1922. He was ordered to a new destroyer, the *La Vallette*, but had to wait several months to get Navy transportation through the Panama Canal to the West Coast to board her. He determined to use this time productively and got a scholarship at the University of Chicago, to take courses in history and psychology. Shortly after signing on to the *La Vallette*, Rickover had so impressed his skipper that he was made engineer officer of the ship, despite his lack of rank or experience, becoming the youngest engineer officer in the squadron, less than a year after leaving the Naval Academy.

He served on the destroyer for two years, learning a number of lessons that stayed with him for life. He learned to like life at sea and the opportunities the Navy provided to learn. He took a Naval War College correspondence course in strategy and tactics, which set him apart from most ensigns, particularly those who were technically inclined. One incident left an especially clear mark in his memory, and it underlined the price that sometimes accompanies a "minor human error." In a heavy fog the ship's navigator was plotting a course from radio bearings being received from a radio station ashore, but unfortunately he was plotting the bearings with respect to a nearby lighthouse. The ship went aground, and although the damage was easily repaired, the captain was court-martialed. The concept of personal responsibility was vividly impressed upon the young ensign.

Rickover completed his tour on the *La Vallette* with excellent fitness reports, and in January 1925 he reported to the battleship *Nevada*. He tackled that assignment with his usual energy and thoroughness, reading operating and maintenance manuals and tracing pipes and electrical cables from one compartment to the next. He apparently attracted favorable attention from the other engineering officers, because he was soon appointed electrical officer, an unusual responsibility for an officer only three years out of school.

The ship's commanding officer was an unusual naval officer in two regards: he was open and relaxed with his junior officers, and he was intellectually inclined. When he found, to his surprise, that his young electrical officer had not only taken the Navy's course on strategy and tactics but had developed considerable knowledge and insight on the subject, he asked him to help work out the war games for the upcoming maneuvers. This was a heady experience, and Rickover managed to carry it out without interfering with the engineering project he had started: to install a complete five-hundred-unit shipboard battle telephone system. As a result of this and other improvements, in June 1925 he was promoted to lieutenant, junior grade.

Graduate Work at the Academy and at Columbia University

On the day Rickover reached his fifth year as a commissioned officer, he had completed the required sea duty and seniority for postgraduate training at the Naval Academy. He applied that very day, passed the selection process, and reported back to Annapolis. He chose to work for a master's degree in electrical engineering. This entailed a year at the Naval Postgraduate School, at the Naval Academy, followed by further work at Columbia University. He was excited to find an entirely different approach to teaching at Columbia, not the rote memorization so common then at the academy. He moved into nearby International House, which, as he had hoped, was full of graduate students from all over the world. It was the sort of intellectual hothouse he thrived in, and there he met Ruth D. Masters, a graduate student in international law whom he married after she returned from her doctoral studies at the Sorbonne in Paris.

After graduation, Rickover was assigned to another battleship, the *California*. But he was fonder of life on a small ship, and he knew that in the submarine service young officers were moving up quickly in their careers. So he went to Washington to volunteer for submarine duty and was told that at age twenty-nine he was too old to begin such a career. His application was officially turned down. Leaving the building, he ran into his old commanding officer from the *Nevada* and emotionally told him what had happened. He was told, "Don't worry, that can be changed." Three days later he was officially advised to reapply, and he was accepted.

Submarine School and Sea Duty on the *S-48*

After completing the required courses at the Navy's Submarine School in New London, Connecticut, Rickover was assigned as engineer officer of the *S-48*, an old submarine whose sister ships had all had unfortunate lives: two had sunk and one had had a serious battery explosion at sea. The *S-48*, last surviving ship in her class, ran into her own bad luck not long after Rickover reported aboard, when one of her main batteries caught fire. These monstrous batteries are similar in principle to automobile batteries but large enough to propel the ship when submerged. When the hydrogen gas they generate is not harmlessly neutralized in the catalyzers, a highly flammable and dangerously explosive situation quickly develops, which can spread to the other batteries and destroy the ship. The skipper ordered all men on deck, prepared to jump overboard if the expected hydrogen explosion occurred, then ordered the ship sealed up tight. Rickover decided that the problem was his responsibility and volunteered to go below. He put on a gas mask and climbed down into the dark, smoke-filled hull. The Navy did not give its men much fire-fighting training in those days, and Rickover groped around in the dark for something that might smother the fire without causing the corrosive battery acid to overflow into the bilges or to short out vital electrical systems. He finally smothered the fire with blankets and prevented one of a submariner's greatest nightmares: a battery-gas explosion at sea, which nearly always ends in disaster.

Although disaster was averted, the *S-48*'s propulsion motors were a continual source of trouble. Rickover finally decided that the design of the motors themselves was at fault, so he redesigned and rebuilt the motors, and thereafter they caused no further trouble. No notation of either of these events was put into his personnel file. But he was later commended by the secretary of the Navy for diving into the ocean and saving a "messboy" who had fallen overboard and was drowning.

Lieutenant Rickover had qualified for command and became executive officer (second in command) of the submarine *S-48*. But he did not like to socialize ashore with the other officers, and he was not considered by the submarine high command to be the easygoing, swashbuckling command figure that other officers and men would like to serve under. His was a life-style that was out of step with most submariners at that time. When the *S-48* put into Coco Solo in the Panama Canal Zone, Rickover was joined by his new bride. With her new Ph.D. in international law and his recent completion of a Navy course on the same subject, he preferred to spend his time with her, discussing global matters and riding back into the interior to learn more about the local culture, instead of joining his shipmates in card games or in drinking sessions ashore. But he never became skipper of a submarine. It was the first time in his career that he had failed to make an important goal he had set for himself, and he was deeply disappointed.

At the Office of the Inspector of Naval Material

In 1933, after three years aboard the *S-48*, Lieutenant Rickover was assigned to the office of the inspector of naval material at Philadelphia, whose job it was to ensure that material and equipment manufactured for the Navy met Navy specifications and were delivered on schedule. It was not an exciting job, nor one where Rickover could make an obvious difference in anything. He took the opportunity to study and learn a great deal about manufacturing and about American industry. He was still worried about submarine battery design and operation, so using what he had learned aboard the *S-48* and from his special project on batteries at Columbia grad school, he revised the chapter on storage batteries in the Bureau of Engineering manual. He also brushed up the German he had occasionally tried out at International House and translated *Das Unterseeboot*, a treatise on submarine warfare by Admiral Hermann Bauer, commander of all German submarine flotillas during most of World War I. Rickover believed that it was important for American military personnel to have access to this information, not previously available in English. This book is still available as a reference in the Navy's NavSea Library.

During this period Rickover read a great many books relevant to his career. One that particularly impressed him was *Peacemaking 1919* by Harold Nicolson, which implied that close personal ties among the diplomats may have impaired their abilities to consider only their nations' interest in carrying out the negotiations over the Treaty of Versailles. This shocked him, and he often cited the book in later years to explain why he felt so strongly that persons representing his office should remain completely aloof socially from persons in other organizations whose interests in the job were not necessarily the same as those of his organization.

Engineering Duty on the *New Mexico*

In 1934, after two years ashore, Rickover was ordered to another battleship, the *New Mexico*, as assistant engineer officer. In those days naval ships all ran on oil, and the distance they could travel was limited by their rate of oil consumption, which was enormous. When we see pictures of an aircraft carrier task force steaming at full throttle to trouble spots thousands of miles away, we may not realize that these ships can generally travel only four days at full power—about three thousand miles—and then they must be refueled. This may not be a problem in the Mediterranean, but in the Pacific or the Falklands it is a significant limitation. So one measure of performance in naval vessels has always been their level of fuel oil consumption. Ships compete with others in their class to achieve minimum oil consumption, and the skipper looks to the engineer officer to see that his ship performs well in this regard.

As soon as Rickover found that his ship stood sixth out of fifteen battleships, he promised his boss that by the following year they would be number one. His first move was to track down where all the oil was being consumed. Two items stood out: space heating and freshwater consumption (since all freshwater was made by distilling seawater in oil-fired stills). It was easy to reduce temperature in all the living spaces and ignore the outraged protests of the crew. But tracking the water usage was more complicated, since there was no way to measure how much was being used in the engine room and how much by the crew. Rickover managed to get hold of a large number of water flow gauges and install them in the appropriate pipelines. He could now measure exactly where water was being consumed, and he could limit water usage in the living quarters without impairing operation of the various engine-room systems. He managed to fire up his engine-room crew to look for light bulbs they could remove and dripping faucets they could fix. The entire ship's crew wore coats most of the time and took the world's shortest showers, but the *New Mexico* did become number one the following year, and she remained so even after Rickover had been detached for other duty. The skipper told him he would have promoted him to engineer officer, but he was too junior in rank.

Command of the *Finch*

On 1 July 1937 Rickover was promoted to lieutenant commander and finally got his first and only command. It was a wretched rust-bucket, an aging minesweeper named the *Finch*, operating out of Tsingtao, China. Her machinery was barely operational, the hull was literally rusting through, the entire ship was filthy. Rickover was the third commanding officer ordered to the ship in less than a year. He responded the only way he knew, by ordering his crew to carry out a stem-to-stern renovation program, chipping and painting, cleaning, repairing. He was not going to command a run-down ship. In September 1937 the Navy announced that officers with fifteen years' service were eligible for "engineering duty only" status, a special elite of professional technicians who would guide the Navy into the increasingly technological future. This EDO classification was intended to allow a few carefully selected officers to concentrate on technical specialties, rather than having to pursue the duties associated with the command of military vessels. Rickover applied and was accepted, which required immediate transfer from the *Finch*, since EDO meant, by definition, no such command billets.

Duty in the Philippines

As a temporary assignment until new orders could be cut, Rickover was ordered to the Navy's Philippines shipyard at Cavite, to serve as assistant to the planning officer, a position created for the occasion. However, the Navy then decided that he should spend a full two-year duty cycle there, since he was doing such a good job of cutting costs and improving productivity in the yard. Disappointed, Rickover had no choice but to make the best of it. He looked into the situation there and discovered, as he always did, that it was in need of a shake-up. Ships came into the yard for repairs and overhaul, usually just copying last year's request form, which was not questioned by the shipyard, and the crew went on a much-appreciated rest and relaxation tour until the job was completed. Everyone seemed happy with this situation except the new assistant planning officer.

As each ship came in for repair, Rickover went aboard and asked the engineer officer to show him exactly what repairs were needed. Usually he was able to point out that the ship's crew was capable of making the necessary repairs, and as a result, the amount of work done at the Navy's major repair facility in Asia was suddenly reduced drastically, at great savings to the taxpayer. When it finally became time to leave for Washington, Rickover sent his wife back by ship while he went overland, to retrace the approximate route of Marco Polo, arriving in Washington in the fall of 1939, to become the assistant head of the Electrical Section of the Bureau of Ships (BuShips, in Navy lingo).

Buildup of the Electrical Section, Bureau of Ships

When Rickover arrived on the scene in 1939, the Electrical Section was a typical government bureaucracy, with only twenty-three people and limited, vaguely defined responsibilities. After his boss went to sea, Rickover took full charge of the section in March 1941. He began to lay off some of the deadwood and to recruit bright young engineers from universities. He bullied manufacturers into lending him some of their best talent on a long-term basis, and by the war's end he had built up the section into a tightly run technical team, highly respected throughout the fleet and the electrical industry, with 343 hardworking engineers and support personnel.

Rickover expanded the section's cognizance to include degaussing (neutralizing the magnetic field around a ship), minesweeping, signaling devices, and fire resistance. His people developed electrical cable that would not permit water to leak from one compartment to another, high-temperature electrical insulation, and materials that were flame-retardant but did not give off noxious fumes. One of their proudest achievements was a casualty power system, with emergency cables and fittings, which enabled a ship's crew to rig temporarily around a damaged section of the ship and bring power to wherever it was most needed: lighting, steering controls, fire pumps, communications, or guns.

Rickover scanned commercial catalogs for electrical equipment and spare parts and found to his horror that many items were listed under more than one number. He found one piece of switchgear carried under twenty-five different listings. He knew this meant that ships and faraway warehouses might well be carrying up to twenty-five times as many spare parts as needed, so he set up a group to rewrite the catalogs, consolidating them into one consistent, nonduplicatory listing. He then had a clear picture of what the Navy needed, but he didn't like what it was getting. He didn't see why the hardware had to be so big, so heavy, and so unreliable under shipboard conditions. He was told it had to be that way, because that was what the manufacturers were building.

"I want you guys to redesign this stuff from scratch," he roared at his startled troops. "But who will build it?" they asked. "Leave that to me," he replied. Selecting a particularly bulky control panel as a test case, he called the president of the manufacturer and told him bluntly, "I will have a new set of plans on your desk within a month. I want you to manufacture panels to those specifications. If you won't, the Navy will cancel all future orders for control panels and work with someone who will. Will you do it?" The president, completely taken aback by such uncharacteristic behavior on the part of a government customer, hastily agreed to send a representative down to work things out. He became the first commercial manufacturer to work to Rickover designs.

In another case, Rickover checked dimensions on all of the lighting transformers the Navy was buying and picked the one with the smallest length, another with the smallest height, and a third with the smallest width. Taking these three numbers, he then told the manufacturers to make him a transformer that came within all three dimensions. No one had ever made such a small transformer for this application, but he now had a new standard.

A serious limitation to wartime naval operations was the need to maintain radio silence. Ships tried to get around this by using blinking lights to signal each other, but these could easily be detected by the enemy. The Navy had been looking into infrared signaling since World War I, but no one really took it seriously. Rickover got his people to look into it, developed it into a workable system, and gave the fleet a means of undetectable nighttime communication.

He almost reached too far when he found that the Navy had no means to combat the Germans' highly secret magnetic mine, which was causing serious damage to British ships before Pearl Harbor. He found that the British had developed a floating cable that they claimed would detonate the mines, but they would not release any information about it. Rickover got a naval attaché in London to send him a piece of the cable, which he then had analyzed. The secret turned out to be that a special high-current generator was needed to energize the cable. He had his people design a complete mine detection and detonation system and tried to get approval for ordering the necessary generators. He was told that British patents and classification would prevent any such action ("Sorry"), so he decided to go it alone. On a completely personal basis, he persuaded General Electric to undertake the development as a high-priority project, and the company was nearly ready to deliver the first generators when the Navy purchasing people suddenly realized that the brazen Commander had made an unofficial contract for about $10 million, big money in those days. He was called onto the mat, but when Admiral Claude Jones, in charge of BuShips Shipbuilding Division, realized the significance of what had been done, he quickly settled with General Electric, and the Navy had a magnetic minesweeping capability.

Mechanicsburg and Okinawa

There were two brief tours of duty after the Electrical Section before Rickover began work on the atom. He had been made a full commander on 1 January 1942 and a captain on 26 June 1943. By the end of 1944 he felt he had made the Electrical Section into a viable, effective organization, and the tide of the war had turned to favor the United States. His son had been born in 1940, and he didn't want to have to tell him in future years that he had spent the whole war behind a desk in Washington. He asked for an overseas assignment. A large repair facility was being set up on Okinawa to prepare and maintain ships for Operation Olympic, the invasion of Kyushu scheduled for November 1945, and for Coronet, the invasion of Honshu scheduled for the following March. Rickover wanted command of that base.

He was granted his wish, with the proviso that he first straighten out the Navy's huge supply depot at Mechanicsburg, Pennsylvania. He was told that it took a month to get a spare part out of there that was in stock, and many months for one not in stock. Rickover agreed to take on this chore. He started by selecting twenty-two top industrial production experts and expediters, and persuading their companies to lend them to him for several months at no cost to the Navy. They dug into every aspect of the operation, and everywhere they looked they found inefficiencies and inadequacies that had built up unchallenged through the years. Only one railroad line fed into the gigantic facility, which moved eight hundred boxcars a week. And there was only one fire engine for the 122 acres of precious war supplies. Rickover totally revised the depot's operations, and (a particular Rickover trademark) set up a school on the base to train personnel on their job and its relation to the overall mission of the facility. When he left three months later, everyone knew he had been there, and parts were being located and shipped out within a few days, not months.

Rickover took charge of the Okinawa base on 20 July 1945, and less than a month later, two atomic bombs ended the war and the great invasion was called off. In October a typhoon demolished the base and devastated the island. Rickover was told not to rebuild the base, so he closed it down, gathered up the scattered clothing, blankets, and other supplies of use to civilians, and distributed them among the homeless Okinawans. He then insisted that all usable machinery and tools be loaded onto each and every ship headed for America. He pressured sailors into working overtime loading up the equipment, promising them that they could go home after the machinery was aboard. He was one of the few overseas base commanders who took the time and trouble to ensure that government material was returned to the States from the war zone.

Mothballing the Pacific Fleet

At this time the war was over and demobilization was proceeding precipitously. Ships were being mothballed for possible future service. If done properly, this can provide battle-ready ships years later on short notice. But if the complicated preservation procedures are not carried out meticulously, the concept of a reserve fleet will prove to be a dangerous illusion. The process was under way on the West Coast and was running into trouble. Rickover was ordered to look into the situation, as inspector general of the 19th Mothball Fleet. He took his usual approach to the problem. He persuaded the captains of the ships as soon as they came in to abandon their plans for weekend shore leave, don dungarees, and crawl with him through the bilges of their ships, looking

for dirt and trash painted over and other indications of unreadiness for
the mothballing procedure. He also straightened out the paperwork that
had been delaying the ships and put the whole process on a production-
line basis. It was an unglamorous task, carried out in a demobilization
atmosphere, but Rickover, as always, treated it as the most important
task in the world. He was determined to do it to the very highest
standards. Less than five years later, scores of these ships were hurriedly
reactivated and pressed into service during the Korean War.

For this work the commander of the 19th Fleet recommended Rickover for flag rank—that is, for promotion to rear admiral.

ASSIGNMENT TO OAK RIDGE

> *To do a job effectively, one must set priorities. Too many
> people let their "in" basket set the priorities. On any given
> day, unimportant but interesting trivia pass through an of-
> fice; one must not permit these to monopolize his time. The
> human tendency is to while away time with unimportant
> matters that do not require mental effort or energy. Since
> they can be easily resolved, they give a false sense of accom-
> plishment. The manager must exert self-discipline to ensure
> that his energy is focussed where it is truly needed.*
>
> H.G.R.

As his work with the 19th Fleet was winding down, Rickover dropped
in on his old Electrical Section and, among other things, had a long talk
with Harry Mandil, who had worked with him during the war. "Here
I am, a senior captain, with lots of valuable experience. The war is over.
What should I do now? How can I use that experience to do some good
for the country? I know a lot about how industry works and what those
people can do if they are pushed. And I know how to push them. But
how do I use that knowledge? What do I do with the rest of my life?"
Of course, Mandil had no pat answer to that question, but history
contrived to answer it.

Rickover was crawling through the dirty bilges of the 19th Fleet,
looking for painted-over banana peels and the like, when he received
word that he had been selected to go to Oak Ridge, Tennessee, to study
nuclear engineering. His response was typical of him. He got himself a

EXTENDING THE EFFECT: MANUFACTURERS

Before he had ever heard of nuclear power Rickover realized that to get the quality of materials he needed for his own corner of the Navy, he must reform institutions and individuals in the world at large. When he made the decision as head of the BuShips Electrical Section to require equipment manufacturers to meet not just some additional Navy specifications, but a level of performance not previously required in the industry, he thereby brought within the range of the Rickover Effect literally hundreds of thousands of individuals who might otherwise never have known his name. It was the first of several such decisions that progressively extended his impact over a significant part of American industry.

pile of books on atomic physics, chemistry, and mathematics and spent his evenings studying.

When he reported to Washington in May 1946, his first step was to review all the reports and memos on atomic energy in BuShips' files. There wasn't much. During the war, Navy physicist Ross Gunn had suggested the possibility of atomic propulsion for a submarine, and he had borrowed another physicist, Philip Abelson, from the Carnegie Institution to work on enhancing the concentration of the fissionable isotope of uranium. But no one was seriously working on building a power reactor of any kind, civilian or military, in the near future. In fact, interest in the subject seemed so desultory that Rickover suspected (incorrectly) that the primary purpose of sending him to Oak Ridge was to get him out of the way.

He found that back in 1939, shortly after the discovery of atomic fission, $2,000 had been allocated to the Naval Research Laboratory (NRL) to study the possibility of applying this new energy source to naval use, but he could find no report on the results of this study. Nothing much happened after that, until December 1944, when the director of the laboratory recommended that the Navy undertake a project unilaterally to develop nuclear propulsion. But this recommendation was turned down, because it was considered unwise for the Navy to proceed independently of the Army's Manhattan Project, which had a monopoly on all things atomic. Then in April 1946 the secretary of the Navy's General Board suggested that the Navy investigate the feasibility of nuclear propulsion, and BuShips responded by reporting its recent decision to send personnel to Oak Ridge for that purpose. A report by NRL led to Navy contracts at the Mine Safety Appliances Company and at the Babcock & Wilcox Company to study the problems associated with the use of sodium-potassium alloys as heat-transfer media. Neither of these contracts mentioned nuclear propulsion, but that possibility was one of the incentives for the work.

General Electric had just proposed a study on a reactor plant for a destroyer, but the Navy had not yet acted on it. Rickover had initially felt that GE was the best hope for a naval plant, but as he looked into the situation there, he developed strong doubts. GE had agreed to operate the government's big plutonium production facility at Hanford, Washington, in return for which the government had agreed to fund a new atomic research facility near Schenectady, New York, to study commercial power. Any naval project at GE would have to take third priority to these major corporate commitments. So just before he left for Oak Ridge, Rickover went to see Gwylim Price, Westinghouse's new president, to try to persuade him to get his company into this new technology. Price seemed interested but made no immediate commitment.

Rickover decided to leave his wife and five-year-old son in Washington, to give himself maximum freedom in housing and study time. (After all, he was going to be there only a year.) He had just met Colonel Kenneth D. Nichols, General Leslie R. Groves's brainy deputy manager for the whole Manhattan District atomic program, and the colonel gave him a ride to Oak Ridge in his Army plane. They had a long and friendly talk during the trip, and Nichols then arranged for Rickover, the senior naval officer on site, to have a front office as deputy manager of the Oak Ridge operations. Rickover took full advantage of the situation to visit all facilities, to study all reports of interest, and to obtain a nearly unique overall view of the situation in atomic energy. He found, as he had suspected in Washington, that there was no one pushing for the immediate construction of a practical atomic power plant of any type or size.

He also combed the list of "students" at the atomic school and located four other "bachelors" with whom he could share quarters: Farrington Daniels, the chemist who had proposed the reactor that was ostensibly the focal point of the Oak Ridge studies; two rising young engineer-managers, John Simpson from Westinghouse (whom Rickover had met and worked with during his Electrical Section days) and Harry Stevens from General Electric; and Sid Simon, a materials engineer from the Cleveland laboratory of the National Advisory Committee for Aeronautics. He arranged for the five of them to be assigned to a comfortable house together, rather than scattered through the spare quarters of the bachelor dormitories. He had now made all the preparations he could; he was convinced that he could not count on significant help from anyone else. It was time to get his own program into motion.

Roddis Gets the Word at Bikini

Four other naval officers had been sent to Oak Ridge with Rickover, and he was determined to find out about them and enlist them in helping him achieve his objectives there. One of these was Lieutenant Commander Louis H. Roddis, Jr., USN. When he got the orders to report to Oak Ridge, Roddis was on Bikini Atoll assisting in the atomic bomb tests for the Navy. He smiled as he heard the familiar voice of newscaster Gabriel Heatter: "The palm trees are still standing on Bikini tonight!"

Heatter was promising the world by radio that the atomic bomb just tested at Bikini Atoll was not the doomsday machine some had prophesied. His voice seemed to say, "I may be reporting the Apocalypse, but you can always count on me to maintain my professionally cool objectivity." He wanted to reassure us that the world as we knew it was still there and would continue to exist, despite the alarums spread by some of his less professional journalistic colleagues.

Roddis could see the palm trees of Bikini out his window. But he had just witnessed that fearful blast, and despite the vast amount of reading he had done to prepare himself for it, it had exceeded all his expectations. The observation station was so far away from the detonation point—"ground zero"—that he was afraid the much-advertised blast wouldn't look like much. He needn't have worried.

I know what he saw, because I went through the same experience myself some years later, cowering in a hand-dug slit trench four thousand yards from the largest bomb ever detonated in the United States. First, there was the incredible light. "Brighter than a thousand suns," the physicists said, and it certainly seemed so. And it kept getting brighter. But what made it seem so unearthly was the complete silence. No boom, no shock, no thump to the chest, just that bright, silent light from which they all averted their eyes. Roddis heard one of the technicians mutter fearfully, "It's getting away from the longhairs!" Then, after an interminable period during which the world stood still and he realized afterward he had held his breath, the earth suddenly turned to jelly. He understood now the terror of earthquake victims. When the very earth, the foundation of all being, becomes insubstantial, what can one count on? And still the deathly silence persisted. Finally, because sound and shock travel five times more slowly through air than through the earth, the shock wave and the sound of the blast smote the observation station. Dirt and sand and bits of twigs and other debris were hurled against the structure, and the long-awaited sound itself was heard. Somehow the sound was the least terrifying of the bomb's effects.

At last, realizing that he had been burying his head in his arms for some time, Roddis sheepishly stood to look out. His first impression was, *How close it is!* It towered forty thousand feet into the sky and looked as if it were almost directly overhead. All possible shades of pink, lavender, red, and yellow were flickering in the cloud. He was surprised that it was still generating light, and way up there! He recalled that J. Robert Oppenheimer, when he saw the first A-bomb detonated at Alamogordo, had reportedly quoted from the Bhagavad-Gita, "Now I am become Shiva, destroyer of worlds."

He now understood in his gut that The Bomb—he would always think of it in capital letters—would require a complete rethinking of military strategy. And he knew that few military leaders were capable of such a reshuffling of the foundations of their world view. That was a terrible thing for the world, but Roddis realized that it was also an opportunity for him. For he was convinced that he was one of the few military officers capable of grasping such fundamental new knowledge and its implications.

This self-confidence was not mere ego-flexing, for Roddis was indeed one of the brightest officers in the Navy. Son of a career naval medical officer and first in the Naval Academy class of 1939, Roddis had served with honor at sea and in a shipyard during the war. He had seen firsthand the carnage at Pearl Harbor. He had been selected for the Navy's postgraduate program in engineering at MIT and graduated with highest honors. He had jumped at every chance to take specialized courses in all the latest technologies and had managed to get himself ordered to the staff of Admiral Thorvald A. Solberg, director of the Navy's test program at Bikini.

Roddis's career had gone well up to now, but he was not sure what would come from the orders he had just received. He was to report to the commanding colonel of the Army Engineer Corps's Manhattan Project in Oak Ridge. This was the secret wartime city where the enriched uranium for the atomic bomb had been made, and where many of the advances in nuclear reactor physics and radiochemistry had been developed. An exciting place, no doubt, inhabited by some of the best minds in science and engineering. But where did *he* fit in?

His assignment to Oak Ridge was due in part to his friendship with Vice Admiral E. L. "Ned" Cochrane, chief of the Bureau of Ships, with an assist from Captain Albert G. Mumma, head of BuShips' Machinery Design Division. Mumma had recommended that the Navy accept the Army's invitation to send a few scientifically minded officers to Oak Ridge, and Cochrane had recommended that Roddis be included. The recognition of his scientific competence was gratifying, but Roddis was concerned about studying nuclear physics with a bunch of academic longhairs while his competitors in the Navy were getting important positions where the action was.

However, one thing he had learned in the Navy was that when orders were cut and signed, there was seldom any point in wishing they said something else. Moreover, this assignment would probably prove to be a good thing. He sighed, noted the reporting-in date, and decided that the best thing he could do in the interim was to do his damnedest on his present assignment. That was always a good decision, he had found. And before long, he found himself at Oak Ridge.

Roddis got out of the Navy car, thanked the driver, and looked around. So this was the Atomic City! It was now the fifth largest city in Tennessee, with seventy-five thousand inhabitants, including workers' family members. About the same number of workers were employed at its various facilities, which meant that large numbers of workers lived outside the gates and commuted as much as two hours each way. Although there were heavy cutbacks of personnel in the electromagnetic separation facility, where the fissionable isotope of uranium was winnowed from the nonfissionable isotopes, the town was still growing fast. The local gag was that there were two ways to get into town: you could stand at a bus stop until a bus came along, or you could stand in an open field until they built a town around you.

The local newsletter had grown from a single mimeographed sheet to a sixteen-page formal letterpress newspaper. Roddis read that this

week was to see work started on an outdoor theater, a Tom Thumb
golf course, a riding academy, a pony ring, and another roller-skating
rink. There were already six movie theaters, any number of dance floors,
and a film classics club. But there were still signs advertising "Tent for
Rent." A crazy, primitive-modern town, he decided, but it didn't look
as if it would be dull. He smiled as he realized that the Navy had been
smarter than the Army in handling its recruits. The Army had drafted
young scientists, engineers, and technicians into its program, and made
enlisted men—privates and privates first class—out of nearly all of them,
whether they were Ph.D.'s or lab technicians. So they lived in crude
barracks at the edge of town, with few privileges, as typical "unlisted
men" in any Army camp. The Navy took the same sort of draftees and
made them officers. The Army was thus required to treat these naval
officers with good quarters, an officers' club (with the only beer in
town), access to cars and drivers, and other perks befitting an "officer
and a gentleman." Not surprisingly, this difference was not lost on the
Army recruits.

Townsite was now known as Jackson Square, and the numbered
dormitories had been given swanky names such as Clayton Hall, of the
Tyler Group. The atmosphere at Oak Ridge was relaxed and joyous.
Roddis was particularly fascinated by the boardwalks that seemed to
drift for miles though the Tennessee woods without touching or spoiling
them, like an abstract plane in a geometry text intersecting an irregular
rolling surface. There was something strange and wonderful—something uniquely Oak Ridge—about walking along one of these magic
pathways and looking at the myriad lights of this incredible city scin-
tillating in the valley below. His orders were vague enough to allow
plenty of time for enjoying this pleasant Shangri-La, and the class schedule laid out for him by the Oak Ridge people was certainly not demanding.

When he returned to the dormitory, his reverie was shattered by a
note in his mailbox from Captain Rickover. He knew of the Captain,
but not much. His orders had read merely that he was being sent to
Oak Ridge for individual study, and that he was responsible to Com-
modore Lee in the Bureau of Ships. But before he left, he had been
warned privately by two senior officers to stay clear of the feisty Captain,
who was considered a troublemaker.

Roddis had first heard of Rickover in the early days of the war,
when Roddis was electrical officer on the battleship *Maryland*. He began

to get notices from Rickover's Electrical Section of BuShips telling him how to modify his switchgear and other electrical equipment to maximize its resistance to battle damage. There were other electrical components aboard, under the jurisdiction of the bureau's Section on Intercommunication and Fire Control (IC&FC), which were not under Rickover. In many cases, these were identical components, but no instructions were coming from IC&FC. Roddis proceeded to make the corresponding modifications to the IC&FC equipment, but he couldn't help thinking about the difference between that Commander Rickover in Washington who was really trying to help him, and the others who didn't seem to be much help. He was now about to meet the man in person.

Dick and Dunford Join the Team

Captain Rickover wanted to see Roddis in the Army Conference Room at 7:00 P.M., which was in a very few minutes. Roddis had no idea what this was about, but he hurried over to the appointed room. To his surprise, he found in the room with the Captain all three of the other officers sent to Oak Ridge by the Bureau of Ships. There was Lieutenant Commander James M. Dunford, a classmate of Roddis's at both the Naval Academy and MIT. With characteristic assertiveness and confidence, Dunford had applied to BuShips for "any special or unusual assignment," and orders to Oak Ridge had caught up with him shortly after he reported in to the Pearl Harbor Naval Shipyard. Many people would have been upset by having to move halfway around the world and back again in a short time, but Dunford had asked for it and was eager to go. There was also Ray Dick, a brilliant reserve lieutenant, a pugnacious metallurgical engineer who graduated first in the class of 1942 at Ohio State and had volunteered for frogman duty during the war. And there was Lieutenant Commander Miles A. Libbey of the Naval Academy class of 1940, more academically inclined than the others.

As Roddis entered, Captain Rickover nodded and, without any prefatory remarks, delivered a few brief statements: "As the second ranking military officer on duty in Oak Ridge, I have been made deputy manager of the entire project here. This has allowed me access to all facilities and to all papers and reports, and has been helpful in sizing up the situation. I have now completed that phase of my work, and I intend to devote full time to our Navy project. I have been told that, as senior naval officer present, I will be responsible for filling out and filing each of your periodic fitness reports. I don't have to spell out for you what that means. I suggest you each keep in close touch with me, as I will be planning how we can get the maximum benefit from this period of study. Any questions? Then that will be all for now."

The meeting had taken less than a minute, yet none of these officers needed any further explanation. They knew that the person who fills out your fitness reports holds your career in his hands. All promotions and further career assignments are heavily influenced by the words in those reports. They were now all working for Rickover. One of his first actions after that was to call them all together, in the presence of the Army clerk responsible for military personnel, and speak to her as follows, with the others listening:

"I want you to understand that most of the paperwork from the Sixth Naval District [which was responsible for personnel records of Rickover's new group] is absolutely useless. It will never be missed if you give it all the deep six. Do you know what that naval term means? It means trash it. Throw it away. So you are to do that. That does not, of course, apply to matters involving the officers' pay. If you ever see anything that you feel might be so important that throwing it away would jeopardize your career, you may put it in a drawer and keep it for future reference. But in no case are you to respond or take any other action on this material. Do you understand? And if anyone questions your actions in carrying out this order, any of these officers, or myself if necessary, will step forward and support you in this."

The Navy left them alone after that, and there were never any repercussions from it.

Formulating a Game Plan

If asked, most naval officers would have said that Captain Rickover was completely out of line in taking command of the other four officers sent to Oak Ridge by the Navy. But Rickover didn't ask. He knew in his heart that they had probably been warned to stay away from him, and he also knew that if anything were to come of his stay at Oak Ridge, it would not come from having the five of them separately follow the relaxed academic study program set up by the laboratory. The official scenario, of an industrial power reactor being built first and the tech-nology subsequently trickling down to the Navy for its use, was simply not going to occur. If there was to be a nuclear-powered Navy in his lifetime, he would have to bring it about himself. He had now taken the first step in that direction.

The nominal focal point of the Oak Ridge industrial visitors was the Daniels Pile, intended to be a prototype of a commercial electricity-generating nuclear reactor. (The word *pile* was left over from the first nuclear reactor, built in 1942 at the University of Chicago squash courts under the direction of the eminent nuclear physicist Enrico Fermi. It consisted of blocks of very pure graphite that formed a lattice in which lumps of uranium metal and uranium oxide were placed. As the pile was built up by hand, measurements of the neutron level were taken to record the slow approach to criticality, when the neutron leakage finally no longer exceeded the neutron production and the process became self-sustaining.)

Captain Rickover had no problem convincing Roddis and the other naval officers now under his wing that the Daniels Pile was a will-o'-the-wisp. Essentially no one at the laboratory believed the official Oak Ridge story that the prototype reactor would be built within eighteen months. Most people would tell you it would probably never be built. In fact, few people were actually working on the reactor design; most of the new students were studying metallurgy, physics, chemistry, and other general courses developed for them, giving an atomic twist to the basic scientific material to incorporate what had been learned during the Manhattan Project's brief but productive existence.

President Harry Truman had signed the civilian Atomic Energy Commission into existence in July 1946, but it had no personnel and did not become a viable entity until early 1947. General Groves had hurriedly signed a contract with GE to study a nuclear plant for a destroyer, apparently wishing to get the work under way before a potentially hostile civilian agency could awake and frown on further military development of the atom. Roddis, Dunford, Dick, and Libbey had now reported in and started to take notes on the courses and reports they were studying. Rickover's first step was to formalize that process. He had each of the officers take a topic and write the "definitive report" on it, a summary of all new information on that topic available through the courses, reports, studies, and dormitory discussions. The subjects ranged from the metallurgical, chemical, and nuclear properties of beryllium to the problems associated with shielding personnel from radiation. When they finished one report, he started them on another. Soon they developed an appreciative audience for what became known as the Naval

Group Reports, which were generally conceded to be the most complete and accurate source of information that was otherwise available only from widely scattered reports and notes or from people's heads.

In November 1946 Rickover had gone to the Naval Medical Center in Bethesda, Maryland, for a hernia operation, when he received word from Colonel Nichols that the Atomic Energy Commission, which was about to pick up responsibility for the atom from the Army, wanted a report stating the Navy's position with respect to nuclear power for naval use. This was a first, an unprecedented opportunity, and Rickover did not intend to lose it. He got his operation delayed, talked the hospital's commanding officer into giving him a fully equipped office, and got the Bureau of Ships to lend him two secretaries. He called Roddis in from his Oak Ridge weekend, and they worked two long days to produce a bold and provocative report. They predicted that within five to eight years the Navy could have its first nuclear-powered vessel, and within ten to fifteen years there could be nuclear power in every major class of ship. The report was forwarded to BuShips for endorsement, and from there it was forwarded to the secretary of the Navy with the cautionary statement, "The opinions quoted herein do not reflect the policy of the Navy, but that of two individual officers."

Back in Oak Ridge, Rickover gathered his group together and paid a visit to General Electric. The atmosphere there was more invigorating, but two weaknesses bothered Rickover. The concern he had felt earlier about the Navy work taking third priority to plutonium production and to the civilian reactor was confirmed; but there was little he could do about that. His second concern was that, like Oak Ridge, GE was approaching the project as a scientific rather than an engineering task. "The problem is 95 percent engineering," complained Rickover. "You ought to put engineers on it." But he gained no converts to this point of view. He did, however, persuade GE to scale down the power level to a submarine-sized plant, and he considered that a step in the right direction.

On 1 January 1947 the Atomic Energy Commission formally took over its new responsibility, but this was still a largely paper move, and it elicited little reaction from the Naval Group. What did get everybody's attention, however, was the shocking news that Captain Albert G. Mumma had been formally appointed deputy coordinator of nuclear matters for BuShips, under Captain Armand M. Morgan, "whether the

nuclear energy is to be used as an explosive or a source of power."
Rickover was stunned. He had assumed that he was the Navy's agent
for bringing in a nuclear power plant, and now this had happened behind
his back. He called his troops together and told them, "I want you guys
to know you are free to align yourselves with Mumma. I have no
intention of trying to hold on to you. He has the title and the official
responsibility, and I have neither."

But there was no doubt in the mind of any of them as to who, if
anyone, could turn the dream of naval nuclear propulsion into reality.
They all replied without hesitation that they would stick with him.

A few months later, Rickover decided to visit General Electric again.
No significant activity was under way at Oak Ridge, and he hoped that
maybe in the industrial world some progress was being made. But he
found that the trends he had seen on his previous visit had continued:
the civilian commitments had further drained effort and interest from
the Navy project; scientists, not engineers, dominated the work; and he
was unable to bring about any changes in the situation. In June 1947
GE signed a contract with the Navy in which the company laid out its
policy with respect to nuclear power, reaffirming all the things Rickover
had tried to change. A mere $30,000 a year was assigned to the scientists
at the GE laboratory to work on the reactor concept, which meant only
two persons working on it. But $2.25 million was assigned to develop
a heat-transfer system, without anyone really knowing what the plant
would look like.

Elsewhere in the Navy the story was the same. Admiral William S.
Parsons was director of atomic defense in the office of the chief of naval
operations. He was convinced that atomic propulsion for submarines
was a proper and important goal. But he was not willing to speak out
for it at that time. He had been involved in the weapons tests at Bikini,
and he knew that conventional naval vessels needed considerable upgrading. He did not want an atomic propulsion program to divert funds or
attention away from that work. He was also concerned, as was nearly
everyone in the program in those days, that there would not be enough
uranium to supply both the weapons needs and propulsion, and he
believed that the nation should put breeder reactors, which were
intended to produce more fuel than they consumed, ahead of all other
reactors until an ample supply of nuclear fuel could be developed. The
BuShips chief now had five captains on his staff advising him on nuclear

power, and they either shared Parsons's feelings on the subject or deferred to his viewpoint. Rickover's voice came in ever more faintly from far-off Tennessee.

Back at BuShips in Washington, a group of submarine officers had been meeting for four months to discuss new submarine designs, and on 9 January 1947 they issued a report recommending a broad effort to upgrade the nation's submarine force. They would do this, first, with improved diesel models, then with chemical closed-cycle systems, and finally with "nuclear power plants for eventual installation." All Rick-over could do was to put his own ideas, as forcefully as he could, into a memo to the bureau. He did this without any illusions that it would change anything at the moment. It was part of what he called his "ortho-dontic approach," the application of continuous, steady pressure over the years in order to achieve eventual change.

Defining the Organizational Approach

Rickover spent a lot of time thinking about how the program should be organized, if and when he finally got some money and authority to move on it. In a typical exchange on the subject he said to Dunford, "That's what I'm trying to tell you, Dunford. There *is* no precedent, or formula, or procedure for what we're trying to do. We're on our own. There's nobody to turn to for advice. We have to think this thing out from basic principles. First, let's look at the legalities of the matter. That's always a good place to start. The authority for designing, build-ing, and maintaining ships rests with the Navy, specifically the Bureau of Ships. So our organization has to have a base there. We have to be able to do things in the name of BuShips—to sign contracts, spend money, and approve ship design features."

Dunford replied, "That's certainly true, Captain. But no engineering duty officer has much real policy-making power. All important decisions are made by line officers."

"I know that. That's why we're having this discussion. We need another base of power. And there's a legal basis for this. I've been studying the Atomic Energy Act of 1946. And it's very clear that respon-sibility and authority for anything atomic lie with the U.S. Atomic Energy Commission, the AEC. If atomic fuel is to be procured, if it is to be fabricated and reprocessed after use, if reactor safety inspections and evaluations are to be made—all these matters require an AEC base. Only AEC officials can sign contracts and make arrangements to deal with atomic materials and atomic secrets. So I need an AEC hat too. In fact, all of you guys, or at least some of you, should have both hats. The question is, How do you set up an organization that operates within two wholly different government agencies?"

"That's where we come up against the no-precedent problem."

"That doesn't have to be a problem. It can be an opportunity. If nobody's ever done this before, there's no way they can tell us we're doing it wrong. That's got to be our basic strategy. If the Navy doesn't like what we're doing, we'll do it with our AEC hat."

"Yeah! We can write letters with our Navy hat on, telling the Navy what we need. Then we'll pick up our AEC stationery and say, 'That sounds like a great idea, Navy. We'll do it.' "

Rickover was suddenly very stern. "Get this, Dunford: We're not playing games here. We'll be very visible. We'll be a prime target for every bureaucrat. They hate to see anybody who has figured out how to get around them. That means we'll have to follow the law scrupulously. Yes, we'll write Navy letters. But we'll send them up through the chief of BuShips, through the chief of naval operations to the secretary of the Navy and the secretary of defense. Strictly kosher. And yes, we'll answer them from the AEC, but we'll get sign-offs from the director of reactor development and then the AEC commissioners. I'm dead serious about this, Dunford. If I catch any of you bastards trying to cut corners on this, I'll slaughter you. The only way we have a prayer of getting away with this is if we're cleaner than a damn hound's tooth. And conversely, if we do it right we'll have the whole damn government behind our every move. We'll even keep clearing it with Congress. Roddis tells me that Joint Task Force One, which ran the Bikini tests for the Navy, involved civilians as well as two or three different military organizations, and it apparently worked well."

"But how do we start it off? How do we set it up?"

"We'll draft a Memorandum of Understanding, to be signed by both agencies, spelling out just how we'll operate. We'll have to get everything we want in it, because that'll be our basic charter. I want offices and phones in both buildings. And a box on each organization chart. It'll have to be worded very carefully. Then we'll have to walk it painfully through all the higher-ups who should sign off on it. And if we push long enough and hard enough, we'll eventually have our marching orders. Now get cracking on the first draft. Get help from anybody you need. Just stay away from the lawyers. I'll get one of the lawyers here to take a quick look at it after we're all done, to make sure we haven't set any traps for ourselves. But I don't want lawyers in on the early drafts. And don't you try to sound like a lawyer. Just write it in plain English. No *whereases*. Get going."

So Dunford had another chore. He had a lot of research to do, and he wanted to talk with some people who had been around Washington. The Rickover Team was beginning to function.

The Naval Group's Grand Tour

In July 1947 the Naval Group was almost through its tour of duty at Oak Ridge. Rickover knew that when they finished, they would probably all be dispersed to various billets around the Navy. He wanted to do one more thing before that happened. "I've been working quietly since January," he said, "trying to set up a tour for all of us to all the major atomic installations in the country. We have to find out who, if anybody, is interested in pushing for a real power reactor in the near future. There's nobody in the Navy who knows anything about this stuff except us. And the goddamned AEC has just one guy with any experience with reactors. One! And he's not an engineer, he's just a physicist. I also want to find out what experimental facilities, test equipment, and data these places have, on metallurgy, heat transfer, nuclear physics, and the other basics. I've read the reports, but usually there's damned little behind the fancy words when you actually go to look at it."

"When do we start, Captain?" asked Dunford.

"As soon as I can confirm the date, we'll leave for the Ames Laboratory at Iowa State College. We'll be away the rest of July and most of August. This is our last hurrah, and I want to get everything I can out of it. I want to preach as well as listen. We're not going to accomplish any more sitting here."

Their trip was an eye-opener, in that they saw some of the world's latest high-tech research facilities and met some of the brightest theoreticians in the physical sciences. Many had fled Hitler's Europe and were establishing themselves in the New World. They met the Naval Group with an attitude of friendly scientific openness. Many agreed with them that the only way to develop a power reactor was to establish a high-priority project to build one, rather than to research it casually in a laboratory.

Dr. Walter H. Zinn, director of the AEC's Argonne National Laboratory near Chicago, seemed to know as much as anyone about the practical side of reactors, although he was more of a scientist than an engineer. He encouraged the group to build a prototype plant on land as soon as they felt that the technology was ready; this would give them a chance to study the problems without committing a ship. He urged them to settle on a reactor coolant first, as this would influence nearly everything else in the design. Other important decisions, such as the design of radiation shielding, could then follow logically.

Dr. Ernest O. Lawrence, director of the Radiation Laboratory at the University of California at Berkeley and inventor of the cyclotron, was enthusiastic, but he warned that the plant could never be built unless the Navy was willing to spend "real cash" on it. If they were bold enough to create a major program, they could attract good people and could interest a major corporation in getting involved. A small, continuing laboratory program would take years to accomplish anything, he insisted.

The major enthusiast of the tour was the eminent theoretical physicist Dr. Edward Teller, who was at that time working at the AEC's Los Alamos Laboratory in New Mexico. He said he was convinced that a power reactor could be built quickly if a major effort were devoted to it. He conceded that the problems were more of an engineering than scientific nature. But he was concerned that most engineers were not trained to deal with radically new ideas. Some of the basic formulas they were accustomed to using without question had to be revised to fit atomic realities. But nonetheless, he agreed that the emphasis should be on engineering.

Then he asked bluntly, "What sort of backing do you have in the Navy?" Rickover hesitated. He did not want to be dismissed as a lone zealot. But he told the whole story, of his inability to get serious backing from the Bureau of Ships, of Mumma's appointment as deputy chief of the Nuclear Power Branch, and of the fact that his own group would undoubtedly be dispersed upon their return to Washington.

Teller was not deterred by this response. He felt that there were a few men of vision around who would back such a project. After the group left, he wrote a long letter dated 19 August 1947 to his friend Dr. Lawrence R. Hafstad, who later became director of research at General Motors and who was at that time executive secretary of the influential Research and Development Board of the Department of Defense. Teller explained that he was "very much impressed" with the "enthusiasm and enterprise" of Rickover and his group, and also with "their detailed knowledge." And he closed with a clear message:

> The reason I am writing this letter as you can guess is my dismay brought about by this situation: I see five Navy men, unusually intelligent, and interested in a detailed, concrete and down-to-earth plan (if down-to-earth is a proper Navy objective), but when I asked them when and how they will proceed, I am met with hesitation that seemed to me to indicate that the whole thing is not at all approved as yet, and that it is perhaps being put in the same class as some of the projects which in more ways than one are way up in the clouds [referring to the ill-fated aircraft nuclear propulsion program].

This letter produced no overt results at the time, but seventeen months later, when Hafstad became Rickover's boss as director of the AEC's new Reactor Development Division, Rickover was glad it had been written. The last action Rickover took from Oak Ridge was to send a long report to BuShips, summarizing his findings and conclusions from the trip. "It is significant," he wrote, "that during our entire tour, of the many scientists contacted, not one was found who had a definite interest in and was working on the problem of furthering nuclear power." He urged that the Navy assign promising young engineers to nuclear power projects at the AEC's laboratories, and that a design concept for a power plant be selected for study and development. And he recommended that his group be designated as BuShips' agent to carry out this program. A week later, having heard no response, he wrote a second letter suggesting that if his previous proposal was not acceptable, his people could be assigned part-time in BuShips and part-time in the AEC.

A Prophet in His Own Land

When they returned to Washington, the members of the Naval Group found their worst fears realized. The group was broken up. Roddis was assigned to work for Captain Mumma, who was still officially in charge of nuclear matters for the Bureau of Ships. Other members of the group were scattered like the Jews after the destruction of the temple: Ray Dick to a research desk in the bureau's Metals Section; Libbey to the

Military Liaison Committee staff of the AEC; and Dunford to the Military Applications Branch of the AEC, which was concerned primarily with nuclear ordnance. There was some hesitation as to what to do with the feisty Captain Rickover himself. Most officers in the bureau were convinced that there was no need for him in the bureau, since there was so little nuclear activity. One suggested that he be returned to Oak Ridge as a declassification officer, to identify documents that no longer warranted military classification. Admiral Earle W. Mills, BuShips chief, knew Rickover from his Electrical Section work and had sufficient respect for him that he decided to override his advisers and keep him around as a special assistant for nuclear matters. But he had no staff, no assigned responsibility, and no authority.

Rickover's elite Naval Group, repudiated and scattered, had hit bottom.

Part II

Building a Decisive Weapon
(1947–1952)

II.

When I came to Washington before World War II to head the Electrical Section of the Bureau of Ships, I found that one man was in charge of design, another of production, a third handled maintenance, while a fourth dealt with fiscal matters. The entire Bureau operated that way. It didn't make sense to me. Design problems showed up in production, production errors showed up in maintenance, and financial matters reached into all areas. I changed the system. I made one man responsible for his entire area of equipment— for design, production, maintenance, and contracting. If anything went wrong, I knew exactly at whom to point. I run my present organization on the same principle.

H.G.R.

Building a Decisive Weapon
1947–1952

RETURNING TO WASHINGTON in September 1947, Captain Rickover crouched like a jungle creature looking for a chance to spring. He continued to meet informally with members of the Naval Group, at times singly, occasionally with all of them. They kept him apprised of what news they picked up from the various far-flung outposts of the atomic community. The news was nearly all administrative, political, or bureaucratic. Little substantive progress was being made in the areas of interest to him. Thus, the problem boiled down to convincing the top levels of the Navy and the Atomic Energy Commission (AEC) that building a nuclear submarine was an important national priority. It was clear that no one else who mattered held that view at that time. Rickover focused on the submarine as the application in which nuclear power would make the most dramatic difference: it would enable the craft to operate submerged for long periods without the need for air to operate its engines. Furthermore, it was the most difficult application; if a nuclear power plant could be put into a submarine, then application to other ships would be clearly feasible.

RISING FROM THE ASHES

The office Rickover was given at the Bureau of Ships had previously been a ladies' rest room, as evidenced by a washbasin and some capped-off plumbing still remaining. His response to this indignity established a pattern for the rest of his career. He played it up, joked about it, and, in every subsequent office until his retirement as a full, four-star admiral nearly four decades later, his decor was "po' boy shabby"—honest but underappreciated. It fit his style and personality and discomfited his enemies. The head of nuclear matters at BuShips, Captain Albert G. Mumma, had given Lou Roddis an office right across the hall from Rickover, partly to keep an eye on Rickover but also to assist when appropriate.

Rickover tried his hard-sell on everyone in Washington he could get to, without success. So he took another tack. He heard that the Daniels Pile project was still struggling along at Oak Ridge, without much progress or enthusiasm but still with some remaining funds. He flew down to Oak Ridge and talked to the few remaining people who were still working on the project. He found that there were enough funds and materials to keep the group going another six months or so. He called the people together and asked, "Would you guys be interested in dropping this turkey and spending your remaining resources studying a submarine reactor plant?"

He got a surprisingly affirmative response. Warming to the idea, he continued. "It ought to be a thermal neutron design, so that it will require a minimum of scarce uranium. We'll use pressurized-water coolant, because we know how to build pumps and pipes and valves to handle that. The shielding we'll have to look into, but I don't want a lot of exotic materials. In a submarine, weight and space are at a premium, but if we can lick that application, we can power *any* kind of ship."

Rickover knew that Dr. Alvin M. Weinberg, the bright young director of the Physics Division at Oak Ridge, favored this sort of reactor design, as did Harold Etherington, the analytically skilled engineer from the Allis-Chalmers Company who was now head of the laboratory's

Reactor Division. The Daniels group reacted to Rickover's proposal with excited questions about safety, ruggedness requirements, saltwater systems, and other aspects peculiar to submarines, and when Rickover left, he felt for the first time that somebody might actually begin to study seriously some of the many problems that would have to be solved in order to send a nuclear-powered submarine to sea.

For several weeks no one in Washington knew that the Daniels Pile had been terminated and a submarine study was under way. Rickover had told his boss, BuShips Chief Admiral Earle W. Mills, and of course Roddis and Mumma knew; but no one else knew. When the AEC people finally found out, they were shocked but, upon consideration, decided that there was no point in trying to resurrect the moribund Daniels project, so they let the work continue. They knew that it didn't matter much, either way. Rickover also knew that it didn't matter much, and that nothing significant would happen until the secretary of the Navy declared the nuclear submarine a military necessity. The AEC would then be obligated to respond, as a matter of national policy. After that, his problem would boil down to ensuring that the effort was effectively and competently run—and getting himself put in charge of it.

Taking on the Navy

The response Rickover got every time he tried to arouse interest among the Navy brass was discouragingly the same: "Dammit, Captain, you're not going to get anyone at the policy-making level interested in your underwater space ship at this moment in history. We're trying to figure out what this new Department of Defense is going to do to us. The enemy right now is the Air Force. They're getting themselves into all the important positions. They'll be getting the key missile missions. We'll be lucky if we can hang on to our aircraft carriers."

Rickover knew all that. He also knew that the chief of the Bureau of Ships, *his* boss, was telling people (based on advice from Mumma), "Nuclear submarines would be great, but it doesn't make sense for the Navy to try to build one now. Let the AEC develop power reactors ashore first. Then the Navy can use the technology to tackle the submarine application, which will be challenge enough."

From time to time Rickover would review the situation with Ray Dick or one of the other Naval Group expatriates. "Trying to persuade all these Navy jokers is a waste of time," said Rickover. "If the secretary declares the nuclear submarine a military necessity, they'll all fall in line. Until then all they'll give us at best is sympathy. But the secretary is a politician. That's his job. He doesn't give a damn what kind of ships we have. He doesn't know anything about ships. He's worrying about the secretary of defense and the Air Force."

"Do we have any leads through his aides or any other staff types that could get us an audience?" asked Dick.

"Naw, that's not going to do it. It's got to be somebody who can speak authoritatively on ships, on what kind of ships a fighting Navy needs."

"That's what the Bureau of Ships is supposed to tell him."

"Oh, hell. No line officer really thinks the bureau knows what it needs. When was the last time you heard a seagoing line officer listening with rapt attention to some character from BuShips?"

"The only real authority on the needs of the fleet is the chief of naval operations, Captain. The rest of the guys are just an amen chorus."

"Right, Dick. That's right. And Chester Nimitz is a submariner himself! By God, we'll draft a letter for Nimitz to the secretary, and I'll take it to him myself. If anyone can understand the advantages of nuclear power to a submarine, he should."

"But don't we still have to pick up signatures from everybody between Nimitz and us?"

"Of course. But now we have a focus. A point of immediate action. Not a vague question of just how much do you favor this project. What the hell! What have we got to lose?"

It took a week for Dick and Rickover to craft the carefully worded letter. They scrutinized every sentence from the standpoint of each of the officers who would have to sign off on it, trying to skirt issues they thought might be touchy. And then they began the tedious task of hand-carrying it to each of the necessary offices, taking it back and rewording each part considered offensive. Admiral Mills signed off, adding a crucial endorsement. Two veteran submarine officers in the office of the chief of naval operations (CNO) provided critical help: Captain Elton W. "Joe" Grenfell and Commander Edward L. Beach. Their well-known wartime experience in submarines lent authority and credibility in the eyes of the line officers. Two months later, on 5 December 1947, the letter got to Nimitz. He was fascinated with the idea and signed the letter immediately. Along with Nimitz's letter were proposed letters for Navy Secretary John L. Sullivan to send to James V. Forrestal, the first secretary of defense, to Dr. Vannevar Bush, chairman of the Research and Development Board, and to Admiral Mills at BuShips. Sullivan also signed. The Navy was finally on record:

There was a military need for a submarine with unlimited endurance at high speed submerged.

Only nuclear power could meet that need.

With sufficient effort, such a submarine could be completed by the mid-1950s.

The Bureau of Ships was to be the Navy's agency for carrying out this development.

Taking on the Atomic Energy Commission

Important as this development was, Rickover knew that the Navy could accomplish very little without the AEC. He had already taken on the AEC the previous month and had come away with only a handful of smoke. Undeterred, he went on to arrange a meeting between some of the AEC officials and Admiral Mills and himself, to discuss in general terms the problems and prospects of nuclear power in the Navy. Admiral Mills opened the meeting with a short speech covering the Navy's view of the situation, and the floor was then open for discussion.

"Admiral, you must realize," began the AEC response, "that our primary function is to carry out the program the Army began, to supply nuclear munitions for the nation's defense. There is a vocal and influential constituency in this country that believes that this responsibility should never have been taken from the Army. They are continually scrutinizing us to prove their case. To prove them wrong must be our first priority."

"Of course, sir."

"There is also the problem of uranium supply. The demand for new types of weapons is increasing, and it is a demand we must meet, by law. Yet the supply of good uranium ore is limited primarily to Colorado and the Belgian Congo. This fact has already distorted our nation's foreign policy, and we are frantically exploring to find new sources. In this situation, another demand for uranium, which if successful could increase at an alarming rate, is not one we view with equanimity."

"We appreciate that point also."

"Moreover, there are programmatic considerations. We tolerated the change informally brought about that redirected the Daniels Pile project toward a submarine application. But as you know, we are just now consolidating all of our reactor work and moving it to our Argonne Laboratory outside Chicago. We give our laboratory directors considerable discretion, and it is not clear what the priorities will be there once the dust settles, which will take some time. You should also understand, gentlemen, that our General Advisory Committee, which is made up of some of the foremost scientists in the world, and which is thoroughly familiar with the latest information in atomic energy, has looked into this matter and has concluded that to undertake the development of a nuclear power plant for a submarine at this time would be technically premature."

None of this was encouraging to Rickover. He knew that the AEC was the organization that would have to take responsibility and provide most of the funding to carry out his program. He clearly had a task ahead of him.

He started with BuShips. The bureau had been officially given the task of developing a ship designated by the Navy as a military requirement. He drafted a letter from Mills to the AEC, stating as follows:

The Bureau of Ships has been tasked by the secretary of the Navy to develop a nuclear-powered submarine.

The responsibility of the Navy to supply the best possible ships for the nation's defense requires that no time be lost in undertaking this development.

The responsibility for atomic matters lies, by law, with the AEC.

The responsibilities of the two agencies for such an undertaking cannot be separated. To ensure proper decision making, the program must be closely coordinated between them.

It took only a month and a half this time to get the letter signed out. It proposed that a single organization be set up, responsible to both agencies and utilizing the resources and facilities of both, as appropriate, and that additional personnel be trained, in order to minimize the demands for existing AEC laboratory people. The gauntlet had been thrown down.

The Attack from the Undersea Warfare Symposium

It might be supposed that an official letter of this apparent import could not be ignored by the responsible cabinet-level agency to which it was addressed. But it was. Rickover had now gleaned enough experience to find this no surprise. He knew that Vannevar Bush's Research and Development Board and the AEC's General Advisory Committee, led by the famous Dr. James B. Conant and Dr. J. Robert Oppenheimer, had responded internally to Mills's letter by going on record that the project should be considered a "moderately long-range" one rather than an urgent one, and that it should be fully under AEC control rather than in the dual Navy/AEC role Mills had proposed. Rickover learned through his informants that the AEC had no intention of replying to his letter in the near future, so he looked around for a position from which to launch his next attack. He quickly found one.

Roddis came over with a request received by the Bureau of Ships to furnish a speaker on nuclear-powered ships at the next annual Undersea Warfare Symposium. "These symposia are sponsored every year by these guys," said Roddis.

"Who are they?" asked Rickover. "Are they government? Does anybody pay any attention to them?"

"They're a group of scientists, oceanographers, marine engineers, and naval officers, operating outside the government but with a lot of government personnel involved. They get some well-known speakers and draw an audience of about seven hundred people, including a lot of top-level people we'd like to reach."

"What do they want?"

"They've asked the bureau to provide a speaker to talk on nuclear propulsion for ships. Mumma thinks we should have three speeches: one by him, one by me, and one by you. He's asked me to write all three speeches and show them to you."

"That's a stupid idea."

"I agree. But I thought maybe we could make something out of this."

"You think there really are some important people at these things? Is there a lot of publicity on it?"

"Yeah. I looked into it. In previous years there've been a number of important ideas that first were aired at one of these meetings."

"Then let's do it right. Let's have one speech. We'll write it, and we'll have Mills give it."

So on 2 April 1948 Admiral Mills got up and laid out the frustrating situation that the naval nuclear propulsion effort was facing. He was an impressive speaker and well respected in this audience of engineers, scientists, and policy makers. He talked not like a temporizing politician but like a determined project director. He stated, "The design and development of a nuclear power plant for a submarine is of utmost importance to the Navy and may be a decisive factor in a future war. Such a design is technically feasible and is almost entirely an engineering problem. When such a plant will be available depends entirely on the initiative and effort expended."

With AEC Commissioner (and later Chairman) Lewis L. Strauss chairing the symposium, and other commissioners and Navy officials in the audience, Mills spoke directly of his problem with the AEC:

> There is another point I must make clear to this audience, and that is that to date the Atomic Energy Commission has never recognized the submarine power pile as a project, nor has it given official status or priority to such a pile. I mention this because the impression is abroad that considerable work is being done on a submarine pile and that it is a project which enjoys high priority . . . If I may be so bold as to venture an opinion, I would guess that less than one percent of the work which will ultimately be required to design a submarine plant has now been accomplished.

Mills closed with a final salvo:

> To date it has not yet been recognized as a project and only a very small effort has been expended toward its accomplishment. Common prudence and the dictates of national defense make it mandatory that this situation be recognized and that work be undertaken without delay. We should use all agencies, industrial as well as laboratory, that can contribute to the solution of this project, so important to the Navy.
>
> I sincerely hope that in the very near future, the Atomic Energy Commission, in accordance with the recommendations of the various committees and of the Research and Development Board, will establish the development of a nuclear power plant for a submarine as a formal project at high priority.

Washington was not used to such public bluntness at high levels. No one in the room missed the point of Mills's remarks or the intensity of his feelings on the subject. Chairman Strauss remarked with forced jocularity, "I never thought an old friend would do that to me." But the commission's written response, which came several weeks later, was an ambiguous promise that the project would be formalized and "prosecuted with a high priority commensurate with the importance of this project."

"Ha!" said Rickover to Roddis, when he saw the letter. "They'll pursue it with the importance they think it deserves, and we know how little that is."

But now Mills had the bit in his teeth. And not only Mills; it was wonderful to see how many other naval officers favored a nuclear submarine project, now that the top levels had signed off on it. The BuShips people had been given a task to do, and the partner the law required them to work with had rebuffed them. Moreover, the Navy shared Rickover's concern that an AEC laboratory full of research scientists would probably not be capable of developing battle-worthy hardware. The Navy preferred working with industry. So Mills, egged on by Rickover and abetted by allies on the powerful Military Liaison Committee, drafted another letter to the AEC, stating that "the most rapid progress, at this time, can be made by utilizing the parallel efforts of industrial organizations, as well as of laboratories, simultaneously to the fullest extent."

Getting Industry Aboard: Westinghouse and General Electric

Rickover was running into a great deal of resistance getting industry and engineers into the project. Not only did the AEC resist Rickover's idea of the project being run by a technical team equally responsible to the AEC and the Navy; the AEC wanted the Navy to let the Argonne Laboratory study the options for an indeterminate time, and then the Navy could pick up the design after Argonne had selected the coolant and laid out the basic concept. Rickover was willing, in fact anxious, to have Argonne train Navy people and the employees of its industrial contractors in the esoteric new technologies of nuclear energy. But he was not willing to be dependent on the laboratory scientists to develop the actual shipboard power plant.

Early in May 1948 Rickover went to Argonne with Admiral Thorvald A. Solberg and Mumma to discuss with lab director Dr. Walter H. Zinn just how far Zinn was willing to go in working with industry. Zinn made it clear that he wanted to retain control of the technical decisions, and that he was backed to the hilt on this position by the

AEC's strong-willed director of research, Dr. James B. Fisk. In March Mills had reluctantly agreed to be less than a fully equal partner, in the face of Fisk's and Zinn's insistence on control. But Rickover wanted to spell out what this would mean, and subsequent discussions convinced Mills that the dual organization originally suggested by Rickover was the only proper approach. Since it was not clear that the AEC would agree to share responsibility for the program at Argonne, the General Electric project began to look like the only program with potential for becoming an industrial naval project.

The Navy had put a great deal of money, by 1948 standards, into the GE effort to develop a liquid-metal heat-exchange system for possible use in a naval vessel. Rickover wanted that program opened up into a full-fledged effort to develop a liquid-metal reactor plant, to parallel the pressurized-water approach. The use of parallel projects was common practice in important developments. The Manhattan District had used two approaches to the atomic bomb—plutonium and highly enriched uranium—and had developed three different processes for enriching the uranium. The Navy too had found the parallel approach a safer road when a lot depended on the outcome. So Rickover found a great deal of support in the Navy for his wish to have a backup for the pressurized-water design.

Rickover and Mills decided to lean on GE to give the Navy program greater emphasis. They were able to impress upon GE the urgency of the program, and they left feeling that the company might be willing to tilt a bit more in their direction. So Mills drafted another letter to the AEC, appending a report of their trip to Argonne and stating the importance the Navy attached to getting the GE program going as a parallel path to Argonne. He also signed an $830,000 contract with Westinghouse for a heat-transfer system study with pressurized water to parallel the GE study with liquid metal.

The AEC's response to all this was to call in Harry Winne and other GE officials on an urgent basis and tell them bluntly that the Navy was acting on its own in suggesting greater emphasis on the submarine reactor, and in fact the AEC desired *less* emphasis, rather than more, on the Navy work. At about this time AEC Chairman David Lilienthal suggested that the Navy appoint a liaison officer to deal with the AEC, indicating that Admiral Solberg might be an excellent choice. The Navy might well have made that choice, had not Solberg been appointed chief of naval research, a position that required him to sever all ties with the nuclear energy project. So Mills held off making any appointment to the relatively powerless liaison position.

Mills had a copy of a report that Admiral Nimitz had written to the Joint Chiefs of Staff of the Armed Services. It had a few blunt paragraphs that he thought should be shown to the AEC, such as this: "The seriousness of the Russian submarine menace is emphasized by the fact that they now have over five times the number of undersea craft that Germany had at the outbreak of World War II."

Mills also knew that the Russians had captured a score of the German Type XXI submarines and the engineers and technicians who had built them. These were the high-speed, long-range, snorkel-equipped boats developed at the end of the war. The commander of the Pacific Fleet had stated, "The new submarine with high submerged speed and great underwater endurance is probably the greatest threat that exists today to safe use of the sea. Until a solution is reached to the problem of how to destroy this submarine, and until the forces are made available for this work, we shall be in a poor position to operate our armed forces overseas against an enemy who has a large fleet of them."

The Navy's Operation Development Force had put it even more simply: "The tactical characteristics of the medium-speed, deep-diving snorkel-equipped submarine have virtually nullified the effectiveness of most of our World War II ASW [antisubmarine warfare] procedures, tactics, and doctrines."

Armed with this information, Mills was determined to face the AEC top brass for a showdown. Through the Military Liaison Committee he arranged a meeting with the commissioners for 16 June, and he brought along two experienced and well-known submariners to lend weight to his message. After the tactical and strategic importance of a nuclear submarine had been described, Mills brought up the General Electric project. He questioned the GE position that the company could not work on both the civilian power reactor and the submarine reactor, particularly if it brought in more engineering help from within the company. The point was discussed, and the commissioners agreed to get back to the Navy within a few weeks. Mills and Rickover left feeling that their views had been sympathetically heard, perhaps for the first time.

The AEC response to the Navy was signed out a month and a half later, not by the chairman or even one of the commissioners, but by the general manager. It was a clear repudiation of the Navy's position.

It directed GE "that as great a portion as possible of the effort on the 'Navy reactor' at Schenectady be redirected towards the early completion of the intermediate-energy power-breeder reactor." And it firmly rejected the Navy's proposal that the AEC work with the Navy as an equal partner and emphasize engineering development rather than scientific research.

In the meantime Mills had decided to appoint Rickover to the AEC liaison position, and when the AEC letter came, Rickover swung into action. He drafted a strong letter to the AEC chairman from Mills saying that the Navy could see "no reasonable hope" that the AEC approach could develop a submarine plant in the required time, and that the Navy would have to have a backup project for the Argonne program. If the AEC was unwilling to cooperate in this effort, the Navy would contract with industry unilaterally. Rickover bolstered Mills's position by drafting letters for Mills to send the secretary of the Navy and to the secretary of defense. By this time he had laid sufficient groundwork that he was able to get all the letters signed within forty-eight hours.

With pressure from the chairman of the Military Liaison Committee, a series of urgent internal discussions were held within the AEC, and the commissioners agreed to meet again with Mills and Rickover. Rickover worked during the few days before the meeting to tie down any uncertainties. He obtained a written statement from GE that the company was "willing and anxious to design and build a reactor suitable for use in a naval vessel." He also called Westinghouse and got assurance that the company was ready to implement his earlier suggestion to set up a separate division to handle the naval project, and that the company stood ready to send six of its best engineers to GE for one year of training. Rickover felt that this would provide impressive evidence that a competitive industrial situation could be established.

Mills and Rickover went back into battle with the AEC. Fueled by the anger of Mills and Rickover, and moderated by the mediation of Donald F. Carpenter, the competent chairman of the Military Liaison Committee, a mutually agreeable arrangement was finally worked out. Rickover now had both the Navy and the AEC officially agreed to work on the project in a serious way.

Getting the Billet

Nine months had passed since Rickover had returned to Washington and had his group disbanded. He still had one more loose end to clean up. He went to Admiral Mills with a simple message: "I need to set up a small working team, patterned after the group I had at Oak Ridge, to take charge of this program. It will have to have status in both the Bureau of Ships and the AEC, and I think we can arrange that without too much fuss." Mills agreed. He had heard the point before, and he couldn't argue with it. But he was not prepared for Rickover's next point: "Obviously, the bureau can't have two people in charge of nuclear power. You'll have to get rid of either Mumma or me."

Mills hesitated. He had great respect for Mumma, but he knew that Rickover was right: the bureau couldn't have two people in charge of nuclear power. He chose Rickover and made him head of a new Nuclear Power Branch (designated Code 390) within the bureau's Research Division. At last Rickover had the tools and the elbow room he needed. All he had to do now was to develop a nuclear power plant.

CREATING THE MEANS

One must permit his people the freedom to seek added work and greater responsibility. In my organization, there are no formal job descriptions or organization charts. Responsibilities are defined in a general way, so that people are not circumscribed. All are permitted to do as they think best and to go to anyone and anywhere for help. Each person is then limited only by his own ability.

H.G.R.

Although Rickover had finally gotten the Navy and the AEC to commit themselves formally to a nuclear submarine project, there was little physical evidence of this commitment. Rickover's first move was to reassemble his old team under his new banner of the Nuclear Power Branch in the Bureau of Ships. Of the four other naval officers whom the bureau had sent to Oak Ridge, only Roddis and Dick were immediately available, and Rickover quickly pulled them in. Dunford joined the team in January 1949, but Libbey decided to stay with the AEC's Military Liaison Committee.

The bureau had also sent three civilian employees, but one of them stayed on with the Oak Ridge Reactor Physics Division, and one went with Harold Etherington to Argonne. Rickover brought in the third,

George Emerson, and then began the slow process of recruiting additional bright young engineers for his permanent headquarters staff. By the end of 1948 he had selected two new officers, Robert V. Laney, Naval Academy class of 1939, and Eugene P. "Dennis" Wilkinson from San Diego State, and two civilian engineers from Oak Ridge, Dr. Jack A. Kyger and William H. Wilson.

Laney had heard about the program in 1946 from his Naval Academy classmates and applied for duty there as soon as he could. He continued to perform important tasks for Rickover until as late as 1983. Wilkinson was a technically minded submarine officer who had trained at Argonne and whom Rickover hoped to get into Naval Reactors. But Wilkinson, with eight war patrols under his belt, was determined to go back to sea. He was to become the first nuclear submarine skipper, in command of the USS *Nautilus*, and was later made captain of the first nuclear surface ship, the cruiser *Long Beach*. He was known far and wide as a formidable poker player. His time in the Naval Reactors program required considerable shore duty, without sea pay, and he was too busy to supplement his shore pay with poker earnings, as was his wont. So he trained his wife in the fundamentals of the game and told her, "Don't take from Navy people. Air Force, civilians, OK." And she handled it just fine.

Jack Kyger, a bright, laid-back Ph.D. chemical engineer from Yale and MIT, also played poker, and there were some killer games in Pittsburgh and in Washington during those early years. He owned a sailboat and he sailed to win, which he did consistently, in his two weeks off each year during Marblehead Race Week. Bill Wilson, whom Kyger had pulled in from Oak Ridge, was a demon bridge player, and Wilson persuaded Kyger to join him in some of the open duplicate bridge games that took place each week in downtown Washington hotels. Kyger had worked on producing the very first production quantities of uranium at the Mallinckrodt Chemical Works in St. Louis, and he and Wilson both had a deep and wide knowledge of materials, both metal and ceramic, which proved to be a priceless asset to the program.

I Find Myself Working for Rickover

Some months later, in September 1948, I organized a three-day symposium at the Oak Ridge Laboratory on radiation shielding of nuclear facilities and invited both potential users and potential suppliers from all over the United States. It was the first time anything of this scale had been attempted for a subject that was highly classified, but it went well. All of the major atomic energy laboratories were represented, as were organizations interested in building both stationary and mobile reactor systems. Reproduction facilities were less common and less developed in those days, particularly for classified papers, and I insisted that each speaker bring 250 copies of his paper before the symposium started, so that they could be bound into a package for each of the participants to take back, with copies left over for the appropriate laboratory libraries and files.

Rickover saw the symposium as an opportunity to get his story across to all of the technical people who might have some useful input, and he came down the night before to discuss how to get the most out of the affair. "What are you going to get out of this thing, Rockwell?" he asked.

"What do you mean, Captain? There will be a chance, for the first time, for users like yourself to talk directly with the laboratory people who will have to produce the data on which your shield design will be based. That's what I'm trying to accomplish."

"Yeah, yeah. I know all that. But we shouldn't pass up a chance to get something concrete out of this. Let's get some commitments out of people."

"I'm not sure I know what kind of commitments you want, Captain."

"I want to know who's going to do what, and by when. Can you work with us tonight? I'd like to have you work out with my people a list of first steps that should be taken to resolve the questions and uncertainties that stand in the way of our designing a shield right now. Could you sit down and design me a shield right now?"

"No, sir. Of course not."

"Why not? What do you need to know first? Let's start to define those things, and then define what we need to do to get that information. Do we need experiments? What kind of experiments? Is the theory adequate? What theoretical work do we need? Who should do it? Hell, do I have to spell it all out for you?"

So I found myself working far into the night in the Oak Ridge "Guest House," as the dormlike hotel was called, with Lou Roddis, Miles Libbey, and Jack Kyger. This was the one night of all nights I didn't need an extra chore. I was not experienced enough to have delegated all of the symposium logistics, and I kept worrying about whether people were getting met at the airport and whether they all had rooms to stay in. But by morning we had a talking paper to lay before the conferees, bringing focus to what had been a rambling philosophical discussion, and I had become fascinated with the intense, silver-haired Captain Rickover and his small, dedicated crew.

Thus, in November 1949 I was not totally surprised to receive a call from the Captain asking if I could attend a meeting in Washington that weekend, at which a group of invited scientists would comment on the problems of providing radiation shielding for a nuclear submarine. Though notice was short, I canceled my weekend plans and went to the meeting. The range of comments was wide, including proposals involving exotic materials and designs, and suggestions for undertaking long and difficult theoretical developments. I somewhat hesitantly stated my conviction that the Navy should stick to simple materials—iron, lead, and water—and use a simplified mock-up approach, such as Everitt Blizard and Charles Clifford were already doing at the lab, leaving a more fundamental understanding of the process for later study. Rickover thanked us all for our contributions, and as we were leaving the room he called me back.

"How much do you make, Rockwell?"

"I just got a raise, sir. It's now a little more than $5,000 a year." For some time that amount had been a sort of milepost to look forward to, and it felt good to be able to claim it.

"We can beat that, can't we, Dunford?" Seeing Dunford's nod, Rickover shouted to his secretary, "Get me Al Weinberg at Oak Ridge." Weinberg was director of research at the Oak Ridge Lab.

"Wait a minute," I protested. "What are you going to tell Weinberg?"

"We need you here. He'll understand that. Hell, he's got hundreds of characters down there milling around. We're trying to do something. He won't want to hold you back."

"I don't even know if I want to come here. What would I do? I don't know if I or my family would want to live here; I don't know anything about Washington."

"If you come here, you'll help me create a nuclear submarine in the next five years. If you stay at the lab, nothing will have changed much in that time. What will you do here? Hell, I don't know! I don't even know what *I'm* going to be doing. Whatever needs to be done. You've got to help us figure out what that is. Wilson, show Rockwell around

Washington until he likes it. Now get out of here. I've got work to do."

And the next thing I knew, I was working for Rickover.

Mandil Enters the Scene

Harry Mandil had gone to work for Rickover while Rickover was still a commander and nuclear power was not even part of his vocabulary. Mandil was born in Istanbul, and he received his B.S. in electrical engineering from the University of London and his M.S. in electrical engineering from MIT. He had worked as a field engineer at the Norcross Corporation in Newton, Massachusetts, designing process control systems for textile mills, paper mills, and chemical plants. This experience taught him a lot about metals and other materials, and about mechanical systems, to add to his electrical knowledge. And he saw firsthand how ideas that look good on paper often fail to measure up in the hard-bitten real world of the factory.

Mandil had good technical insight, but he also had the discipline and temperament not to leap impulsively wherever insight suggested. He was a very thorough engineer, one who didn't have to learn a lesson twice. His field experience showed him the importance of training, operating manuals, maintenance procedures, and the myriad aspects of engineering that are not taught in schools but often make the difference between equipment that works and equipment that fails, sometimes when it is needed most.

When Mandil signed up with the Navy in 1942, he was assigned to the Electrical Section of the Bureau of Ships. He didn't know much about the head of the Electrical Section, one Commander Hyman G. Rickover, a thin, wiry "engineering duty only" officer in his early forties, already turning gray-haired. Shortly after taking charge, Rickover had gotten hold of British battle damage reports. He was horrified to find the damage to electrical equipment caused by mines, torpedoes, and bombs. Little consideration of battle-resistance had gone into the design of electrical equipment for shipboard use. Even before Pearl Harbor, Rickover realized that this was a major area of vulnerability for our fighting ships. Electrical failure could mean loss of propulsion power, lighting, fire-fighting equipment, communication, ventilation— a complete loss of function, a ship drifting dark, silent, and helpless in the presence of the enemy. To correct this situation, Rickover had set up a task force with forty engineers to focus solely on designing and testing shock-resistant equipment to replace existing hardware. In a crash program he was able to develop, build, and deliver tens of thousands of items of replacement equipment for installation in both old and new ships while the war was still under way. To see for himself what form this battle damage took, Rickover traveled nearly one hundred thousand miles a year (in the slow, noisy propeller-driven aircraft of the day), determined to visit every battle-damaged ship that put into port for repairs. He compared what he saw with the British reports and with what he had managed to learn from other sources, and returned to his office with copious notes to be integrated into the ongoing design and development work.

In Rickover's fast-growing Electrical Section, Mandil was soon put in charge of the group responsible for the preparation of electrical power distribution specifications, for both submarines and surface ships, and the development of power distribution equipment such as switchboards, automatic bus transfer devices, circuit breakers, special fittings, and the like.

After the war, Mandil was glad to get out of uniform and back to his civilian job. He was made assistant to the president of Norcross, in charge of all field engineering for the company. But Rickover knew talent when he saw it, and when he started to build up his nuclear power team, he turned his persuasive power on Mandil to get him into the program. It was the kind of program to fire the imagination of any engineer, and before he could have second thoughts on the matter, he found himself in the Oak Ridge school, on the long road to becoming a nuclear engineer and one of the top two or three people on the Rickover Team.

Panoff Is Brought In

Robert Panoff was another one of those top people. Panoff was a tough guy. Not a bully who shouts at people who can't hurt him, like secretaries and kids. He didn't look for fights, but he had grown up as a little guy in a tough neighborhood, and he learned early on that you either stand up or get trampled on. He had decided that he wasn't going to get trampled on. After Pearl Harbor, he was anxious to do his part, but he was too short for military duty, so he decided to finish school and get his engineering degree. Government officials repeatedly announced that the nation needed engineers, and there were plenty of defense jobs where his newly learned skills could be applied to the war effort.

He decided to try for a job in the Navy's Bureau of Ships. He wasn't a sailing buff—he'd never had enough money or time for that kind of activity—but he knew that ships were all engineered hardware, especially naval ships. There wasn't a stick of material aboard that hadn't been designed to be there, and for an engineer like Panoff that was an ideal working environment. He had enjoyed his summer job before senior year at Union College wiring up electrical systems in new diesel-electric locomotives; those too had a natural functional beauty that he just enjoyed being around.

After graduating in 1942, he found a cheap, dormitory-like apartment building near Dupont Circle, where he could walk to work and eat in when he wanted to, and he settled in with the other young government workers. It was almost like a continuation of college. He was still awaiting security clearance and reference checks, but he was confident that he would be at work within a few days.

He proved to be right about this. The war had caused technical organizations to scramble competitively for good engineers, and Panoff had graduated near the top, from a top-flight engineering college. He was soon at a desk trying to figure out how to be useful. A young officer had handed him a five-inch-thick loose-leaf technical manual with a cheap hard cover and said, "It's all in here. Read this, and ask me any questions." Panoff took the manual home with him every night, determined not to ask anyone how to do his job. He would figure that out for himself. Each morning he came in to work with a list of little questions about what he had read: What did this acronym stand for, what was that organization and how did it relate to BuShips, why did they use this particular switchgear?

Panoff found that submarine electrical systems had not had a thorough design review for decades. Changes had been pasted onto outmoded hardware, and the whole system cried out for a complete redesign. He now had a chance to do just that, and he dug into it with enthusiasm. He read manuals and textbooks, ships' logs and battle reports, and even had a chance to examine battle-damaged equipment on American, German, and Japanese ships. He rode submarines and talked to officers and sailors. And he talked with manufacturers of equipment and read their technical reports.

Panoff was in the reception area one day when Rickover came striding out to meet a vendor bringing in an instrument he had just redesigned. The vendor announced proudly that it was now a fully shockproof design. He handed it to Rickover, expecting the Commander to look it over admiringly and perhaps comment on its sleek appearance. But Rickover merely hurled it against the old-fashioned radiator and didn't even wince as it shattered. He then turned on his heel and strode silently back to his office. (He performed this ritual more than once.)

Shock damage was a particular problem for submarines, for several reasons. First, because the confined spaces put components close together and made them especially vulnerable to excessive motion. Second, because the weapon of choice against submarines was depth charges—underwater explosions designed to deliver severe shock to the submarine and all her equipment. And third, because loss of electric power is particularly serious on a submarine, since a submarine, like a whale, can stay submerged only for short periods and then must come up for air. Loss of electric power, even for a short time, could prevent a submarine from surfacing, or even cause her to sink unchecked until she was crushed to death in the sea's dark depths.

Rickover's shock-testing program had now reached the point where full-scale testing, under shipboard conditions, was needed. A large number of tests had been run on scaled-down components, mounted inside scaled-down submarine hulls on foundations that simulated the anticipated shipboard situation. These miniature submarines, heavily instrumented, were then anchored in the Chesapeake Bay, and scaled-down depth charges were exploded nearby. Data from strain gauges, accelerometers, position indicators, velocity meters, and other sophisticated gadgetry, augmented by slow-motion movies of the equipment swaying in ever-increasing arcs until it broke off and sent pieces drifting through the hull, were shown to horrified equipment manufacturers. Rickover also located the most spectacular pictures in the Navy's files, of ships battling incredible waves and other ships limping home, mauled and mutilated by battle damage but still afloat. "That's the environment your equipment has to work reliably in," he would insist. Some of these films and slides were later used to good effect in educating incredulous laboratory scientists as to what naval application really entailed.

An elaborate theoretical basis had been developed to guide the design of these experiments, but modeling a process with scaled-down hardware always has certain inherent limitations. For example, a component can be made half as high and half as wide and half as deep as the original. This will decrease by half the length of lever arms through which shock forces are transferred. But the weight of all parts, which drives the vibration, will now be one-eighth, not one-half, and surface areas may be one-fourth. Resonant frequencies—the frequency of vibration to which the structure is particularly sensitive—will be grossly different. Each of these problems can be gotten around to some extent by ignoring or distorting the others. But with each such step the departure from the actual conditions one wishes to simulate grows more tortuous and uncertain.

The mere logistics of the test program amazed Panoff. There were half a dozen organizations involved: his own BuShips; the Naval Engineering Station, a testing lab of the bureau's; the Naval Research Laboratory, which was entirely separate from BuShips; BuOrd (the Bureau of Ordnance), sister organization to BuShips; and several commercial contractors. The field of action was a large area of open water in the Chesapeake Bay, so the Navy was on familiar turf. It had brought in living barges, large, floating dormitories to house and feed the workers, scientists, and occasional visitors. The Naval Research Lab had mounted all its instrumentation systems in special trailer trucks, which were then rolled onto barges and bolted down, providing vibration-isolated laboratories from which scientists could monitor the tests. Communication and transportation to and from "the beach" were handled routinely. It all worked remarkably smoothly. Panoff realized that this was the sort of operation the Navy handles best.

Panoff knew the great importance Commander Rickover attached to his shock-testing program, and he knew that he was adding additional junior personnel to the project, so he was not unduly surprised to find himself called into the front office to talk about it. There were never any opening pleasantries. "Panoff, you know the difficulties we've had trying to apply the shock-test results to full-scale applications."

"Yes, sir."

"We're finally going to have a chance to do it right. The *Ulua* hull was rushed to completion toward the end of the war, so they could get her off the ways and get a new ship started. The hull is essentially complete, but very little of her interior gear has been installed. With the war over, they've decided not to finish her. I've helped persuade the necessary people to make the hull available for testing full-scale components on full-scale mounts. That'll not only give us valid data right off; it'll also give us a chance to check out the model theory we've been using to apply the data from the small-scale tests. How about it? Can I pry you away from your present assignment for a while to get you into this program?"

Panoff was amazed that it had been put as a question. "You don't have to ask, Commander. You're the boss."

"Goddammit, Panoff, this is an exciting and important program. If you're not clawing at the gates to get into it, I'll get someone else. I don't want anyone in this program who isn't eager to do it. It's too important. Now get out!"

Panoff was finally able to convince the Commander that his response was prompted by surprise, not reluctance, and that he was indeed excited about the program. He considered it not only of great practical importance, but also of considerable theoretical interest and value. He was now about to see up close what it meant to work on a program in which Commander Rickover took an intense personal interest.

So in 1950, when Captain Rickover began to look around for known human assets to build up his new nuclear power team, it was not surprising that he turned to Panoff. And it was not surprising that Panoff accepted, though both of them would say more than once in later years that their relationship was hardly a peaceful one.

Going after "A Few Good Men"

In 1950 civilian physicist Dr. Alvin Radkowsky and Lieutenant Commanders Eli B. Roth and Marshall E. "Bill" Turnbaugh (Naval Academy class of 1939), Sherman Naymark (1941), and Jonathan A. "Bud" Barker (1942), all of whom Mumma had sent to Argonne for a year of more of nuclear training, returned and joined the Rickover team. Rickover had arranged to have the Argonne group reporting to him by the end of 1949, while they were still in training at Argonne. Radkowsky was an ordained orthodox rabbi with a master's degree in electrical engineering; he had earned a Ph.D. in physics from Catholic University while working in Rickover's Electrical Section at BuShips. He was to become Rickover's leading expert in reactor physics.

Roth, like Jack Kyger, was an enthusiastic poker player, though not a consistent winner. His assertive, jocular personality contrasted with quiet, competent Bill Turnbaugh, who went to the Pittsburgh office, where he played a key role for many years. Naymark went from Argonne to the Schenectady office, and Barker came to headquarters in

Washington. Barker was a quiet worker with a good sense of humor, who ended in the curious but important specialty of supervising the design and operation of complex systems to test the effects of radiation on specimens inserted into test reactors.

Rickover required his new recruits to develop for his approval a self-study program that they would follow on their own time. As finally approved, the course required a demonstrated mastery of several specific advanced texts in physics, metallurgy, chemistry, and engineering, plus field trips to various AEC facilities. It would require "a total of 854 hours' study, or 16 hours per week, excluding time spent on field trips or special duty assignments." Then, turning his attention to the longer range, Rickover went with Dunford to MIT to explore what could be done to expand the existing courses on marine engineering and naval architecture. They found the MIT faculty and students enthusiastic about the idea, and a survey course on nuclear physics was added to the regular graduate program. In addition, MIT agreed to set up a master's degree program in nuclear engineering for selected graduates of the regular program, and a curriculum was drawn up and agreed to by Rickover, to begin in June 1949. This program was the source of many of the officers who filled important positions in Rickover's program during its crucial early years; some of them stayed on for two or three decades.

Rickover also wanted to recruit civilians of known quality, as he had done for the Electrical Section during the war. From the several hundred still there he selected, in addition to Mandil and Panoff, Jack C. Grigg. Grigg had graduated from Texas Tech in 1941, and he was working in the Westinghouse student training program early in the war when Rickover's program for recruiting bright young engineers from industry picked him up. He became Rickover's top instrumentation and controls expert and stayed at Naval Reactors nearly three decades.

About this time (early 1950) Rickover received an application from Howard K. Marks, who had come out of Stanford with a master's degree in mechanical engineering and had transferred from the Puget Sound Naval Shipyard to the Portsmouth yard on the other coast to work on the design of a new class of submarines. He had over ten years of shipyard experience to offer, and when he heard that Rickover was recruiting, he decided that nuclear power was the place to be. "After three days of interviewing hell," said Marks, "I was finally hired by the Captain and sent to the Oak Ridge 1950 class, along with Harry Mandil, Joe Condon, Phil Finkelstein, and Bernie Resnick." Marks worked for Panoff at first, then took over submarine systems when Panoff became a project officer, and in 1958 he picked up the corresponding responsibilities for surface ship systems. He took a lot of flack from Rickover, because he was responsible for many critical items, but the Captain always knew he could depend on him.

Later, Rickover recruited Karl E. Swenson, who had spent several years at the Portsmouth Naval Shipyard before coming to the BuShips Submarine Type Desk. The bureau sent him to Argonne back in 1948, and after his return to the Type Desk he attracted the favorable attention of some of Rickover's people, running liaison between the nuclear plant and the rest of the submarine.

Rickover was able to find a few engineers of the caliber and type he wanted at Oak Ridge, but, as with the officers at MIT, he wanted to provide for the future. "We can play the game everyone else will be playing," he said to Roddis one day. "We can steal trained people from the laboratories and then have them stolen from us, or we can arrange to create more nuclear engineers, to train our own, and to create a national asset that will benefit everybody. I choose the latter course."

With Alvin Weinberg, the director of research of the Oak Ridge National Laboratory, Rickover and his people worked out a one-year curriculum to be given at Oak Ridge to acquaint engineers and scientists with the specifics of nuclear science and technology, and the laboratory agreed to accept the first class of twenty in March 1950, with a second class following in September. This was the beginning of what became internationally known as ORSORT, the Oak Ridge School of Reactor Technology, known locally as Clinch River Kollege of Knuclear Knowledge. Graduates were awarded the degree of Doctor Of Pile Engineering, enabling them thenceforth to add D.O.P.E. after their names. By 1958 thirty-five students had been sent from Naval Reactors, and other organizations working with NR had sent nearly six hundred additional trainees. Westinghouse sent 16 for its Naval Reactors facility plus 8 for elsewhere in the company; GE sent 13 for its naval program plus 15 more; Combustion Engineering (the third prototype site) sent 18. Five private shipyards sent a total of 49; six naval shipyards sent 21; manufacturers sent 158; electric utilities sent 34; BuShips groups outside NR sent 19; other government organizations sent 196. ORSORT was turning out about a hundred graduates per year, many of whom went on to become leaders in the burgeoning nuclear power industry. Rickover had delivered on his promise to create new nuclear engineers.

While building up his Navy organization, Rickover had not forgotten the AEC. It was still a skeleton organization, and the few people aboard were fully preoccupied with the task of producing bombs and assuring adequate supplies of uranium and plutonium for that purpose. They were also embroiled in organizing the laboratories and moving reactor work from Oak Ridge to Argonne. They were finally persuaded to announce the creation of a Division of Reactor Development in September 1948, but there was nothing to show for this announcement until the following February, when a director was appointed for the division. Several efforts to recruit a director from industry had failed, and finally Lawrence Hafstad, from the Defense Department's Research and Development Board, who had been a professor of physics at Johns Hopkins University during the war, agreed to accept the position. He was well liked by scientists and had the respect of Admiral Mills, and the AEC was glad to have him aboard. Rickover was not sure that a physics professor would be sympathetic to his approach, but he was willing to try to convince him. Indeed, he had little choice in the matter. He arranged for his group to give Hafstad an extensive briefing and urged that the Naval Group be given a home in the new division. Mills supported the idea, and it was done.

Rickover now had to figure out how to run a program with responsibility split between the AEC and the Navy, and between Argonne and Westinghouse, with General Electric a further largely unknown factor. Obviously not an ideal situation, but one he would have to live with. He moved his group into a temporary building called T-3, behind "Main Navy," where he had been. T-3 was a World War II temporary building, with seldom-functioning air conditioners in each window—stifling in the summer, cold and drafty in the winter. Main Navy, on the other hand, was temporary structure from the *first* world war. It was put up when Franklin Roosevelt was secretary of the Navy, and he protested at the time, "Nothing is so permanent as a temporary government building." (He was so right. The building was in full use until Richard Nixon's presidency.) The AEC had moved into the old Public Health Building across Constitution Avenue, so the Naval Group was within easy walking distance of the offices it had set up for itself in that agency.

During this period Rickover also took aboard a few young engineers from other parts of the Bureau of Ships. Some came from his old Electrical Section, some from Machinery Design and other appropriate sections. Most of these he sent down to Oak Ridge to take the full-year nuclear technology course. A few he put on a self-study program so that they could contribute immediately. Some he hired on AEC payroll, some on BuShips, but all had dual roles, appeared in both organizations' phone books, and had at least phantom offices in both buildings, with both Navy and AEC phone numbers on their desk at each place. This was fearsome and confusing to the bureaucrats in both agencies, and that was just fine with Rickover.

(Years later, when Rickover had become a public figure, a reporter called his Navy number and asked for his social secretary. Dixie Davis, Rickover's unflappable secretary, replied that she was that person, and then turned down an invitation she knew he wouldn't accept. The reporter, undaunted, then called the AEC, which at that time was in Germantown, Maryland. When her AEC extension rang, Dixie picked up the same phone, pushed another button, and answered. The poor reporter retreated in complete confusion, amazed at the ability of the Admiral and his staff to be everywhere at once. Such tricks are common now, but in the low-tech 1950s they were considered dazzling.)

Some of those early recruits contributed significantly to the program and deserve special mention. From the Oak Ridge Laboratory Kyger brought in metallurgist Frank Kerze, a street-smart New Yorker and a connoisseur of knock-knock jokes and wicked puns. Milton Shaw, an articulate, athletic mechanical engineer from the University of Tennessee, who was working at the Navy's Engineering Experiment Station, sought out Rickover and talked himself into a job. He was sent to Oak Ridge and then given responsibility for surface ship systems, and later for the same systems in the Shippingport, Pennsylvania, civilian power plant. From the Naval Academy and the MIT graduate program came Engineering Duty Officers Jack A. LaSpada and Archie P. Kelley (both class of 1941) and S. W. W. Shor (1943).

LaSpada was smooth in rough situations, which I particularly remember from his tour at the Knolls Laboratory, which GE ran for the government. During the labor disputes there, he managed to get his job done without ruffling any feathers. Kelley was known for an incredibly active imagination. For a while he established a ground rule for lunch that the time had to be spent arguing some outrageous scientific proposition or question, such as "Numbers greater than 10^{75} have no real meaning, since that is the sum-total of all the atomic particles in the universe." Tom DeBolt, an electronics Ph.D. from Carnegie Tech who worked for me, stopped that one cold by pointing out that the total amplification of the transatlantic cable was about 10^{110}, achieved by having small in-line amplifiers every few miles. "And that's real hardware, Arch!" What could anyone add to that?

Shor, whose initials earned him the sobriquet Salt Water Willie, had a number of memorable attributes. Rickover and I stayed in his guest room on occasion, in company with fifty-power tripod-mounted binoculars looking out to sea and a large hooded hunting falcon perched restlessly near my bed.

From the postgraduate program that Rickover had worked out with MIT came John W. Crawford, Jr., and Edwin E. Kintner, both of whom appear often in the pages ahead, followed by John J. Hinchey and Arthur E. Francis, who both spent many long, hard years in shipyards as Naval Reactors representatives. Robert L. Moore, also in the 1951 MIT group, first came to NR headquarters and then left to become the BuShips supervisor of shipbuilding at Electric Boat, outside Rickover's aegis.

John Mealia was recruited from the Oak Ridge school, and as of this writing he is still at Naval Reactors and has nearly four decades of service there, longer even than Admiral Rickover. From the University of Wisconsin came chemical engineer, scoutmaster, and choir soloist Theodore J. Iltis, who became head of the Coolant Technology Branch. Edward J. Bauser, who had entered the Navy from the University of Minnesota and the Naval Postgraduate School, had war duty on cruisers and design experience in BuShips. He applied for NR in 1949 and was told that he needed more math and physics. After taking advanced courses on his own, he was accepted and sent to MIT. After a training period at NR, he worked in the field, first at the AEC's Chicago Operations Office and then at the Idaho prototype, until his retirement from the Navy in 1958, after which he joined the staff of the Joint Congressional Committee on Atomic Energy. Joseph A. Murphy came from Fordham and stayed nearly twenty years. Raymond F. Fraley brought a maritime background and later went to work for the staff of the Advisory Committee on Reactor Safeguards. And John Michels came from the University of Pennsylvania and retired in 1989 after thirty-six years of service.

This intensive recruiting program had only begun to make itself felt when I reported in to Naval Reactors in November 1949; at that time the headquarters crew consisted only of Dunford, Roddis, Dick, and Emerson, from Rickover's original team, plus Kyger and Wilson from

Oak Ridge. Engineering Duty Officers Laney and LaSpada were there until September 1950, when they left for extended duty at Schenectady to oversee the construction and operation of the *Seawolf* prototype plant. Archie Kelley, another engineering duty officer, was there when I arrived, and he stayed on at headquarters for some time. There was also John Gray, who left a year later and in time became manager of the Atomic Power Division, Duquesne Power and Light, responsible in that utility for building and operating the world's first commercial nuclear power station under Naval Reactors. (Max Rodin, a genial mechanical engineer from Notre Dame, with a master's degree from Purdue, was surely there during the early days. But neither he nor I can remember exactly when, and the record does not say. Similarly for Paul Grant and Art Clark, for whom the record is even sketchier.)

Rickover arranged for his people to give training lectures to the other sections of the Bureau of Ships, from the most senior officers to the junior technicians. He subsequently expanded this practice to include lectures on the shipboard application problems to scientists and engineers at Argonne, Westinghouse, GE, Allis-Chalmers, and Oak Ridge, and on nuclear science and technology aspects to Navy and shipyard personnel. Training was clearly a top priority, as Roddis, Dunford, Mandil, Panoff and I, and his other senior people found out, sometimes giving two three-hour lectures in one day to save travel time. He also reversed the process, bringing in professors and research scientists to lecture his own engineers on various specific aspects of physics, metallurgy, chemistry, thermodynamics, and mathematics where they or he felt the need. He topped this off by persuading Dr. Samuel Goudsmit, an internationally famed nuclear physicist and editor of *Physical Review*, to spend a summer with his engineers, sitting evenings on our back porches or staying late at the office, to talk and answer questions about the basic concepts, philosophy, and procedures of science. Goudsmit was on a first-name, beer-drinking basis with most of the top theoretical physicists in Europe, and the president had sent him into Europe, just behind the front lines, as World War II was winding down, to determine how much progress the Germans had made on the atomic bomb. He had some wonderful stories.

"The Pinks"

Since mid-1949 Rickover had used another training and work control procedure, one for which he became notorious and which quickly became known throughout Rickover-land as "The Pinks." Roddis thought he understood it, but he quickly discovered that his understanding was inadequate. This was before the days of photocopiers, and Dixie kept carbon copies of all correspondence on pink tissue paper, for her boss's nightly perusal. One evening, as he was getting ready to leave, Captain Rickover looked at the stack of pink copies and said to Dixie, "That looks smaller than usual. Are you getting copies of everything that's typed up in here?"

Dixie replied, "Yes, sir. That's everything that's going out today."

"Dixie, that's not what I asked you. Do you have a copy of every piece of paper that was typed by anyone in this office today?"

"Well, not everything, Captain. I mean, there are some unfinished drafts and things like that. The men don't want that kind of thing coming up here."

"Dammit, Dixie, their wants are none of your business. You work for me. I told you I want *everything* that's typed in here. Who told you to hold back stuff?"

"Well, Commander Roddis, for one."

"Get him up here. On the double."

"Yes, sir."

After a remarkably brief moment, Roddis burst in and was greeted with "Who gave you authority to withhold information from me? And to countermand my instructions to Dixie? Where do you get that authority?"

"I don't know what you're talking about, Captain."

"I'm talking about the pinks."

"Sir?"

"You refused to give Dixie some of your pinks."

"Oh. No, Captain. All I said was that there was an unfinished draft Kerze is working on for me that I hadn't even seen myself yet. I didn't . . ."

"Roddis, my orders to Dixie are simple and unambiguous: Each night, I want to take home a copy of every sheet of paper that is typed in here. You have no authority to modify that order. Do you understand?"

"But Captain, you'll be pulling me in here to explain and defend something I haven't even seen yet!"

"That's your problem. It's up to you to see that I don't know more about what's going on in your shop than you do."

And thus Roddis, and soon everyone else in the Rickover operation, came to understand the power and the impact of the simple little management tool called The Pinks. Through it Rickover could quickly discover whose work he had to watch carefully and whom he could give a longer leash. He could see intended commitments in draft form and, if necessary, stop them before they were committed. And it gave him great opportunity to teach "word engineering," the art of saying what you really intended.

One time he caught me using the editorial *we*, as in "we will get back to you by . . ." He explained brusquely that only three types of individual were entitled to such usage: "The head of a sovereign state, a schizophrenic, and a pregnant woman. Which are you, Rockwell?"

The Support Staff

From the very early 1950s on, Admiral Rickover needed four secretaries to keep up with his frantic activities. While many of his staff found that one good secretary could keep up with all the work of four to six engineers, no one doubted that all four of Rickover's competent secretaries were indeed fully occupied with real work. Throughout this book I refer to Rickover's secretary as Dixie Davis, but there were others. Some were WAVEs, female naval personnel, and some were civil service. The distinctions were blurred among strictly stenographic duties, clerical tasks, and administrative functions, some of which required considerable skill, tact, and perseverance. There was Theresa Leone, a dedicated and competent WAVE warrant officer, and others whose anonymous service kept the organization running.

But most of all, there was Jean Scroggins. She seemed to be a reasonably bright, pleasant young woman when she arrived in the early 1950s, but she soon proved to be much more than that. When the Admiral retired in 1982, Jean had become an institution, listed in the Navy phone book as "Jean E. Scroggins, J-Item Engineer," which requires some explanation. The Admiral was in the habit of continually raising questions—based on the pinks, on reports from the field, from every conceivable source. To keep these from getting lost prior to resolution, he used to scrawl a question or a comment on a piece of correspondence, directed to a particular person in the organization, along with a deadline for getting an answer. Jean kept track of these and issued a weekly report on the status of these "J-Items." Each week your name would appear on this list with the number of J-Items resolved that week, the number of new items added, and the number outstanding. Some of these might be quite trivial and quickly answerable, but not until someone got back from a trip. Others were complicated, and attempts to get the Admiral to remove them on the basis of superficial answers were seldom successful.

Obviously, the implementer of such a system would not find that the function endeared her to the participants, but Jean's good sense, good humor, and gentle persistence kept her both effective and well liked. She was finally made a special assistant to the Admiral, and when he retired, her job was abolished and she retired on the same day he did.

In addition to the secretaries, there were WAVE officers who carried out important administrative functions. The first was Lucille S. Thompson, whose father and stepfather had been at the Naval Academy at the same time as Rickover, although they were not classmates. Lucy was in charge of Rickover's office from 1950 until she left in 1954. The next two WAVEs were brought in a year later, directly from Officer Candidate School: Wilhelmina Klein and Kathleen D. Beck. Willie was the first person assigned as military personnel officer, and she organized all the interviews. When she married while at NR and became Mrs. Small, we argued that she hadn't changed her name—just translated it.

Kate Beck became an administrative officer, and she could hold her own with Rickover in repartee. He often repeated the story of how he saw her late one afternoon with the phones ringing, papers piled on her desk, and people trying to get her attention. Spotting a half-eaten sandwich on her desk, he asked with mock sternness, "Eating lunch on company time?" To which she replied, without missing a beat, "That's yesterday's lunch, Captain!" So when she married Bob Panoff, we all knew they had created a perfect match. She stayed at NR until she had to leave to have her first child (of six).

The following year Ethel Weyant came and was put in charge of budgeting and contracting matters. That was a year before any of the Supply Corps officers arrived to take over this work. In 1953 she was joined by Margaret Polatty, who also served as information officer for the program. It was characteristic of all these first WAVEs that although we were very aware of their lively presence as persons, they performed their functions so well and so quietly that we had little feeling as to what they did in detail. Rickover's office continued to function, the money came in when needed, and the interview schedule ran smoothly.

Thinking back, that could not have happened without some very efficient handling.

In 1953 Rickover told BuPers (the Navy's Bureau of Personnel) that he wanted another woman officer, and they sent over Rebecca A. Lloyd, a recreation major from North Carolina with a master's degree in education (personnel administration) from New York University. Rickover hired her and, to her amazement, told her that she was going to be one of the eggheads. He asked if she had taken chemistry, and she said no, but she had taken a physics course once. He assigned her a self-study program in chemistry and told her that he was putting her in charge of secondary system chemistry and heat exchangers. He told her new boss, Jim Cochran, that he'd better not see her at a typewriter.

Most of us figured he had probably done this to humiliate Cochran because he was presumably unhappy with how chemistry was being handled. But Becky Lloyd said that she took Rickover at his word: he just wanted to get a woman into the technical work, and he thought she could do it. "He seemed to be impressed with the fact that I had worked my way through college, including the master's degree, without any help from anyone," she said recently. "He valued hard work and

---

EXTENDING THE EFFECT:
PLANNING AND BUDGETING

Another whole book should be written about the philosophy and procedures developed by Naval Reactors to arrive at and carry out long-range planning and budgeting. Rickover saw that the usual practice of "winging it" from year to year, and assuming that Congress is an adversary rather than an ally in the process, would just not work. By laying out requirements years in advance, by having the same people present the same story year after year, and by making Congress a party to the problems as well as to the achievements, Rickover created an atmosphere of stability and a predictability that was the envy of other major programs across the country. Unfortunately, the persons who envied these results seldom took the trouble to understand what measures were required to achieve them.

motivation a lot more than credentials. That experience really changed my life. I learned that I could do things I would never even have considered trying before." Nearly twenty years passed before women began graduating in significant numbers from engineering schools.

In 1953 Vincent A. Lascara, NR's first Supply Corps officer, reported in, and Weyant and Polatty were incorporated into his organization. The following year Sally Higgins and Kathleen Ann Bashe joined Lascara's group, and later both married NR Supply Corps officers. Sally Higgins was the semiprofessional singer about whom more is told later in these pages.

In the Military Personnel function, Mary Catherine Bellas replaced Willie Small in 1955, followed successively by Joan Zook, Julia DiLorenzo, and Rachel J. Sarbaugh. Rae Sarbaugh held the post from 1960 to 1974, becoming a treasure trove of anecdotes and history much valued by anyone who ever had occasion to try to reconstruct just what happened during that period.

GETTING STARTED WITH THE WORK

> One must create the ability in his staff to generate clear, forceful arguments for opposing viewpoints as well as for their own. Open discussions and disagreements must be encouraged, so that all sides of an issue will be fully explored. Further, important issues should be presented in writing. Nothing so sharpens the thought process as writing down one's arguments. Weaknesses overlooked in oral discussion become painfully obvious on the written page.
>
> H.G.R.

Rickover's strength, and many of his problems, derived from the effort he put into organization and training. When he was doing it, sending much-needed personnel away for a year's training at Oak Ridge or MIT, developing lecture series for others, and the like, he was convinced that this was the most important thing he could ever do. And looking back, he would not have done it differently. Yet he fretted over his belief that not much was getting done toward developing the necessary hardware when key people were tied up with training. He would complain to visitors that nothing had been accomplished in the previous few months.

But by 1950 Rickover had amassed—in fact, created—an imposing array of trained technical talent and facilities and the organizational structure and authority to use them effectively to develop a nuclear submarine. He was now anxious to start moving toward that goal.

He had persuaded the AEC to sign a contract with Westinghouse on 10 December 1948, even before the formation of the Reactor Development Division and the Naval Reactors Branch within that division. Under this contract the AEC would pay for the construction of a new facility, where Westinghouse agreed to house scientists and engineers, and to work with Argonne personnel to develop and build a water-cooled, thermal-neutron reactor plant for a submarine. A month later the AEC approved the acquisition by Westinghouse of the old Bettis Airport near Pittsburgh for the new Westinghouse Atomic Power Division, or WAPD, as it became known. To get money for all these projects was not easy. "Getting the money is my job," Rickover would say. "You guys just get the work done." And a great deal of his time was spent justifying cost projections, budgets, and past expenditures, backed up by an exceptionally competent group of Supply Corps officers. The net result was that we almost always had the money we needed. But we knew that this didn't happen automatically, and that an unprecedented amount of time and skill was required, on a continuing basis, to make it so.

By this time there was enough technical work going on that Rickover devoted more and more of his time to it. He was nervous about letting the Argonne scientists run unmonitored with the ball, and the Westinghouse team was not yet assembled. Week after week, at the end of the day he would fly up to Pittsburgh, to be met by his representative there, Lawton D. Geiger, an engineer with construction and management experience, who had been the Manhattan District manager at the Ames Laboratory during the war. Geiger was assisted by Lieutenant Commander Eugene P. "Dennis" Wilkinson. As they drove to the Bettis site, Geiger and Wilkinson would answer Rickover's probing questions, so that when they arrived, Rickover was ready with a full agenda. The Westinghouse people would be already assembled in the conference room, and there would be sandwiches and coffee for Rickover and his people. After the meeting he and his staff would rush to catch the 1:00 A.M. sleeper train back to Washington, so they were able, in effect, to put in two full days' work in two different cities within a twenty-four-hour period.

Most of the focus in any reactor discussion was reactor physics, which in turn relied mostly on sophisticated mathematical techniques—Bessel functions, Laplace transforms, and higher-order differential equations. This was a subject you could lecture on and do experiments on. But Rickover had a simpler question: "What are you going to make the damn thing out of?" The reactors that made plutonium for The Bomb were made of graphite and ran at room temperature. The experimental Materials Testing Reactor being developed at Oak Ridge also ran at room temperature. Aluminum was a good fuel-cladding material for these reactors: it did not absorb too many neutrons, and it didn't corrode at room temperature. But the submarine reactor was something else. It had to run at high temperature in order to generate steam for the propulsion turbines, and aluminum would not stand up under those conditions. High-temperature steel alloys also presented a problem: they absorbed too many neutrons. So Rickover's question was an important one, and of course it was one the Argonne and Westinghouse scientists had been puzzling over for some time.

Creating a Zirconium Industry and a Hafnium Industry

Back in December 1947, when Rickover, Dunford, and Roddis had made a quick trip to Oak Ridge to try to fan up the dying embers of the reactor study Harold Etherington had been making with the last of the Daniels Pile group, they picked up an interesting idea. Sam Untermyer, a nuclear engineer in the group, had suggested using the rare metallic element zirconium for the fuel elements. Only a shoebox-full of the metal, in an impure form, had been produced in the whole world, although the ore was plentiful. But it seemed to be capable of maintaining its strength at the required high operating temperature, and it appeared to be resistant to corrosion.

"Why haven't we heard about this before?" asked Rickover.

"We always thought it was a neutron absorber," replied Untermyer. "But recently Herb Pomerance, in the physics group here, discovered that zirconium almost always contains about 2 percent hafnium, another element that is very hard to separate from zirconium. Pomerance has now obtained some zirconium without much hafnium in it and discovered that pure zirconium should be practically transparent to neutrons."

So Rickover was ready when Sid Krasik, the head physicist of the Westinghouse-Bettis group, and Joe Dietrich, who headed up the reactor design effort at Argonne, suggested zirconium.

"What do we have to do to make zirconium fuel elements?" asked Rickover.

There were plenty of people ready to answer that one. A process had to be developed to separate the hafnium from zirconium in large quantities. Then a process to produce zirconium in tonnage lots would have to be developed. Neither process existed, even on paper. Next, tests would have to be run to check corrosion resistance, strength, and neutron absorption, and these tests, in turn, would probably show the need to develop a suitable zirconium alloy. Pure metals seldom have all the properties required for a particular application, and nobody knew how removing the hafnium would affect corrosion resistance, strength, or other critical qualities. There would also be the problem of incorporating the uranium into the fuel element. Just solving the zirconium development and production problem would require a major national program.

The main problem associated with the development of reactor-grade zirconium was the preponderance of unknowns and the interaction among them. Until a production method had been developed, it would not be known how pure the metal could be made. Then, after large quantities of metal were available, a suitable alloy would have to be developed with the necessary corrosion resistance, high-temperature strength, and resistance to radiation damage in the reactor. The ingredients of this alloy would determine its nuclear characteristics, which would markedly affect the reactor physics and the design of the reactor. In addition, the trace amounts of corrosion products that leached into the reactor coolant might affect the radiation shield design, which in turn strongly affected ship weight and characteristics. Yet all of these questions had to be pursued in parallel in order to meet the rigid schedule. Rickover realized the overriding importance to the program of solving the zirconium problem, and to back up Geiger he put Mandil on it, assisted by Frank Kerze and Bill Wilson, both of whom were outstanding metallurgists Jack Kyger had brought in from Oak Ridge.

Much to Rickover's distress, the AEC decided that zirconium procurement should be handled by its Division of Production, which delegated it to the commission's New York Operations Office. Rickover urged the AEC to let Bettis manufacture the material for the *Nautilus* reactor, but the AEC overrode this recommendation. The New York office contracted with four different companies for development and production of zirconium. Removal of the hafnium would be done at Oak Ridge. Six other organizations were also investigating various aspects of zirconium. There was little coordination of all this effort.

Rickover was told that one of the problems was the lack of a firm, official requirement for a specific quantity of zirconium with stated characteristics. So early in 1950 Kyger and Geiger worked with Bettis to calculate the amount and rough specifications for the zirconium needed for the *Nautilus* prototype reactor, known as Mark I. They concluded that they would need at least thirty thousand pounds, and in March 1950 they wrote the AEC establishing this requirement, and stating that they saw little likelihood that it could be met by the contractors presently existing. They requested permission to procure zirconium directly.

The AEC refused this request and in April 1950 contracted with Foote Mineral Company to deliver thirty thousand pounds of crystal bar zirconium by 30 June 1951. This procurement envisioned that zircon sand from Rutile Mining Company would be chlorinated by Stauffer Chemical Company and further processed by the Titanium Alloy Manufacturing Division of National Lead (TAM). Oak Ridge would remove some of the hafnium, send some of the oxide to TAM, and convert some of the oxide back to tetrachloride, which it would ship to the U.S. Bureau of Mines, which would convert it to sponge metal. TAM would essentially duplicate the BuMines process. Some of the sponge metal would be sent to Electro Metallurgical Corporation for melting, then to Simonds Saw and Steel Company for forging and rolling, and then to Argonne for physics experiments. Foote would convert the tetrachloride to sponge and then to crystal bar for delivery to Bettis. (The actual situation was even more complicated than this description.)

Predictably, this plan failed miserably. By July 1951, a month after the scheduled delivery date, Argonne had received less than a quarter of the material promised for its experiments, and Bettis had received none of its thirty thousand pounds of crystal bar. So nearly a year and a half after Rickover's request, Bettis finally received permission to design, install, and operate a crystal bar plant to "supplement" the shipments from Foote. The following month Rickover was given overall responsibility for zirconium procurement. Since Foote's sponge metal was friable and hard to process, he canceled that operation. The TAM sponge had excessive impurities and was inefficiently produced, so that process was also canceled. This left BuMines producing sponge. It was not consistently corrosion-resistant, and thus could not be used directly in the reactor, but it was sufficiently ductile and pure to act as feed to the crystal bar plant. Hafnium separation was still being carried out at Oak Ridge, but Rickover asked BuMines to get into that process as well, and BuMines ultimately replaced Oak Ridge in that function.

Before any zirconium had been delivered to Bettis, Rickover and other AEC officials had agreed that the government should not stay in the zirconium business any longer than necessary, and steps were taken to create a competitive zirconium industry. In March 1951 the AEC issued a press release stating its intent to obtain zirconium and hafnium from commercial suppliers, and it sent a prospectus to twenty-six promising candidates. Thirty-four companies attended the contract discussion, expressing grave doubts on the quantity required and objecting to the fixed-price requirement. No contracts were awarded. A new invitation was issued to thirty-five firms, but no responsive bids were received. This provided the legal basis to negotiate a "best obtainable deal," and a contract was finally negotiated with the Carborundum Metals Company for two hundred thousand pounds per year for five years. Ultimately, other companies were brought in, production levels of thousands of *tons* of zirconium per year were achieved, and the price was brought down from over $300 per pound to about $5. Zirconium became the fuel-cladding material used in nearly all the world's nuclear power plants.

When Secretary of the Navy Dan Kimball testified before Congress in 1952, he said he asked Westinghouse how the company was able to set up and operate these new facilities so quickly and so successfully, when all previous efforts by others had failed. The reply, Kimball told Congress, was "Rickover made us do it."

During this period (August 1949 to December 1951), Russia detonated its first A-bomb, and the chief of BuShips issued an internal memo stating that the nuclear submarine was a serious project, with an estimated sea date of January 1955. The Korean War started, and President Harry Truman authorized the *Nautilus* in the 1952 shipbuilding program, with the January 1955 sea date. Studies were begun on a nuclear-powered aircraft carrier. And Rickover was passed over for admiral for the first time.

EXTENDING THE EFFECT:
THE MATERIALS INDUSTRY

Naval Reactors engineers had found that various kinds of equipment supplied by commercial manufacturers had to be custom-made, to radically different standards, to meet naval reactors requirements. Then we discovered that the materials industry would also have to come under our purview. The special requirements for hundreds of tons of reactor-grade stainless steel were the first indication of this. Later, we became involved in the development, purification, and production of tens of millions of pounds of zirconium and hundreds of thousands of pounds of hafnium. For Shippingport we needed tonnage lots of reactor-grade uranium oxide. And we discovered that welding rods, supplied as a standard commercial product by dozens of vendors, had to be upgraded for our needs. Before long there were literally scores of companies involved in producing these materials, and they all eventually felt the impact of working to Rickover's unprecedented standards.

Deciding to Build the Prototype Plant inside a Submarine Hull

Zirconium was not the only subject to occupy the Captain's attention during this period. By the end of 1949 Argonne was still evaluating three reactor systems in parallel: water-cooled, gas-cooled, and liquid-metal-cooled. Rickover was anxious to bring the selection to a head. Until the coolant had been selected, everything else about the system was up in the air: radiation shielding, pumps, heat exchangers, even the pipes and valves. Liquid metal was being pushed by GE, and Rickover could see no point in Argonne also spending time on that concept. Gas-cooled systems are inherently larger and higher-temperature than water-cooled, and these characteristics made it more difficult to squeeze the final plant into a submarine hull and required the use of exotic, high-temperature-resistant materials. Rickover increasingly focused on pressurized, high-temperature water, and by March 1950 that concept had been selected as the design basis.

To further focus the effort, Rickover called a meeting to discuss the design of the land prototype plant, which would proof-test the design prior to building the shipboard plant. The Westinghouse and Argonne engineers did not think of this as a controversial subject. They had sketches and plans for a plant in a very large building, in which the components could be spread out for easy instrumentation and maintenance. They were stunned when the Captain said bluntly, "That won't do. The land plant will be built into a simulated life-sized submarine hull. And the hull will be under water, so we can test the effects of water on the radiation shielding design."

The engineers howled in unison at the idea. "Let's test it first under the best possible conditions, and then, when we've proved out all the separate parts, we can squeeze the design down to fit into the ship." This was the normal way in which such developments are carried out.

But Rickover's position was simple: "We don't have time to do it that way. The plant is supposed to drive a submarine and work under those conditions. I want to prove that out on land before we take it to sea. If we did it your way, it would take another step, another five years. We'll build the prototype and the shipboard plant almost simultaneously, with the shipboard plant just enough behind the prototype to let us correct mistakes and apply lessons we've learned ashore."

Years later, when the AEC's aircraft nuclear propulsion program built a land prototype, another advantage of the Rickover approach became clear: no problems were encountered in the submarine prototype plant that were not also applicable to the ship. In the aircraft prototype, the idea of making the prototype simpler by making it different from the final model led to numerous problems unique to the prototype, problems whose solution did not contribute to the actual aircraft.

"Suppose Your Son Were to Serve on This Submarine"

Rickover's most awesome personal performances occurred when he was faced with a near-consensus opposition, when a wide spectrum of people were in agreement that what he wanted to do was just plain wrong. In such a situation he sometimes asked an embarrassingly simple, emotional, or personal question, one that would have seemed completely phony if someone else had asked it but that turned the tables under Rickover's uniquely powerful personality. I remember a particularly vivid example.

The question concerned the head, or "lid," of the submarine reactor pressure vessel, a massive, thick-walled steel vessel that held the reactor core and its control mechanisms. The initial design showed the head welded securely onto the body of the vessel. But Eugene Wigner, the Nobel laureate physicist, had suggested that the weld might possibly become impaired by the reactor operating conditions, so we had added gigantic bolts weighing hundreds of pounds each to hold the head in place against the inside pressure. At that point a number of industrial pressure vessel experts asked: Now that the head is bolted down, why do we need a weld? A simple gasket would provide adequate leak protection.

But Rickover replied, "Why not keep the weld, to give further assurance of leak-tightness? Let's have both belt and suspenders." The objections to this were two: It wasn't necessary, and it would make removing the head for core replacement just that much more difficult, especially since the weld would have to be cut, and later rewelded, in a highly radioactive environment.

To resolve the question Rickover called in the most respected gasket and pressure-vessel experts from industry and academia: pressure-vessel code committee members, vice presidents and chief engineers from Foster Wheeler, Babcock & Wilcox, and Combustion Engineering—the best brains and authorities on the subject in America. They met first with Mandil, Panoff, Kyger, and other senior technical people on Rickover's staff, and with only one exception they were unanimous in declaring that there was no need for a weld. Mandil went into Rickover's office to explain that he had been unable to persuade them to change their minds on this point. He expected to be handed his head. But Rickover just said, "Let's go talk with them," and they went into the conference room.

Rickover was still a lowly captain at this point, with little prestige or recognition inside or outside the Navy. After being introduced to the visitors, he slowly asked a simple question: "Suppose *your son* were to serve on this submarine, with his life dependent on its safe operation. Would you be willing to let his life depend on the continued integrity of a gasket to hold back every droplet of the highly radioactive water? Or would you rather have a weld backing it up, just in case?" And he looked around the room into the eyes of each visitor.

The room was absolutely silent. I was mortified; it was so corny. Rickover hadn't added anything technical to the discussion. I felt sure that no one was saying anything because everyone was too embarrassed for him. It was as if the priest had blurted out an obscenity in a church meeting.

But I was dead wrong. First one of the visitors, and finally all of them, spoke about as follows: "Well, I suppose you've got a point there, Captain. There's no reason not to put in a weld. In fact, it's probably a good idea."

"So you all recommend a weld, then?" asked Rickover. And they all assured him they did.

All I could say was "Well, I'll be damned!"

Killing the Breeder

Although Rickover was pushing the GE reactor approach on all possible fronts, GE itself kept subordinating its small naval reactor effort to its dream of an Intermediate Power Breeder Reactor, or IPBR. *Intermediate* referred to the fact that in a liquid-metal reactor, with no water present, the neutrons are not slowed down to the thermal energy of the water molecules as they are in the water-cooled Westinghouse design, which was called the Submarine Thermal Reactor, or STR. Intermediate-energy neutrons are not as effective in causing fission as are thermal-energy neutrons, so the GE design required a great deal more scarce uranium to do the same job. On the other hand, GE believed that the intermediate-energy neutrons would prove to be more effective in converting the nonfissionable uranium isotope into fissionable plutonium, and even creating more fuel than it burned, which is called breeding. However, the goal of breeding proved more and more unattainable in this design, and shortly after Rickover signed up Electric Boat to work on the prototype, the AEC canceled the IPBR project. "The Navy will have to do its breeding ashore," quipped Rickover.

The cancellation of the IPBR did not cause an immediate embrace by GE of the naval reactor project. GE's primary responsibility in atomic energy was to ensure sufficient production of plutonium for bombs at the Hanford facility that it operated for the AEC. The primary interest of its scientists, engineers, and technical management was nuclear power for the production of electricity. There was concern in many quarters that if GE were to undertake a significant naval reactor project, its commitment to these primary interests might be compromised. Since Rickover now had a hull and was in danger of losing his backup reactor

"COURT ORDERS SANITY TEST FOR ROCKWELL"

One morning during the early days of the program I walked into my office to find a headline cut from the newspaper and pasted to my door: COURT ORDERS SANITY TEST FOR ROCKWELL. I knew where it had come from, but I didn't know who had put it there. There was a George Lincoln Rockwell gaining notoriety at the time as founder of the American Nazi party. Although such activity is hardly a cause for laughter, this particular Rockwell was giving rise to headlines such as PENNSYLVANIANS JEER ROCKWELL; JURY ASSERTS ROCKWELL IS "A NUISANCE"; NAVY DISCHARGES ROCKWELL; ROCKWELL TOLD TO SUPPORT FIRST WIFE, 3 CHILDREN; ROCKWELL SHOULD NOT BE TOLERATED; and ROCKWELL RALLY URGED AS LAUGH.

Of course, it turned out that Captain Rickover was the cause of these gems appearing in increasing numbers on my door. He apparently got a chuckle out of spotting them in various newspapers during his travels and saving them for my edification. He had soon decorated my door with several dozens of these tidbits and then broadened the scope to include art auctions (ROCKWELLS FOR SALE), military hardware ads (ANOTHER FINE PRODUCT BY ROCKWELL), even initials (REPUBLICAN STEAMROLLER CRUSHES T.R.). He finally closed it off with TOO LITTLE KNOWN ABOUT ROCKFISH.

plant for it, he therefore undertook to alleviate these concerns.

He went first to Senator Brien McMahon, chairman of the Joint Congressional Committee on Atomic Energy. McMahon was one of the very first congressmen to take an interest in atomic energy, and one of the chief architects of the Atomic Energy Act of 1946. At that moment he was an active proponent of increasing the nation's stockpile of nuclear weapons. When Rickover had convinced him that a submarine program at GE need not interfere with the operation of the Hanford facility, McMahon became a strong advocate for the submarine. Rickover then went, with Lawrence R. Hafstad, to the Research and Development Subcommittee of the Joint Committee and gave convincing evidence that postponing the IPBR was not a blow to civilian nuclear power, that other approaches would undoubtedly prove more attractive. In the meantime GE could develop its nuclear skills best by working on a practical reactor plant, the one for a submarine.

The following day, 4 April 1950, Rickover and Rear Admiral David H. Clark, who had succeeded Mills as chief of BuShips, discussed with the AEC general manager, Carroll L. Wilson, their intent to build a submarine prototype plant at the GE West Milton facility near the company's headquarters at Schenectady. The next day Clark and Rickover went to GE. In both meetings they found a high degree of receptivity. Rickover had previously invited Harry E. Stevens, one of the roommates he had chosen for his year at Oak Ridge, now a project manager at GE, to bring some of his colleagues down to Washington for an informal briefing on the Naval Reactors program, and that had undoubtedly helped smooth away some of GE's questions and concerns. GE therefore submitted a formal letter to the AEC, proposing that half the staff of the Knolls Atomic Power Laboratory at West Milton, New York, be devoted to supporting the Hanford plutonium production facility, and the other half be switched from the IPBR to the naval submarine project. Rickover told the AEC that it would be possible to begin construction on the prototype in 1951 and have it operating in 1953.

The story of how that crucial GE letter was written epitomized the early Rickover operations. Rickover had been working on GE management, and they had finally indicated that they were willing to undertake a serious naval reactor program. But time was critical. After a series of meetings and phone calls, Rickover and Roddis met Harry Winne of GE in the railroad employees' YMCA in the upper stories of New York's Penn Station, and Roddis hammered out the letter on a rental typewriter, feeding quarters into the slot until they had a letter both sides could agree on. "I don't think I ever collected from the government for those quarters," recalled Roddis.

Bringing in a Shipbuilder

That settled, Rickover realized that it was not too soon to bring in a shipbuilder. There would be many problems in mounting a new type of power plant in a submarine, such as providing for hull compression during submergence. Foundations had to permit components to slide outward as the system heated up, but to hold fast under external forces such as shock from depth charging or wave motion against the hull.

Systems had to continue to operate stably in various extreme ship's attitudes and with hull compression at great depths. And other shipbuilding considerations such as weight distribution, atmosphere control, and the like could best be handled by a shipbuilder.

The matter was brought to a head by a call from Lieutenant Commander "Danny" Brooks, a Rickover supporter in the Naval Operations offices in the Pentagon. Brooks reported that the 1952 shipbuilding program was being firmed up, and that if the Naval Reactors people wanted to request a nuclear ship in that program, they would have to get an official request out of BuShips that very day. The next chance would come a year later. Dunford was suffering from a very painful hemorrhoidal operation he had had that morning, and he had planned to go right home. But Brooks came over and met with Dunford, Roddis, Dick, and Laney to come up with a projected sea date. January 1955 was about the latest date that would require the ship to be in the 1952 shipbuilding program. Since they were pushing the AEC to proceed at full speed on the propulsion plant, they did not dare ask for the following year and have the Navy appear to be any less intent on building the ship for it.

Dunford drafted the letter and, after a few rounds with Rickover, got his approval. He then went home to bed, and Roddis carried the letter around BuShips for the necessary sign-offs, with Rickover phoning ahead to smooth the path. The chief of the bureau, Rear Admiral David H. Clark, signed the letter, but Forrest Sherman, the new CNO, did not sign off on it for another three months.

Rickover didn't wait for the CNO. With Dunford, Roddis, Dick, and Charles H. Weaver, head of the Westinghouse Bettis Laboratory, he headed for the Portsmouth Naval Shipyard at Kittery, Maine. (For reasons I've never understood, the *Portsmouth* Naval Shipyard is in Kittery, while the *Norfolk* Naval Shipyard is in Portsmouth, Virginia.) There were two submarine shipbuilders on the East Coast: the government yard at Kittery and the private Electric Boat Company at Groton, Connecticut. Since Westinghouse had traditionally made electrical equipment for the Portsmouth boats and GE made equipment for the Electric Boat submarines, Rickover felt that the Portsmouth yard would feel comfortable working with Westinghouse on the *Nautilus*. He presented his story, of the status and plans for the ship and the prototype, and asked the shipyard commander, Rear Admiral Ralph McShane,

"Would you be willing to take on the job of assisting Westinghouse in the design and construction of the land-based prototype for the world's first nuclear-powered ship?"

McShane called in his planning officer, Captain John J. Scheibeler, an engineering duty officer from the class of 1924. Scheibeler heard the story and responded with a surprisingly blunt NO. The yard was already underfunded and understaffed, and he did not see how it could take on this additional task. Rickover said he estimated that it would require only one man full-time at first, with perhaps thirty by the end of the year, which was nearly ten months away. Moreover, he would arrange to get necessary funds and approval for increased manpower. But the answer did not change. It may be that Scheibeler or McShane could envision that if Rickover were to get the funds and the manpower, he would ultimately take control of the operation, and they didn't want that. Whatever the reason, the answer was a clear no. Fighting back his disappointment and his anger, Rickover asked simply, "Do you mind if I use your phone?"

"Go ahead," said McShane.

Rickover put in a call to O. P. Robinson, general manager of the Electric Boat Company. "O. P.? Will you help me build the prototype for the first nuclear submarine? The damn Navy yard isn't interested. I'll need some of your best people. You will? Great! I'll be down there tonight. We'll settle the details." And he and his people walked out of the Portsmouth yard and took Weaver's Westinghouse limousine to Robinson's home that very night. In short order they got agreement from Electric Boat to provide the necessary naval architects, marine engineers, submarine experts, and construction personnel to assist in the prototype construction and to build the ship herself.

The story about Electric Boat picking up the *Nautilus* option on the first bounce is well known. What is less well known is that Rickover had been there two months previously to discuss the prototype plant for the GE reactor. He had met with enough enthusiasm to return a week later with GE people, and a fairly intensive and friendly exchange had ensued. Rickover promised to arrange a lecture series on nuclear technology for Boat Company personnel and to send some of them to Oak Ridge for further training. Negotiations on the GE plant were continuing but not yet complete when Rickover arrived at Robinson's house, hours after being turned down by Portsmouth for the Westinghouse plant. Agreement was quickly reached in principle that Electric

Boat would assist in the design and construction of both prototypes. This violated Rickover's general rule to always have two parallel paths available, in case one fell behind. But in this case, he had little choice in the matter.

GETTING A SHIP

> *Complex jobs cannot be accomplished effectively with transients. Therefore, a manager must make the work challenging and rewarding so that his people will remain with the organization for many years. This allows it to benefit fully from their knowledge, experience, and corporate memory.*
>
> H.G.R.

Rickover still had nothing firm on the ship herself. His BuShips letter to the CNO had not yet been acted on. The name *Nautilus* would not be picked officially until two more years had passed. Like the frontiersmen in the old forts, running around firing from one position and then another to create the impression of great strength and activity, Rickover volunteered to talk about the nuclear submarine in every forum that would listen. On 9 February 1950 he appeared alone before the powerful Joint Congressional Committee on Atomic Energy. On 28 March he briefed the secretary of the Navy's General Board, which reviewed each proposed shipbuilding program for the secretary. In that instance he put on his AEC hat and told how much the commission was doing to develop the reactor for the Navy. He made it clear that it would be embarrassing if the Navy did not have a hull ready, after having gotten the AEC to develop a reactor plant at its own expense and in its own facilities. The General Board agreed and approved the project, and the secretary's approval followed shortly. The board even reversed the recommendation of the Ship Characteristics Board that the ship be considered a test vehicle, without torpedo tubes. The shipbuilding program was submitted to Congress and approved by President Truman on 8 August 1950 as part of the authorization act. Rickover now had official authorization for the first nuclear submarine, and it would be a full-fledged fighting ship. That same month construction was started on the *Nautilus* prototype at the National Reactor Testing Station at Arco, Idaho.

The Craft of Building Submarines

A shipyard is a wild and fascinating place. People who work in a shipyard are a special clan, different from autoworkers, or electronics manufacturing personnel, or the widely scattered operators and maintenance people in an automated oil refinery. And submarine builders are a special breed of shipyard workers.

One of the first things I noticed in the shipyard was that some of the men always wore old but jaunty-looking heavy leather jackets, making them look like veteran fighter pilots. I thought at first that this was an affectation, but then I learned that these men were welders or weld grinders, and the jackets were to protect them from burns. Welding, particularly in the confined spaces of a submarine hull, meant splattered metal and molten slag, and burns went with the territory. The company even gave scar bonuses, if the burns were bad enough. I also learned early that you could tell a man's trade by the color of his hard hat. The welders wore blue and their grinders orange ones. The bosses wore nice white ones, the radiation monitors yellow, and the testers brown. There were two shades of green: light for the machinists, dark for the riggers.

Since shipyard work is all steel-on-steel, the noise level was intense. Trucks bouncing over the rough roads loudly jostled their loads of steel beams, castings, and forgings. Riggers picked up the steel noisily and dropped it with a clang onto the loading areas. Diesel engines and jackhammers competed for attention with high-pitched grinders smoothing up welds and sledgehammers easing stubborn pieces of steel into place. Trucks, fork-lifts, and cranes all had their shrill alarm beepers warning passersby to keep clear. And inside the tin sheds and the more permanent buildings, a hundred lathes, drill presses, routers, and sheet-metal formers kept up a constant din.

But it was working inside the submarine hull that gave submarine work its special character. Workers experienced in surface ship work were always taken aback when they first entered a hull under construction. I paused at the bottom of the temporary wooden stairway going up to the hatchway on the top of the huge steel cylinder. It was nearly thirty feet in diameter and seemed to go forever in both directions from the ladder. I could not understand why workers continually griped about lack of working space inside it. But once I stepped inside the hatch, I understood. There were only two hatches to let in air and daylight, and one was nearly filled with air-hoses and electrical cables. Every person entering or leaving the hull had to do so through the other hatch, the one I had just climbed through.

Inside the hull was a different world. I had a quick flashback to my English teacher vividly recreating Dante's description of the entry into the realm of the damned. The spaciousness I had envisioned had been eaten up by the scaffolding, deck structures, temporary passageways, electrical cabling, flexible ventilation ducting, water hoses, ropes, pulleys and cables of all sorts, and the tools and equipment of the workers: welding units, chipping hammers, tool kits, grinders, pipe cutters, and myriad other devices that seemed to occupy every possible space. The heat was unbelievable. Not only heat from the bodies crammed into all available locations and positions, but heat from the welders and even more heat from large metal sections that had to be preheated too hot to touch before they could be welded. The noise from all this activity reverberated back and forth off the steel and echoed back into my ears at a painful level. The acrid smoke and dust were so thick I felt choked, and they blotted out everything more than a few feet away. Almost every day, it seemed, the heat and smoke got too much for somebody, and the watch crew had to be alert for the first slump of a worker who had just passed out. The alarm would sound, and the crew would drag him out into the comparative open space around the ladder, then up and out the hatch and down the stairs to the waiting ambulance.

The slim shaft of sunlight streaming down the hatchway and the blinding intermittent flashes of blue-white light from the welders merely intensified the darkness. Most of the workers carried droplights on long cords and hung these near their work. I suddenly had a new appreciation for the task of the welders, weld grinders, and weld inspectors. In some cases, men smaller than jockeys had been hired to slither back into impossible niches, where they did their high-precision work holding a dental mirror to see around a final corner, sometimes with a long extension on the welding rod. Not only sparks but molten metal, slag, and occasionally tools or small parts were continually raining down through this space, and the wooden scaffolding often caught fire. Emergency crews were always standing by for this situation, quick to rush in with fire extinguishers. Nobody wanted to test whether the hull could be evacuated in time if the fire extinguishers failed to put out the fire quickly.

I also quickly learned that, in a submarine, weight and space are critically important. Everything that is put into, or taken out of, a submarine is weighed at the site. If it is moved fore or aft, port or starboard, that too must be recorded and corrected for. A submarine operating submerged must be able to be brought to neutral buoyancy, and, in addition, it must balance fore and aft, port and starboard. Then, by flooding proper tanks, the commanding officer must be able to decrease the buoyancy still further, but not too much, and he must be able to blow the water from the tanks so as to bring her to the surface, again in proper attitude. Since the maximum operating depth for a submarine may be only two or three times her length, inability to control the boat's diving angle may cause the bow or stern to exceed permissible depth, even while the depth gauges show that her depth at the center is satisfactory.

This sensitivity to buoyancy makes a submarine particularly vulnerable to what on a surface ship might be tolerable damage to the hull or seawater piping systems. Add to this the fact that a submerged submarine is under tremendous pressure; water will roar through a slight flaw, enlarging it, whipping pipes about, spraying salt water over electrical equipment, shorting it out, and plunging the ship into helplessness and darkness. Like an airplane, and unlike a surface craft, a submarine cannot survive without power. Unless she can get to the surface and maintain watertight integrity, she is soon lost.

All of this means that a submarine is of necessity a concentrated package of highly engineered machinery, every inch a challenge to designers and constructors. Even equipment associated with food preparation or report writing must be specially designed for submarine use. Food, for example, must be stored in every hard-to-reach cranny that can't be used for other purposes. And great planning is required, so that as food is pushed back into these recesses between beams, it can later be retrieved for consumption in somewhat the order needed. No crew wants to discover during the last few days of a patrol that only pineapple juice is left, because that is what was stored first.

Not only are weight, space, and weight distribution controlled during submarine construction, but many plasticizers, solvents, and other volatile chemicals are prohibited within the hull from the moment construction begins, because traces of such materials would contaminate the closed atmosphere of the ship and create health problems for the crew. One that surprised me was mercury. I had played with mercury in lab courses at school and never thought of it as a source of toxic vapor. I also knew that a common testing device for marine systems was the mercury manometer, a simple glass U-tube partially filled with the silvery liquid, which measures the difference in pressure between one side of the tube and the other. But I found that mercury manometers were specifically forbidden aboard submarines, even during construction. This problem was reported over two hundred years ago, on a British sailing ship, and again on a World War I Italian submarine, when mercury spilled out into the straw where live pigs were kept (yes, on a submarine!) for fresh meat. The crew became deathly ill and some died. Mercury poisoning was later found to be the cause. Substances that would never cause a problem in a well-ventilated surface ship or in a facility "on the beach" (as sailors call any place ashore) can prove deadly in the closed atmosphere of a submarine. Everything on a submarine has to be engineered; nothing can be left to chance. And this was the kind of challenge that submarine builders liked.

Pierce Goes Nuclear

Joseph D. Pierce was a guy who really belonged on the waterfront. He was a big, powerful, blunt-spoken man who could make himself heard over the construction din in a submarine hull. He had a special talent for understanding the problems of shipyard workers, and for coaxing them to achieve beyond their horizons. But his fatal flaw was his practice of flatly stating the bare facts to his bosses whether they wanted to hear

---

EXTENDING THE EFFECT: SHIPBUILDING

Nuclear power had a greater impact on shipbuilding than the advent of steel hulls or the change from rivets to welding. With eleven shipyards geared up for nuclear work, over a hundred thousand workers and their supervisors and managements had to learn an entirely different way of carrying out their various tasks. Almost explosively, the Rickover Effect suddenly encompassed nearly a dozen huge organizations from Pearl Harbor to Kittery, Maine, and all their many suppliers and subcontractors. Many of the innovations developed during this period, such as building full-scale wooden mock-ups to check maintenance and repair procedures, have become standard in the industry.

---

them or not—and conversely, trying to meet their stated objectives whether these were reasonable or not. As a waterfront supervisor, he was one of the best. But a politician he was not.

He began his career during the war, not in a shipyard but in Rickover's Electrical Section, working on submarine electrical systems. After the war he leapt at the chance to work on the GUPPY conversion program. The acronym stood for Greater Underwater Propulsion Project (with the Y added for phonetic esthetics). Fifty-two submarines built during the war were to be modernized, using everything we had learned from studying German U-boats and from our own submarine warfare experience. Submarines ran most of the time on the surface, propelled by four specially designed diesel engines. In fact, the Navy's prewar program to develop small diesel engines for submarines was deliberately used by the government to encourage the development of commercial diesel engines in small-enough sizes for trains, trucks, and buses. Before that, diesel engines had been made only in very large sizes, to propel large ocean liners, tankers, and freighters. The submarine diesels not only propelled the ship on the surface; they also charged the huge, heavy batteries that were the only source of power submerged. The batteries were of very limited endurance, so a submarine had to limit her speed and range submerged, and look forward to the next time she could surface and recharge the batteries.

The snorkel, that marvelous Dutch invention that the Germans had put to such effective use, was to be adapted for the GUPPY. The snorkel system used a very large pipe to bring in air for the diesel engines, with a float valve at its opening, which slammed shut momentarily when the intake was overridden by a wave. This enabled the diesels to be run while the ship was at periscope depth, and therefore difficult for the enemy to detect. The engines kept running whether the snorkel valve was open or closed. When it closed, the engines sucked air out of the submarine, causing painful pressure on the eardrums, until the wave washed over, the valve reopened, and the eardrums popped painfully back. The snorkel provided a significant military advantage, but its operation was wearing on the crew.

The ships were also to have their deck guns removed and the conning towers streamlined. Four torpedoes were to be removed, to make way for larger batteries, and on some of the ships one of the diesel engines was sacrificed for battery space. These changes were expected to increase underwater speed on batteries to a maximum of fifteen knots (from nine), and also to increase the distance that could be traveled between battery charges. All of this was to make the ships more truly "undersea boats," as the Germans called them, rather than surface ships with a very limited capability to duck under the water for brief periods and travel short distance at slow speed while submerged. The British and Russian navies also adopted the snorkel and, in addition, were looking at exotic propulsion systems, such as hydrogen peroxide turbines. But the Americans considered these systems highly unreliable and perhaps even dangerous, because of the instability of the peroxide.

Pierce was excited about these new design concepts, and on these studies he often found himself working with a young engineer in his section named Bob Panoff. A mutual respect sprang up between them, born of admiration for the technical insight and engineering competence consistently shown by each of them. They both liked the challenge of producing a really high-performance machine, and they had confidence that they could create a vehicle of which everyone could be proud.

In February 1950 the scenario suddenly changed. The Navy had committed to undertake the design and construction of the world's first nuclear-powered submarine. Pierce didn't know whether the idea of a nuclear submarine was a far-off pipe dream or a serious project. But one day in May Panoff told him that he was transferring from the Electrical Section to Rickover's nuclear power staff, and he urged Pierce to think about doing so himself. Pierce demurred but decided at that moment that maybe he should begin to take nuclear power seriously. The Electrical Section had deteriorated after Rickover left, and he felt increasingly stifled by the bureaucracy. He wanted to get his hands on hardware, so he left and went to work for the Electric Boat Company, where he soon found his natural niche as a waterfront supervisor.

He was to stay at the Boat Company for thirty years.

Recruiting Submarine Drivers

Toward the end of 1951 things were going reasonably well for Lieutenant Commander James Calvert. He had been born in Cleveland in 1920, and he attended Oberlin College prior to the Naval Academy. He was known for his quiet, dignified demeanor, coupled with an admirable war record: two silver stars and a bronze star. He wore his love of country and love of the Navy on his sleeve, and he made a point of teaching Sunday school wherever he was stationed. Handsome and personable, he was the kind of person you could picture as superintendent of the Naval Academy, and indeed, he was given that billet at the appropriate point in his career. His tour of duty at the Submarine Detail Desk of BuPers had gone along with no serious mishaps, and he would soon be released for duty on one of the Navy's newest Guppy submarines. He loved sea duty, and not just for the extra pay. He still remembered vividly his first war patrol.

He was fresh out of the Naval Academy at that time, but he was already on his first submarine war patrol. He had read a lot about submarines, but the books and stories always emphasized the submerged operations, and he was not fully prepared for the fact that real submarines carry out most of their operations on the surface, even in war patrols. Top speed on the surface was eighteen to twenty knots and range was thousands of miles, whereas top speed submerged was eight or nine knots and range at high speed was at best fifteen to twenty miles. Of course, submarines could, and did, spend a lot of time submerged, sitting quietly and listening, or moving very slowly on their battery-driven electric motors. But even then they usually traveled at periscope depth, because depending entirely on sonar to know where you were and who else might be nearby was a somewhat uncertain business.

There was a lot to get used to on submarines. First off, there was the unique smell of diesel fuel. It permeated everything. It was not particularly objectionable to the men as they came aboard, but when Calvert went ashore after a few hours on the ship, it was not long before somebody noticed the smell and commented that he must have just come off a submarine, as the smell of his clothes was clear and unmistakable, and they stayed that way until they were laundered.

The second thing that struck the newcomer was the crowded conditions. Surface people called it claustrophobic, but that wasn't quite it. It was just plain crowded. Things were hard to get at. Newcomers, particularly those whose hair was receding, usually had a fresh scar or two where a valve or other protruding piece of machinery had been inadvertently bumped into. You had to learn the submariner's trick of running down the passageway, grabbing the top portion of the flange on the approaching hatchway, pulling your feet up, and swinging through to the other side, all in one motion, without losing speed. The closest Calvert came to claustrophobia was the subconscious feeling, as he swung from one compartment to the next, that the "open spaces," the less crowded area of the ship, must be either just ahead or just behind him. But of course, there was no such place.

Calvert quickly adopted the submariner's clear understanding that his life was very much dependent on the skill and speed with which his shipmates could carry out the emergency operations they were constantly drilled in, such as rig for collision, fire, surface, dive, and the myriad normal operations that could also lead to disaster if done incorrectly. He likewise accepted the responsibility this situation placed on him for the lives of all the others. He was sure no other service forged such bonds.

Submarines on patrol are limited not only in space, but also in material supplies and energy. This made simple procedures, like taking a shower, unique. The shower stall was less than two feet square and just about six feet high. The procedure was to run the water just long enough to get wet, then turn it off and soap. After soaping, a quick rinse was permissible. There were to be no leisurely hot rinses, melting out the muscular knots of the day. Flushing a toilet (or "head," as they call it) was even more restricted. When a submarine is submerged, it is surrounded by water under great pressure. Clearly, one cannot merely flush to sea under such conditions. So the system is designed to flush to an inboard tank, which can then be pressurized later and its contents blown overboard. The actual alignment of valves and piping varies from one class of ship to another, so there was even a story going around that the admiral in charge of all submarines in the Atlantic (ComSubLant, in Navy parlance), trying on an unfamiliar ship to flush without first venting tank pressure, had managed to spray his gold-braided uniform with his own effluvia.

If Calvert needed any confirmation that much of a submarine's fighting would be on the surface, he had only to look at the armament aboard in addition to the torpedoes. Different ships varied in the amount of firepower they carried. Most had one 5-inch cannon mounted on the deck; some had two. Some had .50-caliber machine guns on the deck, and some had additional guns of this type on the bridge. There were twin 20-millimeter machine guns stowed below, which could be hurriedly hassled up the ladder and affixed to the deck mounts. There were two 40-millimeter automatics mounted permanently on the bridge, cadmium-plated to protect them from the seawater. And there was a plentiful supply of small arms. A submarine suddenly and unexpectedly pouring all this firepower into a tanker, a troopship, or an escort vessel could be a terrifying and deadly force indeed. Submariners fought hard and fast in a surface fight, because they knew that if they could not knock out their opponent quickly, they would surely be destroyed themselves. Unlike surface ships, submarines had no excess buoyancy, and a single hole in the hull could be enough to finish them off.

Calvert was on the bridge, reveling in the fresh night air. To get there he had climbed a ladder up out of the main pressure hull, a cylinder about sixteen feet in diameter at its largest with a little more than two hundred usable feet of length inside. Above the main pressure hull, and connected to it through the hatch Calvert had climbed through, was the conning tower, so called because this was the place from which the ship was controlled, or "conned." Critical sonar, radar, speed and depth information was displayed here, and the officers monitoring this information had direct communication with the rest of the ship, through telephones that could be either kept private to the person called or broadcast over the ship's loudspeaker system. The conning tower was not a tower at all, but a horizontal pressure hull eight feet in diameter and sixteen feet long. When things were busy, there could be as many as fourteen of the crew's sixty-eight-man total in the conning tower at one time.

A ladder in the conning tower led up through a watertight hatch to the bridge in the open air above. As the youngest officer on board, Calvert was junior officer of the deck. He knew all too well, however, that before this patrol was over he would have the deck by himself, and that he had better learn all he could from every day and every maneuver. This time, the exec was officer of the deck, and the ship's captain was also on the bridge. The ship was pitching in the heavy seas, and every so often a sheet of solid black water lifted itself over the prow and drifted lazily through the air, over a hundred feet, to hit the curved windscreen on the bridge. The three officers would duck beneath its protective surface and the water would cascade down behind them, to drain back into the sea. Calvert marveled that the other two officers seemed to do this instinctively, without even looking forward at the onrushing wall of water.

Four lookouts had been posted since entering combat waters, and these men had strict orders to keep binoculars to their eyes at all times, monitoring both air and sea for any signs of the enemy. The three officers also swept the horizon with their glasses. Calvert was surprised how heavy the binocs became, and he admired the ability of the lookouts to continue to scan for an entire hour between watch reliefs. Suddenly the forward starboard watch shouted, "Smoke on the horizon, Captain.

About 60 degrees." The captain reached over to his right and pushed the press-to-talk button that activated the phone system. "Conn, do you have a sonar contact about six zero?"

"Checking, Captain . . . Yes, sir, there's a possible, about six-oh degrees relative. Range, maybe twenty thousand yards."

"Let me know as soon as you can estimate her course, and anything about her size or type."

The submarine had traveled nearly three thousand miles, zigzagging surreptitiously across Japanese-controlled seas, surfacing only at night, vulnerable at all times to superior firepower, her only protection being to remain hidden. Now she had found what she had come for, an enemy target, and she initiated pursuit at full throttle. With all four diesels running wide open, she was able to start closing the distance between herself and her prey. Calvert could feel the blood pounding in his temples and his throat beginning to dry, as he anticipated the imminent battle, his first.

Suddenly there was a cry from one of the lookouts: "Aircraft coming in fast off the port bow. Coming right at us, sir."

"Battle stations! All hands to battle stations. Dive! Dive!" the captain's voice rang out urgently over the loudspeakers. *Ah-uuu-guh! Ah-uuu-guh!* blared the klaxon. The officers stepped back from the hatch as the lookouts scrambled through. Then the junior officers and last, with the ship's deck disappearing under the foaming green water, the captain jumped through the hatchway, pulling the wire lanyard as he went, slamming the watertight hatch shut. One of the lookouts, who had been standing by at the bottom of the ladder for this purpose, jumped up on the ladder and spun the dogs tight. The entire process had taken fourteen seconds.

"Get me the bathythermograph card," called the captain. "How deep is the first temperature layer? We're going to have to hide out for a while."

The depth charging from the airplane was bad, but not like the movies. Glass popped out of gauges and light bulbs burst, but bodies weren't thrown around. And submariners don't yell; their survival demands silence. By the time they could resume aggressive tactics, there was no target within range. Driven from the surface by the antisub patrol plane, and limited to a crawl by the energy stored in its batteries, the once-mighty submarine was reduced to hiding to save her own skin. *Damn*, thought Calvert. *So much effort and so much danger to get so close, and then to have to throw in the towel. Think what we could do if we had a submarine that could really stay submerged and run fast for long periods. We'd be invincible.*

And now, in 1951, there was talk of a nuclear submarine, one with practically unlimited endurance! Calvert wondered if he would see such a ship in his lifetime. He was looking forward to getting back to sea, and then the call came. Captain Rickover had a nuclear submarine building, and he had asked BuPers to send over for interview the "two best young submarine officers available" for eventual assignment to the nuclear submarine. He planned to take on four such submariners and train them thoroughly while the ship was being built—a period of several years.

This training plan was a drastic change in the normal order of things, but the idea of having anyone, especially an engineering duty officer, interview line personnel prior to assignment was even more appalling. Apparently BuPers management was going along with the request, because Calvert, as in-house expert on junior submarine officers, was asked to nominate two candidates. He did so, and they were ordered to Washington for the interview. Shortly thereafter, the chief of BuPers received a fiery phone call, stating that if these were the two best young submarine officers in the fleet, then the Navy's future was dim indeed. The natural result of this unexpected blast was a demand from the Front Office to Calvert: Who was responsible for this fiasco?

Calvert reported, visibly shaken, with the complete record of the officers in question, back to their graduation date. It was finally agreed among Calvert's superiors that these were indeed among the Navy's best. But if the irascible Captain Rickover wanted to try again, they would send another pair of candidates. This process was repeated, week after week, but the feedback was no more positive. Then suddenly, the requests for more candidates stopped. Rumor had it that Rickover was now interviewing naval aviators, and some suggested that even Air Force officers were being considered.

One day Rickover telephoned and remarked pleasantly that he liked the look of the first two fellows he had interviewed, and would BuPers please arrange to have them report in as soon as possible. Calvert had had his first experience with the notorious Captain, although he was not to meet him for another four years.

EXTENDING THE EFFECT: RECRUITMENT AND TRAINING

Rickover's insistence that each new recruit be examined, tested, and trained as if he or she were being groomed for the position of company CEO was intended for use only in his own program. But he extended this process, first to his field personnel, then to his contractor and shipyard people, and even to such persons as the public health officers assigned (at his request) to monitor his various operations in the field. But many of these Rickover-trained people ultimately went on to positions of importance in the nonnuclear Navy and in the commercial nuclear industry, and even into industrial positions other than power generation, and they have tried to apply the lessons learned to their new environment. Many of these lessons have been codified in policy statements, procedures, and manuals produced by these Rickover alumni.

The Aircraft Carrier Project

In addition to the two submarine projects, Rickover soon found himself involved with a nuclear aircraft carrier study. He and his people had looked into the question of nuclear propulsion for large surface ships in early 1950, and they had concluded that so long as uranium was in short supply, it did not seem advisable to use it for this purpose. At that time they tended to view the idea of a nuclear-powered carrier as a diversion from the important task of developing the nuclear submarine, where the advantages of nuclear propulsion were indisputable. But Admiral Forrest P. Sherman had become CNO shortly after the supercarrier *United States* had been canceled, and the "admirals' revolt" that followed had left morale at a low ebb. As a naval aviator, Sherman was a strong believer in carriers, and after the invasion of Korea, and about the same time that Truman authorized construction of the *Nautilus*, Sherman asked BuShips "to explore the feasibility of constructing a large carrier with an atomic power plant, and to determine time factors, cost factors, and characteristics." Rickover asked Argonne, Oak Ridge, and the GE group at Knolls to prepare quick feasibility studies. These were completed within two weeks, and ten days later Rickover handed Sherman a memo for his signature to the Joint Chiefs of Staff, proposing to complete a land prototype in 1953 and a shipboard plant in 1955. Sherman deleted the reference to the shipboard plant and signed out the memo.

With the shortage of uranium still critical and the military services pushing the AEC for more uranium and plutonium for weapons, the Navy was reluctant to push the commission too hard for a carrier plant. In July 1951 Sherman died, and a month later the AEC asked Westinghouse to prepare an engineering study, under the direction of the Civilian Reactors Branch of the Reactor Development Division. The rationale for this unusual assignment was that the plant should also produce plutonium and make electricity, and if Rickover were to do it, he might just scale up a submarine reactor. During those early years there was a strong belief in the reactor community that Rickover's pressurized-water reactor was only one of dozens, if not scores, of approaches to reactor design, and that Rickover was just too unimaginative to exploit all these potentials. A large number of these concepts were actually built by the AEC as expensive "reactor experiments," but they never led to a working power plant. The dream of miracle performance from exotic power cycles has proved completely illusory, as essentially all of the world's nuclear power plant builders have independently come to adopt Rickover's design concept and technology. But in those days the search for an ideal reactor plant cycle was a strong motivating force in nuclear power development.

Westinghouse completed its study in January 1952, presenting six possible reactor types, of which five were considered feasible. No choice among the five was recommended, and the Naval Reactors group was asked to choose one. The group concluded that the pressurized-water design was best, and this choice was endorsed by both the Navy and the AEC. The AEC assigned development of the carrier prototype to Westinghouse and gave Rickover responsibility for directing the project. If there was to be such a project, Rickover wanted it safely under his control.

The *Nautilus* Keel Laying

About the same time, BuShips signed a contract with Electric Boat to build the *Nautilus* and contracted with Westinghouse to build the *Nautilus*

A "FAT SLOB" ALMOST GETS FIRED

In the midst of all these happenings, Panoff rushed into Rickover's office to ask why he had just fired a man they had recently put in charge of an important part of the technical work in Rickover's headquarters group, a man they had worked long and hard to recruit and train, who by all reports had been doing well.

Rickover looked genuinely surprised. "What the hell are you talking about?"

Panoff was equally surprised. "He's cleaning out his desk. He told me you fired him."

"Where did he get that idea? My God, I didn't fire him. We need him around here. He's just beginning to get that shop into shape. What's gotten into him?"

"He said you called him in here a while ago and told him he had screwed everything up and you'd be better off without him. In fact, you said the world would be better off if he'd never been born."

"Aw, he shouldn't take it personally, for God's sake. Why would he take it personally?"

"Captain, you called him a lazy son of a bitch, a fat slob, and an incompetent. How else is he going to take it?"

"Well, tell him I didn't mean it. That is, tell him I don't want to fire him."

"You'd better tell him, Captain. It won't do any good for me to do it."

"Oh, all right. Jesus! You guys don't work for me; I work for all of you. I spend half my time smoothing feathers and trying to talk people out of quitting. *I* don't have that option. Nobody worries about ruffling *my* feathers. You guys can quit any time. You can give me crap and create all sorts of problems for me, and I have to stay here and keep trying. All right, get him in here. Dixie, get that fat slob up here."

plant. Less than two months later, as if that were not enough, the CNO asked BuShips to develop design criteria for a high-speed submarine. Rickover decided to exploit the momentum. He would have a "keel-laying ceremony" for the *Nautilus*. A submarine does not have a keel, but any of her bottom hull plates could be considered keel plates. Wouldn't it be wonderful, he thought, if he could get President Truman to lay the keel for the *Nautilus*! He had recently been privileged to discuss the naval program with the president, and the president seemed genuinely interested. But Rickover followed protocol by going through Senator McMahon. Not only was McMahon the acknowledged spokesman for atomic matters on the Hill, but the *Nautilus* was being built in his state. McMahon agreed enthusiastically, and although he was dying of cancer, he telephoned the president from his sickbed and the president agreed to speak.

The ceremony was an impressive one. Top political, Navy, and AEC officials were present, along with officials of Westinghouse, General Electric, and Electric Boat. Truman was effusive in portraying the future of nuclear power, and the importance of the Naval Reactors program and Captain Rickover's leadership in achieving that future. Gordon Dean, chairman of the AEC, echoed these sentiments, adding, "If one were to be singled out for special notice, such an honor should go to Captain H. G. Rickover, whose talents we share with the Bureau of Ships and whose energy, drive, and technical competence have played such a large part in making this project possible." A few weeks later Navy Secretary Dan Kimball pinned a second Legion of Merit medal on Rickover, calling his program "the most important piece of development work in the history of the Navy."

The next day Captain Rickover was passed over for admiral a second time. Since he had also completed thirty years of active duty, he would be required to retire from the Navy by 30 June 1953. There was no precedent on the books under which he could continue on active duty after that time.

Part III

Putting the Atom to Work
(1950–1957)

III.

When doing a job—any job—one must feel that he owns it, and act as though he will remain in that job forever. He must look after his work just as conscientiously, as though it were his own business and his own money. If he feels he is only a temporary custodian, or that the job is just a stepping stone to a higher position, his actions will not take into account the long-term interests of the organization. His lack of commitment to the present job will be perceived by those who work for him, and they, likewise, will tend not to care. Too many spend their entire working lives looking for the next job. When one feels he owns his present job and acts that way, he need have no concern about his next job.

H.G.R.

Putting the Atom to Work
1950–1957

BY THE END of 1950 Captain Rickover had most of the organizational raw material he needed to carry out his program. The Navy had officially established an urgent need for a nuclear-powered submarine, and President Harry Truman had approved it, with a January 1955 sea date. The Atomic Energy Commission (AEC) had finally agreed to Rickover's plan to establish a group with responsibility and authority within both agencies, and had agreed in principle to work with industry in carrying out the project. Westinghouse and General Electric had been brought in, and the basic administrative procedures were in place. Rigorous training programs had been set up at Oak Ridge and MIT, as well as at headquarters and within the laboratories involved in the program.

THE BASIC TECHNICAL PARAMETERS

In addition to the administrative aspects, some critical technical decisions had been made. The coolant was to be hot pressurized water. The

117

structural materials in contact with the coolant would be a high-temperature-resistant stainless steel. The reactor fuel cladding would be made of a zirconium alloy not yet defined. The radiation shielding would be of common materials: mostly steel, lead, and water ("Water has no cracks," Rickover used to say), and the radiation levels to which people might be exposed would be conservatively low. All this was for the Westinghouse/Argonne *Nautilus* plant and its prototype. The GE plant would be cooled with liquid metallic sodium, and the structural material would be a type of stainless steel, but other details remained up in the air while the company struggled to maintain some of the characteristics of its commercial power-breeder concept.

If these basic technical decisions had not been made, no approximation, even rough, could be made of the plant. With these parameters set, various reactor and plant concepts could be compared and system designs begun. However, there was still a high probability of complete failure. We explained the paradox this way: We can decide that the reactor will be made of a zirconium alloy, with certain assumed nuclear, metallurgical, and mechanical properties. We know, for example, the approximate properties of a zirconium alloy with 1 percent iron in it, and we can start with that. The physicists and the mechanical designers can then begin to get into detailed design and analysis. During this period we have to learn how to produce and fabricate this material, and how to measure its nuclear properties, its corrosion resistance, strength, and radiation resistance; this requires lots of difficult and time-consuming tests. At the same time, component and system designers can begin plant layout studies. And yet there is no guarantee that any of this will work out. There may not be *any* alloy that is strong enough, or corrosion-resistant enough, or it may fall apart under the fierce radiation bombardment in the reactor. So we proceed as if we knew quite precisely what we were doing, yet we are aware that we are on completely unknown ground and that it may not work at all.

To meet the January 1955 sea date for the *Nautilus* and to maintain at least a little lead time for the prototype over the ship, construction of the prototype had to begin at once, so ground was first broken in Idaho in August 1950, with many of the important design parameters still unsettled. The Electric Boat Company had no experience building a ship two thousand miles from its shipyard in Groton, Connecticut, and the high desert presented many unique problems of its own. (For example, all water had to come from new wells drilled over a thousand feet deep.)

One day Carlton Shugg, a highly competent Naval Academy graduate and former deputy general manager of the AEC, now manager of Electric Boat, called me with a possible problem. He had been quietly comparing health data from employees who were issued radiation detection badges with data from employees who were not involved in radiation work. There was a small but statistically noticeable difference in white blood count between the two groups, although the radiation badge readings indicated that the men wearing them had not been exposed to a biologically significant level of radiation. Clearly, this was something that had to be followed up on.

I suggested that it might have nothing to do with radiation, and instead might be associated with working in Idaho, where the work hours were longer, stress, smoking, and coffee intake greater, and the altitude higher than in Connecticut. Further analysis showed this to be the case; employees who worked at Idaho tended to show slight decreases in white blood count, even before the reactor was started up and there was still no reactor radiation whatsoever. Such minor variations in physiology are apparently common. It was the kind of "problem" that had not been noticed before, because no one was looking that closely. The greater sensitivity to possible safety hazards that characterized the nuclear field turned up this sort of situation more than once.

The Benefits of Starting with a Submarine

There is no question that choosing a submarine as the first application for nuclear power was choosing the most difficult option. The destroyer, which GE and many naval officers had spoken for, would have been easier. A larger surface ship would have been easier yet. Why, then, did Rickover pick the submarine?

The most obvious answer is that nuclear power confers a unique advantage on submarines—the ability to stay submerged indefinitely—whereas the advantages to surface ships are less clear-cut. This alone was sufficient justification to warrant the extra effort and risk of tackling the submarine first.

But there was a less obvious reason, which in retrospect may have been even more critical. Submariners do not have to be convinced of the vital importance of the highest standards in hardware reliability and personnel training. More than people in almost any other profession, they are made aware daily that their lives can be snuffed out by a faulty valve or a poorly trained sailor. So in working with submarine operators and shipyards and suppliers, we found more ready acceptance of our demands for extraordinary quality and discipline than we would ever have found in the surface Navy. Once we had established that level of excellence as a pattern and a precedent, it was easier to carry it over to the surface Navy, and then into the civilian power industry, than it ever would have been to start it there.

In a similar vein, it would have been almost impossible to get any shipyard up to that level if we had had to do it entirely within the yard. But the land prototype in Idaho offered an almost monastic ambiance where the extraordinary could be established, away from the peer pressure of normal shipyard operations, and then transplanted once it had taken root.

In Defense of a Parochial Viewpoint

Rickover had cornered much of the nation's high-temperature stainless steel for his projects—some six hundred tons—and was under great pressure to release some of it for jet fighters being built for the Korean War. Lou Roddis had a call from a staffer in the office of the secretary of defense, warning that Rickover was about to create a serious national emergency and Roddis would be smart to get him to back off. Roddis hurried into the Captain's office to pass on the warning, but it didn't take Rickover long to figure how he felt about the matter:

"Roddis, you want me to take a statesmanlike position, to rise above my parochial viewpoint, to consider the good of the nation as a whole, and perhaps the good of all humanity, is that it? Well, I'm not going to do it. You're not in a position to judge just how urgent or important their need really is. Neither am I. What I *do* know is that I have been ordered by the president of the United States to have a ship ready to go to sea by January 1955, and I intend to do my damnedest to make that happen. If the president and the secretary of defense, who have responsibilities for both programs, ask me to back off, I will. But all we know at the moment is that some staffer thinks it would be easier to get the stainless steel from me than to do what I did and go out and find it. Well, he's going to find it's easier for him to get a shovel and dig it out of the ground than to get it from me."

Roddis was willing to let it go at that, but Rickover wasn't through.

"You guys are always telling me I should be more reasonable. People would like me better, and life would be beautiful, if I'd only be reasonable. Well, I don't see any advantage to the Naval Reactors program of being reasonable. Suppose they start talking about cutting back the Reactor Development Division budget. Everybody is supposed to be reasonable and absorb part of the loss. Do you think anybody'll say, 'Let's talk to Rickover, he'll be reasonable?' Hell, no. They'll do anything they have to, to keep from talking with me about it. They'd rather take the cuts themselves. So tell me: Is my attitude beneficial to the project, or not? I'm not asking what's the best way to have lots of friends and get invited to parties. I'm asking what's good for the project."

Roddis said he couldn't argue with that, and Rickover wrapped it up with "All right. You've had your sermon for the week. That leaves you free to come in here Sunday. Now quit trying to make problems for me. I've got enough real ones already."

And no more was ever heard on the matter.

Setting the Radiation Standards

Meanwhile, I was struggling with the design of the radiation shielding. "The simplest locations to calculate are those places where a person could stand right against the shield," I said to Bob Panoff one day. "The radiation goes from the reactor through the layers of shielding, and you can calculate how much shielding is needed to a reasonable degree of accuracy. And we know what further experiments and what improvements in theory are needed to get better accuracy. But this situation doesn't apply to much of the reactor."

"Why not? What do you mean?"

"Take the bottom of the ship, for example. Directly under the reactor. There's no point in shielding that to a level where someone could stand against it all day, right?"

"Yeah, but you can't get away with *no* shielding at all. You do come into dry dock sometimes, and you might have divers have to inspect the hull."

"Right. And you'll also have radiation reflecting off the water back into the hull, and you have to calculate that."

"How close can you calculate that—the reflection of radiation back into the hull?"

"Not very well."

"So what are you going to do about it?"

"The Old Man has agreed to build the hull of the prototype plant inside a water tank, so we can actually simulate the situation we'll have on the ship. He doesn't want any surprises, particularly when it comes to radiation."

The reactor would not be the only source of radiation. The entire reactor coolant system, with all its piping, pumps, valves, and heat exchangers, would contain water irradiated by circulation through the reactor, and thus present a source of radiation that had to be shielded. Therefore, Panoff and Milton Shaw and Howard Marks devoted considerable attention to laying out the system so as to minimize the shielding required for this equipment.

One day I was called into Rickover's office and found that the Captain had also been stewing about the shielding problem. "Rockwell, we have to formalize our radiation standards. We've been operating with sort of an informal agreement so far, and up to now that's been enough. But we now have to tell people just what our codes and standards are in this area."

"I've talked with all the radiologists, health physicists, and biology experts I can get to, Captain, and there seems to be general agreement that there's no need for us to use the civilian standards. There's a lot of margin in the civilian standards, and we could use a higher radiation level and still be considered very conservative by all the civilian experts."

Rickover replied, "You know I went out to see Hermann Muller, the Nobel laureate geneticist. He's very conservative about radiation, but he said that for a military project, we could undoubtedly get away with a higher dose than the civilian standard. But you know what? I'm not going to do it that way. How much do you think they would let us shave from the civilian standard?"

"Factor of three. Maybe a factor of ten. We could probably give the crew ten times the permissible civilian dose."

"How much weight would this save us, compared with using fully civilian standards?"

"Gee, Captain, I can't estimate that. We don't even have a shield design yet."

"How much, dammit, *how much*?"

I rolled my head back, muttered a little, and finally said, "Ten percent, maybe fifteen."

"Of the radiation shielding, or of the plant weight?"

"Of the shield."

"Aw, hell, Rockwell! That's nothing! Why have we screwed around with this thing so long?"

"That's a lot of tons, Captain. It'll make a bigger ship. You could put in a lot of sonar or whatever for that kind of weight."

"Is that *your* problem? Your job is to protect the crew from radiation. There are other people worried about getting the sonar aboard. You can be sure *they* don't care how much radiation the crew gets, so *you* damn well better. What if some kid on the *Nautilus* fathers a two-headed baby? If we haven't met all applicable standards for radiation protection, is that mother going to worry about your damn sonar? No, sir, I'm going to use civilian standards throughout, the ones approved by the United Nations medical advisers, the World Health Organization, the whole nine yards. Now I want you to put that into the form of specs; specify exactly how the radiation levels at various locations, in the ship and near it, should be set, so that the civilian standards will be fully met. I don't want any corners cut, you understand? I don't want there to be any doubt or ambiguity that we've met all applicable civilian standards, with margin to spare. What are you grinning about, Rockwell?"

"Captain, you know that guy Williams at Battelle? He keeps going around saying we should use pure gold for gamma shielding. He has calculations showing that we could save most of that 10 percent if we would just use a couple of hundred tons of gold instead of an iron and water and lead design. He says there's tons of gold at Fort Knox, not doing anybody any good, and you won't use it for political reasons. He's making quite a pest of himself."

"We should never have cleared that clown for this program. The next time he brings that up publicly, I'm going to tell him that scientists tell me the best material for neutron shielding is *white Protestant babies*, and there are a lot of them around, not doing anything. But despite their excellent nuclear properties, I'm not going to use them. For purely political reasons." Here he got a gleam in his eye. "And I'm going to start calling him Gold Shield Williams, every time I see him or refer to him in public. That'll stop the bastard."

The Production of Sponge Zirconium

By the summer and fall of 1952, significant milestones were beginning to whiz past like telephone poles past a speeding car. Rickover had been assigned the aircraft carrier project, and a formal public announcement was made. Lawton Geiger had created a zirconium production program that was a miracle that bedazzled everyone who knew of it. But it was still not clear that enough material with the required properties could be produced to meet the needs of the prototype and the research program, and also the requirements of the shipboard plant, whose deadlines were coming up fast. As for the aircraft carrier plant and other naval ships that might follow—nobody dared think about that for the moment.

At an evening meeting with the Westinghouse people at Bettis, Harry Mandil, who had been talking with the Bettis people all day, stated the consensus to the Captain: "We're going to have to expand our production facilities for crystal bar zirconium pretty soon. We can barely make the fuel elements for the Mark I prototype with the units we have, and we have to get started on the shipboard core before long. Can I bring you a specific proposal for approval in the next few days?"

This seemed like a reasonable and noncontroversial proposal, so no one was prepared for Rickover's response. "I want to use sponge metal."

There was a startled chorus of "What?! Are you serious? We can't do that!"

But the Captain was firm. "The crystal bar process was a very ingenious laboratory method for increasing the world's total supply of pure zirconium metal from less than an ounce to many pounds. But it's a tricky and expensive laboratory process. My God, can you really picture us making tons of crystal bar, to fuel hundreds of ships, by depositing metal, atom by atom, out of hot iodide vapor onto special electrodes? No, sponge metal is the way we'll have to produce zirconium sooner or later, so we might as well get started."

Geiger tried his hand at injecting some realism into the scene. "Captain, the process for making zirconium sponge is still mostly a dream. The only product we've made so far is full of impurities, and it's brittle. It may take years to prove out a suitable process and put a line into production."

The Bettis people asked, "We have the Mark I core process all lined up, and the first fuel elements are actually under construction. Do we throw all that away?"

The Captain was ready for that one. "No, it's probably too late for Mark I. But for the ship . . ." This too elicited a chorus of protests. He had spoken heresy. "But Captain, we've told everybody from day one that Mark I equals Mark II—the prototype has to be just like the ship.

No exceptions. You spilled lots of blood convincing us all that nothing was to be put on the Mark I prototype that wouldn't be suitable for the submarine. Are you now scrapping that rule?"

Rickover's response was surprisingly low-key and patient, almost tutorial. "Let me show you some Rickover math." He went to the blackboard and wrote in big letters, "Mark I = Mark II," and read aloud, "Mark One equals Mark Two." He then wrote under it, "Mark II ≠ Mark I," and read, "Mark Two does not equal Mark One. The first equation says we won't postpone tackling any shipboard problems just to get the prototype on line. But the second equation says we can always make an improvement in the second plant, if there's a better way to do something. If we need to. And here we need to."

There was a stunned silence for a moment, then Mandil spoke. "Captain, there are two or three tests I'd have to see positive results on before I could support using sponge metal in the ship. I think the chances of those results being positive are not good. I'd like to give you a memo describing the situation."

Rickover's response was typical of him. "Fine, give me a memo. But I want to be ready to start tooling up for large-scale sponge production in three months. I have to leave now. I've got to catch a plane."

And amid further cries of protest that three months was too short to prove anything, he left. To everyone's amazement, a process for making large quantities of satisfactory-grade sponge zirconium was indeed worked out, and the first reactor core for the ship was made from zirconium sponge.

Problems with Structural Materials

Zirconium was not the only material problem the project faced. The stainless steel from which the pumps, valves, and piping were to be made was to be subject to new and unusual conditions, for which little information was available. Initial corrosion tests showed nasty black film covering the test specimens. Even more troublesome were the problems with bearing materials, on which pumps and valves depended. As data from the laboratory tests began to come in, they were not all good. Late in 1952 Mandil called an internal meeting to discuss the latest test results. As expected, the Captain did not take the news lightly. He opened the meeting with "Mandil, you're the bearer of this news. Everybody here hasn't heard the whole story, so just review it quickly."

Mandil responded, "We've finally gotten the first dynamic hot-water tests from the labs. You know, we've had hot autoclave corrosion tests, which looked OK, and bench tests of mechanisms in air, and in room-temperature water, and these looked all right too."

"Never mind the good news, dammit. Get to the problem."

"We just got results from some bearing tests and some preliminary valve tests in pressurized water at full operating temperature. Some of the bearings froze and some of the valves tended to seize up. Now, these results are only preliminary, and the test equipment may be at fault."

"Dammit, Mandil, if the problem goes away, we won't have to worry about it. But as of now we have a problem, and we'd better anticipate the worst. Rockwell, did you know about this?"

I admitted I did. To which the Captain replied, "Why the hell didn't you tell me about it? Are you afraid I might take some action you wouldn't approve of? Or did you want to get some cozy cover story all prepared?"

"Captain, these results are very preliminary. I'm not sure they mean anything at all. I wanted to get some more information before . . ."

"Rockwell, what's the worst this can mean? The very worst. Suppose a thousand other tests all give the same answer. What does it mean?"

"Well, if we can't get past this point . . ."

"That's what I asked, dammit!"

". . . then we'd have to conclude that a pressurized-water reactor system won't work. But . . ."

"And this is the news that you wanted to keep from me! Listen, Rockwell: Don't you ever withhold bad news from me again, thinking it might go away. *I'll* decide when to worry about it. Understand?"

"Yes, sir. I guess I figured this was Mandil's area. I didn't want to take over his turf."

"Rockwell: Are there any implications here for safety? Does it matter to you if pumps or valves freeze up or reactor control rods stick?"

"Yes, sir. That would be disastrous, but . . ."

"Dammit, then it's your responsibility to tell me so. One hundred percent your responsibility. It's also 100 percent Marks's, because the pumps and valves are his. And if he weren't out of town, he'd be here and I'd be chewing him out too. And it's 100 percent Panoff's, because he's submarine project officer. And it's 100 percent Geiger's, because he's in charge of the Pittsburgh office. The existence of these other guys doesn't change your responsibility one whit. Do you guys all understand that? I don't want to have to keep going over that point again."

It turned out that the sticking of valves and bearings and the buildup of radioactive corrosion products were two aspects of a real problem, which came within a hairbreadth of dooming the entire pressurized-water reactor concept, the concept on which nearly all of the world's nuclear power plants are based. The dilemma was solved by means that Rickover was never really comfortable with: it was found that if an overpressure of hydrogen gas was kept on the reactor coolant system, the chemistry of the system would be chemically reducing, rather than oxidizing, and the two problems would not occur. Rickover had the submariner's fundamental aversion to hydrogen, based on a legacy of battery explosions, but he accepted the solution as a stopgap measure. In time, a practical means of providing the proper chemistry was worked out.

Training Lessons

The point about the inescapability of responsibility was basic Rickover dogma, and he never missed an opportunity to drive it home. He circulated copies of John Grier Hibben's "Essay on Responsibility" to all the staff and expected them to read it and learn from it. Circulation of reading material had become an important training technique, and the variety of materials he circulated was bewildering. A government memorandum defining "Completed Staff Work" and another on how to prepare a proper memo to a superior ("FDA: The Facts, Discussion, Action Format") were unsurprising in that context, as was the original text of Elbert Hubbard's "Message to Garcia." But other messages were more unexpected, such as a long chapter from a book on life during the Thirty Years' War, or Dylan Thomas's prose poem *A Child's Christmas in Wales*.

One esoteric example that I remember was an excerpt from a book entitled *Chinoiserie: The Vision of Cathay*, by Hugh Honour, which began as follows:

> In China, letters are respected not merely to a degree but in a sense which must seem, I think, to you unintelligible and overstrained. But there is a reason for it. A rose in a moonlit garden,

the shadow of trees on the turf, almond blossom, scent of pine, the wine-cup and the guitar; these and the pathos of life and death, the long embrace, the hand stretched out in vain, the moment that glides forever away, with its freight of music and light, into the shadow and hush of the haunted past; all that we have, all that clings to us, a bird on the wing, a perfume escaped on the gale—to all these things we are trained to respond, and the response is what we call literature.

The staff read these things, pondered them, and kept their copies, even after they left the program. Some pieces they copied and sent to their children, passing the Rickover Effect on to the next generation.

A paper that particularly intrigued many of the engineers involved the way scientists and engineers evaluate situations, make judgments, and communicate their reasoning, as compared with the way executives and other decision makers do these things. Panoff and I discussed this one far into one rainy evening. I had been on travel and had not yet read the paper; I had just skimmed through it and planned to read it more carefully later. So Panoff told me what he had gotten out of it.

"Well, this guy says that some people, particularly scientists—and I guess that would include engineers and most of us—we tend to see things in terms of similarities. If we do something wrong, it bothers us, as it would anybody. But we try to understand the mistake in terms of general principles. And when we find where we went wrong, and see that the basic principles that rule the world are still in place, then we feel OK. It was only a little mistake; everybody makes mistakes, right?"

"Yeah, natch. But what's the point? How else can you look at it?"

"Ah hah! You've just revealed yourself as a 'similarities man.' No surprise there. But the 'difference men,' mostly business executives and certainly including our Beloved Leader, see things in terms of differences. Each morning they look for changes from the day before. Should they buy or sell? Fire or hire? Every difference, no matter how small, is scrutinized to see what action is required, either to correct for an incipient problem or to take advantage of a perceived opportunity. And when the similarities man—you or me—has decided that his little mistake is OK because the principles are still in place, all the difference man can see is that you were wrong, not right. Black, not white. There are no grays in his world."

"I'll admit that sounds familiar. So what do we do about it? Just wring our hands?"

"No, there's a way. Just stick with me. A similarities guy always wants to present his story step by logical step—I know I do—starting with 'Now, you'll agree that so-and-so' and ending with the logically inescapable conclusion. But the Captain always cuts me off by screaming, 'I'm not agreeing to anything yet. Where are you trying to lead me?' The difference man wants the big picture first, then he'll fill in as many details as he thinks he needs. In fact, I've gone in there with all my arguments lined up and documented, and—having read this article—I give him the punchline first. I ask for what I want, with no backup. And sometimes he just says, 'OK,' and when I try to give him all the backup and rationale, he just yells, 'Get out of here, Panoff, before I change my mind.' "

He paused, looked around, and then said, "Wait a minute, let me try something."

He picked up two partially filled water glasses and poured the fuller one into the other, to bring the levels about equal. He put them down in front of me and said, "You haven't read the article yet. Just tell me about these two glasses."

"Well, they are physical objects, not an abstraction or an idea. They are man-made. They are made of glass and contain water. They . . ."

"Can't you see any differences between them?"

I looked long and hard at the glasses and then said, "Well, nothing significant. This one seems to be a little fuller, maybe."

"Believe it or not, I tried the test on the Boss. He was amused, but he went along with it. I asked him to describe the two glasses. 'Which one?' he asked. I asked him to consider them together. 'That's ridiculous,' he says. 'One has a chip and the other doesn't. One is fuller than the other. One has a dirty fingerprint on it,' and he went on and on. I'll have to admit, the article really helped me see why I was having so much trouble communicating with the Old Guy."

Rickover's concern for informing and motivating his people was not confined to the professionals. He also sponsored a series of after-work lectures and seminars on atomic energy and submarine basics, for secretaries, stenographers, and clerks. Attendance was strictly voluntary, but the percentage who chose to give up their spare time was high. As a bonus, when the course was finished he took the attendees, plus some key clerical personnel from the Bettis site, on a weekend trip in Navy planes to the Mark I prototype plant in Idaho, where they were given a tour and a question-and-answer session before being whisked home. The impact on morale was dramatic and long-lasting. And the government was adequately reimbursed by increased productivity and extended work hours.

Starting to "Own" the Design

Looking back on a successful design effort, it is hard to recall how certain decisions—now so clearly correct—could have been so hard to make at the time. In the early days of the program, the Argonne Laboratory people were the reactor experts; the rest of us were outsiders, or rather newcomers. We knew we had a lot to learn. We tended to think of the Argonne people as scientists and ourselves and the Westinghouse-Bettis people as engineers, and we attributed our different outlooks to that. But that isn't quite the story. A number of the Argonne people had degrees in engineering and thought of themselves as engineers. But they generally lacked industrial experience, and they didn't have the corporate pool of industrial talent to draw on that was available at Westinghouse and in the Navy. So although they were engineers, they were research engineers, and that is a very different skill from industrial engineering—neither inferior nor superior, but quite different.

Accordingly, the first design concepts for the submarine reactor came out of Argonne, and the engineers in the newly formed Bettis group responded as they did when they got an idea from their in-house research people. They would seldom question the basic concept, and they would proceed to see that the necessary pumps, valves, motors, and pipe sizes were properly engineered. And that is how we slid into the reference design for the control drive mechanism that moved neutron absorbers into and out of the reactor core.

It was a complex device in the tradition of the inimitable Rube Goldberg. The designers wanted to avoid putting a rotating shaft through the pressure vessel wall, so they created rotation by means of hydraulic motors inside the vessel. They did not want to have a penetration for each control rod, so they had one large one and moved the individual rods through a complex mechanical linkage. Inside the vessel were three large master gears, or "wobble plates," which operated on off-center shafts, which imparted a rotating motion to threaded nuts, which drove lead screws up and down, carrying the control rods with them. When asked to describe how it worked, we would joke that "the big wheel's run by faith, and the little wheel's run by the grace of God." And if asked, "Will it work?" we would grit our teeth and say we were going to make it work. What else could we do? It was unthinkable to consider a basic design change on such a crucial part of the system at that late date.

Each part of the system was being engineered to give maximum assurance of operability, and there were backups for several of the critical components and materials. But Rickover was not convinced that it made sense to depend on such a complex design, all sealed up within the radioactive reactor vessel. He sent Jack Crawford, a young naval engineer on his staff, and Erling Frisch, a highly experienced Westinghouse designer, on a tour of all the facilities developing the many different motors and mechanisms comprising the design. Crawford's report on the magnitude of the effort persuaded the Captain to bite the bullet. He convened a task force at Bettis to address the problem from scratch. They emerged several weeks later with a much simpler design, radically different in concept from the Argonne approach, and Rickover, with complete concurrence from his staff, chose it as the reference design.

It is clear, in retrospect, that this decision did not delay the program, and the original design might well have doomed the project. But at the time, it took courage and vision to make such a decision. None of us had the guts to recommend it to Rickover before he himself decided to consider it as an option. Once the change was made, a major taboo had been broken. The design was beginning to be ours.

Selecting Hafnium As the Control Material

By December 1952 Rickover and his people were becoming more and more concerned about the design of the nuclear control rods. Designed and developed at the Argonne Laboratory, they consisted of a silver-cadmium alloy, clad in stainless steel. Dr. Alvin Radkowsky, Rickover's chief physicist, was convinced that hafnium, the neutron-absorbing element removed from zirconium ore, would be a much better control rod material. It should share the strength and corrosion resistance of its sister element zirconium, and it would avoid the problems associated with having a low-melting alloy clad in a high-melting metal of very different mechanical and nuclear characteristics. But the Argonne physicists were not confident that hafnium would be sufficiently effective as a neutron absorber. The silver-cadmium alloy was clearly more effective in absorbing the low-energy "thermal" neutrons that made up most of the neutron population. The argument turned on whether the ability of hafnium to absorb higher-energy neutrons would make up the difference.

Radkowsky devised a nuclear physics experiment that Argonne could run, to test the comparative effectiveness of the two competing designs, and I insisted that Argonne and Radkowsky agree in advance exactly what numbers, developed from what method of analyzing the experimental data, would be sufficient to declare hafnium the winner. If this could not be agreed to in advance, I was sure there would be no agreement after the fact. Radkowsky proposed that the test would have to show hafnium as 15 percent better to warrant changing to hafnium, and Argonne readily agreed, confident that this would end the matter. But the test showed that hafnium was better, by more than the required 15 percent.

On 15 December a meeting was held at Bettis, to evaluate the latest autoclave corrosion tests on the Argonne control rods. These were called "accelerated corrosion tests," designed to show in a few weeks or months how much corrosion might be expected in the plant over a period of years. This was the kind of measure we had to adopt in order to keep barely ahead of the frantic construction schedule. On the morning of the meeting, the rods were pulled out of the hot autoclaves (great, high-pressure, electrically heated vessels) and examined carefully. It appeared that in at least one case, the cladding had swelled slightly and pulled away from the inner alloy. This could be very serious in the reactor; it might mean that the alloy would no longer be adequately cooled at that spot, and further distortion could then take place, which might bind the rod so that it could not move. That evening, when Rickover was shown the results, he called for a hammer and struck the rod a single sharp blow. The cladding broke loose from the alloy, and Rickover announced that hafnium was no longer just a backup effort.

Shortly after that, at a meeting with his senior people in Washington, Rickover made the final decision to use hafnium. It was a serious decision; no one knew what it would take to prove out hafnium or how much this might set the program back. In the midst of this crucial meeting the Captain got a phone call. He listened for a moment and then said calmly, "Call me back later. I don't have time now to get mad." We all cracked up, and shortly thereafter the meeting concluded and the decision was made. And hafnium is now used, not only in naval plants but in reactors throughout the world, and it has proved to be an excellent material.

STARTING UP MARK I

It is a human inclination to hope things will work out, despite evidence or doubt to the contrary. A successful manager must resist this temptation. This is particularly hard if one has invested much time and energy on a project and thus has come to feel possessive about it. Although it is not easy to admit what a person once thought correct now appears to be wrong, one must discipline himself to face the facts objectively and make the necessary changes—regardless of the consequences to himself. The man in charge must personally set the example in this respect. He must be able, in effect, to "kill his own child" if necessary and must require his subordinates to do likewise.

H.G.R.

Looking back, it's hard to realize how little was known about nuclear power reactors in early 1953. When you know, in hindsight, that something works, it's hard to recall how it might have failed completely. The great natural uranium "atomic piles" at Oak Ridge, Savannah River, and Hanford, Washington, which produced plutonium for the atomic bombs, were a totally different beast from the tiny water-cooled, highly-enriched-uranium Submarine Thermal Reactor (STR) in the Idaho desert. The physics, the chemistry, the metallurgy, and the engineering behind those special-purpose behemoths were as inadequate for the STR as the Wright brothers' technology was for the space shuttle.

The nearest exemplar, from a nuclear physics standpoint, was the Materials Testing Reactor (MTR), which the Oak Ridge reactor group had just finished building. It was small, but it ran in an open tank at room temperature and produced no external power. The Oak Ridge physicists were convinced that the control mechanism for the reactor must be a very sensitive high-speed device, capable of responding every few milliseconds, or thousandths of a second, to a rapidly changing neutron level. The Argonne physicists agreed, and they insisted that the same requirement would apply to the submarine reactor. It was one thing to design such a delicate device to operate over an open tank, at room temperature, on a stable platform; but to operate such a device reliably through a high-pressure seal in a thick-walled pressure vessel on a pitching ship seemed out of the question. Radkowsky felt sure that such high-speed response was unnecessary, and Sid Krasik, at Bettis, was equally certain. I watched the single MTR control rod quivering up and down in tiny, rapid, random-sized oscillations, and I was convinced that the rod was responding not to changing demand from the reactor, but to electronic noise in the circuitry. I pleaded in vain for the MTR operations people to run a simple test in which the response of the rod would be progressively slowed until it equaled the sluggish STR system, but no one would take responsibility for such a test. So I bit my nails and kept telling myself that I was right. I didn't see how the problem could be solved if high-speed response proved to be necessary.

The control consoles of the submarine plant were like nothing in the nuclear world. Up to that time reactors had been laboratory devices, used for research, and their controls and instrumentation reflected that heritage. This was appropriate. There was no need for these devices to have the ruggedness and compactness needed on a warship, or even on a commercial power reactor. So there were instruments on tables or makeshift racks temporarily rigged up to gather data for a particular test or experiment.

But the submarine prototype plant looked like a submarine engine room. True, there were some special test instruments temporarily set up on a balcony outside the hull, which Rickover had allowed to exist only until preliminary nuclear and safety data had been taken. But inside the hull, you were clearly in a Navy engine room. In fact, one of the first questions raised by the safety reviewers was, What are those funny little clips on all the instrument and control panels? When told that they were coffee mug holders, there was momentary consternation. The reviewers considered it poor protocol for operators to have any food or drink at the controls. But when they finally realized that all Navy equipment is so equipped, and that coffee (called Brazilian Blood) is considered essential to a sailor's existence and well-being, they relented.

There were three panels, each only a few feet square, side by side, to control the entire plant, a sailor seated at each. The first, on your left as you faced them, was the reactor control panel. Next came the steam plant controls. The third panel was the electrical system. That was it. (The same functions in a central station power plant ashore required panels nearly a hundred feet long.) This was the place from which the reactor, the steam plant, and all of the electricity generation and distribution for the ship were controlled. There were, in addition, other panels containing switchgear and the like, from which local functions could be manipulated. The ship controls, directing the ship up, down, right, and left, were forward in another compartment, with the periscope, the sonars, and the navigation equipment. The ship control aspects of the submarine were not simulated in the Mark I prototype.

Scram

Finally, the time came for the cautious approach to "initial crit," meaning the first time that the reactor is brought to criticality, the point where the nuclear chain reaction is self-sustaining. As the core design was being settled, Rickover had always kept pushing for the higher value of uranium loading. At one point I got into an argument with him on the subject. "Look, Rockwell," he said. "You may be completely right. The lower figure may be enough. You bright guys may have hit the number right on the head. But humor me. I'm just trying to be conservative. I just want to make sure the damn thing starts up. What's wrong with erring on the high side? I'm willing to pay for a little more uranium."

To which I replied, "Hell, Captain, I'm not trying to win any gold stars for getting the right answer. I want to be conservative too. I just want the damn thing to *shut down*. Isn't that important, too?" And so it went. But now it was March 1953, and the approach to initial criticality began. Some people had seriously suggested that the first start-up be made from a special test station a mile away and monitored by television, but this idea was quickly dropped. A hair-triggered conglomerate of eighty different safety circuits was standing by ready to shut down, or "scram," the reactor instantly on indication of any of the scores of possible problems that had been anticipated. This system proved so effective that, for a while, it looked as if the plant would never get to criticality. The control rods would be eased out at a predetermined cautious rate, pausing at each increased level to take masses of physics data and analyze it, comparing it with calculations previously made. Then, suddenly: SCRAM, the rods would drop in, and a long wait ensued while the cause of the shutdown was determined from the numerous operating and test instruments. When it was finally determined that the shutdown was understood, the tedious process of pulling out control

---

EXTENDING THE EFFECT: CONSTRUCTION

The role of the Navy's Civil Engineer Corps construction people in getting the Naval Reactors facilities and prototypes built on time, to unprecedented standards and in unbelievably short times, is a miracle I mention here only in passing. The need for maintaining surgical cleanliness in assembling some of the largest components of their kind ever built, and the use of shipyard-trained people in the high desert terrain of Idaho—these are stories that should be told. Some of the lessons learned in these tasks were carried to other construction jobs after the personnel completed their NR projects and moved on. But the story of those early construction projects is an epic tale in its own right.

---

rods would start all over again, from the beginning. (Reactor operators always talk about "pulling out" control rods, because control rods on the first reactor, in a squash court at the University of Chicago, were actually hung on ropes and pulled out by hand. But the STR has control rods that are pulled out by an electric drive mechanism.)

The problem of unwarranted scrams dogged the Mark I on into the power testing program. There was no desire to lower the protection of the reactor from real problems, but scrams were traced to such spurious causes as lightning striking an electric power line in Montana, or an operator walking through the reactor compartment. Finally, enough information was obtained on the characteristics and stability of the reactor that the number of emergency scram circuits was lowered from more than eighty to fewer than twenty. This, plus further intensive training of the crew, led to reliable operation with a minimum number of scrams. But this process took several painful months.

(Later, when Sid Krasik returned from the 1955 Atoms for Peace Conference in Geneva, I asked him if he concluded, from talking with the Russian scientists there, that the reports of Russian reactors were genuine. Krasik said he felt sure they were. "How can you tell?" I asked. "The written reports are sure vague." Krasik answered, "I asked one of the scientists if they had had any trouble with scrams. He rolled his eyes back, slapped his forehead, and took on such a pained look that I knew he'd been there. He wasn't faking that look.")

At 11:17 P.M., 30 March 1953, the STR Mark I reached initial criticality. (Clocks on Eastern Standard Time showed two hours later in Washington and in Pittsburgh, and initial crit went into their books as 31 March.) The power level was less than one-hundredth of one horsepower, and it stayed in that range, or below, for nearly two months, while low-level physics, radiation, and radiochemistry data were taken, and the engineers anxiously awaited the start of power testing.

The Important Role of the NRX

The technical philosophy of Rickover, heartily endorsed by his people, was to test everything that could be tested, at as early a stage as possible. So little pieces of zirconium and stainless steel were corrosion-tested in pressurized-hot-water kettles, called autoclaves, and other specimens were tested for strength, creep, and other important characteristics. In some tests, reactor radiation was simulated (but not very accurately) with Van de Graaff generators, the huge "atom smashers" of prewar science fiction. In other tests, heat generation was simulated with electrically heated elements, but the electric fields created by the heaters changed the electrochemistry of the water and clouded interpretation of the test results. Nuclear parameters for the reactor were mocked up in room-temperature "critical experiments" at Argonne and Bettis. But the biggest unknown was, How would a full-sized fuel element act, in hot, pressurized water and simultaneously in the presence of the intense nuclear bombardment experienced in an operating reactor? The cooling water would be decomposing and recombining in the radiation field, creating unknown chemistry conditions. Fission products being formed in the fuel might cause intolerable swelling and distortion. An adequate rate of cooling under these conditions was not assured. A few small samples were inserted into nuclear test reactors, to check the effects of radiation damage, but this was a very difficult procedure, and the tiny samples yielded only limited information. There was no test facility in the country that could test a full-sized fuel element.

In Canada, however, there was a reactor that could provide such a test. In the beautiful wilderness area near Chalk River, Ontario, the Canadian government had built a small reactor in 1945, and in 1947 it built another, a test reactor called NRX, that was of sufficient size and power to make such a test feasible. Security laws, however, made the use of this reactor by the United States problematical. The Atomic Energy Act of 1946 was more restrictive than its security predecessor, the Espionage Act of 1918. Under the Espionage Act, military allies who were foreign nationals could and did routinely obtain secret military information. But the Atomic Energy Act specifically forbade the giving of atomic energy information to any foreign national, and it also forbade the shipment of enriched uranium out of the country. Since this was the "McCarthy Era," such restrictions were not to be taken lightly. So Rickover disguised his test fuel section as a "materials test," and the shipments across the border were carried out in utmost secrecy.

In a move that was characteristic of him, though it would have been astonishing for anyone else, Rickover reported his illegal action to Congress, said that these tests were important to U.S. national security, and insisted that Congress change the law—which it did. This was the paradox that few understood about Rickover: he would flout some rules and scrupulously abide by others. He had the insight to know which rules he must follow and which he could ignore. His would-be imitators seldom understood the crucial difference.

The tests in NRX revealed important and sobering information. Only a few months before the *Nautilus* Mark I prototype plant was to start up in Idaho, the first fuel test sample was returned for examination. There were indications of significant buildup of a black deposit on the surfaces of the fuel element, which was unceremoniously named *crud* (short for Chalk River Unidentified Deposit). Apparently, the minute amounts of iron, nickel, chromium, and other metals picked up from the stainless steel and circulated in solution through the system were being precipitated out in the radiation field of the reactor. This was a potentially devastating problem. It had appeared after only a few months of operation, and in the prototype plant it could well continue to build up, coating the heat-transfer surfaces of the fuel and causing overheating and possible meltdown. There was also the possibility that, after staying on the fuel surfaces long enough to become very radioactive, the material could slough off or redissolve and then build up on piping and equipment outside the reactor, causing a much higher radiation level after shutdown than had been anticipated in the design. Efforts to explore this problem intensified, but there was no way it was going to be settled before the plant started up.

Unexpectedly, NRX played another important part in Rickover's program. Shortly after the Mark I fuel tests were finished, there was a power surge in the reactor, leading to a partial meltdown of the fuel. The NRX design was very different from Rickover's reactors. Rather than using uranium enriched with the fissionable isotope U-235 and cooled with ordinary water, the NRX used natural uranium and was cooled with heavy water. Heavy water absorbs far fewer neutrons than ordinary water does, and this makes it possible to use natural uranium. But because heavy water is less efficient at slowing down neutrons, the NRX had to use more of it, and so the reactor was more spread out than U.S. reactors, with the fuel elements farther apart. This basic design difference made it easier in the NRX reactor to find room between the fuel elements to insert experiments and test specimens. But it also led to a very different mechanical design, so that the accident caused the fission products to pour down into the basement below the reactor, contaminating large parts of the facility. Although there was no public hazard, cleaning up the facility and restoring the reactor was clearly a major task.

Rickover took the news as an important opportunity to repay his Canadian friends for the invaluable help they had given the program, and to learn unique and important lessons in doing so. "There has never, in the history of the world, been a situation involving large-scale radioactive contamination of equipment and facilities," he said to me. "This is a chance to learn some real-world lessons, to get some experience you can't simulate by playing with dishes of chemicals in a laboratory. I want to send fifty people from Bettis, fifty from GE, and fifty from the Boat Company . . ."

I was somewhat overwhelmed. "You'll swamp 'em with 150 people, Captain. Aren't you overdoing it a bit?"

But Rickover had no doubts on the matter. "I won't send them all at once. Jesus, give me credit for some brains, Rockwell. But this isn't going to be settled overnight. It'll be months before they get that reactor back on the line. I want a large number of our technical people to get some direct, hands-on experience out of this. I want to get some of the submarine officers into this too. Iltis can be our coordinator on the thing. Don't you understand? When Providence hands you an opportunity like this, you've got to have the vision to seize it."

By the time the cleanup was finished, 214 persons from the Naval Reactors program had expended thirteen hundred man-days of effort on it, using special decontamination equipment, radiation instrumentation, and personnel protection gear developed in the United States and shipped in. Wooden mock-ups were used to check out proposed procedures, equipment, and techniques developed at the site. This work gave NR designers and operators unique and invaluable experience making repairs and modifications to piping and equipment in a highly radioactive environment, as well as experience in decontamination and recovery on a wide variety of surfaces.

Mark I's Transatlantic Trip

On 30 May 1953 Captain Rickover took AEC Commissioner Thomas E. Murray with him to participate in the first power operation of the Mark I prototype plant in Idaho. Murray had been a prominent business executive and was highly respected as the first engineer to serve on the Atomic Energy Commission. He had understood and backed Rickover's struggles to arrive at this crucial day, and the Captain wanted him to have the honor of opening the throttle valve and allowing steam generated by the reactor to enter the turbine for the first time. When this had been done, and it was clear that the power plant was operating smoothly and steadily, Rickover and Murray climbed up out of the hull and walked down the wooden stairway to the floor of the building. From there they walked back to where they could gaze in silence at the shaft of the power plant turning slowly under the power of nuclear fission. It was an emotional moment; the atom had at last been made to produce a useful quantity of power.

On 25 June 1953 the plant topped off a series of cautious power increases and for the first time achieved its full rated power. An important milestone had been reached, but there was still great anxiety among the technical people at headquarters and in the laboratories. The Chalk River crud phenomenon was still not understood, and there was also little information as to the dimensional stability of the fuel and control elements under operating conditions, even without corrosion buildup. Because of this, there was concern that warpage and blockage of cooling passages could occur. These kinds of problems tended to be cumulative, so that satisfactory operation during the first few hours was no assurance of continued good operation.

In this situation, Commander Edwin E. Kintner, who was Rickover's man in charge of the Idaho site, called Jack Kyger back at Naval Reactors in a state of great concern. "You know, we were carrying out

"DON'T OVERLOOK THE OBVIOUS"

One of the hardest Rickover lessons to learn was one I never heard him preach in so many words. Perhaps he thought it was too obvious. But he sure demonstrated it memorably, on more than one occasion. It was a simple point, merely this: Don't take the obvious for granted. If it's important, you'd better check it out, along with all the minutiae.

I will never forget an occasion when this lesson was demonstrated to me. I had an important long-range task coming up, and I needed a bright young assistant to take charge of it. We had a number of excellent youngsters out of Naval ROTC and Officer Candidate School who were completing their terms of obligated military service, and we were deciding which ones to offer jobs as civilians. I finally chose a likely candidate and spent about two hours describing what the job would entail. I was impressed by his eager interest and by some of his suggestions on how he would go about it. I checked with other Naval Reactors supervisors, who also gave him high marks. So I went in and told the Admiral I had selected the man for this job, and described his background and the discussion we had had.

Rickover concurred, and as I was walking out, he asked me to bring the candidate in for a minute. When I did, the Admiral simply asked him, "Are you planning to ship over?"—that is, to come aboard as a civilian. The young man thought a minute and then said, "No, I don't think so." I couldn't believe what I had heard! I jumped to my feet and screamed, "Then what the hell have we been talking about all morning?" He replied calmly that he presumed we were talking about what he would do *if* he stayed on; it sounded interesting, but he was about to accept another job. I was speechless. I looked at the Admiral and shrugged my shoulders. I had nothing to say. He just smiled and said, "You'd better get someone else."

our forty-eight-hour full-power run to get the physics and thermodynamic data we need, and found at the end of twenty-four hours that we had what we needed. We were about to shut down and start the examination of the plant for any damage or abnormalities. Well, you know the Old Man is out here, and he ordered us to stay at full power. This didn't bother me very much, since we had originally planned to run forty-eight hours, although I didn't see much point in it. But now we're about through the forty-eight hours, and he wants to go one hundred hours!"

Kyger was shocked. "Why in the world would he do that? What did you tell him?"

"I told him that I thought the extension of the run was unwise, in light of the Chalk River data and all the other uncertainties. In fact, I said that I felt so strongly about it that if he insisted on continuing the run, I would not accept responsibility for the plant."

"What did he say?"

"He said he would take full responsibility, and he has decided to simulate a full-power submerged run across the Atlantic. He has posted a chart of the Atlantic Ocean in the control room, and at the end of each four-hour shift the crew plots the position of the ship on the chart."

"Brother! How crazy can you get? You know, it's only two weeks until the Selection Board decides whether to make him an admiral or kick him out. You'd think he'd at least wait two weeks. I'm going to get the senior people together and I'll get back to you."

At the forty-eight-hour point the plant seemed to be doing well, but about ten hours later, troubles started to show up. The electric generating sets started to spark, because of carbon dust from the brushes that had begun depositing on the windings. One of the main coolant pumps began to make noises for reasons that could not be determined. And the nuclear instruments became erratic. At sixty-five hours one of the main condenser tubes failed, causing steam pressure to drop rapidly. The Westinghouse people recommended to Rickover that the plant be shut down immediately.

At this point Kyger phoned Rickover. "Captain, I've met with most of the senior people here, and we urge you to shut down long enough to check out the condition of the plant. There are too many things that can wreck the plant at this point. Why do you want to risk it?"

Rickover's reply was firm and calm. "This plant is for a warship, not a floating laboratory or a test-bed. She'll have the best weapons, sonar, and other military hardware aboard. That's why I insisted that we run all those shock tests in the Bay, with full-size equipment, using real, large-scale depth charges. This plant must be fully ready to fight. You guys have no imagination! Don't you see the effect this long run will have? No submarine in the history of the world has ever run continuously more than twenty miles at full power. This run will show people that this thing is real. It's not a toy. If I let you shut down the plant, it will be weeks before we're back on the line again. No, I'm not going to let you talk me out of this. It's too important, dammit! That's non-negotiable, so let's drop it."

And despite the trepidation of his advisers, Rickover stuck to his guns. Each crew that took its shift was determined not to be the one that caused a shutdown, and everybody took pride in repairing, adjusting, and keeping everything on line. Finally, after ninety-six hours of continuous full-power operation, the chart showed that the "ship" had made landfall at Fastnet, Ireland, and the Mark I's simulated transatlantic cruise was complete. Now there could be no mistaking that nuclear power had been effectively harnessed to do real work on a practical scale. Rickover's only comment was (paraphrasing Pasteur) "Nature seems to want to work for those who work hardest for themselves."

Subsequent examination showed no damage or problems requiring more than minor adjustments and improvements. The steps taken to combat the crud problem had been successful, and the plant went on to two years of nearly continuous operation and testing on the first reactor core. Until 17 October 1989, over thirty-six years later, the plant was in full operation as a testing and training facility.

Ironing out the Procedures

Admiral Rickover always insisted on operating by the book. To those who knew him only by reputation, such a characterization may seem surprising, for he was often portrayed as a person who had little regard for rules or protocol. This is not the paradox it may seem. Rickover was keenly aware that there are two kinds of rules. He understood that laws of nature, such as the effects of gravity, or radiation, or excessive temperature or pressure, cannot be gotten around by fast talk, political influence, or any other subterfuge. On the other hand, man-made rules are a different entity. Some, such as laws passed by legislative bodies, must be obeyed, and he was scrupulous about this. Others, such as bureaucratic procedures defining how one may carry out assigned responsibilities, sometimes can and should be circumvented, he felt. In particular, those procedures that "everyone" followed because "it's just our policy" he not only spurned but did so with great pleasure.

For a system as complex, expensive, and unforgiving as a nuclear power plant, Rickover's insistence on formal operation was absolutely rigid. In a national environment where most customers tolerated receipt of operating and maintenance manuals months after delivery of the hardware, Rickover would not pay for an item until the manuals were delivered. "It's not complete. It's not yet operable. It's no good to me until I have the manuals," he would shout, and there was no negotiating the point.

So when Mark I started up, there was on board a complete set of manuals, hundreds and hundreds of pages, with cut-away drawings and exploded views, test procedures, preventive maintenance rituals, emergency procedures—everything the designers could think of. Each section was originally written by one of the designers responsible for that item, but the product only proved the truism that most engineers can't write. After a tremendous effort at Naval Reactors, Bettis, and Electric Boat to make these manuals clearer, more complete, and more accurate, a professional organization that specialized in writing technical manuals was called in. The result was even worse. I recall one sentence that ran nearly two pages. Finally, the outside tech writers were thrown out, the material was returned to the design organizations, and with various compromise solutions and a great deal of effort, a satisfactory set of manuals was completed, approved by Naval Reactors, and sent to the Mark I site. The designers were tired, but proud of their product, at last.

But this was not to be the end of the saga. For when these procedures were sent to the plant, they were found, in many places, to be clumsy, vague, unclear, tedious, and sometimes just plain wrong. The plant's operating crew—sailors and officers selected from the cream of the Navy's submarine forces—had been given nearly a year of special training in both the theoretical and the practical aspects of nuclear power, and they were not about to follow blindly any procedures they considered inadequate. These sailors were exceptional people. Many of them had given up submarine pay—generally equal to another 50 percent added to their pay—to volunteer for this alien duty in the desert. You generally think of submariners as carefree bachelors, but these were serious people, and most of them were married. No Navy quarters were provided, and the crew had to find housing for their families in town, and look forward to 140 miles of commuting, or more, each day.

So there ensued months of long and raucous arguing between operators and designers, face to face and over the long-distance phone lines, with Naval Reactors engineers in the middle. But out of it came a greatly improved set of operating and maintenance manuals. The crew had turned in 133 carefully thought-out changes; 80 percent of these were accepted. This valuable result could never have come from the Navy's traditional method of turning a ship over to the Navy crew only after the shipyard felt that all the bugs had been ironed out.

During all this, while back in Washington, I got a telephone call from Kintner. It was about midnight at the site, and thus 2:00 A.M. in Washington, and my wife made no comment as the conversation continued for about an hour. But as I was signing off I made the mistake of saying, "Thanks for calling, Ed."

That did it. "Maybe you had to take the call, and maybe you had to talk for an hour," she said, now fully awake. "But did you really have to say, 'Thanks for calling'?"

GOING AFTER THE NAVY

> It is a sad comment on the decline of individualism in America that the critic has no friend in court. He is tagged "controversial," the worst that can happen to anyone in a conformist society. The "controversial" tag makes him by definition a "flawed" personality, not group-adjusted, one-sided, ill-informed, frustrated and motivated by ill will.
>
> H.G.R.

Sometime in January or February 1953 Panoff beckoned Mandil and me into his office and closed the door, an unusual occurrence in Naval Reactors, where open doors were the norm. He asked us, "Are we just going to sit here and let the Navy put Rickover out to pasture?" I was still boiling over a recent incident. An admiral had said to me casually, "By the way, you fellows might be interested to know that there are lots of people over at the Pentagon who would like to see a destroyer named after Rickover. The sooner the better." In my naiveté I had muttered, "That's nice." Panoff had to remind me that destroyers are named after *dead* naval heroes. To the question of helping Rickover, I

EXTENDING THE EFFECT:
OPERATING PROCEDURES AND MANUALS

The idea of prescribing *exactly* what an operator will do under all imaginable circumstances has been approached in some particularly hazardous industries, and nuclear power gave this objective a new emphasis. But a warship, unlike a laboratory or an industrial facility, cannot be inflexibly bound by rigid procedures—her crew may have to take unusual action to survive. (For example, there are circumstances in which the safest mode for the reactor is shutdown. But if a ship is fighting a storm or an enemy, being suddenly adrift without power may not be the safest condition overall.)

In this situation, Rickover directed that the designers consider and analyze every identifiable operational requirement, and define the appropriate procedure for it. But he did not stop there. He required that the operators be given sufficient knowledge of the processes and design limitations of the plant that they could intelligently judge alternative procedures if an emergency were to arise.

The operating and maintenance manuals that resulted from this directive provide a new standard for intelligent operation of any complex machinery. By insisting that manuals be delivered at the same time as the machinery (instead of the common practice of delays of a year or more), Rickover gave operators a chance to test out these procedures at the prototype plants, in close contact with the designers.

The difference between civilian plants that have applied these lessons and those that have not beggars description.

could only answer, with considerable frustration, "What can *we* do?"

Panoff had obviously been trying to find an answer to that question, but he wasn't there yet. He said slowly, "I've been reviewing this thing, and here's what I've found. The Selection Board that passed over Rickover last June sent the list of admiral selectees to the secretary of the Navy and to Harry Truman, both of whom approved it. But because of the shuffle of political parties in the last election, the Senate Armed Services Committee, who are the last guys to approve it, have held up on this action, waiting for the new Congress to get settled. So it's still not a completed action."

"But has Congress ever changed anything on one of those lists?" asked Mandil.

"No, never. All they can do under the law is to reject one of the nominees, which results in the whole list being sent back to the Navy to reconvene the Selection Board and get them to submit a new list. But they've never even done that. Not in the whole history of the Navy. But they could."

"And if they don't, with his thirty years of service, that means he'll have to retire by the end of next June. At the age of fifty-three, for Pete's sake! How can they do that? What happens then? Who else could run this show?"

"They'll just bring in some ringer from a shipyard in Guam or somewhere, and all of us troublemakers will quit. Then things will quiet down, and this will become a normal Navy project, if it doesn't die out altogether. Don't forget: Most officers don't make admiral, so it's not looked at as punitive in the Navy. It's routine. Nobody will notice. It's a basic part of Navy philosophy that any officer can run anything. He can find out what it's all about and run it, and then turn it over to another officer, all in the span of a year or two. As I say, nobody will notice."

"Well dammit, I'll notice. I agree we shouldn't just sit here and let it happen. But what can we do? We don't have any clout. We're just 'staff.' This town's full of staff. You couldn't exchange a hundred of 'em for a cup of coffee."

"Well, I intend to do something," said Panoff. "Rick sure as hell would do something if he were in our shoes."

"What can you do? Do you know somebody?"

"No, but I can use a phone book."

"Who you gonna call?"

"Well, Rick's family congressman, the one his father still votes for, is Sid Yates, of Chicago. I've never met him, but I'd like to."

A Few Phone Calls

Panoff found Mr. Yates's number in the Congressional Directory and called his office. "Miss, this is Robert Panoff, and I have Messrs. Mandil and Rockwell with me. We are civilian engineers, working for Captain Rickover on the Navy's nuclear propulsion program. It seems the Navy is about to force the Captain to retire, in the prime of life, and leave this important national program adrift. It just can't be run in a routine way, and we thought perhaps the congressman would be willing to advise us on what we could do to prevent this situation. I will be glad to put the matter into a letter or whatever you might need. [*Surprised*] He will? Two-thirty this afternoon? Yes, ma'am, we sure will. What room is that, please? Thank you. Thank you very much."

He hung up and turned to Mandil and me. "How about that? She said he'd see us!"

"I've been thinking, Bob. I don't think we should tell the Captain what we're doing. He may figure it out, but it's better he doesn't know. Everybody will think he sent us, and I'd like him to be able to say he doesn't know anything about it."

"Right." Panoff dialed the Captain's secretary and said, "Dixie, will you please tell the Captain that Mr. Mandil, Mr. Rockwell, and I have a personal errand to run this afternoon. We'll be gone a couple of hours, starting about two." He hung up the phone and turned to us. "Now we'd better think about what we're going to say."

(We never told anyone what we were doing, and no one told us of any efforts others might be making. Years later, I learned that Lou Roddis, Jim Dunford, and Bob Laney had gone to BuShips Chief Admiral Homer N. Wallin and told him that they intended to talk with people in Congress about the situation. Wallin warned, "Your careers in the Navy will be finished if you do." They told him that they figured they had already passed that point, and they did indeed talk to a number of the same people we did.)

That afternoon we found ourselves talking with Congressman Yates, who seemed sympathetic but told us, "I understand your concern, but the problem is that the House has no role in the approval of admiral appointees. That function rests with the Senate Armed Services Committee. I could make a speech on the floor, and perhaps get some mention of it in the papers, but it wouldn't have much effect."

Panoff responded eagerly. "We'll gladly take what we can get, Mr. Yates. I'd be pleased to draft some suggested remarks for you to work from, if you wish."

"That would be fine," said the congressman. "But our best bet is to contact Scoop Jackson. He is on the Joint Committee for Atomic Energy and is a great fan of the Captain's. As you know, he used to be here but was recently elected to the Senate. I know him well, and I'll be glad to set up a meeting for you."

He soon had the senator on the phone and said, "Scoop, I'm flattered that you still deign to talk with your old friends in the House, now that you are settled in the Other Chamber. Yes, well, thank you. Scoop, I have a couple of young men here who are concerned about Captain Rickover's situation . . . yes . . . yes . . . and they'd like to talk to you about it. I told them I couldn't help much from here, but perhaps you could. All right, not tomorrow then. Sunday? Fine. Two P.M. What's that room number again? Fine, they'll be there. Their names are [*looking at his papers*] Panoff, Mandil, and Rockwell. You're civilian engineers, right? Fine. Thanks a lot, and let's get together some time."

He hung up the phone, turned to us, and said, "OK, boys, the ball is in your court."

We expressed our appreciation to the congressman for his prompt and effective action, then asked, "Mr. Yates, should we also try to approach Senator Saltonstall? He *is* head of the Armed Services Committee, where the list of proposed admirals has been sent for action."

Yates's response to this was noncommittal. "You're welcome to try, boys. I don't know the gentleman, or I'd help you."

Flushed with our unexpected success so far, we walked down to the Old S.O.B., as the Old Senate Office Building is affectionately known in some quarters, and went into Senator Leverett Saltonstall's office. We stated our business to the receptionist, who asked just one question: "Are you from Massachusetts?" We confessed that we were not, and she excused herself and went into the inner office. In a moment she returned and said, "His message is simple, gentlemen. He says this matter is of only peripheral concern to his constituents, and he is pressed by many matters that concern them directly and urgently. In that situation, he feels he cannot devote his limited time to the matter. I'm sorry, but that's what he said."

Somewhat sobered by our first setback, we thanked the receptionist and left. Back at the office, we started on another tack. Poring over a city telephone directory, we finally found the Press Club (under *N* for National Press Club) and called the number listed. This time it was my idea. Panoff asked dubiously, "Is this really going to work?"

"I don't know," I said. "But what have we got to lose? Ten times as much effort as anyone else would consider reasonable, right? That's what the Old Man says you should put into anything you do. [*Talking into the phone*] Hello, I'm looking for a Michael Amrine. Is he registered there? Oh, you don't. Well, does anyone there know where I could find him? He's a sort of free-lancer, at least he was several years ago. I think he worked for North American Alliance. Well, could you just ask around? Someone might know him. No, he doesn't owe me any money. I have a story for him. You know, a scoop. Yeah, I'm sure they do. Please, just ask . . . He is? Honest?! My God, no kidding." I turned to Panoff and said, "Somebody saw him at dinner. They're trying to get him to the phone. Geez, how about that? I saw the guy once, in Oak Ridge, years ago, and haven't seen him since. He's the only reporter I know. And now . . . Hello, Mike? OK, I'll wait. Thanks, thanks a lot. Mike? Mike Amrine? This is Ted Rockwell. From Oak Ridge, remember? God, am I glad to talk to you. I've got a great story for you, man. Are you still writing? Great! Well, this is not only a hot story, but an exclusive. Can you get it into the Boston paper? You can? Really? Oh, man. How soon can we get together? Anyplace you want, fella. We'll be right over."

The meeting with Senator Jackson had gone well, and now, a few days later, we found ourselves holding a Boston paper with headlines trumpeting the Navy's imminent retirement of Captain Rickover and editorializing on the injustice of it. We marched triumphantly into Saltonstall's office with the paper and were granted an audience.

"It looks as if your constituents share our concern on this matter, Senator."

The senator grinned knowingly and said, "OK, boys, you got me. I've asked a few of the committee members and other interested senators to join us." And in a few moments Senators James Duff of Pennsylvania, Estes Kefauver of Tennessee, Henry "Scoop" Jackson of Washington, and some others we did not recognize were ushered in. We were asked to state our case, and Panoff, swallowing hard, did his best:

"Gentlemen, we thank you and especially Senator Saltonstall for being willing to hear us out on this matter. As you know, the Navy has submitted a list of thirty-nine names proposed for promotion to admiral. Since the Naval Appropriations Act of 1916, the Senate has been asked to concur on the Navy's selections for flag rank, which are passed on through the secretary of the Navy, and now we have the secretary of defense, and then the president signs off on it. And this duty of the Senate has fallen on the Armed Services Committee. Under the terms of the Officer Personnel Act, this committee can reject any nomination on the list. But if it does so, then the entire list is considered rejected, the Selection Board must be reconvened, and a new list must be sent through the channels to the Senate for reconsideration. I might add that since 1916 the Senate has never rejected the list of nominees submitted by the Navy. Today we are asking you to consider taking such a historic step on this particular occasion. As I'm sure you realize, we're not asking for anything for ourselves. We're not worried about losing our jobs. But we are greatly concerned that if Captain Rickover is forced out of the Navy, this important national program will founder and die."

Senator Duff responded first. With his steely voice, his iron-gray brush cut, and his rugged visage, he was a formidable figure. "Why should that be? Are you saying he is indispensable? Most Americans are suspicious of such a claim."

Panoff replied, "No, he could be replaced. But he has years of specialized training in nuclear power that no one else in the Navy has. And, in addition, he is extraordinarily effective at getting things done."

I pulled a paper from my pocket and said, "Only one day before his rejection by the Selection Board, the secretary of the Navy, Dan Kimball, gave Rickover a medal and said [*reading*], 'Captain Rickover, more than any other individual, is responsible for the rapid development of the nuclear-powered ship program.' And he added, 'Rickover has accomplished the most important piece of development in the history of the Navy.' And the *very next day* the Navy promoted thirty-nine other captains and passed over Captain Rickover."

Mandil added, "In fact, the Navy has now written the Captain and asked him to stay on another year as a twice-rejected captain, because they admit they don't have anyone qualified to replace him! And I'm sure you realize, an officer who has twice been repudiated by his management, so to speak, and who has been publicly told that his tenure is severely limited, has very little clout when he wants to get things done."

Senator Jackson spoke up. He had ridden with Rickover across the country and out into the Pacific Ocean for a nuclear weapons test a few months previous. They had talked long and hard, and Jackson had come away impressed. "I can vouch for the Captain's unique talents, from watching him from my seat on the Joint Committee for Atomic Energy. He is indeed a national treasure. But what are you asking us to do? The Congress, and even the president and the civilian service secretaries, are quite properly reluctant to tell the Navy who its senior officers should be. Once you start down that road, it's hard to hold the military responsible anymore."

Kefauver asked, "Did the Captain send you down here?"

"We did not tell him we were coming, sir. If we had, he probably would have forbidden it. We're here on our own, as citizens."

"What do you suggest we do?" asked Jackson.

This was the question Panoff had been waiting for. Holding up an envelope, he said, "We have obtained an advance copy of the testimony that will be given before your committee this week by Admiral Wallin, chief of the Bureau of Ships."

Saltonstall asked immediately, "How do you come to have that? I expect the Navy would not want you to see it."

Panoff nodded agreement with this last statement but said merely, "I would rather not say, sir, except that several people in the bureau were given copies for comment. I have copies here for each of the members. We have annotated it, to note statements we consider incorrect or misleading. We are also prepared to suggest questions that may be helpful in giving you a more accurate picture of the situation. The main thrust of the Navy's statement is that things are done in the Navy by systems. Officers, being well-rounded individuals, rotate through various positions in the system. Rickover, they claim, just happened to be standing there when this particular bus came by. Any other officer of his rank would have done the same things he has done. And they have others of captain's rank who are ready to step in to replace him. Isn't that a comforting picture?"

Duff spoke up. It was clear that he did not intend to be misunderstood. "I am willing to listen to your suggested questions, but I am no parrot. I will not read off someone else's words in the conduct of my duties. If I don't understand it well enough to say it properly, then educate me and I will try again. But I will speak always in my own words."

We expressed complete satisfaction with that position, and passed out copies of the paper to each of the senators. Panoff then worked through the document, paragraph by paragraph. "The first one, two, three, four paragraphs are just early history, trying to convince you that the history of nuclear power in the Navy precedes Rickover. You will note, however, that the only money mentioned in these paragraphs is $2,000 for the Naval Research Laboratory. Then, in paragraph five,

Admiral Wallin states that technical personnel were not available until 1948. The facts are that in the fall of 1947 Captain Rickover's well-trained group were ready to start the project, as described in Dr. Edward Teller's letter of 19 August 1947, attached. The next paragraph mentions Captain Harry Burris, but he retired last year and is no longer available. From then on, most of the testimony refers to steps taken by, quote, the Bureau of Ships, without mentioning that most of the actions cited were initiated and carried out by Captain Rickover, who remains strangely anonymous in this testimony. Then, after two paragraphs describing the training of certain minor naval individuals, the statement mentions the need for training them with the Manhattan District, which is just what Rickover and his people did . . ." And in this manner we worked through the entire testimony.

After we got back to the office, we received a call from Mike Amrine, saying that he had been asked to make a major speech before the American Society of Newspaper Editors and Publishers, which was having its annual convention in Washington. The theme that year was "Freedom of Speech," and Amrine had prepared a great story on the Rickover problem, but he was having trouble clearing it with the Navy. It was in the hands of Admiral Evander W. Sylvester, deputy chief of BuShips, and Amrine had gone down to see him. Amrine told him that he had been asked to give this address, and he could either give them the Rickover story or he could tell them how Sylvester wouldn't release it. He said Admiral Sylvester just sat there like Br'er Rabbit, looking at his hands and then looking at his feet, and finally he said, "Oh, take it," and stamped the Navy release on it. So then he had both stories.

I was still somewhat overcome by the events of the day. "I keep thinking about all those senators taking time to talk with us and work with us on this thing," I said. "These are really important Joes. They're the movers and the shakers you read about under the big headlines. We can't deliver any votes to them, and we don't have any money for their campaigns. We can't do anything for them politically. Yet they listened. That's damned inspiring. It's like *Mr. Smith Goes to Washington*. It makes me proud to be an American. The system actually works, like they taught us in high school! I never thought it would. You know, everybody thinks of Rick as getting around the system, cutting corners, pulling fast ones. But that's not really what he does. It's just that he's willing to put lots of effort into making the system work. That's all we did. And it worked."

Panoff was not quite so sanguine. "Yeah, that's all very true. But the Old Man is still a twice-rejected captain about to be forced into retirement. The Senate has never, I mean *never*, turned back a Navy selection list since they got the ball in 1916. This Selection Board got letters from senators and congressmen, and even a pretty direct pitch from the secretary of the Navy. Top industrialists wrote letters—you've seen some of them. And the Selection Board rode right over that. They meet in secret, they keep no records, and they don't have to explain their actions or their reasoning to anyone. No one has ever beaten that system before, not even on behalf of some popular war heroes. Do you really think they'll do it for a lousy little engineering duty officer?"

Congress Forces a Deal

After hearing the testimony from Admiral Wallin, chief of the Bureau of Ships, the Armed Services Committee halted the hearings for a few days and let the press build up some pressure. Clay Blair, Jr., Time-Life's aggressive reporter, and John Giles, of the *Washington Star*, added fuel to the fire Amrine had started, and other reporters joined in the fray. The previous December Wallin had published "the complete, authoritative story" on the *Nautilus* in a ghost-written cover story for *Collier's* magazine. The article identified Wallin as "head of the bureau in charge of building the history-making sub" and described the backup work being done by the bureau and the AEC. But Rickover's name was not even mentioned in the article, and this added to the rising public resentment. Senator Richard Russell, who had not been briefed by us, was nevertheless disturbed to the point of telling a reporter that this seemed to be the worst injustice since the World War I flying general, Billy Mitchell, was court-martialed for being too outspoken an advocate for military aviation. Senator John Sherman Cooper was also quoted as saying that it appeared to be a grave injustice. Senator Jackson told reporters that he planned to ask Senator Saltonstall to investigate the matter formally. Congressmen Chet Holifield and Melvin Price also pushed from behind the scenes, providing the articulate support that was so important to Rickover throughout their long stay on the Joint Committee on Atomic Energy. Other key members of Congress quietly warned President Eisenhower's political advisers that the situation was getting out of hand, and the White House conveyed to the Navy its strong desire to settle the matter quickly.

Amrine had kicked up a fuss with his story in the professional magazine *Editor and Publisher*, relating how the Navy had tried to censor his articles. The *Washington Post* devoted some twenty-four column-inches of news space and an editorial to *Time*'s complaint that its story had been held up sixty-seven days and that the magazine had been pressured to change the "slant" of the story. *Time* got hold of an internal Navy memo, prepared to rebut the story, which admitted, "This Time-Life article as a whole cannot be said to be false, since perhaps 90 percent of the raw factual data appear to be accurate." The memo suggested, "To combat the effects of the article . . . a story [should be] placed in a magazine friendly to the Navy and highly competitive to *Time*, to appear before the *Time* article does . . . This would have to be handled with extreme delicacy, preferably by the Chief of Information personally."

The Navy had been particularly upset that the *Time* story claimed that Rickover's demise would have serious impact on the morale of his people. The AEC had marked this part "Delete—not true." But the accompanying AEC memo conceded, "However, if Rickover is forced to resign from the Navy on retirement schedules, these things probably will happen: (a) morale of the AEC Naval Reactors Branch will be affected; (b) some of Rickover's staff will leave; and (c) there will be a time lag that usually occurs when there is a change in a key post."

The *Post* editorial concluded, "In short, this appears to have been an attempt to censor an article not so much because of wrong facts as because of opinions and interpretations which officials found distasteful. This is very perilous ground, indeed. It is the sort of approach, if condoned, that could be used to muzzle all sorts of legitimate criticism; as such it ought to have the prompt attention of the President."

But it wasn't until Congressman Yates introduced a bill proposing to restructure the Navy's selection process by adding civilians to the Selection Boards that the Navy knew it had a bear by the tail. Saltonstall's committee upped the ante by announcing that it was holding up action on all thirty-nine admiral nominees pending an investigation of the Navy's entire promotion system. The Navy knew that Congress was reluctant to order that a given individual be promoted, but it was less sure of Congress's reluctance to revamp the entire selection process. And the Navy wanted to keep the lid on that can of worms, at all costs.

The Navy had offered to call Rickover back to the same billet, as a passed-over captain, for an undefined period, but Rickover had refused, saying that he would have no real authority under such circumstances. There was some talk of a presidential appointment to flag rank, but no one seemed to know whether or how such an appointment could be made and what precedent *that* would set. The only alternative was the one finally outlined by Navy Secretary Robert B. Anderson, in a letter dated 6 March 1953 to Committee Chairman Saltonstall:

> I propose, therefore, to take the following action:
>
> (a) Convene at once a Selection Board to recommend Engineering Duty Captains for retention on active duty for a period of one year with a requirement in the precept that one of those recommended for retention be experienced and qualified in the field of atomic-propulsive machinery for ships. Should Captain Rickover be recommended for retention under this precept, he will not be retired on June 30, 1953, and will be eligible for consideration for promotion to the grade of Rear Admiral by the Selection Board which will be convened in July 1953.
>
> (b) Include in the precept of the Selection Board which will be convened in July 1953, a requirement that one Engineering Duty Captain experienced and qualified in the field of atomic-propulsive machinery for ships be selected for promotion to the grade of Rear Admiral.
>
> The action proposed above is authorized by existing law. It will serve to give Captain Rickover another opportunity to achieve the grade of Rear Admiral under precepts as favorable to him as the law permits.

As Rickover said to me the next day, "Congress is unwilling to tell the Navy who, by name, should be admirals, but they have told the Navy they will not approve the thirty-nine proposed names until my status is settled satisfactorily. The secretary of the Navy has now proposed a deal. He didn't actually say they had to promote a 125-pound Jew, but he came as close as he could. This will give me all the advantage the law allows. They may still screw me, but we'll have to take it and hope for the best. I know you guys have stuck with me through all this, and I appreciate it. I also heard that a number of top industrial officials wrote strong letters to the Navy supporting me. I don't know how much arm-twisting it took to bring that off, but I hear it helped. Now let's get to work. We've lost a lot of time with all this nonsense." And he did not talk about the subject again for several years.

Incredibly, despite the direct instructions from above, the Navy still fumbled with the problem. The March 1953 Selection Board retained several captains in addition to Rickover, apparently just to maintain the charade of routine naval procedure, regardless of the fact that the board would never have even existed under naval routine. The following July, when another board met to select engineering duty admirals under the precept described in Secretary Anderson's letter, the engineering duty officers on the board refused to select Rickover. The line officers on the board, not wanting the whole selection system to come under outside scrutiny, broke tradition and cast the votes to make Rickover an admiral. Admiral Wallin, with a year and a half to go as chief of BuShips, was transferred to the naval shipyard at Bremerton, Washington. The issue was finally settled. Or so it seemed.

THE LARGE SHIP REACTOR PROJECT AND CIVILIAN ATOMIC POWER

> As machines relieve us of the brutal, tiring, and time-consuming labor that had been the lot of the majority of men from time immemorial; as they enable us to universalize affluence and leisure, we face a choice: we may take these benefits and live the life of the idle rich of old, pursuing a good time and not bothering about the quality of our own life or the life of the nation. Or, we may decide to emulate those—and there were many—who in the past considered wealth and leisure a trust, to be utilized for self-improvement and for improvement of their particular societies. The choice is for each individual to make. Moreover, each individual, under our form of government, has a right to speak out publicly in favor of making better use of science and technology than is possible under present conditions.
>
> If those who agree with this new viewpoint become a majority; in other words, if a consensus is reached through public discussion of this issue, the American people may decide to take action. The action may displease powerful vested interests, but this is how we govern ourselves. The status quo has no absolute sanctity under our form of government. It must constantly justify itself to the people in whom is vested ultimate sovereignty over this nation.
>
> H.G.R.

Ironically, the Mark I extended full-power run had brought the dream of a nuclear-powered aircraft carrier closer to a technical reality just when the carrier was being killed for budgetary and political reasons. President Eisenhower delivered the final blow by announcing that it was more important at this point in history for the nation to turn its attention to peaceful uses of the atom. To that end, Rickover was ready to reassign personnel from the proposed aircraft carrier plant and develop a plant for civilian electric power production. And with a great deal of help from AEC Commissioner Murray, that is what finally happened.

There were several forces lined up against giving the civilian project to Rickover. There were those who were disturbed at further encroachment by the military into the civilian scene. And there were those who felt that pressurized-water reactors represented only one small slice of the wide spectrum of possible reactor designs: there were liquid metals, gases, organic fluids, and other untried coolants; there were heavy water, natural water, beryllium, graphite, and other neutron moderators; there were highly enriched, slightly enriched, and natural uranium fuels, in the form of alloys, oxides, carbides, or even hydrides. All these exotic materials, in various combinations, offered an endless path of alluring research. How could anyone decide now, they argued, without trying at least a few of the other approaches to reactor design?

In response to this situation Rickover published, in a technical journal of the field, his classic definition of the differences between new reactor concepts ("paper reactors") and real reactor plants. He noted that a paper reactor generally has the following characteristics:

It is simple.
It is small.
It is cheap.
It is lightweight.
It can be built very quickly.
Very little development is required: it will use off-the-shelf components.
It is in the study phase; it is not being built now.

By contrast, a real reactor has the following characteristics:

It is complicated.
It is large.
It is heavy.
It is being built now.

It is behind schedule.

It requires an immense amount of development on apparently trivial items.

It takes a long time to build because of its engineering development problems.

There were also industrial interests who felt that this was the opportunity to break away from the "dead hand of government" and take off on their own. (Rickover, the terror of bureaucracy, enjoyed the irony of finding himself so labeled.) They were convinced that they didn't need a government bureaucrat like Rickover to tell them how to build a power plant; they knew that business a lot better than he did. Opposed to these interests were those in the government, particularly in the Interior Department and the Tennessee Valley Authority, who wanted to see the government build the first civilian power plant, as a bulwark against a private monopoly developing. There was yet another faction in the AEC, which was determined not to be pushed around by the Joint Congressional Committee on Atomic Energy. It was this last factor that tipped the final balance when the committee sent an urgent message to a high-level AEC meeting, stating that it was adding money to the commission's budget for a power reactor "initiated by Congress," noting that the committee would maintain a "more than usual interest" in how the program was carried out, and warning against "too heavy emphasis on the Navy aspects." Commissioner Murray, who backed Rickover in this matter, challenged the commission to decide whether the AEC or the Joint Committee was going to run the nation's atomic energy program.

And as if that weren't enough, there were many naval officials who were not anxious to see Rickover's power grow, and there were others in the Navy who sided with those in the AEC and industry who felt that Rickover's stick-in-the-mud technology was holding back truly revolutionary advances in weight and size reduction and in thermodynamic efficiency. So all through this period, starting with the chief of naval operations' proposal in December 1950 to build a Large Ship Reactor prototype, the program to develop a reactor plant for use on a large surface ship had been on-again-off-again, sometimes competing with, sometimes supported by, the interest in building the first commercial nuclear power station for the generation of electricity.

Finally, in July 1953, as the Korean War was ending, the AEC assigned the civilian power project to Rickover and his team. And a year later, after the Russians detonated their first hydrogen bomb, President Eisenhower approved the order of the Joint Chiefs of Staff to reinstate the Large Ship Reactor program. So Rickover emerged from that turbulent period the predominant world figure in nuclear power. The *Nautilus* had been launched by Mamie Eisenhower, and the keel had been laid for the submarine *Seawolf,* which would be powered by the GE sodium-cooled reactor. The AEC had approved the Submarine Fleet Reactor (SFR) program, to develop simpler and smaller (but slower) follow-on reactor plants for the forthcoming nuclear submarine fleet. And the AEC had just approved the Submarine Advanced Reactor (SAR) project, under which GE would develop and build the most advanced nuclear power plant feasible.

The aircraft carrier prototype project was under way, and the world's first commercial atomic power station was under development at Shippingport, Pennsylvania. Russia and England had large reactors to produce plutonium for atomic ordnance, some of which produced some by-product electricity. But nowhere in the world had anyone tried to build a practical nuclear facility for producing electricity on a reliable commercial basis. That task was now Rickover's.

Learning to Think Civilian

In July 1953 Captain Rickover called a meeting of his senior people and said, "I have an important announcement to make. It's not yet public, so keep your yaps shut. As we have all been hoping, we are about to be asked to build the world's first civilian nuclear power station, to deliver electricity to the nation's electric system. You know that the project to develop a plant for an aircraft carrier has been canceled, and we don't know when, or even if, it will be reactivated. Now listen carefully; it's important that you understand this next point. A lot of companies and scientists are mad that we are getting this project. Not because in their objective judgment we're going to screw it up. No, they're mad because *they* wanted it. So they will try to show that we're looking at the job as a scam to keep the aircraft carrier project alive. People have already made that squawk. They keep pointing out that the civilian power plant is supposed to be about the same power capacity as the canceled shipboard plant. It is therefore essential that we give them no basis for such a complaint. I mean this, now. I'm not talking

THE AEC AS ADVERSARY

Rickover alumni tend to remember the Atomic Energy Commission as an ally in their battles to build nuclear-powered naval vessels. But when it came to commercial atomic power, we often found ourselves attacked by other AEC groups who resented our taking over what they considered to be their private turf.

After Chairman Lewis Strauss and Commissioner Thomas Murray left the AEC, the new chairman, John A. McCone, set up a committee to recommend a course for nuclear power development. It was an open secret that McCone and others hoped and expected this committee to recommend shutting down Shippingport, despite its successful operating record. Rickover managed to get Mandil and Radkowsky put on the committee and, after six to eight weeks of intense debate, they persuaded the committee to recommend that Shippingport continue operation, much to everyone's surprise.

On another occasion, Congress urged the AEC to set up a parallel alternative program to complement Shippingport, built around a gas-cooled reactor rather than a water-cooled one. Congress expected that this project would be assigned to Rickover, but instead the AEC gave it to the Oak Ridge Laboratory. This program never actually led to a commercial reactor, or even to a demonstration facility. But it was kept out of Rickover's hands.

for the record; I'm telling you guys how I want this project run. If we never get to build an aircraft carrier reactor, so be it. But by God, this will be the best damn civilian power station humanly possible. Do any of you have any questions on that point?"

Roddis asked innocently, "Is the carrier job really dead, Captain?"

Rickover exploded furiously. "Goddammit! We're not talking about the carrier project. Didn't you hear anything I said? I don't want to hear anything about that project again. From any of you. Do you get that? If we do ever get such a project—and I'm not even looking for it, understand—I'll assign it to an entirely different team. So forget that project until and unless you hear differently from me and from no one else. Have I made that clear? Does anyone want me to repeat it? Dammit, you guys are hard to get through to, sometimes."

There was complete silence for a few moments. Then Rickover began again. "Now let's talk about the civilian power project. We'll call it the Pressurized-Water Reactor, or PWR for short, to distinguish it from all those crazy thermodynamic cycles that everyone else wants to build. The only thing Navy about it is that we're going to keep it as simple as possible. Utility operators love automation and gadgets. You know how hard I fought to keep that junk off the submarines. Operators love to sit in a central air-conditioned control room and flip little electric switches. I want a guy who starts a pump to go to where that pump is and turn it on from there. If it leaks, or smokes, or vibrates, or grinds its bearings, he'll be right there to hear it and do something.

"You know, I saw one of those plants where they pumped some waste water into a tank for treatment. The whole thing was done automatically. An inlet valve opens, stays open a predetermined number of seconds, the pump starts up, the valve closes, all that crap automatically. The operators sit there doing nothing. In fact, they're usually reading comic books. The control panel has no mimic board to show where each valve and pump is in the process. It just has switches. They don't do much training, because the union wants to rotate the operators around from one place to the next, and they don't stay on any one job long enough to learn it. The union claims this is good for their careers. The instruction manuals are lousy, and there are almost no operating procedures. Management thinks operators are stupid and unmotivated, and so it selects and trains them on that basis. And what do they get? Stupid and unmotivated operators."

I commented, "It looks as if we have our work cut out for us, Captain."

"You're damn right we do. Does that bother anybody?" There were denials all around, and Rickover continued. "I want to get an electric utility company to operate the plant, and we'll make them pay for the honor by picking up a big share of the cost. And we'll insist that they put their best people on it, and we'll select, train, and crew-quiz 'em. I want to use this opportunity to introduce quality into American industry. I want to set new standards for metallurgy, quality control, welding. I want to work with the technical societies, the ASME, ASCE, ASM, and revise their codes and standards . . ."

He continued on in this vein for some time, as we gradually came to realize the magnitude of the task we had undertaken. Not only were we going to have to educate several new shipyards on how to build nuclear ships, and to train the hundreds, perhaps even thousands, of officers and enlisted personnel who would operate them; we were also going to have to revamp much of the civilian electric utility industry and its suppliers. This could not be done from the outside. It would require us to create, by education and training, the knowledgeable and demanding customers in the commercial world who would provide the only hope of getting quality equipment. I suddenly felt a little panicky, and very tired.

Rickover's Power Base in Congress

It is widely acknowledged that Rickover's ability to survive and triumph owed much to his relationship with Congress. Such a statement usually conjures up a picture of sleazy lobbyists slipping money under the table in a smoke-filled room. But that was obviously not Rickover's game.

EXTENDING THE EFFECT: THE ELECTRIC UTILITY INDUSTRY

It is hard to picture how the civilian nuclear power industry would have started up without the Naval Reactors precedent. The scientific discoveries and technological developments, the suppliers and support industries, the design concepts of the plants themselves—all were directly spun out of the Rickover program. Nearly all the world's nuclear power plants are direct technological descendants of that program.

But an even greater factor was the vast educational and training system Rickover had set up. Once the glamour of long months at sea, or long hours at the laboratory or shipyard, had worn off, Rickover's operators and designers were easy prey for the industrial recruiters who eagerly snatched them up.

Today these people still enliven the industry, and to varying degrees they carry the Rickover Effect to the corners of the world.

He expressed his views and his needs openly and officially to assembled committees. It has been estimated that over the years, Rickover presented over a million words of testimony before various congressional committees.

He had read deeply in history and constitutional law, and he was firmly convinced of two things: First, Congress was the ultimate seat of power in America, and properly so. Second, there were certain clear barriers separating the three branches, and these must be respected. So although he and his people worked many long hours with congressmen and their staffs and shared a great deal of information, Rickover repeatedly made clear to all his people that they were never to thwart or subvert any of the constitutional or statutory restrictions. "If I ever catch any of you characters slipping an Executive Department memo or report to Congress, I'll nail him to the wall," he would say. Other people who were publicly more circumspect than Rickover often assumed that he was casual about cutting corners in private. They never understood how wrong they were in that regard.

I was trying to explain all this to one of the newer officers one day. "Military people generally assume that Congress is an enemy, or at best an untrustworthy friend, and not a very bright friend at that. So they go before Congress and give them a cock-and-bull story, a P.R. pitch. Rick works just the opposite. He treats them as valued senior advisers and members of his team. He tells them he has lots of troubles and he needs their help. They know he's leveling with them, and he's made them believe in his program—he's made them partners in it—and so they knock themselves out to help him when he asks for it. If you haven't been around this town, you can't appreciate what a novel approach that is. To the congressmen, it's a breath of fresh air."

Congressional hearings tend to be long and dull, for the most part. So it is difficult to get the flavor of one by reading through the voluminous record. But my recollection of a typical hearing, leaving out the dull parts, goes something like this:

CHAIRMAN: Thank you for your testimony on the state of your very important program. You have made remarkable progress since you last reported to us. I am sure I speak for all members when I commend you for the completeness, honesty, and clarity of your presentation.

RICKOVER: The law requires me to keep this body fully and currently informed, Senator. I take that obligation seriously and I do my best to fulfill it.

FIRST SENATOR: I can tell you are being completely honest with us, Admiral.

RICKOVER: How can you tell that, Senator?

SENATOR: By your eyes, Admiral. I always look at a man's eyes when he testifies. Some of the people who come up here are pretty shifty-eyed.

RICKOVER: Hell, you can't see my eyes from there, Senator. You'd better sit up closer if you're going to do that. You're pretty far away to be making such an important judgment.

SECOND SENATOR: I didn't understand your statement about turning back money to the Treasury. I must have misunderstood you. Would you go over that again, please?

RICKOVER: You understood me perfectly, sir. I said that we found we could carry out our program this year for about a million dollars less than we budgeted for. Your committee was kind enough to give us all we asked for, and so we have a million dollars left over. The only honorable thing to do with that money is to turn it over to the Treasury, and that I have done.

CHAIRMAN: That is unprecedented. I literally have never heard of such a thing in all my years in government. Is there a procedure or a form for doing this?

RICKOVER: No, sir. In fact, the Treasury doesn't know quite what to do with the money. But I'm sure they will find a use for it someday, and I don't want to take any more of the people's money than I absolutely need.

CHAIRMAN: Well, I certainly commend you for such an unusual and conscientious action.

RICKOVER: Senator, I have always been honest and open with the Congress. It sounds corny to say it, but this Chamber houses the voice of the people, and I cannot lie here. You realize this is totally contrary to Navy practice. They tell you everything is fine, and you should just trust them and not ask too many questions. So you give them the money they ask for, and in a few months they're back, asking for more. It seems they had problems they didn't tell you about, and now they need money to solve those problems. I consider you people a trusted ally, not an adversary.

CHAIRMAN: We recognize that and appreciate it, Admiral.

RICKOVER: Before I came up here, my boss in the Navy, the chief of the Bureau of Ships, called me in and asked me what I was going to say. I said I would be glad to go over it with him, but he should realize that I might be asked whether I had been instructed or limited in any way by the Navy in what I could say. I told him that of course I would have to be honest and tell them that I had been required to review my testimony with my naval superiors before I could present it. I asked him if he wanted me to do that. For some reason, he said, "No, just go ahead and tell them whatever you want." [*Laughter*]

SENATOR: What do you think of this general who is running the nuclear airplane project? Is he doing a good job?

RICKOVER: Let me ask you, sir: What do you think of the senior senator from your state?

SENATOR: [*Laughing*] All right, I won't pursue that one. But would you tell us what you consider the chances are of having a successful nuclear airplane in the foreseeable future?

RICKOVER: Dim. [*More laughter*]

SENATOR: What can you tell us about the explosion of the experimental Army reactor at the Reactor Testing Grounds in Idaho? Are there some lessons we can learn from this?

RICKOVER: My information on that subject is like yours, sir: secondhand. I'm sure you will uncover the technical facts of the matter through your investigation, which I understand has been under way for some time. But the lesson, I suggest, is this: You have yet to bring forth an individual in that program who will say to you, "I am responsible." They rotate people and delegate responsibility in the usual military way. You do not have that problem with my program. I have many people carrying out tasks in the program, and I hold them accountable to me for those tasks. But if anything important goes wrong in my program, is there any doubt in your minds who is responsible? I will tell you right now, in case there is any uncertainty about it: I am responsible. And I will never try to tell you otherwise. You may call me up before you, and I will answer for whatever happens.

CHAIRMAN: We understand that, Admiral, and we value it.

RICKOVER: Don't be fooled. I heard an Army general testifying the other day to the Atomic Energy Commission about the proposed nuclear-powered battle tank. The commissioners were concerned about safety, and they asked this general some questions about it. He looked them in the eye and said with great earnestness, "Gentlemen, I take full responsibility for this project." But that general won't be around when and if that project ever comes to fruition. He'll be rotated or retired. I won't. That's the difference.

SENATOR: Admiral, I don't understand how you, as an officer designated "engineering duty only," can select and reject captains and crew members for the Navy's operating ships. I understand that engineering duty officers are not even permitted to command a ship of any size.

CHAIRMAN: If the senator will permit an interruption for a personal anecdote, I was once on a nuclear-powered cruiser when Admiral Rickover was demonstrating the propulsion plant for a congressional committee, and I overheard an old chief petty officer explaining to a new recruit the meaning of the various signal flags that were being flown. "This one is for the Admiral," said the chief, referring to the fact that the task force commander was aboard. "You mean Admiral Rickover?" asked the lad. "No, he's an engineering admiral," said the chief. "He couldn't take command of the vessel." To which the lad replied with great sincerity, "If he wanted to take over this ship, I don't know anybody who could stop him."

RICKOVER: [*To Senator*] The question you asked is an important one. I'm glad you asked it, because many people are confused about it. I do not carry out that function as a naval officer. Recall that the Atomic Energy Act assigns responsibility and authority for public safety to the Atomic Energy Commission. I am assigned by the secretary of the Navy, for my primary duty, to the director of reactor development, United States Atomic Energy Commission. I have additional duty, for my convenience, in the Navy's Bureau of Ships, because the Bureau of Ships is responsible for building and operating Navy ships, and the Atomic Energy Commission has no authority in that matter. There is also a Reactor Safeguards Committee, which Congress and the public look to as an outside body of expert opinion to independently evaluate and advise on all matters of public safety involving atomic energy. This Safeguards Committee has repeatedly insisted in writing that I continue to carry out this function for the commission, because they trust me to do it responsibly and competently. So you see, it is not a Navy function I perform.

CHAIRMAN: Thank you, Admiral. As usual, your testimony has been most helpful and enlightening. We look forward to having you come here, and we urge you to call on us whenever you think we can help. This meeting now stands adjourned.

I was always quick to point out that honesty and a quick wit were not sufficient to gain support on the Hill. Still, I admit that we tried to take advantage of what we knew—you couldn't afford to be stupid. For example, we knew that Senator Clinton Anderson, chairman of the powerful Joint Committee on Atomic Energy, was taking medication that made him somewhat laid-back in the afternoon, after he had taken it, and irritable and aggressive in the morning. If we wanted him to get mad about something, we'd bring it up in the morning. If we had bad news and were worried about his reaction, we'd bring it up in the afternoon.

But if you wanted their support, you had to have some results. Rickover used to say, "You gotta show 'em samples." And at every opportunity he would take over models, pieces of exotic metals such as zirconium and hafnium, photographs of test rigs, mock-ups of fuel elements—hard evidence that there was solid accomplishment behind the talk. He took the committee members to see his facilities, and later they rode the ships: the first submarine *Nautilus* in 1955, the first high-speed attack submarine *Skipjack* in 1959, the first Polaris missile submarine *George Washington* in 1960, and the first nuclear aircraft carrier *Enterprise* in 1962. They never doubted that they were dealing with a person who was actually creating important, working hardware in the real world.

Technical Intuition

One of Rickover's greatest assets, as leader of a technically sophisticated project, was incredible technical intuition. When he insisted on going against the advice of his technical advisers, they often tried to explain to him afterward why they opposed him, how logic and the technical facts seemed to be against him. Although Rickover was a strong proponent of logic and data, he also recognized that sometimes intuition urged otherwise. He was not embarrassed or apologetic over the dichotomy, nor did he try to justify it. He would just shrug his shoulders and ask ingenuously, "Why am I always right for the wrong reasons?"

I remember a typical instance in the early days of the GE reactor. I was at the Knolls site, trying unsuccessfully to convince the people there that there was a heat-transfer problem. I had discussed it with Rickover but felt that he hadn't understood my analysis. What I didn't realize was that Rickover understood the essence of my argument and agreed with it. I found this out when he was suddenly on the phone to GE, his high-pitched scream coming in over the conference phone speaker.

"Dammit, I want you to look into the heat transfer through that head assembly. Don't you understand? It's a real problem area. If that sodium doesn't freeze, we won't have a seal and we'll have a mess on our hands. Mandil and Rockwell have talked to your people about it, and they just brushed them off."

The GE official was sure of his ground. "Rick, I've been assured that our calculations . . ."

"Goddammit! I don't care about your lousy calculations. I'm telling you there's a problem there. Don't argue with me. Look into it."

"We also have a lot of test data that support the design."

"Dammit, the stainless steel is going to conduct the heat through there like a damn express train. Look, I'm not going to keep arguing with you. If you're not willing to give this problem the attention it deserves, I'll go to your president. You know I'll do it."

"Yes, you've done it before. I'll get right on it, Rick." But the phone was already dead.

One of the GE engineers was furious. "Why do you let him bluff you? If he goes to the president of the company, he'll make a fool of himself. He didn't know what he was talking about."

Another chimed in. "Yeah. He said the *stainless steel* would conduct all the heat. The fact is that the stainless carries only a percent or two of the heat. It's the sodium that's the conductor. He's just plain 3-D wrong about that."

The first engineer was back, saying to me, "Ted, you and I discussed this thing this morning. I thought I'd convinced you it's a nonproblem. I say we forget it. Let the Old Boy rave."

But his boss had the last word. "You guys have a few things to learn. First, Rickover is the customer. We don't ignore our customers. But more important, I've been around him long enough to know that when he points off somewhere and says there's a problem there, you'd better check. If you ask him to justify his concern, he may give you a rationale based on wrong facts and faulty logic. But his engineering intuition is eerie. He usually turns out to be right, regardless of the reasons. So get on this one, and take it seriously. I want a report by the end of the month."

As it worked out, the GE managers let their engineers convince them that there was no problem, and in fact they used the incident as an example of undue interference with the company's technical judgment, in a memo addressed jointly to Rickover and the GE top brass. Rickover's intuition wasn't vindicated until a large-scale electrically heated mock-up showed that the heat transfer via sodium convection in the cracks was twenty times what the engineers had calculated. It was possible to correct the problem at that time, but it would have been a lot easier if it had been done when Rickover first raised the question.

Another example of Rickover intuition involved air conditioning. Strictly speaking, the amount of air conditioning on the ship was outside Rickover's jurisdiction. He was to supply the power plant; all other aspects of the ship were the responsibility of other parts of the Bureau of Ships. It was also clear that cooling the prototype plant did not require much air conditioning in the cool, dry Idaho desert air. But Rickover knew that in 1917 the British had built some submarines with steam-powered propulsion systems, and he also knew that they proved inoperable because the heat and steam leakage made living conditions on board intolerable. So he was liberal beyond reason in specifying the amount of air conditioning to be provided. Electric Boat had calculated that sixty tons would do the job, and that is what the company recommended. Panoff and Dunford decided to add a 100 percent safety factor, and the BuShips air-conditioning people agreed to go along. Rickover later decided that whatever had been agreed to should be doubled, so at the last minute he ordered that the air conditioning be doubled again, to 240 tons. This caused quite a stir at the time, because it was not easy to add equipment so heavy and bulky to a submarine so late in the design process. Today you don't hear about the *Nautilus* air conditioning; who would be interested in such a mundane thing? But we now know that the ship would probably have been inoperable without the extra air conditioning ordered without adequate justification by Rickover and his annoying intuition.

"Everything Has to Be Built Special"

Back in 1952, when Mandil brought up the problems with sticky bearings and seizing valves, the solution led into unexpected territory. The meeting had been interrupted by one of those telephone calls in which Rickover blasted some poor soul mercilessly. The group sat uncomfortably through the grilling, but after Rickover slammed down the phone he said calmly, "I'm not interested in fixing blame in this situation. At least not yet. This is a technical matter, and I want to discuss it technically. Forget about schedule, cost, everything else. Let's evaluate the technical situation. Mandil, how serious do you consider this problem? Are we talking about a quick fix in the next few weeks, or is it something fundamental?"

"Captain, it's pretty fundamental. I think the problem is our lack of basic understanding of the mechanisms of friction and lubrication in water at this temperature. No one has ever tried to operate machinery in that sort of environment. It may not work."

"There's nothing in the Old or New Testament that says it's gotta work. I have to face that possibility."

Roddis gave the subject a different twist. "I've never been excited about the idea of a sodium-cooled reactor system—I mean, who likes a material that burns in air and explodes in water?—but we may be glad we have a sodium-cooled reactor system as a backup project if we can't fix this thing."

Rickover's response was typical. "Yeah, and if the oceans were made of sodium, some damn-fool scientist would be pushing a water-cooled reactor for submarines. Let's get back to the problem."

Mandil wanted to be sure everybody understood the gravity of the situation. "Our laboratories are working on the fundamental problems, but the valve companies and the pump and bearing people consider our project a pretty minor part of their business. They just won't put the people and resources on it. It's a major problem to us, but it's peanuts to them."

Imperceptibly, Rickover slipped into his statesman role. "We were supposed to develop the nuclear reactor and all the stuff that's never been done before. You'd think that was challenge enough. American industry, in its infinite wisdom and ingenuity, was supposed to supply

EXTENDING THE EFFECT:
LARGE EQUIPMENT MANUFACTURERS

Rickover's efforts to upgrade the quality of small components—valves, switchgear, control equipment, and the like—had been difficult, but reasonably successful. But when we started to ask for the largest pressure vessels of their kind ever made, requiring some of the largest castings and forgings, then we ran into a new problem. Only a few companies made such items, and these companies were quick to tell us that what we wanted, particularly in the area of quality control, "just couldn't be done." We were told that those in the industry knew what was possible and what was not, and that we had just better relax and accept it.

We got the same story everywhere. But one day, one of the NR engineers—I think it was Mandil—was in one of the manufacturer's plants when he noticed a roped-off area. "What's going on over there?" he asked. "Oh, that has nothing to do with your work." But Mandil persisted, and he found that the company had roped off a special area where vessels were made for a German company. It seems that the Germans weren't buying the argument that the company's normal quality control procedures couldn't be changed, and finally the company agreed to provide special procedures and controls for that work. Rickover had found the doorway, and he was quick to dart through it. "It may cost a little more to get something made right in the first place, but you can bet it will cost less in the long run," he said.

pumps, valves, bearings, and all the easy stuff. Well, it isn't working. And I'm not going to let that basic problem kill this program." He got up, walked back and forth a moment, then turned back to the group. "We'll have to set up our own programs to develop this hardware, through industry of course, but we'll direct it. I'll contact the presidents of the appropriate firms and get them to set up special divisions for this work. Dammit, I'll have to insist they put their best people on it, or they'll assign all their deadwood to it." He paused. "I'll make 'em pay for the facilities out of their own money. We'll have to set up a whole new contract structure for this. I want to see that they do the whole thing for an absolutely minimum profit margin. After all, we're handing them a plum."

Roddis couldn't picture it happening. "Will they do it, Captain?"

Rickover's answer was characteristically blunt. "If they ever want any other Navy business, they will. Now get out of here. I've got work to do."

This represented a fundamental change in the basic philosophy of the program, a tremendous increase in the scope of responsibility and the breadth of technical coverage. Perhaps it was inevitable, but I marveled that it had happened in the flicker of an eyelash. The consequences to American industry were marked: the concept of quality was about to be upgraded to the Rickover definition, long before Japanese competition forced such a revaluation across an even broader front.

REACTOR SAFETY

> As a guide to engineering ethics, I should like to commend to you a liberal adaptation of the injunction contained in the Oath of Hippocrates that the professional man do nothing that will harm his client. Since engineering is a profession which affects the material basis of everyone's life, there is almost always an unconsulted third party involved in any contract between the engineer and those who employ him— and that is the country, the people as a whole. These, too, are the engineer's clients, albeit involuntarily. Engineering ethics ought therefore to safeguard their interests most carefully. Knowing more than the public about the effects his work will have, the engineer ought to consider himself an "officer of the court" and keep the general interest always in mind.
>
> H.G.R.

Checking the Radiation Levels

As the Mark I prototype inched its way toward full power, spot checks had been made of the radiation levels, to ensure that there were no gross defects in the shielding design or installation. No obvious problems were found, but now that high-power operation of the plant had become routine, a complete and thorough survey of the entire shield design was in order. Maps of the whole shield surface had been drawn up, with locations specified more or less uniformly over the surface where radiation measurements would be made. I had insisted that the expected radiation level at each of these locations be calculated ahead of time, which led to bitter complaints from the laboratory. Not only was this a lot of work, but there were many places where the geometry of the actual shield was so complicated that no one was sure how to calculate it. But I was adamant. "If we don't decide now what we expect to find, we'll never agree as to whether any of the measurements are unexpected. Measurements that are not what we expect to find mean either that our theory is weak in certain particular regards, or that the installation is faulty at that point. I don't want any ambiguities on that score."

So we ended up with the data sheets in the form of maps of the shield surface, with *calculated* numbers shown at each location, and space to put in the *measured* numbers. This situation immediately proved its value during the test, when some gold foils were inadvertently switched with some indium foils. The marked difference in the activation levels was apparent as soon as the test numbers were entered on the data sheets, alongside the expected numbers. Questions were immediately raised and the mix-up discovered. If the numbers had been sent back to the laboratory to be analyzed days later, it would have been difficult to pinpoint the source of the error.

Rickover had arranged that the shield test be performed with the best people possible. I would coordinate, and John Taylor of Bettis and Ed Czapek of Electric Boat, along with some helpers from Ev Blizard and Charlie Clifford's shielding group from Oak Ridge, would place the instruments and tabulate the data. In addition, Rickover had persuaded GE to make Henry Stone available from the Knolls Atomic Power Laboratory to participate. Not only would his assistance be valuable to the *Nautilus* project, but he would gain priceless experience for the GE design. I was delighted to work with such a team; they were all extraordinarily bright, and they worked with the comfortable air of professionals who regard their colleagues highly.

The National Reactor Test Station is a four-hundred-thousand-acre fenced-off reservation, half the size of Rhode Island, in the Valley of the Lost Rivers on the Snake River plain near Arco, Idaho. During World War II it was a naval ordnance testing range, and the local people are used to staying clear of it. It is a place of stark and dramatic beauty.

The Mark I prototype building stands high on the desert flatland, with the spectacular peaks of the snow–clad Rocky Mountains rising abruptly behind it. We hear a lot about the deserts of the American Southwest, but most of us don't know much about our northern deserts. The names on a map of the region give the flavor of the place: Craters of the Moon, Lost River Sinks, Twin Buttes Extinct Crater and Cinder Cone, Blizzard Mountain, Great Rift. There is no Paradise Valley, Emerald Forest, Silver Springs, or Crystal Lake here.

My first trip to the site had been a shocker. It was one of those unseasonably warm days in Washington that sometimes come unexpectedly around Washington's birthday in February. With the weather almost warm enough for shirt-sleeves, government workers flock to the parks and lesser green spaces to eat their brown-bagged lunches in the sun. I was wearing my mesh-toed summer shoes, a short-sleeved shirt, and summer pants when I got a sudden call to get on the plane for Arco. I always kept a raincoat and a small bag with extra toiletries and a clean shirt at the office, so I grabbed these and headed off. At Salt Lake City I changed to the northbound puddle-jumper and was met at the Idaho Falls airport by Jack McGaraghan, Rickover's big, capable Civil Engineer Corps engineer at the site. McGaraghan reported that, with the temperature at 35 degrees below zero and a strong wind drifting snow across the roads, the Navy car might not be able to make the seventy-mile trip to the site. "The state police are warning that if we start out and have to turn back, we might not make it back, either. I've brought a snow shovel. I'm game to try it if you are," he announced.

Of course, we tackled it, and although we had to get out several times and shovel through the drifts, we did indeed make it. But the trip was a memorable one for me as an easterner. We saw an elk, several large groups of antelope, and miles of purplish gray desert covered intermittently with snow. Near town there were vast areas where crops had flourished under spray irrigation, from wells over a thousand feet deep, but then farther out there was nothing but scrub and tumbleweed. McGaraghan explained that farmers planted wheat on this land and waited for rain. Sometimes they planted thousands of acres, renting huge machinery for the task. Most years it didn't rain, and the farmers went heavily in debt. But every few years the rains came, and the farmers became rich. The local joke during those years was that the farmers would trade in their Cadillacs when the ashtrays filled up. And then there would be years without rain again.

As we approached the site, we saw a remarkable spectacle. Between many of the buildings ran insulated steam and hot-water piping, and sitting on the piping, clearly visible in the nearly full moon, were rows of jackrabbits, huddled together shoulder to shoulder on the warm piping. As the car pulled up to the administration building, I saw another local sight. At first I thought they were parking meters. But then I saw McGaraghan reach under the car radiator, pull out a cord with an electrical plug on the end, and plug it into the "parking meter." "Block heater," explained McGaraghan. "Without 'em your oil would be so thick at the end of the day, you'd never get the car started. They're pretty common out here."

My trip to Idaho for the shielding test was considerably more pleasant. It was summertime, and the hot sun and the cool, dry breeze were a delight. The availability of food was still severely limited: the cafeteria during certain hours, vending machines at other times. No commercial restaurants for seventy miles. But I always thrilled at the sight of the huge submarine hull, thrust through an even larger open water tank (referred to locally as McGaraghan Sea) like a mighty arrow through a giant apple. Even at those rare times when no construction work was going on, there was still a constant roar of ventilation fans, motor-generator sets, pumps, pneumatic air hiss—the constant sound of a properly operating plant that is so reassuring to an engineer. Later, on submarine test runs, I would wake up suddenly in the night whenever a pump or fan stopped or started running unexpectedly. A sudden, unanticipated change in the reassuring roar of normal activity signaled possible trouble.

The shielding test did produce some minor surprises. Normally, you expect the radiation level to drop off as you move away from the reactor, and generally it did. But at the center of one of the bulkheads, just the opposite occurred: the radiation level increased as you moved back from the reactor. I had some problem with this at first, but I noticed that the effect had been predicted and was shown in the calculated values on the data sheets. John Taylor showed me why. The main source of radiation at this bulkhead was two large components, located at either side. Up close, the radiation from these units had to travel obliquely through the shield, traversing a long path of shielding material. As one moved back from the shield, the radiation traveled more directly through the shield, becoming less attenuated than if it had traveled the long, slanting path. Of course, after moving back a few more feet, the normal drop-off with distance began. Since the measurements matched the calculated values quite well, and were well within the design requirement, there was no problem. Except for the area around the top of the reactor, where the geometry was complex and some further refinements were necessary, the shield, as built, proved to be conservative, and well within the design limits.

Getting Safety Approval

The crucial arbiter of reactor safety was the statutory Advisory Committee on Reactor Safeguards (ACRS), an independent group of prominent scientists and engineers, set up to be an additional watchdog on the Atomic Energy Commission. Although the committee was not mandated by amendment of the Atomic Energy Act until September 1957, it was recognized by one and all as the authority on reactor safety matters. Since it had no line responsibility to build anything, and drew no money or support from anyone in the atomic industry, the Safeguards Committee provided another layer of independent expert evaluation of safety matters, and it often raised general safety questions, in addition to those related to a particular reactor under review.

Rickover realized from the start that it was essential to convince the Safeguards Committee of the safety of naval reactors, and to seek its advice as to what would be needed to provide that assurance. I had known the chairman, Dr. C. Rogers McCullough, slightly, from his days at Oak Ridge, and Rickover sent me, first alone and then with the Bettis physics chief, Sidney Krasik, to discuss the matter in general terms with McCullough, well in advance of the needed date.

Krasik suggested that the review be broken into phases. "First, let's just look at going critical, getting physics data at essentially zero power. Since there would be virtually no fission product inventory during this period, it would be like running a low-power research reactor. You have a number of those already operating at universities and research laboratories in inhabited areas. You've agreed they pose no public hazard, and this would be a similar situation. Why don't we have the first review cover just this phase, with no approval asked for power operation?"

McCullough agreed that approval of such operation would probably not be difficult to get, but would it be meaningful? Weren't we just putting off the important decision, and what did we gain by that?

I suggested that each phase would be a learning experience for both parties. "We would be learning about your reasoning and requirements, and you would be learning about how the Navy builds and inspects things, how we train and drill people, and this would permit us to advance slowly from stage to stage, based on solid knowledge and understanding." This was explored and discussed for several hours, at the end of which McCullough agreed to think about it, and to discuss it with his colleagues on the Safeguards Committee. There was no attempt at pressure, no hardball tactics. No one was in a position to pressure the committee. Its members met in secret, deliberated among themselves, and published their findings. Since none of them depended on the committee for income or reputation, they could operate on a completely professional basis. But they were facing an unprecedented situation, and they were determined to proceed with proper caution and deliberation.

Meanwhile, the *Nautilus* was nearing completion in the shipyard, and her prospective commanding officer (PCO), Eugene P. Wilkinson, known for some reason as Dennis, was at the yard watching the ship take form. One day, as Rickover was talking with me for the *n*th time about safety clearance for the *Nautilus*, he had an idea. "Dixie, get me Wilkinson at the Boat Company," he called out. "Rockwell, we've had trouble getting the Safeguards Committee to really understand the kind of discipline we have on submarines, where everybody's life depends on everyone carrying out fire drills and collision drills and all that stuff with great speed and precision. All these reactor safety guys know about is laboratories full of scientists. I'm going to give 'em a submarine ride."

His phone buzzed and he picked it up. "Wilkinson?" He slammed down the phone and shouted, "Dixie, he wasn't on."

"They said he was right there, Admiral," she said.

"Well, let me know when he's actually on the phone." His phone buzzed again and he picked it up. "Wilkinson? Listen carefully now. You're familiar with the Advisory Committee on Reactor Safeguards? Congress looks to them to be an independent watchdog on the AEC. They are very important people. If they think we're not properly addressing reactor safety issues, they can shut us down. Got it so far? OK, now listen. I want these people, all thirteen of them, to see firsthand how a submarine operates. I want you to arrange for them to be taken out on a diesel submarine and witness fire drills, collision drills, all that stuff. I want them to come away overwhelmed by the discipline and skill of these crews. Of course, I want to go along, and I want three or four of my people too. And you . . . All right, take more than one boat. Yeah, three's OK. Can you handle that? . . . As soon as possible. Let me know when you have a date. Better make it two or three possible dates, and then I'll start negotiating with the committee members. Wait a minute. Rockwell wants to add something."

I picked up the other phone, while Rickover stayed on his. "Dennis? One point. You know there's some question in the minds of some of the Safeguards Committee members that the reactor control mechanisms might not operate properly if the ship were to keel over suddenly more than 45 degrees."

"Why the hell are you getting into that?" roared the Admiral. "He's not the guy . . ."

"Just a minute, Admiral. I know the ship can't get anywhere near that position. But I can just see Dr. McCullough, the chairman, asking some kid on the boat, 'Did you ever hear of a ship rolling more than 45 degrees?' And the kid's eyes will light up and he'll say, 'Yes, sir. I remember one time in the North Atlantic . . .' "

"Good point! You'd better get around and warn those bastards to lay off the sea stories. They can wreck the whole thing for us. Let me know as soon as you've set it up." And he slammed down the phone.

The trip went as planned. All thirteen members attended eagerly and seemed impressed with what they saw. There is no doubt that one can have a great deal more confidence in the emergency actions of a well-trained submarine crew than in any group of laboratory scientists, no matter how brilliant the scientists may be. The weather was superb, the crew went through the drills with professional precision, and as they were returning to the submarine base at New London for drinks and dinner, I was relieved. Standing on the bridge with the cool evening breeze blowing on my face, I heard a young officer ask, "What did you think of that, sir?"

"Very impressive, I must admit," replied Dr. McCullough. "It's clear that your men are highly trained and competent." But then he asked, "By the way, have you ever known a ship to roll over as much as 45 degrees?"

I smiled with satisfaction as I heard the anticipated question. Rickover was sure right that it paid to put extraordinary effort into anticipating every contingency, no matter how unlikely. But my blood froze as I saw the lieutenant's eyes light up and heard him reply, "Yes, sir. I remember one time in the North Atlantic . . ." Talk about anticipating the unlikely!

McCullough turned to Wilkinson before the sentence was complete and asked sternly, "Commander, you assured me this could never happen. But this man says he's seen it. What am I to make of that?"

Somehow Wilkinson pulled it off, as he answered with great assurance, "Aw, Doctor, you know you can't believe anything a submariner tells you," and they all broke into hearty laughter. It wasn't until I was deep into my drink at the sub base that I could finally settle down. But the question was to come up again.

Dealing with the Public

The launching of the *Nautilus* had gone beautifully. Mamie Eisenhower had charmed the reporters and smashed the traditional champagne bottle fairly across the ship's bow. The predictions Harry Truman had made at the keel laying, about the significance of this ship and the important events that would surely follow in her wake, were echoed and amplified at the launching. But there were still those in the Navy who could not bear to see Rickover vindicated. Drew Pearson reported as follows in his nationally syndicated column:

> President Eisenhower picked up a newspaper shortly before the launching of the atomic submarine *Nautilus* last week, and almost spilled his breakfast coffee. What he read was a news report that the *Nautilus* was not battle-worthy, was merely a test, and in effect was not an important naval vessel at all. The President was furious . . .
>
> The allegation that the *Nautilus* wasn't battle-worthy; that her torpedo tubes were added only as an after-thought; and that her delicate equipment would not work at high speeds, was prepared first by Comdr. Slade Cutter. Later it was put in a memorandum signed by Parks [Navy press chief].

Slade Cutter had also been fingered in the press as the officer who tried to hold up the stories on the Navy's efforts to retire Rickover at age fifty-three. These charges hit the submariners particularly hard, since Cutter had an outstanding war record and was remembered fondly as Intercollegiate Boxing Champion and the midshipman who beat Army by kicking a field goal to score the only points in a rain-drenched, muddy battle.

But Rickover could not dwell on such pettiness. The imminent start-up of the *Nautilus* reactor raised another question in his mind. What would be the reaction of the good people of New London when they learned that they had an operating nuclear power plant in their midst? Of course, the building of the *Nautilus* was anything but secret. Her presence and nuclear nature had been publicized on an international basis. But had he done everything to communicate with the local citizenry, to answer any questions or concerns they might have? He was thinking about this when I approached him one day to say, "I hear that somebody's trying to get a group together to draft a model state law for radiation protection. I don't know yet who's involved."

Rickover reacted to that immediately. "I want you to get on that committee. It's important that any model state law be a good one. Then we can use it as a basis for our own regulations. Work with the American Standards Association, or whoever is involved, but see that they do it right. And another thing, you ought to get together with Shugg, up at the Boat Company. One of these days the people in New London are going to realize they have a nuclear power plant operating in their front yard, and they may have a lot of questions about safety and radiation. At that time Shugg should already have laid the groundwork by talking with them about it. I don't want them to feel we sprang something on them."

I replied, "I've already done that, Admiral. I helped him with some talks he gave to Rotary clubs, Kiwanis and groups like that."

"How did it go?"

"Very ho-hum. There were few questions and almost no interest. The crowds were completely relaxed. The Boat Company is their livelihood, and they accept whatever goes on there. Shipbuilding communities have gone from wooden ships to steel ones, from riveted hulls to welded ones. Nuclear power is just one more step to them. Besides, everybody sees nuclear power as the wave of the future, and they're excited about it and ready for it. Nobody has any worries about it."

"Well, keep an eye on it," warned Rickover. "These things can change. Dixie, bring me the pinks."

The Safeguards Hearings

The Safeguards Committee agreed to the phased hearings, not because of pressure, but because there didn't seem to be any better way. The committee members were also convinced that Rickover would do almost anything to meet any reasonable demand they might impose. "I'm in this for the long haul," he kept telling them. "I've got no incentive to slide something through that won't stick. If you guys aren't completely comfortable, sooner or later I'll have to pay the price. And the sooner I smoke that out, the easier it'll be to fix it."

The first phase passed quickly. There was really no hazard inherent in the zero-power operation that the Safeguards Committee had not already approved for various research reactors. The committee recommended approval, and the AEC approved it.

The next phase involved power operation, but just enough to check out the power plant, and not enough to build up a significant inventory of fission products. Some committee members asked whether these tests could be run at sea, rather than alongside the pier, but Rickover and his people convinced them that to do this before the power plant and the crew had been checked out would create additional hazards and would not contribute positively to public safety. Again, there was no unprecedented reactor hazard, and approval was finally granted.

Throughout these hearings, one member seemed troubled by concerns not expressed, and Rickover decided to find out why. The member was Dr. Edward Teller, a brilliant and politically active theoretical physicist, known internationally as the father of the hydrogen bomb—a person whose concerns carried considerable weight. Rickover did not want Teller to feel pressured, so instead of approaching Teller himself, he arranged for me to visit him in San Francisco. After some preliminaries, Teller finally stated his concern. "I'm really not worried about the *Nautilus*. I have confidence in that type of reactor, when it is properly designed, built, and operated. And I think you people are doing that. But I don't have that kind of confidence in the sodium-cooled reactor that GE is building. It is an inherently different problem, no matter how well it's built. And I do not think it politically possible to approve a reactor built by Westinghouse and then turn around and disapprove one built by General Electric."

So the cat was out of the bag! I expressed, as strongly as I felt I could under the circumstances, my conviction that the GE reactor plant could be evaluated on its own merits, and I urged Teller to consider the *Nautilus* case solely on its merits. But I knew I couldn't lecture Teller on politics, so I thanked him for his willingness to discuss the matter openly, and I took my leave.

Rickover was glad to have the problem out in the open, and he talked with Teller about the importance of not clouding a scientific judgment with political considerations. "It's a matter of ethics, Edward. We've got to do what is ethically and scientifically valid, regardless of the politics."

He can get away with a speech like that, I thought. I was in the room and had heard his little sermon. *I sure could never pull it off. But he said we, not you. That's part of it. And he has established himself as one of the few major doers in the world who can lecture other people on ethics. Very few people can do that and be taken seriously.*

Finally, the day came for the critical safeguards meeting, the one to consider operation up to full power, in and out of New London. The last phase, to cover refueling after two or more years of operation, would raise some new technical issues, but it would surely be an anticlimax. This was the important one. Electric Boat had made its private dining room available and had planned an elegant lunch, with souvenir *Nautilus* tie clips and good wine. The agenda had been rehearsed and choreographed, and there were large colored charts and test specimens of zirconium and hafnium. The key people from Bettis and the Boat Company were there, ready to present their technical data and considered judgments. All that was needed was to start the proceedings.

Rickover opened the meeting by introducing the participants, and then he turned the meeting over to Dr. Krasik. Krasik cleared his throat, looked down at his notes—and was interrupted by a question from Dr. Teller: "The last time I was in New London was at the time of your famous hurricane. My train was held up three hours, because there was a small boat lying bottomside up across the railroad tracks. What if that had been the *Nautilus*?"

The agenda had been shot down in flames! The question of the ability of the control rods to operate under extreme angles had reappeared, in dramatic form. But by the time the Safeguards Committee had been satisfied on this one, the remaining questions were easy, and full approval for *Nautilus* operation was recommended and, shortly after, confirmed by the AEC.

The Faulty Piping Incident

Cold testing was nearly complete and hot testing was being carried out on the *Nautilus* steam plant, using steam from shore. The reactor had not yet been started up, but it was only 16 September 1954, and we hoped to start sea trials before year's end. If the test program continued to go as smoothly as it had to that point, there should be no problem

EXTENDING THE EFFECT:
RADIATION AND SAFETY STANDARDS

Rickover's program involved the world's first large-scale industrial operations involving radiation and radioactivity. The atomic bomb program had preceded it, but that was largely self-contained, subject only to military rule and interacting very little with the world at large. Rickover was determined that he would meet civilian standards and not hide behind military exemption. But in many cases, no civilian standards existed, and Rickover's people took the first steps to define radiation and safety standards for industry and to write model state laws.

Rickover's crew-quiz procedure became the model for examinations by the Nuclear Regulatory Commission (which didn't even exist when we started crew-quizzing). Our methods of presenting plant designs and procedures for outside safeguards review, and our manuals, checklists and other techniques, were adapted for commercial use by Rickover alumni, and these in turn became exemplars for the rest of the world.

meeting the initial sea trials deadline. But then it happened. Just before midnight a small steam line burst, filling the compartment with steam. The well-trained crew immediately shut the steam supply line and popped the safety valves on the dockside boiler. There were no serious injuries and, of course, no radioactivity released. It was a minor incident, not unusual in the shipbuilding business.

Piping in the engine room was supposedly a routine, nonnuclear matter. But Rickover was concerned about the implications of this accident. Why had it happened? What did it imply as to the other piping and the shipyard inspection system in general? Electric Boat and the Navy's local supervisor of shipbuilding launched a thorough two-week investigation, and the findings were not comforting. The pipe that had burst was not the seamless pipe it should have been, but was a rolled and welded pipe, normally used for stanchions, handrails, and the like, not for carrying high-pressure steam. There was no way, either by searching the records or by inspecting the installed piping itself, that one could be completely sure which type of piping had been used throughout the engine room. In addition, since Electric Boat had also installed the steam piping on the Mark I *Nautilus* prototype and the Mark A prototype for the GE plant as well, the same conclusions applied to those two plants. Only the small piping was in question, but there were thousands of feet of it already installed and insulated. Such a failure at sea could mean the loss of a ship.

Rickover did not take long to decide what to do. "Rip it all out and replace it. Every damn inch." He was told that this most likely would mean a massive delay in the sea date, but he just said, "Replace it as fast as you can, but it's got to be absolutely right, however long it takes. We're not going to sea with faulty piping."

Nor did he stop there. "We've got to find out how this sort of mistake was made, and how it got through the inspection system. I want to look back on this as a red-letter day, the day we straightened out the quality control system on piping."

"UNDER WAY ON NUCLEAR POWER"

> *Traditionally, the professional man follows certain tacit or explicit rules of conduct which vary in detail as between different professions. Basic to all of them, however, are two rules: first, the obligation to reject lay direction in the performance of professional work—that is, the duty to maintain professional independence; and second, the obligation to use professional knowledge and techniques solely for the benefit of their clients . . .*
>
> *Service ceases to be professional if it has in any way been dictated by the client or employer. The role of the professional man in society is to lend his special knowledge, his well-trained intellect, and his dispassionate habit of visualizing problems in terms of fundamental principles to whatever specific task is entrusted to him. Professional independence is not a special privilege but rather an inner necessity for the true professional man, and a safeguard for his employers and the general public. Without it, he negates everything that makes him a professional person and becomes at best a routine technician or hired hand, at worst a hack.*
>
> H.G.R.

As the year 1954 was winding down, Rickover worked toward meeting the January 1955 sea date for the *Nautilus*, promised so long ago at the end of 1949, when he had just emerged from his converted ladies' rest room office and was trying to put together staff and facilities to begin the Naval Reactors program. The *Nautilus* had been placed in service on 31 July, under control of her Navy crew, with Wilkinson as officer-in-charge (OIC). On 20 September 1954 the ship's reactor plant was transferred cost-free to the Navy, under a special Memorandum of Understanding drafted by Rickover and approved by the Navy, the Defense Department, and the AEC, and the ship was commissioned. After commissioning, Wilkinson shed his titles of PCO and OIC and became at last a full-fledged commanding officer.

The *Nautilus* Reaches "Initial Crit"

As New Year's Eve approached, everything that could be checked out without the nuclear reactor operating had been checked. It was now time to "go critical," to pull out the control rods slowly, recording the neutron level, until the critical point was reached, where the power level begins to rise of its own accord, without any further movement of the control rods. The power level would then be allowed to rise until it reached a point where the water temperature began to warm up, and then the decreasing density of the water would stop the power rise. Low-temperature, zero-power physics data would be taken, and then the reactor would be warmed up and high-temperature data would be taken. Then, if all looked satisfactory, the slow and steady rise to full power could begin.

I had been there for several days, watching the early tests, and I shared the general feeling that things were going well. But like everyone else, I couldn't avoid the tension that went along with anticipating the moment on which so much depended. There didn't seem to be any way anything could go wrong—so much preliminary testing and calculation had been done—yet until the reactor was actually producing power, you could never be sure.

On 30 December the process began. The Bettis physicist, Frank Jankowski, took the readings, recorded them in the log, and read them off to me. I plotted the numbers on a big sheet of red graph paper in a strange manner: the horizontal axis read "total inches of rod withdrawn" and the vertical axis read "$(cps)^{-1}$." The "inches of rod withdrawn" meant merely the amount the neutron-absorbing hafnium rods had been pulled up out of the core, as read from the rod position indicators. The neutron-counting meter Jankowski was reading from gave counts per second, abbreviated cps. To get $(cps)^{-1}$ I had to calculate the reciprocal— that is, I had to divide his reading into the number 1. Thus, if he read 100 counts per second, I would divide 100 into 1 to get $\frac{1}{100}$ for my value of $(cps)^{-1}$.

The reason for plotting the data in this unusual way was simple and practical. Reactor physics theory predicts that as control rods are pulled out of a reactor, data plotted in this manner will proceed in a straight line and cross the axis at the critical point. That is, as the neutron counter reads higher and higher values, the reciprocal of this number approaches zero. Thus, when the neutron level is still very low, the operator can extend the line he is plotting to see how many inches of rod withdrawal will bring criticality, the point where the neutron level gets very high. The operator thus always has a feeling for how near he is to criticality, an important thing to know.

Initial criticality started out smoothly that night. (*Why do crucial events always take place at night?* I wondered. *Was anybody ever born in the daytime?*) The first three points marched straight down the expected line, headed for an appropriate rod withdrawal number. The fourth point was exactly the same value as the third, departing from the straight line. But because the neutron readings were still so very low, this didn't seem unduly worrisome. When the fifth point dropped nicely back into line, everyone broke into smiles. But the *next fifteen points* were all the same: fifteen points, all showing the same neutron level, as the rods were withdrawn, bit by bit! At that rate the reactor would never go critical, would never start up, even after all the control rods were fully withdrawn!

The physicists kept assuring everyone nervously that the neutron count rate was so low that these numbers didn't mean anything. "How can you put any weight on a reciprocal count rate of 0.02? That's only 50 neuts per second. Wait until we get up a couple of decades, when the readings have some statistical validity. Then it will all smooth out." But they sounded pretty wistful.

In this situation, you could argue, "Let's pull the rods out faster and get into the meaningful range." But you could also argue that when things don't look right, you go more cautiously, not less. And so we split the difference and continued at the same deliberate pace, and the sixteenth point started on down the desired slope again. Other points followed, and finally, just before midnight, we reached criticality. We were well within the expected range, and the physics tests began.

I could not get any shielding checks at that low power, but I could start checking the radiochemistry of the water, which I did. I made a few spot-checks of the ambient radiation levels to rule out any gross surprises. After a few quick naps and some further tests on the plant, everything seemed to be right on target. Another day had passed, and I decided to see if I could get home for New Year's Eve. I arrived at my house at five minutes to midnight and found a New Year's Eve party under way. I walked in dirty, smelly, dead tired, with a five-day growth of beard. Cold sober, I silently watched the merriment for a few moments, then kissed my wife and stumbled into bed.

At Sea at Last

A little more than two weeks later Panoff and I were back at New London for initial sea trials. The plant had been brought to full power on 3 January, and the Boat Company crew had just finished up the last of the pipe insulation. The ship's crew had completed its "fast cruise," which was a simulation of a seagoing trip, with the ship tied fast to the pier but isolated from shore in all respects except communication. This resulted in a new "punch list" of minor items needing fixing, and the yard had nearly completed that task. In pre-Rickover days, all ship operations, through and including initial sea trials, were carried out by shipyard personnel, many of whom were retired submariners. The ship's naval crew then took over the ship without having had much exposure to her prior to that time. Rickover changed that for all time. The PCO and his crew were attached to the ship for the last year or more of construction, watching, learning, and requesting changes. They were now fully familiar with the ship and were actually carrying out the operating, test, and maintenance procedures. And of course, they had all fully qualified on the prototype plant.

On the morning of 17 January 1955 the *Nautilus* was ready to enter the realm for which she had been designed. Rickover and several of his senior people from headquarters were aboard, as were a few Electric Boat officials and some senior submarine officers from the Atlantic Fleet. Karl Swenson was aboard as representative of the BuShips Submarine Type Desk; he was not yet working for Rickover. At 11:00 A.M. the ship cast off the mooring lines and started to back into the channel. (I had had a nightmare the previous night, and it suddenly came back to me. In my dream the streets of New London had been flooded for the sea trials, the way the tennis courts were flooded for ice-skating in my youth. Wilkinson drove the *Nautilus* through the streets like a drunken speed-boat pilot, knocking bricks off the corners of buildings and generally terrorizing the citizenry in his wild flight. I had awakened in a cold sweat.)

The ship was not even into the channel when the engine room reported to Wilkinson on the bridge, "Captain, the starboard reduction gear is making a loud screeching noise. Don't know what's causing it yet. We've switched to electric propulsion [which did not involve the reduction gear]. What do you want us to do?"

The usual response to such a situation would have been to return to shore and check out the problem. But much to Rickover's dismay, a significant crowd had turned out to witness this unannounced but historic event, and he was not about to abort the trial without a struggle. He was on the bridge at Wilkinson's side, and hearing the problem, he made a suggestion. (He was not in a position, legally, to issue an order.) He noted that electric propulsion on this ship was hardly adequate to maneuver her in the strong currents of the channel, and Wilkinson agreed. Rickover suggested, "When you get into the channel, why don't you continue on the port turbine alone while we try to find out what's wrong with the starboard reduction gear?" And he went below, to peer over the shoulder of engineman Tom Reece and hand him tools.

Wilkinson agreed, and for twenty-six agonizing minutes the *Nautilus* continued her slow maneuver into the channel. From the shore there was no problem apparent, and people continued to call, blow kisses, and wave, while the crew members on deck forced smiles and carried on. Finally, the bridge speaker carried the message from the engine room: "We've located the problem. It was a loose screw on a retaining collar, which had worked out far enough to rub on the metal casing. We're admitting steam to the starboard turbine now. We're about ready to answer all bells." One lousy little screw, three-eighths of an inch thick and one and three-quarters of an inch long, had created a noise like the intermittent scream of badly worn automobile brakes!

With all systems operational, the *Nautilus* glided smoothly out into Long Island Sound and prepared to signal her escort tug, the *Skylark*, that she was ready to begin sea trials. "Dennis, this is a historic moment," said Panoff with mock seriousness. "Have you composed a suitably memorable message?"

Wilkinson was a bit of a character, and he replied, "Aw, Bob. They've wrecked all my good submariner's lines. Last night I yelled 'Up periscope,' like they do in all the submarine movies, and the navigation officer says, 'Captain, you just push that little button there, and it comes up automatically.' And they tell me these new scopes don't pour seawater down your neck either. Hell, the romance is gone. I said just tell 'em, 'Under way on nuclear power.' "

Neither Panoff nor Wilkinson realized how famous that phrase would become. But Panoff noticed that the crew was already starting unconsciously to copy the skipper's country-boy phrases and his habit of closing one eye and cocking his head, and he concluded that the crucial process of building a crew from a group of strangers was well under way.

As they steamed past Block Island and hit the open waters of the Atlantic Ocean, the ship encountered heavy seas: twelve-foot waves, ice forming on the deck, and the ship rolling up to 27 degrees—a condition officially designated as Sea State Five. Neither the ship nor the crew was comfortable on the surface in rough water, and the men looked forward to the submerged tests. Everyone felt too miserable to razz the sailors who were getting seasick, and a few got lumps and gouges from slamming into protruding valves and flanges. Large pieces of the aluminum superstructure were torn loose, along with one of the running lights and some of the teak decking. Panoff considered trying to get a quick nap at one point, but as he went to the crew's living quarters to find an empty bunk, the ship took a violent lurch and a sailor's body was thrown from his bunk onto the deck. Panoff decided to forget the nap.

"What are we waiting for? Let's dive!" was heard more and more as the hours dragged on. Finally, the word leaked out. The Navy P.R. people had promised *Life* magazine a chance to photograph the first dive from a helicopter, but the weather had kept the photographer away. When Rickover heard that, he said, "Oh, hell! When they finally find us, we'll do a dive for 'em. If they want to tell everybody it's our first dive, who cares? Let's get on with the test program." And in a few moments, the welcome *ah-uuu-guh, ah-uuu-guh* was heard on the ship's klaxon, and the first dive began.

More than fifty dives were performed before returning to port, a new Navy record for sea trials. Unlike the diesel boats, which required exquisite timing to close off the diesel air intakes at just the right moment, the *Nautilus* could surface and submerge at will, almost like a porpoise. The test personnel turned to their various tasks. One group monitored the compression of the hull as the ship dove cautiously from one test depth to the next, pausing at each predetermined depth to complete the hull measurements and to check the various seals and other vulnerable points for leakage. Another team of technicians had fastened strain gauges onto the main shafts through which the turbines turned the propellers. The strain gauges measured the amount of twist in the shaft at each power level and were thus a precise indication of the horsepower delivered by the plant. Since the shafts were rotating, the strain gauges could be read only with the help of a stroboflash unit, timed to flash at exactly the same position of the shaft on each rotation. These measurements were slow and tedious, but they were considered the ultimate measure of the plant's performance.

The crew was delighted with the stable yet responsive performance of the system. If the skipper asked for more speed, the steam plant operator would open the throttle, which admitted more steam to the turbine, and the propeller would immediately start to turn faster. Since the energy to accomplish this was coming from the reactor, it would start to cool down. But the cooler water in the reactor, being denser, would more effectively slow down the neutrons, and since slow neutrons are more effective at causing fission, the reactor power would start to increase. When the power level of the reactor equaled the demand from the turbine, it would level off. Very little operation of the control rods was required. The crew had never seen any other propulsion system so user-friendly, although that term was not in use in those days.

The crew was also pleased with the aircraft-type joystick controls for the rudder and diving planes. There was one anxious moment when the stern planes stuck with the boat on a down angle. The diving officer immediately reversed propellers, blew ballast tanks, put bow planes on full rise, and threw hard right rudder, all of which halted the potentially dangerous downward plunge within thirty feet. Quick action was then required to prevent a precipitous ascent with uncontrolled surfacing where other ships might be operating. But this too was quickly controlled.

After the appropriate crew members had demonstrated their prowess at ship control, Admiral Rickover was given a chance to try his hand. The Admiral had been pleased with the performance of the ship and her crew, and, as Captain Wilkinson put it, "When he thinks no one is looking, I've caught him smiling." He had dispatched a birthday greeting by radio to his wife back in Washington, and he was no doubt pleased to be able to sign it "from the *Nautilus* at sea." When he felt the great ship respond to his fingertip touch on the wheel, he could not help but feel immensely gratified. When he finished his maneuvers after fifty-two seconds, he turned and barked out a ridiculous series of staccato orders, with a completely straight face: "Take her down and put her on the bottom, all ahead full, left full rudder, take charge Captain Wilkinson," leaving Wilkinson to countermand those orders with all deliberate haste.

Panoff worked with the engine-room crew on their test program. I concerned myself with the radiation survey and constant rechecking of the radiochemistry of the reactor coolant water, both of which seemed to be completely satisfactory. Finally, after four nearly sleepless days, the required tests were complete. The Admiral had monitored the four-hour full-power run submerged, followed by an emergency full astern, which he felt was about the most severe test one could give a propulsion system, and all agreed that it went flawlessly. It was time to head for home.

Rickover's team did not pay much attention to the navigation charts and the ship's course. That was none of their business. But Panoff came to me and asked, "Did you know Dennis is taking the shortcut through the Cape Cod Canal?"

I said this was the first I had heard about it. Panoff went on to explain that this would put the ship several miles inland, within a few feet of shore and the public. "Is that going to give the safety people any heartburn?" he asked.

"We'd better tell Rick about this one," I agreed.

Rickover's response was immediate and unambiguous. "My God! Is he crazy? The Safeguards Committee will be all over us. We've never discussed operation anywhere but New London and the open ocean. We've got a lot of groundwork to lay before we do something like this. Get Wilkinson in here."

Wilkinson said he had cleared his "flight path" with the Atlantic submarine command, and Rickover forgot about being a mere adviser. "You change it! Now! You could set this whole program back ten years! Why would you do such a thing? What's the incentive?"

"This is the standard return route for a submarine in this location, Admiral. It'll take us hours longer to go around."

"I don't care if it takes a week. Our whole operation is based on the premise that I will discuss with the Safeguards Committee each new step that expands our operations. They've been good to us. They've trusted us. I have assured them we will do nothing in haste. And you want to nullify all that to get home a few hours sooner! Don't you see what you're doing? Now get on the radio and change your return route. Quickly, before word leaks out about using the canal."

We returned by open water, without further incident. On 20 March Rickover arranged for the Joint Congressional Committee on Atomic Energy to meet aboard, "for deep deliberations." This, of course, led to suggestions that the members were now a *"sub*committee," and Rickover warning members, as they went into a steep turn, that he was now giving "slanted testimony." In May the *Nautilus* took a shakedown cruise thirteen hundred miles to San Juan, Puerto Rico, in eighty-four hours, mostly submerged. A highly effective, reliable, and deadly combat ship, she was delivered to the Navy on 22 April 1955.

A number of minor problems arose during the trials, and these provided exciting stories for the press. There were numerous small seawater leaks, one of which kept the skipper's bunk wet and the deck of his cabin under an inch of water. There were several oil leaks and two fires, all of which were quickly dealt with by Engineer Officer Les Kelly and his crew, leaving no residual problems. The drinking water turned salty, and the ship's superstructure took some damage from the heavy seas. Captain Wilkinson tried to put these problems in perspective for the press: "This is my fifth time on a brand new submarine, and I can state on the basis of personal experience that the *Nautilus* gave us far less trouble than the average new construction. These were only builder's trials, designed to get rid of the bugs which invariably crop up at first in such a complex piece of machinery as a submarine. The *Nautilus* doesn't officially join the Navy, as part of the Atlantic Fleet, until this month [April 1955, four months after initial sea trials]."

During this run I had become familiar with the other parts of the ship, especially those parts not included in the prototype. Submarines were no longer the cramped, smelly "pig-boats" of prenuclear days. Submerged, the *Nautilus* displaced about four thousand tons, and was over twenty-seven feet in diameter and almost a city block long. This is nearly half again longer than Jules Verne's famous submarine, and about the same diameter. No wonder Rickover had said, "We've got to stop calling these magnificent capital ships 'boats.' " Earlier submarines had been forced to relinquish nearly half of their space to diesel fuel and batteries, but the *Nautilus* had unprecedented room for living. Her wardroom was four times the size of previous submarine wardrooms. Her crew's mess could feed thirty-six at one sitting, and within a few minutes it could convert to a fifty-seat movie theater. She had an automatic washer/dryer, some machine tools, a photography darkroom, and a six-hundred-volume library. There was an ice cream machine, a cola dispenser, a built-in hi-fi system, and a jukebox that played songs for a nickel. But the ultimate luxury was "one man, one bunk," each with foam rubber mattress, shoe rack, drawer for toiletries, and fluorescent lighting. At least during normal operations, there was to be no more "hot bunking," the traditional submarine practice of waiting for your assigned time to a bunk. Even the color scheme and the decor were selected by one of the country's foremost decorators. Air conditioning kept all occupied spaces between 68 and 72 degrees and at a comfortable humidity.

RICKOVER AND THE THEATER

I had never heard Rickover talk about the theater. He claimed that he had never seen but one movie, "the one where the lady falls in love with the horse," by which I gather he meant Elizabeth Taylor in *National Velvet*. I didn't think he had ever attended a play. So I was interested when he mentioned one day that he had just seen Ralph Bellamy play Roosevelt in *Sunset at Campobello*.

"What did you think of it, Admiral?" I asked.

"It was a very interesting experience," replied Rickover. "Very moving. But I can't understand how an actor can do what Bellamy does."

"What do you mean?"

"I would find it challenging and exciting to produce the performance I saw. But I can't imagine wanting to go all the way back to the beginning and produce that same development of character all over again the next night. I just can't imagine being able to do that. I can't imagine anyone *wanting* to do that."

It sure beats life in the trenches, I thought, and I couldn't help but contrast it with the verbal picture in Michael Gannon's *Operation Drumbeat* of a German U-boat setting out on a two-month transatlantic World War II patrol:

> [There was] an odor compounded of stale, humid air, diesel oil, sweat, urine, semen, soiled and fusty clothing, battery gas, bilges, cooking odors, and Colibri, the eau de cologne used by the bridge watch to remove salt spray from their faces. By two weeks, the U-boat's interior would deserve to be described as a sewer pipe with valves, and the reeking, putrescent atmosphere would be having its expected effect on any fresh food that remained. After three weeks, the loaves of black bread, a German sailor's staple food, would be covered with a white, fluffy mold; the crew would call them rabbits and eat only the centers. The sausages that hung everywhere from overhead pipes would wear their own white mildews, and the lemons that everyone on a U-boat sucked to prevent scurvy similarly would grow white coats amid the damp and the stench.

ATOMIC POWER ASHORE

> *In Greek mythology, Antaeus was a giant who was strong as long as he had contact with the earth. When he was lifted from the earth he lost his strength. So it is with engineers. They must not be isolated from the real world . . . The Devil is in the details, but so is salvation.*
>
> H.G.R.

The nuclear Navy was now a growing reality. The keel had been laid for the second nuclear submarine, the *Seawolf*, which would take the liquid-sodium-cooled plant being developed by GE at the Knolls Laboratory. The Navy had included in the 1955 shipbuilding program four more nuclear submarines with reactor plants of a new design, designated SFR, for Submarine Fleet Reactor. One of these plants was put into the *Halibut*, a submarine designed and built at the Mare Island shipyard to carry the air-breathing missile Regulus. Combustion Engineering, Inc.

had been selected to build and operate a third Naval Reactors laboratory at Windsor, Connecticut, where a prototype power plant would be constructed for a small hunter/killer submarine, the *Tullibee*. BuShips submarine designers had been evaluating a radical new hull form, designed for the first time for optimum submerged performance, based on the experimental submarine *Albacore*. This work had now reached the point where the Department of Defense had requested the AEC to develop a plant for this new class of high-speed submarines. The Large Ship Reactor project, for application to an aircraft carrier and other surface ships, was back on the track and moving. And looming in the background was the mighty radar picket submarine *Triton*, to be powered by two of GE's Submarine Advanced Reactor plants.

"Open Skies" and "Atoms for Peace"

But President Eisenhower still dreamed of developing the Peaceful Atom, to "deliver electricity to the factories, farms, and homes of all the peoples of the world," and to counteract the image of Hiroshima as the atom's only legacy. His breathtaking "Open Skies" proposal, to use America's high-flying spy camera technology to monitor world peace and disarmament, had been summarily rejected by Khrushchev. The United States organized the first of several international "Atoms for Peace" conferences in Geneva, and began negotiations that ended a year later in the establishment of an International Atomic Energy Authority, headquartered in Brussels. Eisenhower was determined that the atomic arrows in one talon of the American eagle would be complemented by a credible atomic olive branch in the other. And Rickover's commercial central station power plant at Shippingport, Pennsylvania, was to be his means to that end.

Shippingport Goes On Line

President Eisenhower had been anxious to demonstrate as soon as possible some concrete action toward achieving the goal of commercial atomic power. So his ground-breaking ceremony at Shippingport on 6 September 1954 took place before many of the key design parameters for the plant had been set. On 26 April 1955 Rickover made the important decision that the reactor fuel elements would be made of uranium oxide clad in zirconium-alloy tubes. This was a totally different design concept from the naval reactors and required the development of an entirely new technology on a crash basis. But this development was

EXTENDING THE EFFECT:
TECHNICAL INFORMATION

In addition to the codes, standards, procedures, manuals, and other informational material directly associated with his plants, Rickover decided early on that he would also publish a series of Naval Reactors Handbooks, declassifying and making public for the first time as much of the technology and its scientific background as he could pull together. Each book was a major technical tome—the definitive work on the subject. He arranged with Jim Beckerley, head of classification for the AEC, to obtain rapid security reviews of these books. He set new ground rules for generically declassifying much work that had previously been considered secret, and he cleared the way for declassification of more basic technology from other programs.

There were about a dozen of these books, and although they were published over thirty years ago, many of them are still in print and being cited in the scientific literature.

remarkably successful, and it became the basis for nearly all the world's nuclear power plants.

On 6 October 1957 the first reactor core was installed, and on 2 December the plant reached criticality for the first time. For this event there was a brief celebration, with a group picture taken that was later signed by all present. On 18 December the plant delivered its first electricity through the Duquesne Light Company's commercial transmission system to customers in the Pittsburgh area and beyond. On 23 December 1957 Shippingport reached design capacity. Commercial atomic power was now a reality, just four and a half years after the task had been assigned to Admiral Rickover. Three years later, commercial plants based on this design began to spring up around the country, and shortly after that, around the whole world.

Part IV

Upgrading the Quality of U.S. Industry
(1955–1960)

IV.

The wise use of technology calls for a higher order of thinking than we have so far accorded it. We have largely left it to the management of practical men. I submit that we now have scientific knowledge of such immensely dangerous potential that we ought to bring a broader range of intellectual power to bear upon its use.

I think one can make a general statement that the practical approach to a new scientific discovery is short-range and private, concerned with ways to put the discovery to use in the most economical and efficient manner, little thought being given to side effects and future consequences. The scholarly approach—if I may use this term—is long-range and public; it looks to the effects which the use of a new discovery may have on people in general, on the nation, perhaps on the world; present and future . . . What is important is to recognize that each approach is necessary to illuminate the problem and help solve it. To exclude the one or the other prevents finding a way to reconcile technology and democracy . . .

Conservation has had extremely hard sledding in this country because we worship practical men and have little respect for scholars. This is not an intelligent point of view in today's world.

H.G.R.

Upgrading the Quality of U.S. Industry
1955–1960

NAVAL REACTORS' LONG-RANGE OBJECTIVES

THE CHANGE IN perception as to the real, long-range objectives of the Naval Reactors program did not occur in sharp stages. It did not even occur in the same way for all members of the Naval Group. Admiral Rickover, for example, was a man whose whole career was aimed at developing better weapons, so the nuclear submarine was a natural objective for him, especially during the height of the Cold War. Bob Panoff, however, was drawn to naval ships not primarily because they were military, but because they epitomized for him engineering in a nearly pure form. "Everything on a naval vessel has to be engineered to the limit," he used to say. "Where else can you practice engineering in such a pure and concentrated form?"

I was intrigued from the start of my Oak Ridge days with the idea of providing humanity with an entirely new source of energy. But I do not feel defensive about having worked on The Bomb, although numerous historical revisionists had tried to make its development look, after the fact, as if it had been both unnecessary and immoral. But I never found that view credible; I know people who were scheduled for the November 1945 and March 1946 invasions of Japan but returned safely home after Hiroshima. And most historians don't credit that view either; they point out that some of the U.S. firebomb raids on Japanese cities were even more devastating than Hiroshima. I would not have wanted to work on, say, an improved version of napalm, but I had no problem seeing naval nuclear propulsion as the path to civilian nuclear power, which indeed it proved to be.

The submarine operators, of course, saw nuclear power as a submariner's dream, providing them the ability to carry out missions for which submarines are uniquely fitted, but for which prenuclear submarines were frustratingly restricted. In addition, after completing their naval service, many of the submarine operators became an important element in the nation's civilian nuclear power industry.

But despite all the unevenness of the transition when viewed up close, there was in fact a continuing change in the perception of the mission, a change brought on by the technological facts of the situation more than by any political or psychological considerations. The initial task, of course, was to develop a weapon—the nuclear submarine—and that was considered challenge enough. It was assumed at first by Rickover and his small crew that most of the science and technology for doing this would flow from the mighty atomic bomb program, a multibillion-dollar national enterprise employing some of the world's most brilliant scientific minds, and encompassing whole towns throughout the country created for, and devoted to, developing nuclear technology.

But Rickover was the first to realize that this would not in fact happen. And that was the first step down the road to ever-larger objectives for his program.

Once it became clear that Rickover's program was in fact the only one likely to produce a practical nuclear power plant, the pressure to assign him the civilian nuclear power also began to build on all sides. The peaceful atom was seen as a potentially powerful antidote to the fearsome A-bomb, and nearly everyone, from President Dwight Eisenhower to the proverbial man in the street, wanted it; people wanted it safe and reliable, and most of all, they wanted it NOW. Rickover was viewed as the obvious person to accomplish this, and he and his people were as anxious as anyone else to deliver this boon.

Rickover's experience, supported by a significant amount of naval history, taught that the way to get new technological products was to turn to American industry. For the nuclear power program, this proved both frustrating and ultimately rewarding, time after time. First, in the case of zirconium and hafnium production, and later with special pumps, valves, heat exchangers, and control systems, industry on its own failed to deliver. So Rickover reluctantly had to take over these developments, to provide the necessary jump-start. But these programs were finally brilliantly successful, and ultimately a competitive commercial industry was developed. To accomplish this Rickover had to expand his vision, and his supervision, to encompass a large number of industrial products that he had hoped to be able to buy in the open market. And thus he found himself spending increasing time and effort aimed at upgrading the level of American industry, preaching the need for "zero defects" and "quality first" long before foreign competition burned the same message into the hides of an even wider industrial audience.

Industry's first reaction to such a message was often to hire a "quality control expert," to bestow titles on promising or prominent executives, and to compose advertisements and slogans. The next step was to publish quality control manuals and write voluminous procedures, which were immediately perceived by the persons who had to carry them out to be impractical and were therefore more often honored in the breach. Quality control and quality assurance societies sprang up and sponsored seminars and training programs. Speeches on the subject filled the air. But it became clear to Rickover that the key ingredient in assuring quality lay not in physical manifestations but in a frame of mind, a point of view. And as in the case of zirconium production, he found that he could not define the problem from afar and count on others to do it right. He had to become intimately involved for a considerable time, before the extent and nature of the problem could be made clear.

An example of this occurred when Dave Leighton was nuclear power superintendent at the Mare Island Naval Shipyard. A nuclear-qualified welder was trying to get at a nearly inaccessible location on a stainless steel tank to make a weld. As he bent the welding rod to reach the spot, the rod broke. Normally, a welder would throw it away and get another, but people in the nuclear program are required to report any unusual event to their supervisor, and the welder knew that these rods don't

---

"WE'RE IN THE EDUCATION BUSINESS"

My eldest son, Bob, once asked me, "What is your real objective in the Naval Reactors program? Ultimately, what do you do? Why are you in it?"

I started to enumerate the various major projects we were engaged in, but Bob cut me off. "No, no. That's not what I mean. When St. Pete asks you what you did all those years, what was worthwhile about it, what will you tell him? What is it of value that you want to leave behind as your legacy? Will you give him a list of hardware? I don't think so."

I thought a minute and then said, "I guess what I really feel good about is the way we've changed people's thinking. We've gotten a few industrial people to really think about quality and professionalism as a priority in their lives. And we've started a few kids down the road to being really high-class engineers. More than a few. And that may prove to be important. One example of this is the Admiral's speech at the National Metal Congress in New York in 1962, entitled *The Never-Ending Challenge*. It was full of bluntly worded technical details and we got a huge number of requests for copies. It apparently got through to a lot of people in industry."

"So you're really in the education business."

"Yeah, I suppose you could look at it that way. I guess we're ultimately in the education business."

usually break when they are bent. So he reported it, and the supervisor called in the welding engineer.

Within a matter of minutes, the welding engineer had stopped all nuclear welding in the shipyard. Metallurgy tests showed that the broken welding rod, or electrode, as they are called, was made of stellite, a hard and brittle material; but it had been taken from a can of electrodes marked stainless steel. The yard personnel started radiographing cans of stainless steel electrodes and found to their dismay that several cans each had a few electrodes of the wrong material. So the problem was not just one of mislabeled cans.

Leighton reported the problem to Jack Hinchey, his counterpart at the Portsmouth Naval Shipyard, and between the two yards they uncovered wrong materials in several cans, from five different electrode manufacturers. He called Rickover, who at first was reluctant to get into investigating quality control procedures in the entire welding electrode industry. But he soon realized that he had no choice. He put Harry Mandil on the problem, and Mandil was able to determine the point in the manufacturing process where the wrong materials were being introduced. Mandil hammered out agreements with the manufacturers whereby electrodes for Naval Reactors would be manufactured in such a way as to avoid this problem. But presumably other programs were still unknowingly vulnerable to this serious hazard—and may still be vulnerable to this day. "I have often wondered," said Leighton, "whether some of the problems of manufacture we read about in other programs may have been caused this way. We would still be in trouble if we had not been willing to go far outside our assigned area of responsibility."

Ironically, most of this recognition of the need to upgrade American industry on a broad basis developed while we were immersed in the task of building submarines.

THE *SEAWOLF* TAKES CENTER STAGE— BRIEFLY

Nature is not as forgiving as Christ.

H.G.R.

The Elusive Advantages of Thermal Efficiency

The Holy Grail for power plant engineers is thermodynamic efficiency. From the beginning, the goal has been to get higher temperatures, greater power gradients, to push materials to the limits for this purpose. In automobiles, this shows up in more miles per gallon. In airplanes, it's higher speeds and higher altitudes. And in naval vessels, it means more miles between dangerous, open-sea refuelings. So for the engineering community, it was a shock and a hard pill to swallow when Naval Reactors chose to pursue pressurized-water cycles, rather than the higher-temperature coolants such as gases or liquid metals.

Mark Ireland, of Newport News Shipbuilding, used to complain, "You guys are setting back power plant design by fifty years. You're asking us to look at operating temperatures and pressures that we passed by decades ago."

We would explain that the problem of having to refuel a destroyer every few days was not applicable to nuclear power. That problem had been solved. A nuclear ship could literally run for years without refueling. Now was the time to take an entirely new look at optimizing power plant design. But the problem was not in the brain; it lay deep in the gut. It was like asking a horticulturist to grow ugly flowers, or a chef to make an unsavory stew. This was the basis for much of the pressure on Rickover to find something—anything—other than pressurized water for his power plants. Pressurized water was, in a very real sense— well, tacky. "Surely we can do better than that," said the scientists.

But Rickover's position was supported by a long and painful history—prior to nuclear power—of efforts around the world to develop higher-temperature power plant systems. General Electric had put many years and much of its resources into trying to develop a system based on mercury, a metal that is liquid at room temperature. The desired thermal efficiency was achieved, but the many problems of working with an expensive and highly toxic material led to a reluctant abandonment of the cycle. To Rickover and his people, there were good and valid reasons that water has remained the coolant of choice for nearly all of the world's power plants, ever since the invention of the steam engine.

Liquid metal was doubly attractive to GE as a reactor coolant. Liquid sodium was not only capable of high-temperature operation at low pressure; it was also nearly transparent to neutrons. This meant that it offered a possibility of operating with a significant fraction of the power coming from fissions caused by "intermediate-energy" neutrons—that is, neutrons of higher energy than those slowed to thermal equilibrium with the atoms in a water-cooled reactor. This reactor concept was called the SIR, for Submarine Intermediate Reactor, to distinguish it from the STR, the Submarine Thermal Reactor, which powered the *Nautilus*. GE was anxious to explore the potential of the intermediate reactor for breeding more fuel than it consumed, and although the company did not achieve breeding, the lure of high thermal efficiency remained. (Ironically, long after GE abandoned the idea of breeding in the SIR, Rickover's reactor at Shippingport, Pennsylvania, demonstrated breeding in a pressurized-water system.)

The GE group at the Knolls Atomic Power Laboratory (KAPL), under the direction of Naval Reactors, did develop a workable sodium-cooled submarine plant. The prototype was built at the West Milton site, near Schenectady, New York, and another such plant was installed in the submarine *Seawolf*. We ran it for less than two years, and after seeing that the water-cooled plants did indeed work, we refitted the ship with a pressurized plant like the one in the *Nautilus*. The question remains: Why was the liquid-metal reactor approach abandoned, and what of value was left behind from the liquid-metals development work?

The merits of a power plant finally rest on many things, of which thermal efficiency is only one. The SIR provides an excellent example of how these things often tend to work in opposite directions. The reactor raised its incoming coolant temperature over ten times as much as the STR, and it offered an outlet temperature of 850 degrees Fahrenheit, compared with the STR's measly 500 degrees. This enabled the *Seawolf*'s steam plant to run with modern, high-temperature superheated steam conditions, as opposed to the *Nautilus*' low-temperature, low-pressure saturated steam. Definitely more satisfying for the design engineer. But what about the customer, the captain on the ship's bridge? What does he get out of this?

The higher-efficiency steam plant is lighter weight, which is advantageous, but this is more than offset by the heavy radiation shielding required by the activated sodium, which gives off high-energy gamma rays. The higher efficiency also means that less uranium need be fissioned to produce the same shaft horsepower, but this is offset by the fact that the intermediate-energy neutrons produce a large number of captures without fission; that is, the fissionable U-235 isotope captures a neutron to make U-236, which does not then fission and is just a worthless by-product. Thus, although the SIR does its work with fewer fissions, it consumes just as much fissionable uranium, so there is no saving in fuel consumption, and its fuel inventory is larger.

Up to this point we have a standoff, as far as the naval customer is concerned. His SIR power plant is just as big and heavy, and it consumes just as much fuel, as a lower-efficiency STR. Sodium has only one real operational advantage: if the system can be kept absolutely oxygen-free, the corrosion and the transport of radioactive corrosion products throughout the system are essentially zero. This is obviously useful when major maintenance and overhaul are carried out. But sodium's operational disadvantages are serious.

First, sodium as a reactor coolant becomes a thousand times more radioactive than water, and it remains too "hot" for maintenance for a week or so, as compared with water, whose radioactivity decays another thousandfold to tolerable levels during the few minutes it takes to gain access to the compartment. Second, sodium metal burns in air and explodes in water, presenting a potential hazard during operation and a serious impediment to maintenance. And third, it freezes at about 200 degrees Fahrenheit, so that electric heaters must be fastened to all equipment and piping to keep it from freezing when the reactor is not operating. These electric heaters require a great deal of power, at the very time when the reactor is shut down and not producing power. All these inherent characteristics of sodium create enormous problems for operating and maintaining a fighting ship.

The crucial factor that doomed the SIR was the operational success of the STR. Once that had been established, there seemed little reason to put up with the problems and hazards of sodium. This decision had the advantage that we could now throw all our resources into making sure that the pressurized-water plant would work and work well. And it had the disadvantage that, without the continuous competition of another cycle, one might be tempted to rest on his oars from time to time. But with Rickover calling the shots, that didn't seem to be a genuine problem.

Getting Safety Approval

When the *Seawolf* keel was laid in a quiet ceremony on 15 September 1953, the difficult characteristics of sodium were well known, to Rickover and his people especially. They had worked with Richard N. Lyon at Oak Ridge, and later with C. B. "Doc" Jackson at the Mine Safety Appliances Company, to produce the most authoritative technical reference book on the subject, *The Liquid Metals Handbook*, in three editions, 1950, 1952, and, later, in 1955, each with considerable new material over the previous editions. But the *Nautilus* had not yet been launched, and the success of the pressurized-water reactor concept was by no means assured.

However, by the time the *Seawolf* was launched on 21 July 1955, the *Nautilus* had completed her dramatic thirteen-hundred-mile full-power submerged run to Puerto Rico, and the keel had been laid for the first of five new submarines with SFR power plants. Sodium now had a hardy competitor, and it would have to demonstrate its worth. But serious troubles lay ahead.

Rickover knew that getting approval for *Seawolf* operations from the Advisory Committee on Reactor Safeguards (ACRS) would be difficult under the best of circumstances, and with the influential Edward Teller having declared his grave concerns, the task would be even harder. He was therefore more than casually interested when I brought him rumors that Teller was thinking of resigning from the Safeguards Committee. Rickover held off approaching the committee, although the hour grew close. Finally, Teller did retire, and Rickover let GE release its report on the first phase of *Seawolf* operations for the committee's review. When I got my copy of the report, I looked at the distribution list and was horrified to see Teller's name. GE had neglected to remove it. Frantically I called to find if all copies had been mailed, and whether someone at GE had remembered to pull Teller's copy out at the last minute. But no such luck; it had gone.

With GE's concurrence, I called Teller's secretary and found that Teller was out of town and the report had not yet been opened. I explained simply that there had been a mistake, that the report was not intended for Dr. Teller, and would she please mail it back to GE. She agreed to do so, and I thanked her kindly, hung up the phone, and then slowly let out the breath I had been holding.

Rickover defused some of the Safeguards Committee's concerns over the SIR plant in the *Seawolf* by suggesting preemptively that the committee might wish to require severe limitations on in-port operations, and that Rickover would have to return for committee approval at each expansion of the ship's operating sphere. On this basis, approval was granted, but it was clearly a tentative asset. The Safeguards Committee expressed its reservations in very explicit terms: "The Committee believes that the operation of the *Seawolf* should not be unrestricted." The *Seawolf* had been approved, but at a price.

The safeguards approval of the *Seawolf* was a prime example of the unprecedented personal power that Rickover held over the nuclear Navy. On the one hand, the restrictions Rickover helped place in the Safeguards Committee approval letter, which were then approved and endorsed by the Atomic Energy Commission (AEC), were seen by many of the Navy's operations people as a raw power play. And indeed they were. But it was equally true that probably no one but Rickover could have obtained any safeguards approval at all. And I was convinced that even *he* might not have obtained approval if he had not offered a serious degree of limitation and control. Louis XIV's memorable phrase *"L'état c'est moi"* applied also to Rickover. Anything that helped him helped the program, and thus the idea of conflict of interest in his case was largely meaningless. He had reinforced his control over the Navy and over GE, but it is not at all clear that any other option would have worked.

An interesting sidelight on the GE-Rickover relationship was revealed when GE proposed to put Ken Kesselring in charge of the Knolls site. Not only was Kesselring a model GE manager, of the type NR always found difficult, but he was a close relative of the famous Nazi field marshal. Nevertheless, he was clearly considered the most promising technical leader by his peers at GE, and he was technically competent. Rickover promptly approved the nomination, and after Kesselring's death many years later, the GE prototype site at West Milton, New York, was named in his honor.

Leaks

The SIR system had large steam generators and superheaters, in which hot sodium from the reactor heated up water to make steam to run the turbines. Heat-exchanger tubes of any type sooner or later develop small leaks, which in a pressurized-water reactor result in water leaking into water. But in the SIR, a leak would result in high-pressure steam and water leaking into the sodium, which could cause a disastrous explosion. Even if the leak were a tiny one, the reaction of sodium and water at the leak would create sodium hydroxide—lye—which would quickly corrode the tiny leak into a large one. To prevent such an occurrence, the SIR heat-exchanger tubes were made double-walled, with mercury in the space between the sodium and the water. In this design, sensitive mercury detectors in the steam and sodium systems could signal the start of a leak before sodium and water contacted each other. However, fabricating such a design was tricky, and the presence of toxic mercury on a submarine would always be a concern, no matter how carefully it was isolated from the atmosphere.

Finally, the SIR prototype started up and logged two thousand simulated miles at full power, in response to the simulated transatlantic trip of the STR prototype two years earlier. The initial jubilation was short-lived, however. A month later, mercury was detected in the sodium, indicating a leak in the steam generator, and not long after that, both superheaters showed leaks. By this time, the *Seawolf* had already been launched and the options for correcting the leakage problem on the ship were severely limited. At the minimum, there was a way to get rid of the mercury. Sodium has the ability to form a lower-melting alloy with its sister element potassium, and this alloy stays liquid down to room temperature. Leakage of this alloy into the sodium would not cause any chemical reaction, but it is harder to detect. The mercury in the prototype was therefore replaced with sodium-potassium alloy, and no mercury was used on the ship.

The *Seawolf* started up alongside the pier in the summer of 1956, and at first everything went well. But then superheater leaks appeared during the full-power tests, and the superheaters were isolated. The ship could run without superheaters; the question was whether the steam generators had developed leaks, for they were essential to operation. After several weeks of testing, the *Seawolf* went to sea in February 1957 under severely restricted power and maneuvering limits. By extremely careful operation, her crew kept the ship in service, and she was accepted by the Navy and operated as part of the fleet for nearly two years. When she finally put in to have her sodium plant replaced by a pressurized-water system, she had steamed a total of 71,611 miles, nearly three times around the world. Of this distance, 57,118 miles had been traveled fully submerged.

When leaks on the *Seawolf* followed hard on the heels of leaks in the prototype, Rickover did not wait for the initial sea trials. He knew that the sodium cycle would not die easily, that GE and others interested in "advanced systems" would fight to keep the plant in operation indefinitely. So he moved swiftly and decisively to destroy any routes of retreat. In November 1956 he informed the AEC that he had decided to replace the *Seawolf* power plant with an STR plant similar to the one in the *Nautilus*. Sodium-cooled systems, he wrote, "are expensive to build, complex to operate, susceptible to prolonged shutdown as a result of even minor malfunctions, and difficult and time-consuming to repair." And he secretly had all the replacement fuel elements for the *Seawolf* and her prototype cut into little pieces.

Thus ended the story of the only nuclear propulsion system in the Navy to use, for a time, a reactor not cooled with water.

The Submarine Advanced Reactor (SAR) program gave Naval Reactors another chance to explore all kinds of nuclear plant concepts that might offer greater promise than pressurized-water systems. All of us— at Naval Reactors as well as at the Knolls Laboratory—were hoping to come up with something dramatically better. We looked at all kinds of coolants, moderators, and thermodynamic cycles. We even went so far as to set up NORE, the Naval Organic Reactor Experiment, using a high-temperature organic heat-transfer fluid, sold commercially as Dowtherm and other trade names. But the organic fluid would not stand up under both high temperature and high radiation flux, and in the end, we concluded—again—that pressurized water was the best choice. Knolls came up with a new fuel element design, and we raised the operating parameters a notch, based on experience with previous designs and using the latest analytical and design techniques.

Rickover and the Transatlantic Telephone

Rickover was in England when the *Seawolf* leaks were detected, and it fell to me to pass the word to him. Conveying such unhappy news is always painful, regardless of the nature of one's boss, but with Rickover it was a special treat. He had called in his senior people just before he left and delivered the following message: "I want to go over this code sheet you guys worked out. I'll be at the British Atomic Energy establishment for several days. Dixie knows how to reach me. We've got to assume the Atlantic Cable is tapped, so don't say anything classified over the phone. The nuclear submarine is the most important weapons system we've got. And there's no point in developing a weapon if you then give away the technology. The Russians are ahead of us in missiles. They outgun us in practically every department. But we have a real ace in the hole here. Do you guys realize that when the war started, the Germans had only forty-six operational subs, which meant that they could keep only thirteen on station, far from home? Yet they knocked out four hundred ships, over a million tons, in the first six months of 1942. They damn near beat us right there. What if they had had *nuclear* submarines? Well, that's the weapon we're giving to America, and I don't want to give it to anyone else."

He looked at the code sheet and continued, "Let's see, have you got code words for all of the key phrases that may come up? The *Nautilus* is Romeo, and the *Seawolf* is Juliet. God, you guys are cute. The reactor system is Sullivan—you guys ran out of Shakespeare after two names? What about *deadline*? We need a code word for that."

"How about Brodsky?" I suggested. Bob Brodsky was Rickover's computer and safety specialist. "We haven't used his name yet."

"All right," said Rickover. "Just write it down and give Dixie a copy for me."

And a few days later I had to put the system to work. I got through to the telephone number Rickover had given Dixie and said, "This is Theodore Rockwell, Admiral Rickover's technical director. May I speak with the Admiral, please?"

Shortly thereafter I heard the familiar high-pitched scream: "This better be important. You got me out of a meeting. What is it?"

I spoke into the phone, very slowly and distinctly: "Juliet will not meet Brodsky."

There was complete silence for a moment, then Rickover's voice came over, even higher and louder. "What was that?"

I started to repeat the code message, but I got out only a few words before I was interrupted.

"You're not making any sense, Rockwell. Speak louder."

I started in again, but again I was interrupted.

"What the hell are you trying to tell me? Speak up! Just say it."

At this point the operator tried to help: "Sir, if you would just speak in your normal voice . . ."

But Rickover had an answer for that, and at top volume and pitch: "Goddammit, this *is* my normal voice!"

I couldn't help saying, "That's true, operator. It is."

But the operator hadn't given up yet. "This circuit allows only one person to speak at a time," she said. "One person speaks, there is a slight pause, then the other may speak. If you keep interrupting, nothing will be transmitted."

Rickover hadn't changed his tactic. "What the hell are you trying to say, Rockwell? Just say it."

"Shut up and listen, Admiral," I said. And then I tried again, slowly and distinctly: "Juliet will not meet Brodsky."

"I heard that already! What the hell are you talking about? Who is Juliet? Make sense!"

"We worked out a code, remember? Juliet is a certain ship."

There was a long pause, and then Rickover said, "Oh, yeah. That. Well, I don't have the crib sheet handy. Just tell me. Make it clear but don't give away any secrets."

I decided to bite the bullet. "The *Seawolf* is delayed. She won't meet the scheduled sea date."

"Is it serious? What's happened?"

"It's serious. But it's too complicated to explain over this circuit. I thought you ought to know right away."

"Is it fatal, or can we fix it?"

"We will probably be delayed several weeks. Maybe more."

"I'll get back as soon as I can. Tell Dixie to copy that chapter on the Crusades I gave her to circulate, before I get back with a lot of work for her. I trust you guys are reading that stuff she passes around. I tell her to make a copy for each of you, so there's no excuse." And he hung up.

My only comment, addressed to no one in particular, was "Whew! What a struggle! He's hard enough to communicate with when you're eyeball to eyeball."

The Office Picnic and the Parade of the Dinosaurs

At parties we all heard many Rickover stories about the Old Man being mean just for fun. But I saw his other side more than once. One such interaction occurred at one of the Naval Reactors picnics we had from time to time. After these events, the wives always said to their husbands, "That Admiral Rickover is just as sweet as he can be. I don't see why you men have such a hard time getting along with him." For the picnics did seem to bring out the best of his social skills. I could never quite puzzle it out. Rickover avoided all the social events he could. Conse-

"HE'S MARRIED, Y'KNOW"

Early one morning, Rickover and I arrived at the Washington National Airport on the "red-eye" from the West Coast. As we walked past the Eastern Airlines desk, the woman behind the counter called out, "Oh, Admiral Rickover. Good morning, sir." I explained in an aside, "That's the girl who's dating Gene Rogers." Rogers was one of the Naval Reactors senior engineers.

Rickover quickly picked up the ball and ran with it. "Aren't you the woman who is dating Rogers?" "Why, yes, sir. He's very nice." Rickover, without a smile, said curtly, "He's married, y'know," and kept walking. I asked, incredulous, "You're just going to leave it like that? Why did you dream up such a crazy statement?" To which Rickover responded philosophically, "Rogers needs a challenge. If he can't get himself out of this one, he doesn't deserve the girl."

It reminded me of the time the stereotypical little old lady came up to Rickover, bubbling all over, and gushed, "I know who you are. Now don't tell me. You're somebody famous. Who is it?" To which the Admiral replied, "I'm the late Admiral Richard E. Byrd." And believe it or not, the little old lady went off chirping, "Yes, that's it. Admiral Byrd! Isn't that wonderful!"

quently, he had little practice doing what nearly everyone else does most of the time. And when he did get trapped into some such activity, he was usually pretty surly. But the NR parties were different. These were his people, and he might bark at them all day at the office, but at the picnics he was witty and pleasant, and he managed to charm their wives. It was a puzzlement.

This particular picnic gave me something to remember. The Admiral walked up to my wife and, without any preliminaries, asked, "How do you plan to spend your husband's new raise, Mrs. Rockwell?"

This had been a point of discussion between me and my wife the night before, and I wasn't sure just how she might answer. She had complained that by the time the government had taken out all the increased "dee-ducks," the net increase was disappointing. Actually, she had used a somewhat stronger term, knowing that under Civil Service she would not see another raise for at least fourteen months. I had tried to explain that the Admiral actually put a tremendous amount of effort into trying to get the maximum pay for his people, but the explanation had not had much effect on her. So I listened with particular care for her answer.

She smiled sweetly and said, "I thought we might switch to premium beer."

I was too startled to notice the Admiral's reaction, but he merely turned to my nine-year-old son Bob and said, "There's going to be a big International Naval Review next week off Newport News. Battleships, aircraft carriers, all kinds of ships from all over the world. Parade of the Dinosaurs. There will probably never be another. Would you like to see it? I could get you a seat on a shipyard tug that will go to where you can see better than all the big-shots on shore. I'd even let your parents go with you. Do you think you'd like that?"

Bob didn't wait for any signal. Looking straight into Rickover's eyes, he said, loud and clear, "Yes, sir."

Rickover was now dealing only with Bob. "I'll give you official written orders to represent me at this great occasion. I want you to observe well, and then send me an official report. Will you do that?"

"Yes, sir, Admiral. My father may forget and call you Captain sometimes, but I won't."

And Rickover solemnly shook his hand and turned to my wife. "He's a good-looking young man, but you ought to get his teeth straightened. That will be important to him as he gets older. Promise me you will do that."

She did, and Bob has remarked a number of times since that this one act had more influence on his life than any other.

When he left, my wife asked, "Will he really do that? I mean, about the Naval Review?"

To which I replied, "He certainly will. You can count on it."

Two days later, there arrived in the mail an official Navy letter addressed to Robert Rockwell. It was formal Navy orders, designating him the Admiral's representative for the International Naval Review, and ordering him to give a full report on his return. The affair was memorable, as the Admiral had predicted. The Newport News Shipbuilding and Dry Dock Company, which was to build the first nuclear aircraft carrier, made available one of its work tugs, suitably scrubbed up for the occasion, and Bob labored diligently over his report, pecking it out letter by letter on his mother's typewriter, and reworking it until he had it just the way he wanted it. It was formally acknowledged by the Admiral, with a written "Well done," and Bob has kept the papers to this day.

I have always been intrigued by the fact that while Rickover seemed to take an interest in my children, and the children of others in the program, I almost never heard him talk of his own son, Robert. In all those years I met Robert only once, and we exchanged no more than a brief greeting before he left the room.

GEARING UP TO BUILD AND SERVICE THE NUCLEAR FLEET

> *It is high time we give thought to the proper function of administrators. I suggest that at the top level they set policy and see to it that policy is carried out; that at lower levels they provide the environment and the material needed by the organization's productive workers; and that at the bottom they perform housekeeping and clerical chores. Administration is, or ought to be, a necessary overhead to aid production, and should at all times be kept as low as possible.*
>
> H.G.R.

Gathering Strength

Admiral Rickover's headquarters group was given many official names during its early years: Code 390, then 490, 590, and finally 1500. It was also known as Naval Reactors Branch, Naval Reactors Division, and Naval Reactors Divisions. So we came to refer to ourselves just as Naval Reactors, or NR, and that stuck with us. These changes were due partly to bureaucratic changes in the Bureau of Ships and in the AEC, and partly to Rickover's incessant drive to find ways to pay his people more. He played up the image of his group as unsung, overworked, and underpaid—the kind of psychology used by many charismatic leaders, from Ralph Nader to the "Battling Bastards of Bataan, no mama, no papa, no Uncle Sam." And we were underpaid, as compared with what we could have been paid, and as some were later, in positions of responsibility in the industrial world. But Rickover was determined to do as well as he possibly could for us financially in the civil service, and this meant jobs with higher bureaucratic titles: division directors instead of branch chiefs, and the like.

During those busy two years between Mark I start-up in 1953 and *Nautilus* sea trials in 1955, a number of exceptional engineers were brought in who were destined to play important roles in the years ahead. Richard G. Scott, a mechanical engineer from George Washington University, became one of Harry Mandil's key reactor materials engineers. Some years later he was called by the president of the Mormon church and appointed to the First Council of Seventy (analogous to the Roman Catholic College of Cardinals) and then to the Council of Twelve Apostles. Then came Philip R. Clark from Brooklyn Tech, a smart and steady engineer who succeeded Mandil as head of reactor systems. He left NR in August 1979 to become a senior official at GPU Nuclear, in order to help that beleaguered utility company recover from the Three Mile Island accident. From the University of Kansas came Gene L. Rogers, who retired in 1987 after thirty-three years in NR, most of that time spent in charge of Rickover's group responsible for supporting the operating nuclear fleet.

Webb Institute, an excellent college specializing in marine engineering and naval architecture, supplied many good engineers to NR. In 1954 Webb sent Paul W. Hayes, who stayed until he retired in 1988 as head of submarine systems. In 1955 another graduate, Mark Forssell, joined us, followed the next year by his brother Alan, and each served in NR more than three decades. Dwight H. Harrison, an excellent mechanical design engineer from the University of Kansas; Murray E. Miles, with an M.S. in engineering physics from Cornell; Edwin J. Wagner, a mechanical engineer from Carnegie-Mellon; and Karl E. Swenson, a mechanical systems engineer who had worked at the Argonne Laboratory—all joined the team in rapid succession and served long and productive terms.

The Submarine Atmosphere Problem

One area where Rickover had left quality control to others was the matter of ensuring and maintaining the purity of the air within the submarines. This was clearly outside his cognizance and was the responsibility of another section, or "code," within the Bureau of Ships. But one day he got a call from Commander John "Jack" Ebersole, the doctor

EXTENDING THE EFFECT:
RADIOLOGICAL ENGINEERING

I heard it first from Bob Panoff. A doctor friend was explaining to him the problem of training surgeons. "Working on a living patient is a very different experience from working on a cadaver in the laboratory. With a cadaver you have all the time you need. A living patient may suddenly begin to lose blood, or go into shock, or any number of things that require a series of actions in a very short period, with no time to think or ask questions. Training on cadavers is not enough."

Panoff realized that maintenance in a radioactive environment presented similar problems, and we shouldn't wait until we faced them in the field before trying to devise some solutions. He discussed this with the rest of us and with Admiral Rickover, and the Admiral appointed Jim Vaughn as head of a new radiological engineering group. Based on experience with the Canadian NRX reactor and in the laboratories, Vaughn's group was to try to anticipate some of the problems that would arise, and develop techniques to deal with them. For example, someone suggested we take photographs of the major reactor piping systems before they became buried in insulation and minor widgetry, then take more photos after insulation. Later, when a radioactive system would have to be worked on, a pinhole gamma camera could be set up— a lead box with a pinhole at one end and photographic film at the other. The "picture" it took in the dark would show only a series of bright spots where radioactive material had accumulated in the piping. This picture could then be superimposed on the regular photograph, and you could see where to apply temporary shielding.

Many tricks of this sort were developed, along with the paperwork to ensure that the right photos and other records could be retrieved quickly when needed. Developments like this helped to bridge the gap between laboratory science and field engineering.

assigned to the *Nautilus*. Ebersole was a career naval officer who had received his M.D. training in the Navy and was a specialist in submarine medicine. Submarine medicine was an exciting technical specialty; much research had been done on it, and much more remained to be discovered. The Navy, of course, offered a unique place to practice this specialty, and when I interviewed Navy doctors for the program, I was always amazed how many of them preferred to treat sore throats at Navy hospitals in Philadelphia or Boston than to get into a leading-edge scientific specialty like submarine medicine.

But there were a number of bright young Navy doctors who did choose the submarine specialty, and those chosen for the nuclear program were put through a study and training curriculum specially designed for them. Rickover had insisted that, at least during the early years of nuclear submarines, nuclear-trained doctors and hospitalmen be assigned to each new ship. This was not primarily because of the nuclear aspects, although that was a consideration, but he knew that the unprecedented long-submergence tours might well raise new situations not yet foreseen. Air quality proved to be one such problem. (Looking back with 20/20 hindsight, we could have learned about this problem sooner, by running the prototype as a fully sealed hull. But frankly we were faced with so many unprecedented questions in the nuclear propulsion plant that we did not think much about other problems that were not our cognizance.)

The nuclear training course for submarine doctors was developed from the existing armed forces radiological defense course. It started with twenty-four weeks at Reed College in Oregon, followed by six weeks of field training at the AEC's plutonium production facilities at Hanford, Washington, then five weeks of special courses at the atomic testing site in Nevada and the Sandia nuclear weapons laboratory in New Mexico. After six weeks of further training at the Walter Reed Laboratory, they reported to a submarine prototype and then to a ship. In all cases, they had already completed their M.D. training and were graduates of the Navy Submarine School in New London. The hospitalmen, who were enlisted men without M.D. degrees, were put through a similar program, but with emphasis on laboratory techniques, radiation monitoring, and the like.

The *Nautilus* had just returned from her dramatic eighty-four-hour, thirteen-hundred-mile submerged shakedown cruise to San Juan, and Ebersole had a problem. His voice had an urgent, serious quality to it as he said, "Admiral, this is Ebersole. The air quality on the submarines is terrible. If we don't do something about it before we go to sea again, we'll never be able to stay submerged for very long."

Rickover asked, "Why? What's wrong?"

"The carbon dioxide scrubbers don't work, and the carbon monoxide burners keep exploding and catching fire. It just isn't habitable. You've got to help us."

Rickover's response was quick and unequivocal: "It's not my responsibility. The conventional machinery section of the bureau is handling it. You know that. Dammit, everybody keeps accusing me of empire building and saying I'm trying to take over the whole ship. Do you really think I need any more responsibility? You think just developing a nuclear power plant is not sufficient challenge for me? Why don't *you* try to expedite the bureau? Get your damned BuMed admirals to work on it. They're the customer." (BuMed was the Navy acronym for Bureau of Medicine and Surgery, sometimes abbreviated BuM&S and irreverently called Bums.)

But Ebersole wouldn't give up. "They won't even talk with us, Admiral. There must be a dozen layers of brass between us and them. Can't you help somehow? It will really interfere with these ships demonstrating their potential if we can't get this fixed."

Rickover knew he couldn't ignore the problem. He thought a minute and then said, "All right. I'll tell you what I'm willing to do. I'll set up a meeting for you to meet with the chief of BuMed and his deputy. They're both physicians. You ought to be able to talk with them. But take Rockwell along, to keep you out of trouble. Dixie: Get me the chief of BuMed."

The meeting took place in the beautiful old BuMed offices, which look down on Constitution Avenue from the hill at 23rd Street. The gracious antebellum decor of the high-ceilinged office of the BuMed chief gave a feeling of unreality and remoteness from the gritty world of ships and machinery. Ebersole brought along another Navy doctor, Richard F. Dobbins, who was soon to relieve Ebersole, who went on to the *Seawolf.* The BuMed chief had his deputy with him. Everyone except me was in immaculate blue uniforms with lots of shiny gold braid. A Navy flag and an American flag were standing on either side of the admiral's large desk, and behind him, the elegantly draped window looked out over the city. The chief expressed his understanding and sympathy in dulcet tones: "I understand your concern about the purity of the atmosphere, gentlemen. You've made it quite clear. But

I think you're overreacting." He turned to his deputy. "Don't you, Doctor?"

The deputy responded quickly. "Oh, definitely, sir. Why, I was reading a research report just the other day that said that CO_2 may not be nearly as harmful as we think. I've forgotten the exact numbers, but the point that impressed me was that the author said they had found no indications of permanent brain damage."

Ebersole was horrified. "Permanent brain damage? Are we talking about permanent brain damage as the standard of safety? You'd better not let the sailors hear about that!"

The deputy was conciliatory. "No, of course not. I just thought the research data would be of interest."

Ebersole took a different tack. "Admiral, the solvent used to scrub the CO_2 out of the air may itself be toxic. The scrubbers are not working right, and the solvent splashes all over the place. It dyes everything a bright purple, so it's easy to see where it's been."

The chief thought he had an answer to that one. "I understood that had been tested."

"Yes, sir. I sent a bottle of it to the medical lab in New London and offered to discuss the problem with them. I heard nothing, and then one day I got a one-page letter saying they had shaved the hair off the backs of four rabbits and painted some solvent on the skin. All four rabbits died, but the letter went on to note that we have no basis for assuming that the results are applicable to humans. That was the test, sir. That's the God's truth. What am I supposed to tell the men with the purple splashes on their uniforms?"

Commander Dobbins spoke up. He had been closely following the *Nautilus* experience and later rode on her historic trip under the North Pole. He said, "The carbon monoxide is also high. The CO burners, which are supposed to prevent buildup of carbon monoxide in the air, get coated with grease fumes from the galley and keep bursting into flames and exploding. And they decompose the freon leaking from the air conditioners, to form hydrofluoric and hydrochloric acid, which corrodes everything. In fact, the freon leakage—which you'd never notice on a surface ship—is a problem, even without the CO burners."

"Why?" asked the chief. "I thought the permissible freon level was quite high."

"It is," replied Dobbins. "The freon itself isn't hazardous at these concentrations. But any hot spot—like a lighted cigarette—breaks it

Lieutenant Commander Rickover boards a water buffalo during a tour of Southeast Asia in 1938 with his wife, Ruth. After her death in 1972, Admiral Rickover arranged with the Naval Institute Press to publish her journal of their tour, which includes her sensitive and insightful reactions to cultures that were soon to change drastically under the influence of war and revolution. (*U.S. Naval Institute*)

With atomic power still a dream, Rickover and his team look at a schematic model of the submarine *Nautilus*. Clockwise, starting with Rickover (*standing*), Robert V. Laney, the author, Robert Panoff, Ethel Weyant, "Dixie" Davis, Harry Mandil, Edwin E. Kintner, and Louis H. Roddis, Jr. Several other key members of the group were not available when the picture was taken. (New York Times)

Above: Alexander Squire, a Westinghouse engineer at the government's Bettis Atomic Power Laboratory, looks over some of the first mass-produced crystal bar zirconium, from which nuclear fuel elements were made for the *Nautilus* prototype reactor. (*Westinghouse*)

Left: The Idaho desert, with the snow-clad Rocky Mountains as a backdrop, forms the setting for the STR Mark I reactor plant, the land prototype for the *Nautilus* submarine propulsion system. (*Westinghouse*)

Workmen putting the finishing touches on the submarine *Nautilus* at the Groton, Connecticut, shipyard of the Electric Boat Division of the General Dynamics Corporation. (*U.S. Navy*)

Inside a large building in the Idaho desert, the submarine hull mock-up pierces the sea tank to provide a realistic, full-scale test facility for the submarine propulsion plant. (*Westinghouse*)

President Dwight D. Eisenhower waves a radioactive wand in Denver, Colorado, to remotely cause a bulldozer at the Shippingport site to dig the first earth and start construction of the facility. (*United Press*)

The site of the Shippingport Atomic Power Station, the world's first commercial atomic power plant, built near Pittsburgh, Pennsylvania, under the direction of Rickover's Naval Reactors group and operated by the Duquesne Light Company. (*Westinghouse*)

Above: The *Nautilus* under way in heavy seas. During her initial sea trials, a running light and some deck planking tore loose, and there was superficial damage to her superstructure (called the "sail"). Under such conditions, sheets of "green water" carry right over the top of the sail, forcing the watch-standers to duck behind the ship's windscreen. (*U.S. Navy*)

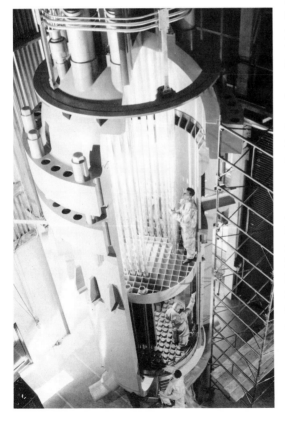

Left: A full-scale model of the Shippingport nuclear reactor vessel. The vessel itself was the largest of its kind ever built—almost 35 feet high, 10 feet in diameter, and 264 tons in weight. (*Westinghouse*)

Crew members man the three stations at the ship's control room, where ship's direction and rate of climb or dive are controlled. (*U.S. Navy*)

The *Skate* bursts out of the Atlantic during early maneuvers. The horizontal bow planes are just coming into view at the front of the ship, and the sonar domes can be seen on the ship's deck. The periscope is up and the sail is nearly surfaced. (R.T. Arnest/© *National Geographic Society*)

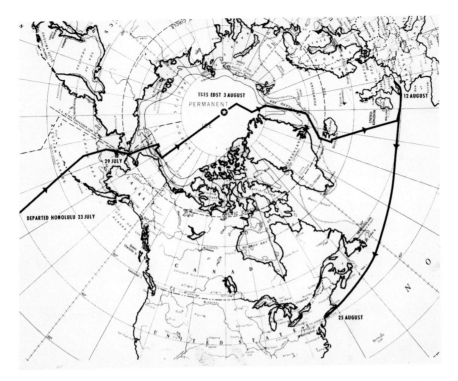

The course of the *Nautilus* as she completed her secret journey to England from Pearl Harbor via the North Pole, followed by a triumphant return to New York. (*U.S. Navy*)

Surface at the Pole! The *Skate* breaks through the ice near the North Pole. (*U.S. Navy*)

Inset: In a midwinter gale, 17 March 1959, *Skate* crew members perform a solemn funeral service near the North Pole for Arctic explorer Sir Hubert Wilkins. By torchlight, they scatter his ashes into the polar night, carrying out a promise made to his widow. (*U.S. Navy/J. F. Calvert*, © *National Geographic Society*)

Rendezvous near the Pole. The *Skate* sailed from her home base in New London, Connecticut, to meet up with the *Seadragon*, sailing from her base in Pearl Harbor. These maneuvers, and others that followed, demonstrated the ability of U.S. nuclear submarines to operate under the ice pack throughout the year, surfacing almost at will, and carrying out all assigned military and scientific missions. (*U.S. Navy*)

The Poseidon missile submarine USS *Sam Rayburn* shows her mighty missile tubes. (*U.S. Navy*)

Above: A Polaris missile, fired from a submerged submarine, bursts from the sea to begin a flawless test flight to a target hundreds of miles away. (*U.S. Navy*)

Left: The two-reactor behemoth *Triton* was launched at Groton, Connecticut, 15 August 1958. Six months later she began her unprecedented voyage around the world submerged. This view of the *Triton* from above shows the astonishing length created by her two independent reactor plants and two engine rooms in series. (*National Archives*)

The *Triton*'s skipper, Captain Edward L. "Ned" Beach, plots the ship's course as she nears completion of her historic voyage around the world submerged. (*U.S. Navy*)

Dr. Edward Teller, noted nuclear physicist, joins Admiral Rickover at the controls of the Polaris submarine USS *Patrick Henry*, after a meeting of the statutory Advisory Committee on Reactor Safeguards was held aboard. (*General Dynamics Corp.*)

The eight-reactor aircraft carrier *Enterprise* under construction at the Newport News Shipbuilding and Dry Dock Company in Newport News, Virginia. (*Newport News Shipbuilding and Dry Dock Company*)

The *Enterprise* under way at full throttle. (*U.S. Navy*)

The *Enterprise* displays her fearful armada of attack aircraft. (*U.S. Navy*)

Four acres of flight deck heels over as the *Enterprise* cavorts like a speedboat. (*U.S. Navy*)

Following page: The *Enterprise* is joined by her nuclear sister ships, the cruiser *Long Beach* (CGN-9) and the guided-missile frigate *Bainbridge* (DLGN-25), now classified as a cruiser. The *Enterprise* crew has lined up on deck to spell out the power behind her speed. (*U.S. Navy*)

Above: Admiral Rickover surrounded by graduates of the 1984 Rickover Science Institute who call themselves Rickoids. The Admiral delivered an inspirational talk to the group and then discussed with each of them individually their plans for the future. (*Center for Excellence in Education*)

Above right: Admiral Rickover addressing students at a high school in Illinois named in his honor. (*National Archives*)

Right: Admiral Rickover with all three living ex-presidents: Jimmy Carter, Gerald Ford, and Richard M. Nixon, at a postretirement party to raise funds for the Admiral's educational foundation. (*United Press*)

Admiral Rickover, some months after retiring at age eighty-two, still managed to exhibit the visionary "can-do" spirit for which he had become famous. (*Eleonore Rickover*)

down into those toxic acids. The cigarette lighters are all corroded, everything brass is turning green . . ."

Ebersole cut in with further specifics. "And the men's throats are always raw and dry, and their eyes burn and are almost glued shut. You can't run a warship under those conditions, Admiral, and you certainly can't run a nuclear power plant either."

The deputy chief had a cheerful thought. "I have a neighbor who is a submariner. Or he was. He's retired now. He told me that they never used to stay submerged overnight. They'd come up each night to charge the batteries. And, of course, this permitted them to completely refresh the air. He said it worked quite nicely."

I had heard all I could take. I arose and said with cold fury, "We are not developing nuclear power plants capable of circling the globe submerged just to have them forced to the surface each night by a lousy air scrubber. Thank you for your time, gentlemen." And I stalked out of the room, hurriedly followed by the two submarine doctors.

We returned to Rickover's office. I described the meeting and added, "It was a disaster, Admiral. I couldn't believe what I was hearing. Have those guys ever been to sea? I mean, since World War I?"

Ebersole wanted to stick to his objective. "Admiral, I know it isn't fair to keep coming back to you with this problem, but I'm sick about it. We just can't send those ships to sea like that. What can we do about it, Admiral? If I knew anyplace else to turn, I would."

Rickover had no problem feeling the doctors' anguish, having submarine experience himself. But he had his own responsibilities to consider. "I've told you, I am not going to take over that development. I'd have the whole damn Navy fighting me, and I don't have any authority. There's no Atomic Energy Commission to back me on this one. But maybe I can do something on the sly." He was suddenly fierce. "If you guys let me be sandbagged on this, I'll never forget it." He sat silently for a moment, then said, "Maybe I could interest old Doc Jackson in getting in on this. He's the guy at the Mine Safety Appliances Company who probably knows more about air purification problems of this kind than anyone else in the world. I'll have him dropped by helicopter onto the *Nautilus*. She's at sea now, testing this stuff, right? I'll have him privately advising me. But I'll tell him not to attract any attention."

The last point was too much for me. I laughed and asked, "Admiral, how do you drop a civilian scientist unexpectedly out of the sky onto a submarine at sea, and not attract any attention? That'll be a neat trick."

But Rickover merely said, "That's his problem. I'll make the arrangements. You guys go now. I'm not making any promises, so just keep your yaps shut."

And in this way Rickover did finally assist in fixing the problem, to the extent that the *Seawolf*, and later the *Nautilus*, performed record-breaking thirty-day fully submerged tests, which highlighted some remaining problems, and before long, Polaris missile submarines were routinely carrying out sixty-day fully submerged patrols.

The Submarine Fleet Reactor Program

On the same day that the *Seawolf* was launched (and over a year and a half before she went to sea), the Electric Boat Company laid the keel for the first of the new Submarine Fleet Reactor (SFR) ships. The *Nautilus* had been at sea only six months, but the new SFR program, as it was called, had an ambitious assignment: to provide a simpler, cheaper, smaller ship design, one that could be built quickly and without a land prototype, based on what we had learned from the *Nautilus*. But the program unexpectedly acquired an additional function. Milt Shaw and Bob Panoff had been trying to get around the problems created by the *Nautilus* shield deck design. That arrangement required a low, horizontal boiler and a number of large penetrations through the shield. Access to the boiler was difficult, and the penetrations created challenging radiation streaming problems. One of the advanced layout concepts that Shaw and Panoff were toying with involved vertical boilers and a shielded tunnel in which personnel could walk through the compartment. The sea around the hull would provide the rest of the shielding.

It was a bold concept and raised many new questions, but the potential advantages were significant. When Shaw and Panoff discussed it with Rickover, he reacted strongly against the new shielding questions, for which answers were not yet available. I too had some problems with it. So both designs were studied on a crash basis, with extensive calculations and physical mockups. Each design offered advantages and drawbacks. So Rickover said, "OK, we'll do both. We'll use the tunnel design for the two SFR boats at Electric Boat. The other yards will have enough trouble just making the old deck design; we won't change that. But Electric Boat can take on the new design."

We were all shocked. The tunnel concept was intended to be a long-range idea, to be explored over the course of developing the next class of submarines. But Rickover insisted that if this was a good idea, then the next class of submarines should use it, and if we were going to commit that many ships to it, we'd better find out now just how well it would work. It was an audacious decision; the keel for the *Skate* had already been laid. Yet less than two years later, the *Skate* was at sea with the new design, and this concept did in fact become the basis for all the fast attack submarines and ballistic missile submarines that followed.

The Role of "NR Reps"

The SFR program also had the burden of developing expertise at additional shipyards, in order to supplement Electric Boat, at that time the only yard experienced in the rigors of nuclear shipbuilding. Two of the SFR boats were to be built at the Portsmouth Naval Shipyard in Maine, and two at the Mare Island Naval Shipyard outside San Francisco. Only the lead ship, the *Skate*, was to be built at Electric Boat.

Rickover was therefore faced with the tremendous task of equipping two new shipyards, government yards at that, to take on a wholly new way of life. He needed officers he could count on, to be his head representatives at each yard. He had to select and train workers in the new features associated with nuclear work: control of radioactivity, high-quality welding and fit-up, surgical-style clean-room procedures for fabricating and assembling reactor system components; and the fundamentals of nuclear science and technology that he insisted be taught to everyone with technical assignments in his program. The senior technical people at Naval Reactors found themselves on lecture duty again, and the interview process for new recruits was stepped up to an even dizzier pace.

Then, during 1956 and 1957, we added more: first, the big private shipyard that had built so many aircraft carriers, the Newport News Shipbuilding and Dry Dock Company in Newport News, Virginia. In addition, Bethlehem Steel Company had a shipyard at Quincy, Massachusetts (later bought up by General Dynamics), and that yard was brought in to help construct and service the anticipated nuclear surface fleet. And in that same period the Ingalls Shipbuilding Corporation at Pascagoula, Mississippi, and then the New York Shipbuilding Corporation in Camden, New Jersey, joined the nuclear club. As the nuclear fleet became an operating reality, we had to maintain, repair, and refuel it, in addition to our construction load. For that purpose, full nuclear training had to be provided to naval shipyards in Pearl Harbor, Hawaii; Charleston, South Carolina; Norfolk, Virginia; and Puget Sound, Washington.

At each of these facilities, Rickover built up an organization that was totally unlike any other "field office," both in philosophy and in practice. It was an extension of his headquarters organization, reporting directly to him, essentially independent of the local staff and management. These field offices were set up not only in the eleven shipyards just named, but also at the Westinghouse Bettis Laboratory near Pittsburgh, the GE Knolls Atomic Power Laboratory near Schenectady, and the three prototype power plant sites at Arco, Idaho; West Milton, New York; and Windsor, Connecticut. And, of course, there was one at the Shippingport Atomic Power Station.

At the *private* shipyards, such as Electric Boat and Newport News, Rickover assigned a representative, whose function (legally) was to be an observer, and whose power to change things derived from Rickover's clout based on his AEC and BuShips responsibilities. At the *naval* shipyards, such as Portsmouth and Mare Island, which were owned and operated by the government, Rickover installed a nuclear power superintendent, who had line authority in the yard and directed the work of hundreds of people. Although this person reported to supervision in the shipyard organization, Rickover obtained the right to file concurrent fitness reports, which assured that Rickover would be listened to. Later, as the number of nuclear shipyards grew, Rickover felt that he should not continue to recruit and train people for these positions, and he urged the yards to undertake this responsibility. He then no longer filed concurrent fitness reports, and although he still had the right to concur in the selection of the nuclear power superintendent, he added an "NR rep" to the yard, just as he had done in the private shipyards.

The Naval Reactors field offices varied considerably in size and character. The offices at Bettis and Knolls had a formal office manager, several dozen engineers, and some fiscal and contract specialists, while at some of the shipyards there was only one senior officer and a few young assistants in training.

One such "NR rep" was John W. "Jack" Crawford, Jr., who was sent to the Newport News shipyard in 1957, when the yard was scrambling to begin work on three very different kinds of ships: an attack submarine, a ballistic missile submarine, and the first nuclear-powered aircraft carrier *Enterprise*, along with her land prototype plant in Idaho.

Newport News had never built a submarine, and *nobody* had ever built a nuclear-powered surface ship. Crawford had served on a Newport News–built ship, the carrier *Yorktown*, during the Battle of Midway, and he was looking forward to his assignment. A Naval Academy graduate, he had earned his master's degree at the naval construction and engineering course at MIT, was experienced in submarine construction, and had been selected by Rickover as one of the first two officers to take the master's-level nuclear engineering course he had arranged there.

"I'm not going to tell you how to do the job, Crawford," said the Admiral. "Just remember who writes your fitness reports. You are to represent me. Your function is to see that Naval Reactors gets what it asks for. Don't worry about my understanding the contractor's problems; he'll have plenty of people carrying out that function. You are to observe what's happening and report in detail. But you're not just a reporter. You are to make things happen. If it's not being done right, get it changed. If you can't, then tell me."

Crawford had seven years' experience and training in the NR program before going to Newport News, so he understood the point of the Admiral's brief message. He was soon presented with an opportunity to apply this understanding. Studying the company's organization, he saw that there was no group whose function it was to monitor and provide quality assurance, independently of the production people. This situation was standard at shipyards at that time, but Crawford knew that it would not suffice for nuclear work. He recommended to the executive vice president that an independent quality assurance group be set up, but the VP replied that there were already too many people reporting to him. Crawford therefore went to the president of the company, who told him that the company's shipbuilding superintendent would never permit a shipyard inspector aboard one of "his" ships.

Crawford had now initiated the classic NR rep procedure: he had discovered the need for an unprecedented action, had suggested it, and had been rebuffed. Now he would see if he had the backing he needed to do his job. He informed Rickover of the situation. On his next trip to the yard, Rickover quietly but firmly told the executive VP that Naval Reactors experience showed the need for an independent quality assurance group, and agreement was quickly reached that one would be set up. To its credit, once agreement was reached, the company set up an effective organization and put one of its strongest young managers in charge.

As the size and complexity of Rickover's wide-flung operation grew, the ground rules for running an effective field office became clearer, although by no means easier. Certain principles were inviolate. For example, although the field rep was to tell the contractor when things were wrong, he was not to tell him what to do about it; that would tend to relieve the contractor of his legal responsibilities. The NR rep and his spouse were not to socialize, in any manner however trivial, with the contractor's people. That would tend to make him an excuse-maker rather than a doer. On a given day of the week, every week without fail, he was to report to Rickover by telephone. If he had no problems, the Admiral might just listen and hang up without comment. But if that happened very often, the Admiral might conclude that the NR rep wasn't looking hard enough. And every week, the rep was to turn in a written report on the week's problems, appending to it reports by each of his assistants. He was not to read any of his assistants' reports until they were complete and signed. He could not change them, but in his own report he could take issue with any of the points raised by his people. Rickover would then scribble his own comments in the margins and pass these letters to appropriate people in the headquarters office.

Once a year Rickover brought in his senior representatives, from Pearl Harbor, Hawaii, to Kittery, Maine, to compare notes and exchange battle stories and lessons learned. One document that always surfaced at these meetings was a memorandum the Admiral had written to Craw-ford and the other field reps in the earliest days of field operations. It was entitled "Responsibilities of NRB Representatives at Field Offices," where NRB stood for Naval Reactors Branch. It had become a classic, and it was frequently quoted when arguments arose between Naval Reactors and one of the field reps:

> It is amazing to me [wrote Admiral Rickover] how officers new to these positions uniformly get themselves into the frame of mind where they conceive of themselves as intermediaries between NRB and the contractor; that is, that their job is to judge who is right—NRB or the contractor, and then to make the decision on their own, in many cases not even notifying NRB. In this way the NRB representative becomes, in effect, NRB's boss. Subtle pressures by a contractor such as making the NRB representative feel that he is "good" and that *he* really

understands the local problems and NRB does not, contribute to this feeling of euphoria and omniscience . . .

Another and more serious mistake arises when the NRB representative decides what he should or should not report to me. Frequently he decides not to report things to me because he feels he can handle the matter better himself; he is afraid that by notifying me of this situation (which *is* his job), I will take ignorant, improper action and upset the "apple cart." Here again, the NRB representative, instead of *representing* me, has become my *judge* . . .

Frequently you must sit back and judge the *contractor* and his performance. Minor events or troubles are frequently clues that show up deficiencies in contractor management, in organization, in ability of personnel, in practices. This will require a great deal of clear thought, but can result in great improvements in the . . . performance of NRB business. Let me know, promptly, of observations such as this.

To achieve the status of a true NRB representative requires the acquisition of God-like qualities; but you can try.

When technical purchasing offices were established for the Westinghouse and GE Naval Reactors programs, a different sort of representational function was thereby established, and an appropriate memo was written defining that function:

An Agent, though selected for a particular task, has no authority beyond the direction and approval of his principal. An Agent's very existence is at the pleasure of his principal, who may always choose a different Agent or elect to act for himself. An Agent has no life expectancy, and deserves none, except as the excellence and loyalty of his performance for the principal induce a preference in the principal's mind toward continuing the relationship.

Rickover Decides to "Deal Officially"

As the scope of the Naval Reactors program grew explosively, the problem of assuring that an adequate number of properly trained personnel would be available at each new site became acute. Rickover and his people took extraordinary measures to alleviate this situation. For example, well in advance of assigning the Newport News shipyard any work on the nuclear aircraft carrier prototype, and with no contractual obligation or mechanism to work with the company, Rickover nevertheless arranged for a carefully selected cadre of its best engineers to attend the Oak Ridge school. These people were all interviewed by NR and were the cream of the crop. Upon completion of the course, this group became the core around which a nuclear power organization and a training program were established within the company. Working closely with the Westinghouse-Bettis engineers, outside the routine shipyard environment, this group was allowed to play a significant role in the design of the aircraft carrier prototype plant in Idaho, an arrangement that benefited both parties and the program as a whole.

Still, Rickover saw that this training would not suffice to give Newport News the experience it would need to build the world's first nuclear-powered aircraft carrier. Accordingly, he arranged for some thirty of the shipyard's foremost construction managers and foremen to be sent to Idaho and assigned key roles there. Such training and experience were literally unavailable anyplace else. As other shipyard needs arose, Rickover made special arrangements to deal with them. For example, Newport News had never operated a nuclear facility and thus had no experience from which to draw or any test engineers trained for such systems. Rickover eased this situation by arranging for several of the company's engineers to be sent to other shipyards already engaged in nuclear work, to be integrated right into the host yards' nuclear plant test organizations.

Rickover expected, of course, that such unprecedented assistance on his part would be matched by full cooperation from shipyard management. Generally speaking, it was. But there was one important exception. When Newport News was assigned its first nuclear submarine, it was agreed that the company would set up a project-type organization, and that Rickover would be consulted on the choice of project manager. The shipyard named one, and Rickover declined to approve. When the shipyard remained adamant, Rickover responded with a stroke of remarkable simplicity. He informed the shipyard that thenceforth, on nuclear submarine matters he would deal with them "officially." Crawford was informed of this decision as he was about to leave for duty as NR rep at Newport News. He did not understand the significance of the decision, and he asked the Admiral about it.

"It means," said Rickover, "that NR will do all that is required by the contract, answer all their correspondence, but offer no assistance beyond that."

The message was clear: Cooperation beyond normal contractual obligations was a two-way street. The shipyard had chosen to stick to its rights, and Rickover was going to stick to his. Who could object to a government official operating on a strictly official basis?

The shipyard tried to work under these conditions for about six months. While the carrier work went forward on schedule, the submarine work languished. Finally, the executive VP took the initiative and offered to reopen the project manager issue. Agreement was quickly reached on one of the shipyard's very best engineers. Rickover immediately provided the fullest measure of informal but crucial support. He arranged for a team of top managers to visit Electric Boat and be shown all they could absorb about managing a nuclear submarine construction program—a uniquely valuable education that could not have been obtained in any other way. Electric Boat would certainly not have volunteered to jump-start a new competitor in this way if EB had not had the same kind of full cooperation agreement with Rickover to which Newport News had objected.

Quaker Meetings on Sycamore Island

Rickover insisted on analyzing every problem from fundamentals, rather than doing what most of us do: looking around to see how other people handle similar problems. He was willing to learn from others, but he did not shun the hard task of thinking things through for himself. As the nature of the program changed, he continually looked for ways to improve his operations. We underlings were all yammering at him about a variety of complaints, but we seldom took time to address the fundamentals of how we should be operating.

In the spring of 1951, hostility and distrust were beginning to build up between Naval Reactors and its new partner, the Bettis laboratory run by Westinghouse. Efforts to pin the blame for this only exacerbated the problem, so Rickover called for a "Quaker Meeting." "Do you know what I mean by that?" he asked. Without waiting for an answer, he continued: "The Quakers have an excellent approach to thinking through difficult problems, where a number of intelligent and responsible people must work together. They meet as equals, and anyone who has an idea speaks up. There are no parliamentary procedures and no coercion from the Chair. They continue the discussion until unanimity is reached. I want you guys to do that. Get in a room with no phones and leave orders that you are not to be disturbed. And sit there until you can deal with each other as individuals, not as spokesmen for either organization."

He sent Ray Dick, Bob Panoff, and Eli Roth to deal with three senior Bettis engineers, one of whom he named chairman. It took ten days to get past the barriers, but the process finally worked. You could not pin down what did it, but all agreed that things were permanently changed for the better after that. Rickover tried the process again in 1952, with the GE people at the Knolls Laboratory. Dick and Panoff joined Robert V. Laney, to bring the Bettis experience into play, but there never seemed to be the same degree of trust, and the process was abandoned after a few meetings. Relations between NR and Knolls grew steadily worse. It was a long time before a reasonably satisfactory environment was developed.

Some time after that, Rickover decided to try the process at home. This time he was concerned not with hostilities and mistrust, but with the broader issue of how we could improve our way of operating. He called in a few of his senior people and said that he wanted us to get together, including some of his field reps, and have a Quaker Meeting. "Go somewhere with no phones and stay two or three days. Then give me a report of your conclusions. Do you have someplace you can go? Don't go where there are kids or dogs. Someplace isolated."

Panoff spoke up. "I'm a member of the Sycamore Island Canoe Club. It's on a completely isolated island, no phones, in the middle of the Potomac River. The only way to get to it is to pull on a rope, which rings a bell on the island, and a guy pulls a raft across, hand over hand on the rope, and carries you back to the island the same way. Except for this caretaker, there's almost never anyone there during the week."

"Jesus! How long does it take to get there? Six weeks?"

"No, sir. It's just six miles from downtown. We can get there in half an hour."

"OK, go."

"What's the question, Admiral? What are we trying to answer?"

"Dammit, that's what you're trying to find out! We're working on all the questions we've identified. What ones have we missed? Getting the right questions is harder—and more important—than getting answers. Now go!"

So we went, and swam, and talked, and ate sandwiches, and surprisingly some useful ideas came out of it. The Admiral didn't always buy all our recommendations, but the mere process of unstructured talk among ourselves proved to be valuable. We did it several times.

The Rickover Conference

As he did for everything else, Rickover had his own approach to the traditional business meeting or conference. I remember finding that out the hard way. (*Is there any other way, with Rickover?* I wondered.) Rickover called me in one day and asked to see the conclusions of a certain meeting with the Bettis people. "Admiral, we haven't had that meeting yet," I said. "That's scheduled for Thursday."

"I know that," he snapped. "Let me see the conclusions."

"That's why we're going to have the meeting, Admiral. To try to reach some conclusions," I said, ingenuously.

"Dammit, that's why everyone else is going to the meeting," said Rickover. "*You're* supposed to be going to achieve certain clearly defined objectives. They should be written out in advance and discussed with me and other appropriate people here before you go. If you can't do that, you shouldn't go. How will you know if you've accomplished what you wanted to, if you haven't defined your objectives in advance? You'll end up agreeing to somebody else's objectives without realizing the implications of what you've done. Dammit, Rockwell, you sure are naive."

One incidental benefit flowed from the practice of defining objectives in advance. I found that if I started the discussion down the desired road, I could often hold back during most of the ensuing discussion and let other participants bloody themselves trying to win objectives that happened to match mine. As the discussion began to wind down, I would see how many of my objectives had not yet been achieved by the efforts of others. I would then speak up, and since I had not fought over many of the previous bitter battles, the others were often more inclined to give me a point or two, in the spirit of fair play.

Another unwritten Rickover Rule for Conferences was that no one left a meeting until the Conclusions and Actions sections of the conference report had been written out at the conference table and agreed to, even if that meant missing your plane and staying overnight. The NR representative always prepared the meeting report. The Introduction and the Discussion sections could be written later. But the Conclusions had to be agreed to by all participants. In those rare cases when one or more participants would not agree with the majority position, the dissenting view was spelled out and attributed to the appropriate party. The Action section was always written in the form of agreed commitments by named parties to do certain things by stated dates.

This laborious ritual seemed unreasonable to me until I'd been through it a few times. But I soon discovered the value of it. Sometimes a meeting would go smoothly, with little argument, and writing the Conclusions seemed to be a needless formality. After all, there was agreement all around. But when it came time to write the Conclusions, it was amazing to discover that there was not so much agreement after all. And sometimes the Conclusions went fairly smoothly but then had to be rewritten when it was found that there was no mutual understanding as to who was committed to what action. I learned to leave more and more time for this little formality of pinning down exactly what was agreed to and who was going to do what.

The more I observed the psychodynamics of meetings, the more I realized the value of having thought through in advance the possible outcomes and their implications, and of having discussed these possibilities with others before the meeting. I then knew the importance of winning certain points and the implications of yielding on others, and I thereby avoided a number of problems that might not have been otherwise apparent.

MANNING THE SHIPS

> *A frank and perceptive editorial in a recent Dupont publication, entitled "The Great Talent Search," remarks wryly that in competing for qualified professional men, business is handicapped since the only incentive it has to offer is money, whereas professional and academic life provide many intangible incentives. It is but a short step from recognition by business that there are other than monetary incentives to the realization that it, too, can provide such incentives.*
>
> *American businessmen are noted for their ingenuity. They could, I am sure, educate their management people to understand that it isn't good business to pay for professional services and then downgrade all one's bright young men to routine technicians.*
>
> H.G.R.

Rickover interviewed *every* officer, and a large fraction of the enlisted men and civilians, who came into his program. Just before he retired, he estimated that he had personally interviewed more than five thousand Naval Academy midshipmen, in addition to civilian candidates and naval personnel from other sources. At first these were all for technical billets, involved in developing the propulsion systems. But the time came, surprisingly soon, when he had to think about manning the ships. While the SFR ships were still on the drawing boards, Rickover started making plans to recruit crews to operate them. It was his intention to take an entirely original approach to this task (as he did to everything else). Not only did he intend to have most of the crew, including all of the officers, assigned to the ship for the last year of construction, learning every detail and giving their input to the shipbuilder before it was too late. But before reporting to the shipyard, the prospective skippers were to spend six months to a year, or even more, in Rickover's headquarters offices, learning directly from his people there and contributing to the writing of operating and maintenance manuals, and in other places where their ship operating experience would be valuable. Each submarine officer picked to interview for this opportunity had a unique and memorable experience.

The Rickover Interview System

The day of a typical interview was just another day for Naval Reactors, but to the prospective commanding officer (PCO) involved, it was wild and crazy and, considering that his career was on the line, a bit scary. There were other persons awaiting interview, but he seemed to be the only interviewee over twenty-one, and certainly the only one with any real naval experience. From what he could overhear of it, Captain Dunford's address to the young candidates went about as follows:

"According to your records, you people are all very bright. Top 5 to 10 percent in your class. You've also been recommended to us as having exceptional character and drive. You have all been, or soon will be, interviewed by at least three of Rickover's engineers for technical aptitude. What we don't know yet is whether you have any common sense. You're about to be interviewed by Admiral Rickover. Some of his questions will surprise you. But I advise you not to put on an act or try to bluff. We've put in a lot of work selecting each one of you and getting you this far in the process. Don't blow it now."

One of the youngsters was trying to make a show of bravado about the whole thing. "What's so special about this program? I'd never even heard of it till they ordered me down here for interview. Then I asked around and got all these scary stories. Sounds like it would be easier to be a test pilot or an underwater demolition expert. I mean, who wants to take all this crap just to be assigned to some kooky research program for God knows how many years?"

Dunford's answer was blunt. "Well, you're here now. If you want to have a career anywhere in the Navy, you'd better figure out how to get through the next few hours with your butt intact."

Dunford went out of the room for a while, and then the stories started. Each of the interviewees vied to see who could tell the most outlandish and terrifying story he had heard about the Rickover interviews. It was like kids telling ghost stories around the campfire.

"The story I like," began one youngster, "is about the guy who had been boning up on the Admiral's methods and decided he wanted guys who were really tough and hard on people. So when The Man asked him how he would run things, he said he would rule with an iron hand. 'Oh,' says the Admiral innocently. 'Maybe you can help me. I've got this one employee who is very good, but he insists on running his private life without regard for the job. I'll let you talk to him.' Now the poor boob knew he'd been sandbagged, but he couldn't do anything at this point. The Admiral had already called in his toughest project officer, and he asks him, 'What do you do after work?' 'None of your damn business,' snaps the project officer, and the Admiral turns to the guy and says, 'What do you say to him?' The poor guy just wilted, and the Admiral says, 'Get out of here, you fool.' "

Another interviewee asked timorously, "Do you suppose he primes his guys for that kind of stuff? How did the project officer know what to say?"

"I gather they don't. Apparently the Admiral just has enough confidence in his knowledge of human behavior to count on how they're going to respond."

"Yeah, but I hear that every now and then it backfires on him. I heard that one time he was trying to impress some big shot with how dedicated all his people are, and he calls in this one guy—Eagle Scout and all that stuff. So he tells this guy, the employee, 'Tell Mr. So-and-So why you came to work here.' And of course the employee didn't have any idea what was going on, so he just played it straight. He said, 'Gee, Admiral, they were about to draft me!' I guess the Admiral wouldn't get any thrill out of these things if he rigged it all ahead of time. I figure he looks at it as a way to keep sharpening his practical knowledge of human behavior under pressure. You can't learn that from a book."

At that point Dunford returned, beckoned to a nervous, slightly overweight candidate, and they went together to Rickover's office. As they went in, the Admiral asked the candidate to wait in the outer office a minute, then turned to Dunford and yelled, "You've been coaching these kids!"

"No, Admiral . . ."

The Admiral ignored his protest and continued, "Look! They all have excellent resumes, and they're supposed to have some spunk and some sense to boot. And you people are supposed to have checked out their practical technical smarts. So what I'm trying to find out is how they will behave under pressure. Will they lie, or bluff, or panic, or wilt? Or will they continue to function with some modicum of competence and integrity? I can't find that out with routine questions. I've only got a few minutes with each one, half an hour at most. I've got to shake 'em up. That's the only way I'll know. So don't undercut me when I'm trying to do something. Don't you dare substitute your judgment for mine. If you've got a squawk, spill it. But don't undertake to change my approach without telling me. Now bring in the kid."

Dunford went to Rickover's outer office and returned with the candidate. The Admiral began brusquely. "Sit down. How much overweight are you?"

"Overweight? Well, yes, sir, I guess I am a little . . ."

"How much, dammit? Can't you answer a simple, direct question? How much?"

"Perhaps fifteen pounds, sir."

"Looks more like twenty to me. Call it twenty."

"Yes, sir."

"How long would it take to get that off?"

"You mean if I really worked at it? I . . ."

"Dammit, if you can't answer my questions, I'm going to throw you out of here. How long?"

"I guess I could do it in six weeks, sir. But . . ."

"I want you to start on that immediately. And send me a written report each week, telling me your progress. Not a lot of excuses. Just how you're making out on this project. Understand?"

"Well, yes, sir, but . . ."

"Look, you're wasting my time. Do you want to work here or not?"

"Yes, sir, I think so. But I have some questions I'd like to go over first."

"You take care of your weight problem first. Then we'll talk. That will be all. Dunford, you stay. Dixie, note in your calendar that this man will be submitting a report to me every Monday for six weeks." He turned to Dunford. "Is that the last one?"

"No, sir, we have three more."

"Damn, did you change that on me? I thought we were finished."

"No, sir, you got tied up in that long meeting. We've been ready for you."

"Well, we'll have to bring them back first thing in the morning. Damn, I hate to be in that position. People will think I did it deliberately, to haze them. I have a meeting tonight, but I'll be back in the morning. That first kid this morning; I liked him."

"Medeiros? He wasn't as good scholastically, Admiral. But he had some very good references, and we thought he had some fire to him."

"He's like me. He's just dumb enough to know he has to use his wits. Most of these young punks are so damn smart they're used to getting by without thinking and without working. That can be dangerous. Particularly with nuclear power. Most of these kids you've been bringing in are real zombies. How did we make out today?"

"If you buy Medeiros, that's two. Out of ten."

"That's not bad. Better than we used to do."

"Admiral, it's terrible. You have no idea how much effort we put into locating and evaluating those other eight. Not to mention the hours senior people here put into each one of them. Three hours per candidate, twenty-four hours today, just here at the office, after we got them in. Now it's all down the drain, and we have to find and evaluate eight more."

"That's the price we have to pay. There's nothing we do that's as important."

"I guess it isn't so serious for the kids just graduating, but for the submarine officers it can wreck their careers. It means they'll never serve on a nuclear submarine. Before long it will mean they're barred from submarines. Doesn't that bother you even a little bit?"

"Sure, it bothers me. Lots of things bother me. I read about a little kid getting hit by a drunken driver. Damn shame. But I'm not in charge of the universe. I'm not even in charge of the Navy. I only have this lousy little corner of the world that hardly anybody else knows about. But it's responsibility enough, and I aim to do it as well as I can. Somebody else has to worry about all the rest of the world. Besides, some of these bastards need a little shaking up."

"Admiral, you can turn a guy down without grinding his face in the mud . . . OK, let that drop. Did you know we've been getting some static from engineering professors and deans about the technical questions we ask? They claim that since they send us graduates in the top ranks of good schools, that should be ample proof that they know the technical stuff. They don't see how we can turn down some of their smartest people on the basis of a few short interviews."

"How do you answer that?"

"Rockwell and Panoff sat down with a couple of deans and professors, and showed them the kind of questions we asked. They had to admit that their students should be able to answer such questions. But Admiral, all this emphasis on personnel and training is a terrific drain on us. You wouldn't believe how much time goes into it. It just isn't efficient use of all this high-powered technical talent you've recruited. Not to mention your own time."

"Efficiency isn't the objective, Dunford, effectiveness is. Don't confuse effectiveness with efficiency. I'm convinced that the only way to be effective, to make a difference in the real world, is to put ten times as much effort into everything as anyone else thinks is reasonable. It doesn't leave any time for golf or cocktails, but it gets things done."

"I understand what you're saying. But it sure looks like the hard way."

"What's the alternative, Dunford?"

"You know the answer to that, Admiral. Anybody else would put a bid in to the Bureau of Personnel for so many lieutenants, and in due course BuPers would serve up that many warm bodies. They would all have the right qualifications—on paper—and would probably carry out their assignments with normal Navy effectiveness. This system has proved to be good enough to run a worldwide fleet and win all the wars we've been in. And all of us technical types could concentrate on trying to build a nuclear submarine."

"And *you* know why I don't do that. If I had done it, none of you guys would be here. Not only would the regular system send us mediocre people, but they would insist on rotating them out of here in a year or two. Before they've even learned anything. You guys may not realize it, but you're here for life."

"If that word gets out, Admiral, you'll never get good people into the program. They know it would wreck their careers to stay in one place."

"We'll have to change that too. Now get out of here. I've got to catch a plane."

Rickover pulled over a stack of forms from his table and started stuffing them into his already bulging briefcase. Dunford looked at them and asked, "Admiral, aren't those the fitness reports and civil service promotion forms for your employees? I've been over all those. So have their group leaders here. You don't have to waste your time on all that bureaucratic crap. That's just clerical stuff."

"Dunford, these forms determine whether these people get promoted and get more pay. I can assure you, none of these people would agree with you that their personnel forms aren't important."

"Admiral, I can't figure you out. You just washed eight guys down the drain with the back of your hand, and now you're going to spend hours on the plane tonight to make a possible small difference in somebody else's career. How come?"

"These are *my* people. That's the difference. Dunford, did you ever really look at the kind of people I've brought in here?"

"Yes, sir, of course. And I've heard people from industry and from research laboratories say that this organization has the highest concentration of bright young engineering talent in the country."

"You still don't get it. Our senior scientist has a master's degree in electrical engineering and a Ph.D. in physics. But he is also an ordained Orthodox rabbi, and highly devout. He has spent many a twenty-four-hour day in an airport because the sun had started to set on a Friday and his religion forbade his traveling. Our senior metallurgist is so highly regarded by the Mormon church that I'm afraid they're going to pull him out of here for a top position in Salt Lake City someday. One of our chemical engineers is a leader in the Church of the Savior, a particularly respected evangelical church here in town. And now I've had a request from one of our people for six weeks off so that he may make the pilgrimage to Mecca required by his faith. These are very spiritual people. They're not just technicians; they are highly developed human beings."

And he headed out the door, as Dunford walked pensively down the hall to ask the PCO to come back the next morning.

The PCO Interview

The PCO did not have long to wait the next morning. He had just started a cup of coffee when Dunford led him into a little office, and there he was interviewed successively by three of Rickover's senior technical people, some of whom had come in from out of town for the purpose. He was surprised by the breadth and scope of the technical questions, but he had little time to think or complain about it, because Dunford was back to take him down the hall to Rickover's office. As he walked silently, he thought, *He'll probably apologize to me for yesterday, and I can be real gracious about it. He owes me one, right?* But he knew the answer to that.

He was ushered into the Admiral's inner office and found that it looked just as he had heard it described. Perhaps even more so. The walls and the ceiling, and even the back of the door, were covered with perforated soundproofing Celotex tile. The floor was beat-up and bare, with a couple of small sheet-metal patches apparently covering up knot-holes. (In fact, one of the patches covered a bullet hole, put there inad-vertently by a jealous husband shooting wildly at his wife in the office below.) The Admiral's desk, table, chair, and bookcases were all used, well-worn, government-issue, civil-servant-clerical decor. Absolutely no sign of rank or pomp. The bookcases were full, with books piled horizontally on top of books vertically shelved. More books, articles, and reports lay on the table and in casual piles on the floor. Models, test specimens, and unlabeled samples cluttered the room. Several unhung pictures were standing against the bookcases, and on the walls were two quotations. One read, "Heaven Is Blest with Perfect Rest, But the Blessing of Earth Is Toil." The other reminded the reader, "Our doubts are traitors / And make us lose the good we oft might win / By fearing to attempt." Rickover's secretary came in from time to time, to pick up a paper, to leave a memo, or to hand him a note. The PCO had never seen anything quite like it.

Dunford introduced him to the Admiral, who motioned for them both to sit down and then asked, "Where did you stand in your class?"

"Second, sir, out of a class of 1,041." The PCO was pretty proud of that. The interview was off to a good start.

But Rickover was shouting at him. "Did I ask you how many are in your class?"

He was rattled by this turn in the discussion. "No, sir, but . . ."

"Just answer the questions, dammit!"

"Yes, sir."

"Do you think I don't know, or couldn't find out, if I gave a damn, how many people are in your class? Do you?"

"No, sir."

"What's that supposed to mean? You don't know?"

"No, sir, I . . ." (*How did this thing get out of control,* he thought. *He's got me defending something I don't give a damn about.*)

"Forget it." Rickover shouted to his secretary in the outer office, "Dixie, get Rockwell up here. On the double."

"Yes, sir."

"Now tell me," said Rickover to the PCO, "why were you only number two? Why weren't you number one? Did you always give your very best effort? Always? Tell me."

"Well, I suppose not always, sir. I . . ."

He was interrupted as I came bursting in the door. "Yes, sir?"

"Rockwell, tell this turkey where you stood in your class." He turned to the PCO. "That's at Princeton, a *good* engineering school. Not that elite boys' school in Annapolis. Well, tell him."

"I stood about where you did, sir. About a fifth of the way down."

"You weren't number one?"

"No, sir. Sorry."

"That will be all."

The PCO was now convinced that Rickover would be mad as hell and take it out on him. But he hadn't seen anything yet. Dixie came back in with a piece of paper and handed it to the Admiral. He glanced at it, wadded it up, and threw it in the wastebasket. He then picked up the phone and screamed into it with a volume and intensity that the PCO had never heard from another human being:

"You damn fool! I spent months straightening out that situation down there, and in two weeks you've got it all screwed up again . . . No, no, that's not . . . You don't even know what I'm talking about, do you? You what? No, you didn't tell me. Look, I've told all you guys a thousand times: Don't use that line 'I thought you knew.' It's your business to see that I know. That's why I require weekly written reports from every field rep. And I tell all you guys, Don't bother me with the good news. And I tell you to phone me anytime in between. Have I ever refused to talk with you? . . . Well, you know why that was. But any other time? No, dammit. So there's no excuse for holding back bad news. Now get into this at once, and get back to me. I *know* it will be late. Call me at home if I'm not here. You'd better start getting on top of things down there. You're not running it. So what time do you get up in the morning? . . . Well, try getting up an hour earlier. Look, if those people are getting behind on their commitments to you, send me a memo with the facts, and I'll send them one of my Friday telegrams. That'll wreck their weekend. And another thing: You and your people must stop fraternizing with the shipyard people . . . The hell you're not! Don't go to dinner with them. Your wives must not get friendly with their wives. You're not even to let your dogs get friendly with their dogs. Understand? Look, when you do that, you become one of *them.* You're just another shipyard employee. You don't represent me anymore; you represent them. You develop great sympathy for their problems. They've already got enough people making excuses for them. Look, they treat you with great respect, so you think they like you. Don't you realize, you fool, they do that because you represent money to them. Money, that's all. If you didn't represent the money I can give them—or take away from them—they wouldn't piss on you if you were on fire. Dammit, I've told you all this before. When are you going to start paying attention?" And he slammed down the phone.

During this tirade, Rickover had stood up; his face was flushed, and he was pounding on the table so hard that he bounced one of the metal samples off onto the floor. The PCO was sure that it would take him hours to recover his composure. And he—the PCO—would pay the price. He was mad at himself for not being able to deal with the situation earlier, although it was obviously a skewed one. He felt that his career in submarines was over, one more victim of the Rickover interview. But the Admiral had now turned and was addressing him in a surprisingly gentle voice.

"I just asked you: Why not the best? Why did you not always give of your best? Wait, I want you to think very hard on that question. Don't go away, I want to talk with you again. Dunford, leave me alone until I call you. I've got some phone calls to make."

Dunford led the PCO out of the office, and they sat in the outer office without saying anything for quite a while. Finally, Rickover called them back in again, and after some interaction, the content of which he could never recall, the PCO was dismissed and returned home, completely dejected. He had been asked to name some books and authors he had read during the last two years. "Not anything you've read in the last month. That doesn't count; you knew you were coming down here." This was an unexpected opportunity. He had read a lot, and some pretty good books too. But now his mind was a complete blank. He fumbled through his mind and finally remembered one book, but not the author. Rickover had responded merely, "Goodbye."

When the PCO got home, he recited the disaster to his wife, and she encouraged him to look through his own library, which had many of the books he had read. He did so, and he managed to recall twenty-four of them. *This is probably a waste of time*, he thought, *but I can't let it drop here. He'll think the whole submarine force is a bunch of illiterates.* So he wrote a brief note to the Admiral and enclosed the list. A few days later he received a call from Dunford, asking him how soon he could report to Naval Reactors for duty.

When he reported in to Naval Reactors, the PCO was given a desk but no assignment of work or responsibility. He watched the others, who always seemed to be on a dead run, and he knew they all had very specific responsibilities and deadlines. After a couple of days he braved facing Rickover again, reminded him that he was aboard, and asked what the Admiral wished him to do. The reply was brief and calm. "Well, why don't you start out by writing me a memorandum proposing what you might do for the next few weeks."

That was clearly the end of that communication, and the PCO left with a hearty "Yes, sir." He was baffled at first; nothing in his naval career had prepared him for this. But he had to admit it was a wise and reasonable response to his question. In fact, as he thought about it, he liked the idea. He talked with Panoff, Dunford, and me, and came up with a program that included several weeks at the Mark I prototype, plus time at Bettis and Electric Boat, and a review of the records of the history of the program and the operating reports of the *Nautilus*. And, of course, an extensive curriculum of self-study of the technical subjects needed for an understanding of the plant. Rickover approved the program without change, and the PCO soon found himself swept up in the brisk pace of the Naval Reactors group.

"My Hero"

There were some other PCOs aboard, and they were startled one day to receive a memo from the Admiral addressed simply "Heroes." They found out that this was Rickover's new title for PCOs, and other memos so addressed arrived from time to time. Whether a PCO had been overheard telling stories of war patrols to an entranced secretary, or just what, they never found out. But the Admiral didn't stop there. He had on his staff a pretty young WAVE officer named Sally Higgins who had considerable talent as a singer, a fact that inevitably became known to Rickover. The Admiral asked her to sing a song for him, which she did, and he then remarked, "I don't deserve any more of this tribute, but I have some real heroes down the hall. I would like it very much if you would drop in on them and sing 'My Hero.' "

Ms. Higgins agreed to do so, and the Admiral added, "Of course, one should remove his or her shoes in the presence of heroes, and I assume you will do that." The song was performed, barefoot as requested, and became a periodic ritual, apparently whenever Rickover felt it was needed. After a while, however, the submariners decided to provide a little guerrilla theater of their own. When Ms. Higgins began her song of homage, the officers rolled up their pant legs to about knee height, a widely recognized signal that the flattery has been poured on so deep as to take on a different odor. They were in that stance when the Admiral dropped by. He got the message, and there were no further lyric tributes.

INTO THE ARCTIC

> *Everything new endangers something old. A new machine replaces human hands; a new source of power threatens old businesses; a new trade route wipes out the supremacy of old ports and brings prosperity to new ones. This is the price which must be paid for progress and it is worth it.*
>
> H.G.R.

Geopoliticians have long eyed the Arctic Ocean as a potentially strategic battleground. Unlike Antarctica, which is mostly Precambrian bedrock fifteen to twenty-five miles thick, covered with solid sheet ice over a mile thick, the Arctic region is all ocean, five times the area of the Mediterranean Sea, covered with floating chunks of ice varying greatly in size and thickness, with occasional gaps of open water. Thus, naval strategists have also been drawn to study this little-known area, lying so close to China and Russia. The fifteen-hundred-mile missiles then being developed for submarine use could reach only parts of Russia, and then from only a few dangerously close and well-defended waters. But from the Arctic, most of the Russian heartland was within reach. Admiral Rickover had said, "Because it is able to hide and even lie still against sonar, the atomic missile submarine cannot be easily traced by the enemy. Search radar would be helpless against it. The enemy would be in the position of trying to find a black cat on a vast and empty plain on a moonless and starless night."

In 1931 a hardy explorer named Sir Hubert Wilkins even outfitted a submarine with topside runners, like a sled, with which he hoped to venture under the polar ice pack and ride, with slight upward buoyancy, with his runners gliding along what he hoped would be the smooth underside of the ice, to surface in the occasional gaps of open water. But the underside of the ice proved to be anything but smooth, and the technology of his day—and the courage of his hired crew—was not up to the task. He gathered a little data from the edge of the ice pack and was then forced to retreat. In World War II German U-boats found that they could duck under the edge of the ice pack and hide after a strike, and after the war a few American submarines tentatively peeked under the edges. But these were very short-term, exploratory moves, and little or no data were taken.

"*Nautilus* 90 North"

In late 1956 Senator Henry "Scoop" Jackson, who had just returned from an Arctic tour, and had previously ridden the *Nautilus* with the Joint Congressional Committee on Atomic Energy, wrote to the chief of naval operations asking if it would be feasible to operate a nuclear submarine under the ice. Arleigh "31 Knot" Burke, who was then CNO, decided to investigate the matter seriously. This was no small task, since the information about the Arctic needed to plan such a trip was almost completely lacking. The first requirement would be to gather a great deal of information about the area: the thickness of the ice at various locations, how much and how fast it changes, the depth of the sea in the region. It was known that the sea was quite shallow over much of the region of interest, and it was suspected that some of the ice might be quite thick in places. This in fact turned out to be true, making submarine operation in the area unpredictable and treacherous.

In addition to problems imposed by the terrain, there were technological constraints. Two kinds of compass were available: magnetic and gyro. Both became less reliable the further north they were taken, and they failed completely in the vicinity of the Pole. After a number of anxious moments in preliminary operations, submarines were fitted with an inertial guidance system, which did not seek north but just kept very precise track of where the ship had been and where she was headed, on the basis of initial values for these parameters put in at the start of the trip and periodically checked against celestial or other reliable information. The device used initially was the North American Aviation N6A system, developed for the Navaho intercontinental missile. The missile itself never became operational, but improved versions of the inertial navigator proved to be a major contribution to navigation, and a particularly crucial component of the Polaris missile submarines to come. There were other devices needed for Arctic work, such as upward-looking fathometers, which were installed for measuring distance to the underside of the ice pack, and iceberg detectors, which look forward to warn of deep-draft chunks of glaciers or coastal shelf-ice that break off and drift menacingly among the ice floes. Because a ship might not be able to surface quickly if a fire or other atmospheric problem broke out, she was fitted with special air-breathing masks, which could be hooked up through hoses to air-supply piping at all watch stations, enabling the men to stay on watch in a smoke-filled compartment.

In early 1957 preparations began for our only operating nuclear submarine, the *Nautilus*, to make exploratory probes under the edge of the polar ice cap between Greenland and Spitsbergen and, "at discretion, proceed under the ice to the vicinity of 83 degrees north latitude and return." A ship at 83 degrees north would be about 240 miles into the ice pack, and about 420 miles from the North Pole, which is at 90 degrees north. On reading these orders, *Nautilus* skipper Bill Anderson, a Tennessee native with eleven submarine war patrols to his credit, asked his operational boss, "How should I interpret *vicinity*? In other words, could I go to the North Pole?"

"We have confidence in the *Nautilus* to do the right thing" was the reply, leaving the final judgment with the skipper, based on what he found on the scene and how the ship and her equipment and crew had been performing.

So on the morning of 19 August 1957 the *Nautilus* left for the first under-ice attempt. A number of problems were encountered, and at 87 degrees north, about 180 miles from the Pole, with both compasses out of operation, the ship turned reluctantly back. The crew had learned a great deal—in particular that neither gyro nor magnetic compasses could be relied on at these latitudes—and returned to apply these lessons to future explorations. (It was after this trip that they received the inertial navigator.) They had been explicitly instructed not to take undue risk to ship or crew.

The following year the *Nautilus* was operating off the West Coast of the United States, giving the Pacific Fleet a chance to work out with a nuclear submarine. A decision had been made that if conditions appeared favorable, another try would be made for the Pole. This time, however, the ice pack would be entered from the west, between Alaska and Siberia, where the ocean was known to be shallow and the ice thick. The *Nautilus* was to attempt to cross the ice pack, from one side to the other, and it was preferable to choose the hard way to get in, rather than the hard way out. The *Nautilus* was scheduled to rendezvous in England with NATO forces, and she was going to try it on a great circle route from Hawaii to England under the North Pole.

This plan was held in strictest confidence, known only to a few, including an enthusiastically supportive President Eisenhower. In view of the many difficulties encountered on the first attempt, and the great lack of information as to conditions at the more formidable Northwest Passage, it was considered prudent not to commit the ship publicly to such an exploit in advance. Therefore, elaborate security precautions were taken, including a cover story about the return trip through the Panama Canal, where a number of the crew—who had not been told of the Arctic plans—planned to pick up merchandise for which they had made deposits on their previous stop-off. Schedules were published for meetings at Panama, work at New London, and social events that, if the secret hopes were fulfilled, would never occur. Commander Anderson made secret trips to Alaska in civilian dress and under a false name, to fly surveys of the ice fields with a chartered bush pilot. The special instruments and equipment for Arctic operations installed on the *Nautilus* were explained in terms of possible future operations off Greenland.

Finally, the time came to leave. The crew was prepared with summer clothing for the Panama visit, and the ship left Seattle "for Panama." Although it was early June, the last ice survey had shown a sudden worsening of the ice conditions, and Anderson was concerned. The concern proved valid, and the ship was finally forced to move south to Hawaii, to create another cover story and wait for the ice to break up. A month later they took off again and, after some anxious moments and some skillful navigation and maneuvering, crossed under the North Pole at 11:15 P.M. Eastern Daylight Time, 3 August 1958, and steamed smoothly on to Portland, England, arriving 12 August.

"No Room at the Inn"

In August 1958 the Navy once again inadvertently backed Rickover into the national headlines. The *Nautilus* was just completing her spectacular trip, fully submerged, from Pearl Harbor to England, passing under the North Pole, and the whole world was rejoicing. The president had wanted to announce the event as soon as the ship cleared the ice pack, so an elaborate procedure had been arranged. The ship would surface secretly off Iceland, and an Air Force H-19 helicopter would lift Anderson off and fly him to Iceland, where he would transfer to a waiting Navy transport plane that would fly him directly to Washington. The president had announced a gala reception at the White House for the ship's captain, and for others associated with the historic event. News of the trip would be announced by the president, and for the first time in peacetime a Presidential Unit Citation would be awarded to a ship.

The Navy's discomfort with Rickover was often viewed with amusement by the media. (*San Francisco Chronicle*)

A large number of dignitaries from the Navy and from other government posts had been invited.

Panoff, Leighton, and I were in Rickover's office, listening to a live radio news broadcast report about as follows: "The White House is giving a gala reception today to welcome Captain Anderson of the nuclear submarine *Nautilus* back from his historic underwater trip from Pearl Harbor to England by way of the North Pole. Much of official Washington is participating. The entire ship's crew has been invited to New York City, where the mayor has promised them an old-fashioned ticker-tape parade."

Incredibly, Rickover had not been included on the Navy's invitation list for the White House reception, and afterward, when congressmen looked for him there and found him missing, there was a predictable uproar. There was a nationally run cartoon showing Rickover standing outside the White House, looking wistfully in at the reception, with the caption "No room at the inn." Rickover remarked dryly, "I thought the senator laid it on a bit heavy when he came up with that 'No room at the inn' line. But it seems to have caught on. The papers like it. And when the Navy said they didn't put me on the invitation list because there wasn't room, he said, 'The guy weighs only 125 pounds soaking wet.' "

But as we were sitting in the Admiral's office, with the reception just winding down, Dixie came in, a little breathless, with an announcement: "Admiral, Captain Anderson is here. He made them stop the entourage, and they're waiting outside the building. Here he is."

Rickover was astounded. "My God, Anderson! That was an audacious thing to do!"

Anderson's reply was matter-of-fact. "Admiral, Bob, Ted, Dave, I didn't want to come to Washington and not stop in to see you. I never have. You understand I can't stay long. But I wanted to pay my respects."

Rickover replied quietly, "I'm really quite moved, Anderson. That was awfully nice of you. Awfully nice. But you'd better not keep the people waiting. Thanks again. I'll tell all my people what you did. It's for them too."

"Yes, Admiral, it is. Well, I'd better go." And he left.

There was silence for a moment, and then Panoff said, "Wow! How about *that*!"

Surface at the Pole

The news of the *Nautilus*'s spectacular trip was received with mixed emotions aboard the first SFR ship, the USS *Skate*. The *Skate* was a totally new ship design, with a totally new propulsion plant and new reactor plant design, all accomplished without a land prototype. She had been conceived, designed, built, and put into service in an incredibly short time, in large part because of the intense personal interest in her taken by Panoff and by waterfront supervisor Joseph D. Pierce and his co-workers at Electric Boat. Her keel was laid in July 1955, just six months after the *Nautilus* first went to sea. She was launched less than two years later, was commissioned just before Christmas 1957, and departed New London on her shakedown cruise the following February. Eight days later she surfaced in Portland, England, and later returned fully submerged, setting records both ways.

She had been primed from the beginning for Arctic exploration. Her crew had studied and been trained in all available Arctic lore, and the ship had been loaded with special navigational and other Arctic equipment and supplies. So her captain, Commander James Calvert, and crew were more than casually interested when the *Nautilus* made her first assault on the ice pack in the summer of 1957. And when the *Nautilus* tried to find the legendary Northwest Passage in June 1958 and had to turn back, they shared the disappointment but felt that they were now ready to step into the fray. "The *Nautilus* had her chance, now it's our turn," was the expectant cry. But the Navy management felt that the *Nautilus* should be allowed to complete what she had worked so hard to do, under difficult and dangerous circumstances, and the *Skate* was asked to stand back and let the *Nautilus* take the honors she had earned.

The *Nautilus* had shown that one submarine could thread her way under the ice, one time, in summer, after several unsuccessful attempts, some narrow escapes, and some extraordinary seamanship. To the *Skate* fell the task of determining whether this was to be a once-in-a-lifetime feat, or whether future nuclear ships could operate in this hostile and largely unknown environment, if not routinely, at least as needed for special military purposes. In addition, the *Skate* was given the task of developing methods for surfacing in, and through, the Arctic pack ice— a task for which she was better configured than the *Nautilus*.

The *Skate* was actually about to dive under the ice in the mile-deep water near Spitsbergen, where the Gulf Stream pushes the ice the farthest north, and head for the Pole, when her crew first received word of the *Nautilus*'s transpolar trip. Calvert was one of the few persons who had known that the *Nautilus* trip was planned, and he had not been permitted to pass this secret information to his crew. He agonized as he and his crew raced northward, talking of the excitement of being first to reach the Pole submerged. Word that the *Nautilus* had beaten them to this honor had a crushing effect on their morale. But they rallied and radioed a message: "TO COMMANDER ANDERSON AND THE MEN OF THE NAUTILUS X HEARTFELT CONGRATULATIONS FROM ALL OF US IN SKATE." Having sent this message, the *Skate* ducked under the Arctic ice pack and headed north.

Although this was a peaceful research mission, the Navy required all submarines in operation to carry a full set of live torpedoes and food and other supplies for sixty days. For the *Skate*, already burdened with eight or nine civilian scientists and technicians and their bulky equipment, this meant stowing away food for eighteen thousand meals, plus a thousand bricks to ballast the garbage that would be pushed overboard during the postulated sixty-day run. Having nearly exhausted their ingenuity in finding places to stow all that food, the crew had still not found a place for the bricks. Finally someone came up with the "Oz" approach: a "yellow brick road" along the crew's passageways, covered with custom-cut plywood that could be kept as clean as the rest of the ship.

The *Nautilus* had confirmed that the traditional magnetic compass, which points toward a shifting pole about a thousand miles south of the geographic North Pole, is of little use in Arctic navigation, and that even the most advanced gyro compass is unreliable within five hundred miles of the Pole. Thus, a ship might find herself circling aimlessly, without realizing it, under a sheet of ice nearly twice the size of the United States. Dead reckoning, the sailor's classic method of navigating by adding speed and course to a previously known position, not only depends on knowing the ship's speed and course through the water; it also requires an estimate of the effect of any drift from wind and current. To have confidence in such a calculation requires periodic corrections from some other source, such as a check against the stars. Two other reliable methods for determining a ship's position are LORAN (measuring the ship's distance from two or more pairs of linked radio transmitters) and a radar fix on a known landmark. Neither of these methods, of course, was available in the Arctic.

Thus deprived of the navigational tools used in other waters, Arctic navigation becomes totally dependent on the remarkable inertial guidance device, supplemented by a radar land fix just before entering the ice floe. The *Seadragon*, *Sargo*, and other submarines that followed were equipped with special optics in the periscope for taking star sightings without having to surface. This proved valuable on occasion, but even they found that the Arctic weather was seldom clear enough for star sighting, and, of course, there were no opportunities to try when the ship was under the ice.

To be useful in the Arctic, a submarine must be able to surface, to fire missiles, to transmit information, to receive signals. Therefore, part of the *Skate*'s mission was to demonstrate that a submarine could surface when necessary during Arctic operations. Her "sail," the protective and streamlining structure surrounding the periscopes and radio masts, had been strengthened, and the latest upward-looking fathometers had been installed to measure the distance to the underside of the ice and to estimate its thickness. As the ship tunneled through the water at sixteen knots, the fathometers drew a wiggly line showing the underside of the ice. This wiggly line occasionally leapt to the top of the page and became a thin horizontal line, which after a moment reverted to a wiggly line further down on the paper. The straight lines at the top of the paper showed open water ponds, and at sixteen knots, which is about five hundred yards per minute, a straight line that persisted for a minute indicated a pond large enough to attempt surfacing.

Surfacing a submarine is normally done by controlling her attitude and position through use of the large diving planes and the rudder. This requires a brisk forward velocity, to provide sufficient water flow over the controlling surfaces. But the *Skate* was going to have to surface vertically, like an elevator, to hit the small ponds or leads (cracks of open water between ice floes) that would provide the only opportunity to surface in the Arctic. The *Skate* crew had practiced vertical surfacing and diving procedures and found that they required exquisite buoyancy control. The *Nautilus* had been "blinded" when both her delicate periscopes were damaged by floating ice blocks too small to be seen by her fathometer. The damage was more than optical; the periscope barrel had also been cracked. Through an incredible twelve-hour repair operation in a howling blizzard, the crew managed to straighten and weld up the damaged periscope, but the incident emphasized the difficulty of surfacing in tiny Arctic ponds.

Supported by the experience of the *Nautilus* and by her own research, training, and improved instrumentation, the *Skate* dashed northward via the deep-water eastern route, reaching the Pole just eight days after the *Nautilus*. After considerable searching and an anxious ascent, the *Skate* managed to surface in a tiny pond just forty miles from the Pole and radio her achievement. She then headed back under the ice to gather water and ice samples, to record bottom terrain and ice thickness, and to practice surfacing in the patches of open water. After completing this work, she proceeded to Bergen, Norway, and then returned for a home-coming welcome in Boston. As she pulled into Boston harbor, among the tooting of tugboats and the whirring of helicopters, a launch pulled up and Admiral Rickover came aboard to congratulate the crew and hear firsthand of her findings.

A special visitor to the *Skate* was Sir Hubert Wilkins, the intrepid Arctic explorer who had pushed his primitive submarine under the edge of the ice pack in 1931. There was considerable mutual admiration between the crew and the grizzled explorer, but Calvert was startled to hear him say, "You must now go in the wintertime. You haven't really opened the Arctic Ocean for scientific investigation—or military or commercial use, for that matter—if you merely demonstrate what you can do in the summertime."

This was an audacious idea. No one visited the Arctic in the winter. Not only was it 60 degrees colder, eternally dark, and whipped by storms most of the time, but the likelihood of finding places to surface was unknown and probably small. But shortly after his visit, Wilkins wrote Calvert a note: "I . . . have given considerable thought to the idea of a winter expedition. You must attempt to bring this about. Do not be discouraged by apathy and resistance, press for it." A month later Calvert received word that Wilkins had died of a heart attack.

Calvert found considerable receptivity for the idea of a wintertime exploration of the Arctic, and additional changes were made to the *Skate* to prepare her for the arduous journey. The sail structure was further strengthened, powerful floodlights were installed in the deck to illuminate the ice from below, and a television camera was mounted in a watertight box in the deck. An improved upward-looking fathometer was installed, and its inventor, Arctic scientist Waldo Lyon, agreed to go along again to supervise its use. At the last minute Calvert got a call telling him that Wilkins, just before his death, had expressed the wish to Lady Wilkins that someday his ashes might be carried to the North Pole in a submarine and scattered to the Arctic winds. Calvert was moved by the request and agreed to try to do so, although the thought of surfacing right at the Pole in the dead of winter seemed a formidable challenge.

The *Skate* did in fact return to the Pole, in 1959, and did so in March, the coldest, most inhospitable time of the year. She experienced main-shaft-seal leakage, potentially the most dangerous casualty of all, and a main-circulation-pump-seal leak, in the dreaded Zone of Inaccessibility, the area farthest from the open sea in all directions. A leaking seal can generally be stopped by tightening down the packing, but when this is done the shaft may no longer turn. A ship with two main turbines and two propeller shafts, like the *Nautilus, Seawolf,* and all the SFR ships, can travel at a good speed indefinitely with one shaft shut down. But later submarines would be built with the more efficient single-shaft hull design, which puts a heavy premium on ensuring dependable shaft seals.

Fortunately, the *Skate* was able to handle her two seal-leakage problems, and she managed to find a tiny spot in the immediate vicinity of the Pole where the ice was thin enough to break through. The night was pitch black, a blizzard was howling, but the crew decided to have a proper memorial service for Sir Hubert. The ship's crew formed a small table on the ice with some boxes and covered it over with green felt cloth. They lined up on either side and held red flares to light the scene. Calvert read from the Episcopal Book of Common Prayer, struggling to be heard above the roar of the storm. Then two of the officers took the urn and scattered the ashes into the gale as Calvert read, "Unto Almightly God we commend the soul of our brother departed, and we commit his ashes to the deep." A rifle squad on the ship's bow fired three times, and afterward they marked the spot with a small American flag. It was an impressive ceremony.

THE BALLISTIC MISSILE SUBMARINE PROJECT

> *All new ideas begin in a non-conforming mind that questions some tenet of the "conventional wisdom." All improvements originate in a critical mind that mistrusts the "image" projected by some powerful organism. The innovator of ideas and the social critic are essential to a free society; they are what make the society free.*
>
> H.G.R.

As early as 1956 there were people in the Navy who felt that it might be possible to launch a long-range missile from a submarine. This was a startling idea, since a nuclear warhead at that time weighed sixteen hundred pounds and the only available missile to carry it stood six stories high, required large quantities of dangerous liquid fuel, and had a marginal fifteen-hundred-mile range. But missile propulsion systems and warheads were continually being improved, and the Navy wanted to be ready. Since the advent of the airplane the Navy's biggest battles have been in the air, against the Air Force, not in the sea where the only foes were foreign. The Navy felt, with considerable justification, that it was vulnerable to losing its air missions, and when missiles came in, the Navy's struggle to maintain parity with the Air Force took on new intensity. If a submarine-borne missile could be developed, it would be an unquestionable national asset, and it would be unequivocally Navy. At first these efforts focused on the air-breathing missile Regulus, but when the solid-fueled missile appeared feasible, Regulus was dropped.

In June 1956 CNO Arleigh Burke asked the newly formed Special Projects Office to work with the BuShips Preliminary Design Section to define characteristics for a nuclear ballistic submarine, based on the developmental solid-fueled Jupiter missile. To ensure that Rickover did not dominate the project, Burke gave strict but unwritten orders to keep all news of the project secret from Rickover. Since the whole project was highly classified and confined to a small working group, this was effective for nearly a year. When Rickover saw the proposed specifications for the first time in April 1957, he objected only to the requirement for under-ice operation. He agreed completely with the importance of under-ice operation, but he believed that no single-shaft submarine should operate under ice. In fact, he tried for a while to insist that all under-ice ships be equipped not only with two shafts but also with two reactors. All of the senior Naval Reactors engineers argued with him on this position, but cost and weight alone were enough to rule out two reactors for all but one submarine, and Rickover finally accepted the inevitable. He did, however, hold out against under-ice operation for the first single-shaft submarines, and he did not relent until a number of single-shaft submarines had demonstrated their reliability.

A critical event in the submarine missile program occurred at an Undersea Warfare Committee meeting at Woods Hole, Massachusetts, in the summer of 1956. Edward Teller informed the participants that a significantly lighter warhead was under development, and by fall the Navy was told that it could count on the weight being reduced nearly two-thirds, to six hundred pounds. The propulsion system was also improving, and by the time the Navy had a submarine missile of its own, called Polaris, it was solid- rather than liquid-fueled, and had become half as high and a fraction of the weight of the old Jupiter. This was a device one could picture being carried vertically in a submarine! The Bureau of Ships now had a preliminary submarine design to carry sixteen of these missiles, each of which could be checked, serviced, and launched while submerged. Burke approved the proposed characteristics in June 1957 and declared that the ship had the highest priority in the Navy.

Burke's priority had the strong approval of President Eisenhower. In August 1957 the Soviet Union launched an intercontinental ballistic missile, and a month later it shocked the world with the first orbiting satellite. In this urgent environment, a completion date for the first Polaris submarine was scheduled for 1960, only three years away. To meet this deadline, drastic action was taken. The hull of the attack submarine *Scorpion* was under construction at Electric Boat. Construction was halted, the hull was literally cut in two, and a missile section, an additional 130 feet of hull, was inserted. The ship was renamed the *George Washington*, launched in June 1959, and commissioned two days ahead of the 1 January 1960 deadline. By the following July the ship had successfully launched two missiles while submerged. And on 15 November 1960 she began her first sixty-six-day patrol.

The Polaris Difference

To get maximum use of these massive ships, two complete crews were assigned to each ship: two captains, two sets of officers, and two entire crews of 130 men each, one designated George Washington (Blue), the other George Washington (Gold). At the end of each sixty-day patrol, there would be a thirty-day period for resupply and a refit and a short machinery readiness check, and then the alternative crew would take the ship to sea, imposing unprecedented reliability requirements on the propulsion plant. And Rickover suddenly found that his recruiting and training demand for these ships had doubled. Polaris sailors claimed the dubious honor of being in the only branch of service that offered two honeymoons a year.

These extended patrols, with no cat-and-mouse games to break up the tedium, were something new for the Navy. The submarines can receive messages, but no messages are sent out, for that might reveal their location to an enemy. Some sailors write letters whenever they feel the urge and then mail out a batch at the end of the patrol.

Life on Patrol

Night and day have no inherent meaning for a Polaris crew; they never look out. Their day revolves around the four- or six-hour watch followed by eight or twelve hours off. But as a link to tradition and a precaution in case they ever need to use the periscope at night, the ship "rigs for red" during nighttime hours: throughout the ship's operational

---

TRACKING THE SUBS

I recall visiting the Readiness Room at the Pentagon, where the location of every naval vessel is shown on a huge map of the world. As I watched, a petty officer moved the little marker that symbolized the *George Washington*. "How current is your information on ship's position, Chief?" I asked. "We're given a new position every fifteen minutes, sir," was the proud response. "But the ships don't broadcast their positions," I objected. "No, sir. This information comes directly from the computer, with the patrol plan that's filed with us just before the ship departs on patrol." "So if the ship sank a hundred yards off the end of the pier and no one knew it, how long would you keep moving that little marker?" I asked. "For sixty days, sir. Then we'd await further input."

areas, all lighting is from pure red lights. This enables personnel to see pretty well using just the cone-shaped cells in the retina, since the rod-shaped cells are not stimulated much by red light. Then, if a crew member has to look out through the periscope to scan the dark ocean scene, his cone cells will already be "night adapted," and he can see nearly as well as if he had been in complete darkness all that time. If a crew member on duty in a red-rigged area has to go momentarily into a brightly lit area, such as the engineering spaces, he wears red goggles. And special playing cards are available for poker or bridge: the hearts and diamonds are outlined in black, because red does not show up against white in pure red light. (I understand that the Navy is now considering substituting low-level white light, which may work just as well.)

Because of the nature of the ship and of the crew, there are always drills to be carried out and studying to be done. At any given moment there will be some sailors studying to qualify for a particular duty or rating. This involves reading textbooks and manuals, tracing piping and wiring through the ship, and attending classes held aboard ship. Other crew members may be reading for pleasure, watching the daily movie, or joining in a sing-along among the missile tubes in what Polaris sailors call Sherwood Forest. In many ways they are like all sailors, but differences keep showing up. One crew tells of having a huge bag of hard candies aboard with different kinds of centers. Peanut butter centers were the favorite, and it soon became a challenge to pick those out from the less desirable others. It didn't take long for the crew to discover that checking the electrical resistance across the candy was a sure way to identify the peanut butter inside.

Although it has never been a problem, it is routine practice to keep checking for any increase in radiation level. When Polaris ships first began operation, each crew member wore two radiation detectors at all times. One, which looked like a fountain pen and was worn like one in a shirt pocket, was a self-reading gamma ray detector. The other was a film badge, clipped elsewhere on the clothing, which, when developed in the ship's darkroom, showed up any neutron tracks and darkening from beta radiation. In the early days, the ship's doctor was responsible for monitoring this information and supplementing it with radiation surveys made by hand-held instruments and checks of the radiochemistry of the reactor coolant water and of the air and other ship's fluids. The doctor always checked before each patrol that all luminous watches had been left behind, because their radiation would exceed that from the reactor and interfere with the radiation control program. A nuclear medical corpsman now carries out these functions, and a modern thermo-luminescent dosimeter (TLD) has replaced the other two types of detectors.

A Lesson on the Military Mind

Rickover's training lessons sometimes came in strange forms. One time I went with him for the periodic ritual of paying his respects to the new CNO. In the outer office we spotted a large and elegant model of a B-52 aircraft, with a bronze plaque indicating that it was the gift of a famous World War II aviator. Rickover said quietly to me as we went in, "Wouldn't that model look nice in our model room? Let's get it."

I was not sure what he meant by that, but I soon found out. I watched in astonishment as Rickover bullied the CNO, in a jocular way, to give him the model. The Top Admiral didn't know how to deal with the situation. He was not used to a lower-ranking officer pushing him for anything, but he also did not want to appear stuffy in the face of good-natured joshing. Rickover finally said, "I'll tell your aide where to send it," and called him in. "Will he send it?" I asked incredulously as we left. "Sure he will. He doesn't know how to say no," assured Rickover.

"Do you know why I did that?" he then asked. "What did you get out of that?"

"Admiral, all I could think of, as I watched that performance, was red-coated British troops, with drums and bugles and flag bearers, marching in formation across Colonial America, while the rebels hid in trees and shot them down with squirrel rifles. This guy doesn't know how to defend himself from soldiers with squirrel rifles."

"You're damn right. Do you think the Russians will agree to play by his rules? Now you know why I refuse to be bound by such thinking. I wanted you to see for yourself."

"Here They Come Again"

The last few months had been filled with mind-boggling exploits. Nuclear submarines had fired the public mind. But Rickover's mind was already racing ahead. "You know, the Joint Committee has been looking for an occasion to needle the Navy to make me a vice admiral. After President Eisenhower announced that he was naming me his special representative for the *Nautilus*'s New York ticker-tape parade, Scoop

Jackson called and told me the committee was going to go for it."

Panoff and I said, almost in unison, "That's great, Admiral!"

"The thing they're worried about is that the secretary of the Navy is now claiming that the president has the power to delegate responsibilty for the safety of nuclear reactors over to the Navy. They claim it's just like the nuclear bombs. I understand the AEC chairman is leaning that way too."

Panoff didn't have to be told what that could mean. "That would eliminate the whole idea of the Navy having to get a blessing from the AEC on reactor safety matters. It would eliminate our entire two-hatted setup."

"Exactly. Everything could be handled in the normal Navy way. Our whole operation would be phased out."

"What do we do, Admiral?"

"Same as always. Just keep working."

"Yeah, but I sure get fed up with the critics. They always seem to have the power and the sympathetic audiences."

The Admiral had an answer to that one, too. "Go back and read that quote from Teddy Roosevelt I passed around to you guys some time ago. To me, that says it all."

So I did. And he was right.

It is not the critic who counts, not the one who points out how the strong man stumbled, or how the doer of deeds might have done them better. The credit belongs to the man who is actually in the arena, whose face is marred with sweat, and dust, and blood; who strives valiantly; who errs and comes short again and again; who knows the great enthusiasm, the great devotion, and spends himself in a worthy cause; who, if he wins, knows the triumph of high achievement; and who, if he fails, at least fails while daring greatly, so that his place shall never be with those cold and timid souls who know neither victory nor defeat.

Part V

Proclaiming the Need for Excellence

(1959–1964)

V

I had applied for the nuclear submarine program, and Admiral Rickover was interviewing me for the job . . . Finally, he asked me a question and I thought I could redeem myself. He said, "How did you stand in your class at the Naval Academy?" . . . I swelled my chest with pride and answered, "Sir, I stood 59th in a class of 820!" I sat back to wait for the congratulations—which never came. Instead, the question: "Did you do your best?" I started to say, "Yes, sir," but I remembered who this was . . . I finally gulped and said, "No, sir, I didn't always do my best." He looked at me for a long time, and then turned his chair around to end the interview. He asked one final question, which I have never been able to forget—or to answer. He said, "Why not?"

Jimmy Carter, *Why Not the Best?*

Proclaiming the Need for Excellence
1959–1964

THE GLOBAL PERSPECTIVE

IN JUNE 1959 I was called to Admiral Rickover's office for an interesting message: "Rockwell, you know Vice President Nixon is planning to visit Russia next month, and he has asked me to go along. I'm going to see that we get to tour their nuclear icebreaker, the *Lenin*. I've arranged to take you and Mandil with me. I've already gotten approval for you from the White House and from the Kremlin. You'll get special passports for the occasion. You'll have to get a flock of inoculations before we leave; you can do that at the dispensary. But I want to do more than that. Allen Dulles, head of the CIA, will be here any minute to discuss it."

I was trying to assimilate all that, and sort out the many questions I wanted to ask, when Dixie called that Mr. Dulles had arrived. The

Admiral said to bring him right in, and in a moment he arrived, with a large manila envelope with papers in it. Rickover introduced me, and we all sat down.

Mr. Dulles, looking just like his news pictures, opened the conversation with a pleasantry. "Your quarters here live up to their reputation, Admiral: adequate but certainly not ostentatious."

Rickover replied in the same vein. "We make shift, sir. I consider that public officials should not expect the citizenry to support them in a lavish style. I live simply at home, and that is all I ask of my professional facilities. Would you like some coffee or tea, sir? That much we do permit."

Mr. Dulles declined with a slight shake of his head and a wave of his hand. And then he got right to the point.

"Open Skies" Revisited

"Mr. Nixon tells me," Dulles said, "that you have suggested that the United States might gain from an exchange of atomic secrets with the Russians, and in fact you would like to see this topic broadened to include a wide range of military information. Would you care to expand on that?"

"Yes, sir. You'll recall that in 1955 President Eisenhower proposed an extraordinary plan to the Russians, which he called Open Skies. The point of departure for that proposal was that we had a clear monopoly on nuclear weapons at that time, and if we offered, unilaterally, to place them under international control while we still had a monopoly, it might be possible to get an agreement with the Russians that would not only defuse the atomic weapons race, but could lead to the declassification and reduction of a much broader range of military weapons and facilities. This disarmament program would be monitored by our remarkable system of aerial surveillance cameras and aircraft, a technology in which we also lead the world. It was agreed that if such a plan could be implemented, it would be in the best interests of the United States to do so."

"Yes, that is correct," agreed Dulles. "But, of course, you know the Russians never went along with it."

"That's true. But now Mr. Nixon seems to feel that the situation might be changing, and the purpose of this trip, as I understand it, is to explore with Mr. Khrushchev whether any thawing of the Cold War is possible. Again, the atomic situation might be the key."

"Exactly what did you have in mind?"

"As you know, when Frol Kozlov, the Reds' number two man, was visiting America recently, I showed him through our civilian atomic power station at Shippingport, Pennsylvania. We were photographed by the national news media exchanging friendly barbs. I patted him on the stomach and remarked that he looked more like the wealthy capitalist, and I was the picture of the hardworking working man. He laughed at that and said it was good to have spent so much time talking about peace. I told him it was all right to *talk* about peace, but now he should go home and do something about it. And then—this is the important part—he suggested that Russia and the United States arrange an exchange of nuclear experts, and I seized the opportunity and agreed. Furthermore, as we were about to go into the plant, he asked me where he should leave his camera. I told him, in front of all the news cameras, that he should take his camera with him, that nothing in Shippingport was secret, and that there wasn't a single place in the plant where classified material or information was stored. That this was a peaceful, public project. And I added, 'Just like your atomic-powered icebreaker ship, the *Lenin*. Isn't that right, Mr. Kozlov?' And, of course, he had to agree. And I went on to say that I would be going over there with Mr. Nixon, and I assumed that I would be given full access to go through that ship, as he was being shown through Shippingport, since there were no secrets involved. And again, he had to agree. In front of all those cameras."

"That's excellent, Admiral. I've seen that news footage, and you did indeed pin him down on that point."

"It would be very valuable to go through that plant, Mr. Dulles. We have no idea right now how far they are in atomic energy. They have presented scientific papers at the Geneva Conferences on Peaceful Uses of Atomic Energy, but these papers are very vague and leave a lot of important engineering questions unanswered. When they were showing us through their exhibit in New York, we asked some questions about the *Lenin*. You know, it has suddenly dropped out of the news, just at the point when they said they were almost ready to start up the plant. They answered our question with '*Nye rabotayet*.' Rockwell here knows a little Russian, and he knew that meant 'It doesn't work.' But the translator said, 'Everything is on schedule.' "

"That *is* interesting. Were you able to get any further information?"

"Rockwell went back afterward and overheard the Russian exhibition people talking in English. Good English. So he said to the kid who had talked to us about the *Lenin*, he said to him in Russian, 'I wish my Russian were as good as your English.' Then he asked him to tell us, in English, about the *Lenin*. The kid was scared silly, because they had insisted that the exhibition people didn't know any English, and that we had to direct everything through the translators. But it was clear that the kid didn't know anything. It was as if we had sent some bright University of Maryland physics students over there. They couldn't answer any questions about the *Nautilus*."

"I see. So you really want to see that plant?"

"Yes, sir. I want to see that plant. But more than that, I would like to take advantage of this particular moment in history, and try to press for a wide declassification of atomic and military information. Tell me, sir: Would you be willing to let Russians walk through the streets of Oak Ridge and Los Alamos, if you could walk the streets of their equivalent weapons development facilities?"

"Absolutely! They already know a great deal about our military facilities, and we know very little about theirs."

"How about shipyards? And ships?"

"The same, Admiral. I would be willing to go all the way to Eisenhower's Open Skies proposal. Assuming, of course, that we get quid pro quo at every step."

"Mr. Dulles, would you be willing to let me make such a proposal, if the opportunity presents itself on this trip?"

"I don't have authority to approve such an undertaking, Admiral."

"Mr. Nixon told me he was in favor of it, if you thought it was a good idea."

"I think it is an excellent idea. That's why I brought along all these plans of the Russian military and atomic facilities, as far as we know them today. I suggest that you and your people go over them carefully, and then you can get back to me." At that point he rose to leave. "I've enjoyed talking with you, Admiral. I expect we'll be talking again before long."

After escorting Mr. Dulles to the door, Dixie returned with a worried look and said, "Admiral, Mr. Dulles left all those top-secret plans and drawings, and they have no copy numbers and no receipts for them. How am I supposed to log them in?"

To which Rickover replied casually, "Just give them to Mr. Rockwell. He'll take care of them." And he hardly smiled at all when I sighed, "Oh, brother!"

Rickover and the *Lenin*

The trip to Russia came off as scheduled, but not quite as planned. For one thing, John McCone, chairman of the Atomic Energy Commission (AEC), decided—*after* we had gotten all our inoculations—that Rickover didn't need any technical staff with him. "This is primarily a political trip," he said; "we'll get the scientists over later." So Harry Mandil and I stayed home and in fact never did get to Russia.

On 25 July 1959 Nixon took Rickover to the Kremlin and told Kozlov that Rickover was empowered to negotiate for the United States on the peaceful uses of atomic energy. Rickover then got up and offered to give the Russians all information on all nonmilitary power reactors including Shippingport; on the plutonium production reactors; on a dual-purpose reactor that would produce both plutonium and electric power; on the aircraft propulsion program; and on the nuclear merchant ship *Savannah*. In essence, Rickover was offering everything except the naval reactors. In exchange, the Soviets would give us all information on their equivalent projects. Rickover even agreed to train Russian engineers at the Shippingport school.

The Russians were astounded, but they were not able to respond to this wholly unexpected offer. The AEC and the U.S. State Department had been discussing a far more pedestrian agreement with the Russians, which they continued to push until it was signed on 24 November 1959. Nothing further was ever heard on the Rickover proposal.

Rickover did get to see the nuclear icebreaker *Lenin*, but that event did not turn out quite as advertised either. The whole party arrived at the Leningrad shipyard on 27 July and were given a quick tour of the yard, then taken to the ship's wardroom for a twenty-minute propaganda film on heroic welders meeting their production quotas. Their hosts then announced that they would have to move on, to keep the trip on schedule. Rickover was furious and told Nixon that he wanted to stay until he had been given the complete tour of the ship he had been promised.

The group left, and Rickover and his translator asked to be shown through the engine room and reactor compartment. The Russians claimed that the workmen had gone home, and that they didn't know where the key to the compartment was. Rickover said he would wait, and sat stony-faced. He asked who all the men in business suits were and was told that they were workers. He walked over to one, inspected his hands, and announced, "In my country, workers have calluses. These guys are spies!" The hosts agreed they were not workers and said they were reporters. "We agreed there would be an equal number of American reporters at all times," said Rickover. "Throw them out." They were asked to leave, and they did so.

Finally Rickover said, "I was promised by Comrade Kozlov, in front of news cameras, that I would be shown everything on this ship. If that does not happen, you will make him appear to be a liar before the whole world. If that happened in America, somebody's head would roll, and it wouldn't be the boss. Get me Comrade Kozlov on the telephone. Now!"

At that point someone magically appeared with the key, and a guide for the tour. The guide, who appeared to be at least eight months pregnant, would obviously have been more of a hindrance than a help in the crowded compartment. Rickover brushed her aside and took his technically trained translator with him, and they made a point of staying in the reactor compartment for a couple of hours, taking copious, detailed notes. Some months later, when V. S. Emelyanov, chairman of the Soviet Main Administration for Atomic Energy, visited America, he made a great show of presenting Rickover with a huge key to the *Lenin* reactor compartment, in the tradition of the "key to the city" ceremony.

The Triton: Around the World Submerged

The U.S. submarine force was still small, only 3 percent of the total naval personnel—about the same in number as the WAVEs, the Navy's female contingent. But that 3 percent had certainly made a splash.

In 1957 the *Nautilus* had been the first to penetrate deeply under the ice, and in 1958 to traverse the Arctic Ocean from west to east. In 1959 the *Skate* had demonstrated the feasibility of operating in the ice pack during the coldest, darkest winter nights, and had proved the practicability of surfacing, almost at will, even at the Pole itself. In 1960 the *Sargo* explored and charted much of the unknown region, and demonstrated that the new ice detector could show the presence of the dreaded icebergs in time to avoid them. The *Seadragon* showed how to go right beneath an iceberg and determine its size and shape. She also found and charted the long-sought Northwest Passage, and traveled for the first time from the Atlantic to the Pacific Ocean via Baffin Bay off

Greenland, through Peary Channel to the Beaufort Sea, and thence through the Chukchi Sea to Nome. These operations were climaxed by two submarines rendezvousing under the North Pole and then surfacing there. Also in 1960, the *George Washington* successfully launched two Polaris intercontinental missiles while submerged, and then headed off for her first patrol.

There seemed little else nuclear submarines could do to prove their capabilities. They had been tested, with spectacular effectiveness, in every sort of war game. (Dennis Wilkinson had even taught the *Nautilus* to "porpoise," a spectacular sight to behold. From full submergence he would bring her up at an ever-steepening angle, while the stewards cursed and vainly tried to keep the silverware, dishes, and glasses from crashing to the deck. The huge ship would then broach the surface and seem to leap into the air like a playful porpoise, before crashing down to resume a more appropriate attitude on the water.) So there was only one remaining challenge to be faced: a nonstop trip around the world, continuously submerged. This task fell to the giant twin-reactor ship *Triton*, 447 feet long and 8,000 tons displacement submerged, 100 feet longer and twice as heavy as any other submarine previously built.

Building and launching this leviathan raised some interesting new problems. She was so long that, on the shipbuilder's ways, her massive bow would block the vital railway that supplied the Electric Boat yard. So a large piece of the lower section of the bow was cut away to let the trains through, and was replaced at the last possible moment before launching. Even so, her stern would have projected far out into the Thames River, so the final fifty-foot section was built on the adjacent ways and delicately lifted into place by two giant cranes working carefully together. But this was still not enough. The ship was seven stories high, from her keel plates to the top of her superstructure (called the sail, because it was the part of the ship most likely to catch worrisome crosswinds on the surface). This was too much height to get under the overhead cranes that straddled the ways, and so the top twelve feet of superstructure was cut off and reinstalled after launching.

The *Triton* first put to sea in September 1959, and she was commissioned on 10 November. Less than three months later, Admiral Wallace M. Beakley, deputy chief of naval operations, asked her skipper if he would be willing to extend her planned shakedown cruise to a round-the-world voyage, continuously submerged. This was a daring suggestion, especially for such a new and untested ship and crew. Not only would the skipper have to complete all preparations for the trip within twelve days; he would have to do so in complete secrecy, inventing a cover story for the crew and others involved in getting the ship ready.

The skipper, Captain Edward L. Beach, a well-known World War II submariner, chose approximately the route taken by Magellan nearly five hundred years earlier. This involved rounding both the Cape of Good Hope, at the tip of Africa, and the dreaded Cape Horn at the southernmost point of South America. A number of adventures occurred along the way, as might be expected. But the training and discipline of the crew, plus considerable ingenuity when unusual repair problems arose, carried them through in classic style.

One problem, which could not have been predicted and was not the fault of machinery or crew, arose not long after they left New London. One of the crew developed kidney stones and became gravely ill. It was clear that he would have to be taken to a hospital. Luckily, a Navy cruiser, the *Macon*, was operating nearby, off the coast of Montevideo. Since the whole voyage was being carried out in great secrecy, it was decided to pass the sick man to the *Macon*, which could get him to a hospital ashore, under a cover story. It was even arranged to do this without opening up the pressure hull to the outside air, which would have broken the "continuously submerged" aspect of the trip. The pressure hull had a hatch that opened into a conning tower, a small, horizontal cylinder that could act as an air lock to the outside. The crewman was carried into the conning tower, the lower hatch was shut tight again, and then, with the entire main hull underwater and closed to the atmosphere, the upper hatch from the conning tower was opened, and the sailor was handed out to the waiting men from the *Macon*. This maneuver was carried out successfully, the sailor not only recovered but maintained his cover story intact, and the *Triton* did indeed complete her historic journey, in sixty days and twenty-one hours.

On completion of the circumnavigation, before returning home, the ship delivered a special bronze plaque designed by Lieutenant Tom Thamm, the *Triton*'s diving officer, to commemorate the replication of Magellan's historic voyage. It depicted a globe in relief, with a wreath of olive branches superimposed. The bottom of the wreath formed the submariners' twin-dolphin insignia, and in the center was Magellan's flagship, the *Trinidad*. Beneath the ship were the dates 1519–1960, and around the edge of the plaque were the words *"Ave Nobilis Dux. Iterum*

Factum Est" ("Hail, Noble Captain. It has been done again"). The plaque was passed to a Navy destroyer, the *Weeks*, using the same technique employed in passing the sick sailor to the cruiser. The destroyer was waiting off the coast of Spain and arranged to have the plaque delivered to the City Hall of Sanlúcar de Barrameda, where Magellan had started his historic voyage. From Spain the *Triton* continued submerged back to New London, where the secretary of the Navy personally delivered the Presidential Unit Citation to the ship.

During the *Triton's* voyage President Eisenhower was embarrassed by the capture of U-2 pilot Gary Powers, shot down in his spy plane over Russia just before a planned U.S.-Soviet summit meeting. The *Triton* had been held to a tight schedule, and now everybody knew why. The president told Captain Beach, who had been his naval aide in previous years, "You've shown that the oceans are still free to all. Of all the things we'd planned to prove for the summit conference, you were the only one to come through."

Giving the Technology to France

The British and the Canadians had provided assistance on the development of the atomic bomb during the war, and therefore, when the British government expressed interest in the late 1950s in establishing a cooperative program with the United States on nuclear submarines, there was considerable sympathy for the idea among a number of top U.S. officials, even though the benefits were primarily one-sided. The proposal was for a U.S.-designed nuclear propulsion plant to be provided to the British for installation in an otherwise British-designed-and-built submarine. Rickover agreed to this approach and to providing support for this one ship through her first refueling. However, he drew the line on any further significant help, because he wanted to encourage the British to develop a complete capability of their own, and not be further dependent on the United States.

This program came about in an interesting way. Rickover and Mandil were touring nuclear facilities in England and Scotland, and they concluded that the British nuclear submarine program would not bear fruit for many years. "England has been a real friend and ally of America for generations," said Rickover. "We should help them."

"But how do we do that?" asked Mandil.

"By giving them outright a submarine reactor plant and the supporting technology," was the reply.

But it appeared that the proud British might be reluctant to accept an American reactor plant for one of their warships. Rickover resolved that question in typical fashion. He met alone with the first sea lord, the famous and colorful Lord Mountbatten, and asked him bluntly, "Do you want a working reactor plant now, or would you rather preserve British pride?"

Mountbatten emerged from that meeting and announced—to the amazement and consternation of his admirals and other officials—that he was prepared to accept Rickover's offer to provide an American plant.

Rickover enjoyed working with the British, who treated him with extraordinary courtesy and respect, and the program worked well. (One British official remarked to me, with obvious admiration, "When that man walks into a room, it's obvious he's in charge, even before he's said a word.") Rickover responded to the British deference by reminding his people that the British were properly proud of their first nuclear submarine, HMS *Dreadnought* (whose motto was "Fear God, Dread Nought!"): "We should be careful not to look as if we were trying to grab any glory from them. She's their ship, let them have full credit." But it seems the British were less sensitive on the point than he had anticipated, for he learned later that the crew had posted a sign over the entrance to the reactor compartment, parodying those in Berlin:

"ACHTUNG! YOU ARE NOW ENTERING THE AMERICAN SEKTOR."

The clear success of the British submarine program suggested another idea to some members of the Eisenhower administration: Why not start a similar program with France? Charles DeGaulle had developed uranium enrichment facilities, nuclear warheads, and intercontinental ballistic missiles to carry them. He had expressed an intent to develop nuclear submarines. The United States was looking for ways to improve its balance of trade by selling more U.S. products abroad. And few things brought in so much money with so little effort as high-technology weaponry. To international fiscal planners in the government, the idea of selling nuclear submarine technology to France looked tailor-made.

Rickover was horrified. He saw no point in developing new weapons just to pass them out to others. He had accepted the British deal as something special, but France! "The head of the French Atomic Energy Commission is a proselytizing Communist," he complained. "He makes frequent trips to Moscow for instructions. He has five hundred known Communists in his atomic program. It's nuts!"

Despite Rickover's protestations, the program seemed headed for implementation. In desperation, Rickover got AEC Chairman John A. McCone, who a short time later left the AEC to become head of the Central Intelligence Agency, to call a special meeting of the AEC commissioners. "No staff, no records, let's just talk about this thing in private. I want you to understand why I feel so strongly about this."

Most AEC meetings had literally scores of staff, outside consultants, lawyers, and miscellaneous experts and dignitaries in attendance. But this one was as requested: all five commissioners, the AEC secretary (not taking any notes), and Rickover and I. I asked the Admiral what the presentation would include, what material should I bring? "Bring everything. We'll play it by ear" was the discomfiting reply.

McCone and the other commissioners took turns explaining the many benefits this program would entail, and Rickover sat silent. They then each explained that they understood the program was not entirely without dangers and drawbacks. Rickover continued his silence. Finally, the talk died down. As one commissioner was feebly trying to keep the discussion alive, Rickover suddenly broke in. With utmost gravity he looked McCone in the eye, and speaking slowly, looking at each commissioner in turn, he asked simply, "Does anyone here doubt how the American people would vote if they were given a chance to express themselves on this issue?" Not waiting for a reply, assuming there was agreement on the answer, he went on: "Knowing that, it is *immoral* for you to proceed otherwise."

There was shocked silence. McCone flushed. The other commissioners looked down at the table and cleared their throats quietly. At last McCone said, "Now Rick, nothing has been settled. This is just a matter that's under discussion. That's why we're having this meeting. No decisions have been made."

Rickover thanked them courteously for taking time from their busy schedules and left the room, with me hurrying after him. I looked at him in awe. "Admiral, I don't know of any person in the world—I mean that, in the world—who could have pulled off that speech. That was incredible."

"Yeah, but will it change anything? I doubt it" was all he said. But in fact the idea of helping the French build a nuclear submarine was not heard from again, for many years.

The Leaky Congressional Hearings

The United States Capitol Building is an amazing artifact. In the early days of the Rickover program, before fear of terrorists closed down public access to some of the most interesting parts of the building, I liked to take my children there on Sundays, when I was not at work and the building was relatively quiet. One Sunday Ed Bauser, the assistant director of the Joint Congressional Committee on Atomic Energy (and former NR engineer), borrowed the massive ring of keys from the Architect of the Capitol and took me and my children on a tour of some of the lesser-known nooks and byways. Before the slick new subway system was installed, there was a little underground Toonerville Trolley that ran from the Senate and House Office Buildings to the Capitol, and we rode this little-known railroad. We sat where Samuel F. B. Morse sent the first telegraph message, and we saw the old direct-current generating station that used to supply all electricity to the building, independent of the city and of everything else. We saw the Senate dining room, the private barber shop, and the ancient printing press that used to print all congressional reports. We climbed down a hidden staircase where British soldiers burst out in 1812 behind the speaker's podium in what was then the House of Representatives meeting hall. And we ascended the spiral staircase between the outer and inner shells of the great dome itself. Carefully lifting up one of the eight-sided panels, we peered fearfully down 250 feet to the floor below, where tourists gazed at the murals, unaware of our presence.

One room I became familiar with over the years was labeled F-88. Room F-88 was typical of a number of tiny, odd-shaped rooms created by carving up this grand old building into bits of turf for the burgeoning number of committees and panels that needed a place in the Capitol. It seemed that none of its lines were at right angles, it was crammed with the maximum number of chairs, and the floor of the long, narrow, winding hall leading to it was stacked so high with committee reports, old copies of the *Congressional Record*, and miscellaneous documents and files that a person could barely navigate its length. I recall an occasion when the Joint Committee was having a series of hearings on international aspects of atomic energy, and top officials of the State Department, the AEC, the Navy, and the Defense Department were crammed into the room for another day of it. I, being the lowest-ranking person in the room, was crowded against the only door—the last person to be seated, the first to push his chair aside to clear the door and lead the parade out at the end of the hearing.

The meeting opened with Senator Anderson of New Mexico complaining bitterly that he was tired of taking extraordinary security precautions before each of these hearings and then reading in detail exactly what had happened in John Finney's stories on page 1 of the *New York Times*. Senator Hickenlooper of Iowa joined in, expressing outrage that these sensitive matters could not be kept from the papers. Others chimed in, and the finger was pointed at the State Department. Livingston T. Merchant, State's senior representative, protested vigorously that his people were not responsible, and after further finger-pointing in various directions and threats of prosecution, the meeting finally got under way.

I remember only one thing from that meeting. When it was over, the participants all burst down the hall with me in the lead. When the narrow hall opened into a wider foyer, I saw John Finney. I knew Finney, but I had never breathed a word of the meetings, or anything else of a classified nature, to him. But there he was, calling loudly, "Ted! Can I give you a ride back to the office?"

Feeling a hundred eyes boring into my back, I tried to accept the offer unobtrusively, and when we were in the car and headed toward town I said, "You dog! If I live long enough to get out of jail someday, I'll never get a job in this town again. How could you do this to me?"

Finney was cheerful. "I know. You don't have to tell me. They were all accusing each other of leaking the story, weren't they? You don't have to answer; it's standard Washington procedure."

"Yeah," I said. "But now they know—or at least they think they do: I'm the goat. Nobody will ever tell me a thing after this."

"Nonsense," said Finney. "No one will ever accuse you of anything. Believe me. The ones who protest the loudest are usually the ones who are doing the leaking. I can guarantee you'll never hear about this again."

And he was absolutely right.

EDUCATING FOR QUALITY

> *The professional person's standing in the community depends, in final analysis, on the public's insight of his work, that is, on the educational level of the man in the street. When specialized knowledge of professional people is incomprehensible to the average man, he is apt to flounder between frustrated suspicion and excessive awe, leading him either to interfere unduly with professional independence or to accept naively every claim made by anyone who calls himself a professional. The relationship between the expert and the public is one of the central problems of our day . . .*
>
> *Thus we observe a widening gap between the experts and the public who depend for their well-being on the work of these experts. This disturbing cleavage exists in the humanities no less than in science. Thus most people are not well informed in such vital matters as the languages and cultures of the various peoples who share this earth with us; the historic, geographic and economic background of current events; the place of American civilization in the estimation of the world; and the real strength of our country in the shifting sands of power relations.*
>
> H.G.R.

It is hard to change the point of view of a person who has been running things for many years, and Rickover concluded that the ultimate hope for achieving quality lay not in the bosses but in education. He therefore began looking into why education was failing to meet its urgent goals and what could be done about it.

Rickover and his people could see this problem not only in industry but also in the young people they were interviewing to operate the ships and to work in various technical positions in the growing Rickover organization. Engineering graduates from the top few percent of some of the best schools in the country were often woefully inadequate when it came to solving, or even just analyzing, simple technical problems. Their professors could not believe that their students were unable to answer some of these questions. "You must be trying to trick or confuse them" was a typical response. But we learned early on that we did not need to be tricky, and in fact it was much more instructive to be completely straightforward in our questions. We didn't ask the kinds of questions that appeared on school exams. Our questions were simpler and more basic. And we found that high grades most often merely demonstrated that the student had learned "test taking" and didn't necessarily understand the fundamentals of the subject.

So Rickover characteristically tackled the problem at both ends. With the help of his wife, Ruth, he researched the American educational system and wrote *Education and Freedom*, which was published by E. P. Dutton in 1959. Later that year he toured Russia with Vice President Richard Nixon, met with the Soviet minister of education, and gathered a great deal of information on the Russian educational system. On his return, he wrote *Report on Russian Education*, which was published by the House Appropriations Committee. We were told at the time that the committee received more requests for that report than any other report in its long history. Later he wrote *Education for All Children: What We Can Learn from England; Swiss Schools and Ours: Why Theirs Are Better;* and *American Education: A National Failure*. These books received wide national attention and, not surprisingly, considerable criticism from the educational establishment, long before such discussion became a national pastime.

Educators versus Educationists

I once brought in a commentary in which an educational professional likened Rickover's efforts to the irritating hammering of a woodpecker against the mighty oak of the American educational system, trying in vain to bring it down.

"Yeah, yeah, I saw that," grumbled the Admiral.

"But I've done a little homework, Admiral," I replied with a grin. "Here's a piece I found saying that woodpeckers don't do any damage to healthy trees. They merely destroy the *bugs* and other *parasitical pests* that endanger the tree. Trees have actually been saved by woodpeckers this way. How about that?!"

"Good," said Rickover with a chuckle. "Draft me a response to this clown. And don't call him an educator. Educators are people who educate. Teachers are, or should be, educators. This character is an 'educationist.' "

One time, Rickover and I were taking the long ride from an airport to a naval facility. Rickover's first reaction was to look with distaste at the admiral's flags flying from small holders on the front fenders, in accordance with Navy regulations. He hated that traditional practice, and always ordered the flags removed or covered. "Put those damn things away," he ordered, and the driver did so.

The young sailor driving the Navy car was a quiet type, not nuclear-trained, and I was looking forward to having some quiet time to collect my thoughts for the coming meeting while the Admiral did the same. Lacking that, I figured I might be able to discuss some of my concerns with Rickover. But neither of these options was to be realized. As soon as we were settled in the car, Rickover addressed the sailor. "Where are you from, son?"

"Michigan, sir."

"Did you graduate from high school?"

"Yes, sir."

"Public high school?"

"Yes, sir."

"Do they have pretty good schools in Michigan? Was yours a good school?"

"Yes, sir. We all thought it was pretty good."

"Where did you graduate in your class? Near the top?"

"Well, I was a little above average, sir."

"Did you study the Civil War? Do you remember anything about that?"

"Yes, sir. We learned all about the Civil War."

"About when was it? Do you recall the dates?"

"Well, I'm not very good on dates."

"Was it more than a hundred years ago?"

"Oh, yes, sir. A lot more than that."

"Two hundred? Three hundred?"

"More like that. Yes, sir. Two or three hundred."

It is hard to report a conversation like that without making it sound like an inquisition. But I noticed that the Admiral managed to sound noninquisitorial, just friendly, and the sailor seemed relaxed. Rickover reviewed a number of topics—history, geography, politics, literature—and the sailor consistently revealed an appalling ignorance. Finally, we reached our destination, and Rickover said, "Thank you for the ride. I enjoyed talking with you. Good luck to you."

And the kid said, with real friendliness, "Thank you, Admiral. It was real nice."

When he was gone Rickover said, "You see why I'm concerned about our educational system? Here's a kid, obviously brighter than average, not lazy, with better-than-average grades from a better-than-average American school, and he is ignorant. Our schools have betrayed him. They took twelve precious years of his life, the years when he was most capable of learning, and taught him almost nothing. What I could have done with him in those years!"

The Admiral's interest in education was more than intellectual—it was born of his own personal longings as a child. "I started grammar school at the age of $6\frac{1}{2}$ in Brooklyn, knowing only a few words of English," he said. "I was probably as poorly prepared academically as any plebe who had ever entered the Naval Academy. Each week of the years at high school, I worked more than 70 hours a week, with no vacation during the entire time. I remember those high school years vividly. It would have been wonderful to have had the opportunity for more study, for reading good books. But I did not have that opportunity."

At the same time that Rickover was taking the national podium to air his views on education, he was also implementing his ideas in his own school system. Those who are familiar with them consider the six-month theoretical schools he established to be equivalent to a good master's degree program. These schools in turn are followed up by in-plant training school, in which fundamentals and principles are stressed, not just memorizing procedures. Tens of thousands of officers and enlisted personnel have graduated from these schools, and the effectiveness of the teaching is continually tested by in-the-field examinations and quizzes. In response to what is learned from these examinations, the curriculum and the teaching methods and texts are continually being upgraded.

Rickover served on the advisory council to Princeton University's Department of Chemical Engineering, and he learned several things there that he applied to his own work. In Princeton's Firestone Library, he saw study carrels, private little "telephone booths" assigned to a student for a period of months, for work on a thesis or other project. The carrels have shelves and a writing surface, and good fluorescent lighting and ventilation. A student can lock up the books and papers he is working with and leave them in the carrel while he goes out to stretch his legs or get a bite to eat. Rickover was always impressed with how difficult it usually is for a student to get undisturbed privacy for study, and he had a large number of similar carrels made for his schools. He also found that the library was open quite late each night and on weekends, and this reinforced his efforts to accomplish the same for the plebes at the Naval Academy.

Rickover and the Doctors

At some point in the middle of all this, I got a call telling me that the Admiral had had a mild heart attack and was in the hospital at the Naval Medical Center, where dignitaries with naval connections—people like Franklin D. Roosevelt and James V. Forrestal—are taken. I hurried over to see him and was relieved to find that he seemed to be in good spirits. He was talking with the medical director of the hospital, who assured him that he would soon be back at the office, unimpaired, if he took care of himself.

"That's a big *if,* Doctor," said I.

"You may be surprised to learn," replied the doctor, "that your boss is an ideal patient. He is behaving admirably."

Rickover had an answer for that one. "Doctor, Rockwell knows I do not suffer fools gladly. But I respect technical competence. And I respect the laws of nature, whether they apply to me or to a power plant. I have to assume you guys know what you're talking about. I have no basis for any other conclusion. If you say I need rest, I'll rest. I assume you know that I need to get back to work just as soon as you believe I can safely do so."

This, of course, was just what the doctor wanted to hear. He responded with enthusiasm. "Excellent! We'll get you out of here just as soon as possible."

Rickover was not interested in small talk. He was always interested in learning new facts about the world, and here was someone who knew things he didn't know. He asked, "Doctor, I'm told your specialty is the use of metal pegs and pins to set bones. Tell me something about that. What problems do you run into? What tricks have you learned?"

The doctor was only too glad to talk on that topic. "We've found out that human body chemistry is very unpredictable and variable. Some patients can keep the steel in their bones for years, and autopsy shows that it stayed shiny and uncorroded. In other patients it corrodes horribly in a matter of weeks. We've studied the biochemistry of these various patients, but we can't yet explain the differences."

Rickover had been listening carefully, and he asked, "How do you specify the steel? What kind do you use?"

"I'm not sure I know what you mean. We have a drawing that shows the size and shape, and the amount of variation in dimensions we can tolerate."

Rickover suspected he was onto something. "Yes, yes, but the material! What material do you use?"

"Why, we just call it medical-grade stainless steel."

"Have you ever seen the specifications for it? Who writes the specifications?"

"We don't really have specifications. Our purchasing people take care of that. I think they just try to get the best price from a reputable supplier."

"Rockwell, get ahold of Mandil. I want him to bring over some of our stainless steel specifications. They're more voluminous than one of your medical textbooks, Doctor. We've found that we have to specify the heat treatment, the crystalline structure, the surface cleaning, maximum impurity levels . . . Any one of these things can affect the corrosion resistance. Believe me, we can help you here. When can I have my people get in touch with the proper people in your organization?"

"Why, that's most thoughtful of you, Admiral. I'll certainly take you up on that. Let me talk with my people, and I'll get right back to you." I never found out what came of that encounter, but I know that Mandil carried the stainless steel specs over himself; Rickover had carried out his side of it.

Rickover was also shocked by the antiquated call system for doctors: no "beepers," just lights on a panel at each floor desk. He called his controls expert, Jack Grigg, to help them modernize the system. But Grigg soon found that the doctors did not *want* to be more easily reached, and so Rickover let it drop.

Rickover's experience with doctors was varied. The stories of his encounters with psychiatrists are legendary. Hearing that the Navy was making a long and expensive psychological study of why sailors get tattoos, he roared, "Because their buddies get them drunk, that's why! Any sailor can tell you that." And sure enough, that was the formal conclusion of this extensive study.

Rickover always enjoyed the psychological examination associated with his Navy periodic physical. A typical exchange went something like this:

SHRINK: Do you like your work?
RICKOVER: No.
SHRINK: Do you like people?
RICKOVER: No.
SHRINK: Are you happy?
RICKOVER: No.
[*Shrink pauses, to figure where to go from here*]
RICKOVER: Are you going to ask any more damn fool questions?
SHRINK: No.

Reportedly, a single word was entered into the psychological symptoms section of the physical report: SANE.

One encounter I particularly enjoyed occurred after Rickover had cut his hand in the machinery during a sea trial. The ship's doctor couldn't stop the bleeding, and then he realized that the Admiral had had a heart attack recently and must be on blood thinner. He started chewing Rickover out, this young lieutenant. "You're supposed to *tell* me you're on anticoagulant, and I would have brought a clotting agent along. That was irresponsible. If you die, they'll hold me responsible and it could wreck my career." And he went on and on. The Admiral just kept looking at this kid in mild amusement and tried to keep from cracking up. He never talked back to him. I had to leave the compartment to keep from laughing right out loud.

A Submarine Crew Quiz

As each ship approached the date of initial criticality, her skipper knew he would soon experience a Naval Reactors Crew Quiz. This was part of the process by which Rickover satisfied himself, and then reported to the AEC, that the training and the performance of this crew were up to the standards necessary to start up a nuclear reactor and take it to sea. This would not be the only such inspection, but it would be the first on the ship, and the skipper would have done everything he could to get ready for it. A typical crew quiz ran about as follows. First, a call came from Bob Panoff, and the inspection was scheduled for a Friday night, to continue on into the weekend, as long as it took.

Panoff, Jack Grigg, and I made up a typical team for those early inspections. We arrived at the ship about 7:30 and identified ourselves and our mission to the deck watch.

"Mr. Robert Panoff, submarine project officer for Naval Reactors. Permission to come aboard for crew quiz."

Grigg and I similarly identified ourselves, and the sailor responded, "Permission granted. The captain is expecting you, sir."

We climbed down the ladder through the hatch and entered the ship's wardroom. The skipper, his executive officer, and his engineer leapt to their feet. "Have you eaten, sir? We can get you something in a hurry, if you like."

Panoff replied for the three of us. "One thing about submarine service: the food is superb. We haven't had any supper yet. If you can give us a bite of something—anything—without a lot of fuss, we'd appreciate it. Actually, we didn't get lunch either. Hey, your galley isn't operational yet, is it? I forgot that. Let's just skip the chow."

But the skipper was up to the occasion. "The cook managed to get some cold lobster, and he made up some salad, just in case. It's all ready." He picked up the phone, dialed, and said, "Bring in three salads, right away."

Panoff started right in. "I want to get right into this. We have a long evening ahead of us. As I think you heard, we had one crew quiz, on the prototype, and we interviewed the people alone so they wouldn't be intimidated by the presence of their officers. But then the officers had trouble believing that their people had done so badly. The officers didn't say so, but it was clear that they were convinced their men had all the answers and we must have tricked them or asked misleading questions. So tonight I'm asking your permission to have one or more of you present for all of the questioning. That way you'll be able to judge the results firsthand. Do you have any objection to that?"

The skipper replied, "No problem. I'm confident about our state of training, and if there is anything wrong, I want to see it myself."

Panoff continued. "Fine. Despite what you may have heard, it's not our purpose to terrorize your people. This is a technical quiz, not a psychological one. We'll keep the questions straightforward, and the men can ask for clarification without prejudice. But we expect them to know the technical material thoroughly. I'm sure you've heard Admiral Rickover say that any one detail, followed through to its source, will usually reveal the general state of readiness of the whole organization. Take the spare parts system, for example. The way parts are inventoried, stored, accessed, and reordered can be quite revealing of the whole organization." He pulled a little widget out of his pocket and asked, "Do you know what this is, Captain?" The skipper and his engineer looked at it carefully. "Do you use these on this ship?"

The engineer was ready with an answer. "Yes, sir. It's a . . ."

Not waiting for a reply, Panoff asked, "How long would it take to get another one? Here, in the wardroom."

"They're stored in the yard, sir. Over in Siberia—one of the new buildings at the north end of the yard."

"How long?"

"Oh, I suppose we could have one within the hour."

"And if it were an emergency?"

"Half an hour, sure."

Panoff looked at his watch and said simply, "Go!"

"I beg your pardon?"

"You now have 29 minutes 55 seconds left."

"Yes, sir!" The engineer jumped to his feet and ran out the door.

The skipper wanted to insert a caution. "It's late Friday evening, you realize. He may have trouble getting the right people at the yard. They keep all that stuff under heavy security."

"Can you guarantee that you won't have any emergencies on weekends, Captain?"

"No, sir. We may have to change our arrangements with the yard to handle things like this. Mr. Rockwell, I've been thinking about that radiation drill you pulled on the prototype last week. They phoned us about it. You had them take wipe samples on various surfaces, and they found high radioactive contamination. So they called a radiation alert. But you told them to go outside and check the hoods of some parked cars. And they were even higher. Those poor guys figured they'd blown a fuel element and were about to shut the whole place down and evacuate. Then you told them it was probably fallout from weapons tests. And they checked and found out it was. Is that just because they're out there in the desert, closer to the testing sites, or is that going to be a problem for me too?"

I asked, "Did you try it here? You could make the same sort of test yourself, you know."

"No, sir. We just haven't had time."

"You would find that you got about the same results. In fact the radiation levels from weapons testing fallout are higher, almost anywhere in the Northern Hemisphere, than we have set for a radiation alert on the ships. You should find lower contamination levels in your engine room than in the parking lot outside. You just have to be aware of that, and not call a false alarm. In case of doubt, you have procedures for differentiating between various radioisotopes. That should pin it down."

Panoff asked, "Have your men been briefed on the meaning of the colors of the various indicating and warning lights?"

The engineer had now come back from setting up the parts search, and he handled Panoff's question. "Lights? Yes, sir. I handled that myself. The complete spectrum, I called it, from *on* to *caution* to *warning* to *danger*. They ought to know that cold, sir."

"We'll see, won't we?" said Panoff. "Let's go."

Grigg had already left to go over electrical and control questions with appropriate crew members, accompanied by the executive officer. The skipper and the engineer ducked through the watertight door into the corridor, following Panoff. A noncommissioned officer was standing watch over some machinery with a large number of red and green lights. The engineer smiled reassuringly at the sailor, then did a double take as he looked at the lights.

Panoff asked, "Chief, do you understand the color system for machinery lights?"

"Yes, sir."

"Will you please explain what you have here?"

"Yes, sir. Glad to," replied the chief. "When I got here last week, these lights were all sorts of colors. You wouldn't believe it. Red, blue, yellow, green. Everything. Even white ones. But I got them all in order."

The engineer could control himself no longer. "My God, Chief! What in the world have you done?"

Panoff cut him off. "Please let him answer. Please explain your system, Chief."

"Yes, sir. Well, you see, red is for port and green is for starboard. So all the lights for the port valves and the port pumps are red, and the starboard ones are green. See how clear it makes it? You can't get the wrong one that way."

"Thank you, Chief. That will be all."

The engineer said grimly, "Chief, I want to see you in the wardroom when this is over. Don't go anywhere."

Panoff said gently, "There'll be more, Lieutenant. The night is young yet."

They went down the passageway to the next watch-stander. I stopped to quiz him, and Panoff went through another door with the skipper, into the engine room. The engineer stayed with me.

"Sailor," I said, "I understand you're qualifying for reactor operator."

"Yes, sir. But I'm not finished yet."

"I understand. You've completed theoretical school?"

"Yes, sir. At Bainbridge."

"And prototype school?"

"Yes, sir. And I'm qualifying for the various watch-stations here on the boat—or ship, we're supposed to call it. I can't get used to a submarine being a ship, sir."

"I'd like to check you out on some basic thermodynamic theory," I said. "Is that OK?"

"Yes, sir. I guess I'm about as ready as I'll ever be."

"Do you know what Charles's Law is?"

"I forget which is Charles's and which is Boyle's. One is temperature and the other is pressure."

"I don't care whether you remember their names. I just want to be sure you know what they mean. Suppose we have a sealed tank, full of a perfect gas. Is air a perfect gas?"

"Any gas follows the perfect-gas law pretty well unless it's under very high pressure," said the sailor.

"Well, air does, anyway. So let's say this tank has a pressure gauge on it that reads 10 PSIG—do you know what that means?"

"Yes, sir, 10 pounds per square inch gauge pressure."

"Right. And let's say it has a temperature gauge that reads 70 degrees Fahrenheit. Now let's say we heat it up until the temperature reads 140 degrees Fahrenheit. What do you expect the pressure gauge to read? Will it change?"

"Yes, sir, it will go up. Boyle's or Charlie's Law says that if you double the temperature in a sealed system with perfect gas in it, the pressure will double too, so the gauge will read 20, right? . . . You look as if that's not right."

"Well, let's think about it a little more," I said. "Suppose there's a second temperature gauge on the tank, and this one reads centigrade. Let's see, 70 degrees F would be about 20 degrees C. And 140 F would be about [*mumble, mumble*] 60 degrees C. So the Fahrenheit gauge says you've doubled the temperature, but the centigrade gauge says you've increased it threefold. Which is right?"

The sailor now looked baffled. "Gee, now I'm really confused. Wait a minute. I got it! From 70 to 140 degrees Fahrenheit isn't doubling. You gotta start figuring from absolute zero, which is 273 degrees below zero in centigrade. I don't remember what it is in Fahrenheit."

"Now we're getting somewhere," I said, getting into it. "Suppose we figured out how much heat it took to double the temperature, then the pressure would go to 20 pounds, right?" The sailor nodded. "But now let's start with the pressure gauge reading zero. We add the heat to double the pressure, but how do you double zero?"

But the sailor didn't bite on that one. "No, I'm with you now. The pressure gauge isn't showing an absolute number either. It reads zero at atmospheric pressure, which is about 15 PSI *absolute*. So if you doubled the pressure, the gauge would go to 30 PSI absolute pressure, or 15 PSI gauge pressure. That's right, isn't it?" He looked pleadingly at me. "Look, Mister, I'm not stupid. They just didn't teach us this sort of thing ʻn school."

I was completely conciliatory. "You did OK. It's clear you're not stupid. And you're not ignorant, either. But you've got me worried about the schools."

While this was going on, the chief previously questioned was relieved of the watch, and, accompanied by the engineer, I went back to quiz the replacement. The chief was looking at a sheaf of papers that he sheepishly tried to stuff into his pocket when he saw me approaching.

"Whatcha got, Chief?" I asked.

Embarrassed, the chief looked helplessly to the engineer, who said, "Tell him, Chief."

"It's a crib sheet, sir. A list of questions we got from the guys at the prototype after their quiz. That isn't really cheating, is it?"

"No, because it won't do you any good. We just want to know if you understand what you're doing. What would you like to be asked about? What do you know best?"

"I just finished studying the charging procedure, sir. Ask me about that."

"OK, Chief, tell me about it. What do you do?"

"Well, when the water level in the pressurizer gets below this point here, I turn on the charging pump by throwing this switch. And I keep watching the water-level gauge, and I turn it off when it gets up to here."

"So what is the maximum amount of water you have to pump in, in inches of water level?" I asked.

"We try to keep it within four inches, sir. We normally don't like it to get any further off than that."

"How long should it take to raise the water level four inches, Chief?"

"Ten minutes, sir."

"Suppose I think it's twenty minutes. How would you check that?"

"I can find that right in the manual, sir. It will only take a few minutes to look that up. But I'm sure ten minutes is right."

He started pawing frantically through the manual, but I cut in. "Suppose you can't find it in the manual. Is there any other way you could check it?"

"I'd ask the other chief, sir. He's pretty smart, and he's been around longer than I have."

"Chief, I'm trying to get down to fundamentals. You taught math at the school, didn't you?"

The chief was puzzled by this turn in the conversation. "Yes, sir."

"Could you calculate from first principles how long it should take to pump four inches of water into that pressurizer?"

"What do you mean, sir? What first principles?"

"Chief, can you calculate the volume of a cylinder four inches high and the diameter of the pressurizer? And could you convert that volume into gallons? And, knowing the gallons per minute the charging pump can deliver, could you calculate how long it would take to deliver that volume of water? Could you?"

"Oh, yes, sir. That's the sort of problem I gave my students all the time."

"Then do it right now."

"Now, sir?"

"Now. Let me see you do it."

The chief pulled a piece of paper out of the drawer and quickly scratched out some figures. He then took out a slide rule and, after a few deft movements, wrote down an answer. With a smile of relief he turned to me and said, "See? Ten minutes!"

"The point is, Chief, that you frigged around with every possible way of getting that answer except by a simple calculation. And you showed that you can calculate it in a few seconds. Why would you do everything else but? Why wouldn't you just calculate it?"

"I guess I just never think of math when I'm on the job, sir. School is school, but this is the real world. That's what they kept telling us at the prototype school."

I jumped at that one. "*What* did they keep telling you at the prototype?"

"Geez, I guess I stuck my foot in it. I probably shouldn't be telling you this . . ."

"Tell him," said the engineer.

"On the very first day the instructors say, 'Forget about all that crap you learned at theoretical school. This is the real world.' Pardon me, but that's what they said, sir."

I responded with great sadness. "Oh, brother! Chief, I'm not mad at you. Thanks for telling me. But we're going to have to do something. If *you* don't ever think of using what you teach, we certainly can't expect your students to."

I turned to walk away, but the chief called after me, hesitatingly, "Sir, I have to tell you something."

"Yes?"

"I want you to know something. I was in the Navy for nearly fifteen years before this program came along. I was a typical sailor like in the movies. You know the type. If the average human being uses 10 percent of his brain, I was using 1 percent. Everybody figured sailors were supposed to be stupid, and who were we to argue? Now I'm working my tail off, but I'm alive. Y'know, I'm actually a thinking human being. And I think about how I just threw away fifteen years of my life because nobody kicked my ass. You know what really woke me up? On my old ship we didn't have toasters, 'cause sailors are too dumb to work toasters, right? So we had cold, hard, dry toast from the galley. Then one day we had toasters on the tables. And I asked around, How come? And you know what I found out? They said Captain Rickover had told the top Navy brass that if sailors were smart enough to run a nuclear power plant, they could damn well run a toaster. And I said, There's a guy I want to work for. And I—well, I wanted you to know that you've done a lot for a lot of guys, 'cause I wasn't the only one. Thanks."

He turned away, and I was really touched. But all I could say was, "Thanks, Chief. I really appreciate your telling me that. Good luck to you."

Saturday continued along in the same vein. In the evening Panoff came in from the engine room with word that Admiral Rickover had arrived and was waiting for us in the wardroom. So we hurried to the wardroom and seated ourselves at the table. The Admiral asked, "Have you finished with your quiz?"

Panoff replied, "No, sir. We still have a lot more to do. We didn't know you were going to get here so early."

"I want to make a tour of the yard. How much time do you want? Two hours enough?"

"Can you give us three? We have a lot to do yet."

"OK. I'll see you at midnight." And then he asked, "Do you have anything to tell me before I leave?"

I began tentatively, "Well, sir, I don't know how urgent it is, but I've gotten a couple of indications of weakness in the theoretical area, and I think it may result from the schools."

Rickover jumped on that. "Anything to do with our schools is urgent. What is it?"

"Well, I haven't checked it, but I heard that . . ."

"Out with it, dammit! What are you trying to tell me?"

"The prototype school instructors may be telling the kids that they don't need all the theoretical stuff. To forget it. Just use what they learn at the prototype."

At this, Rickover exploded quietly. "Goddammit, that's awful! A few words like that can wipe out everything we do at the schools. Dammit to hell! Look, Rockwell, I want you and Panoff to make a survey of the schools. Both the theoretical and the prototype schools. If this is true, and it probably is, we've got to change it quick. Let's take the first ten days of the prototype curriculum and do nothing but relate the operating procedures to the theory. And do a similar sort of thing on the last few days of the theory school."

Panoff was quick to pick up on that. "Yes, sir. We could take the start-up procedure. Ask them what they have to do to start up the reactor. Do they just pull out the control rods? No, they have to start the pumps first. But they can't start the pumps until the system is pressurized, or they'll cavitate. And they can't pressurize the system cold, or they risk brittle fracture. And so on. Yes, sir. We can do that."

"Well, get cracking on it. How did you let it get to this state, anyway? You guys are supposed to be watching it. I'll be back at twelve. Better make it twelve-thirty now. Then I want to go over the whole quiz results." And Rickover headed out into the yard to do his own hell-raising while we worked frantically to finish our task. The schools would get another thorough upgrading.

When Rickover returned, the results were reviewed with him and with the skipper, the exec, and the engineer. After making sure that all of the points had been made clear and that none of them was being contested by the ship's officers, Rickover signed off with a simple statement: "Well, Commander, from what you've just heard you can see you've got a lot of work to do. Your men are not as well trained as you thought. How is it that a couple of outsiders can come onto your ship and, in a few hours, find out more than you know about conditions here? Do you think I would let that happen on my ship? If you had spent last weekend like we spent this one, this never would have happened."

And we departed into the night, to plan another crew quiz.

Rickover's School System

As Rickover made clear in testimony before Congress and in other public statements, he had two alternatives facing him when he started to build up manpower for his program. He could try to lure away from other programs the few people experienced in nuclear technology, or he could train his own people. He decided on the latter course.

Other leaders of state-of-the-art projects have made such a decision, but Rickover's solution went far beyond the usual on-the-job training. He was not content to teach procedures and techniques. He wanted to teach principles and fundamentals, and he wanted to create a change of mind—a whole new way of approaching the job. And he undertook to do this not just with his own employees, but with industrial contractors and their subcontractors, with shipyards and research centers, with the Bureau of Ships and the laboratories of the Atomic Energy Commission, with the officers and enlisted men who operate the ships, and with the medical and public health officers assigned to the program. It was a program of unprecedented scope and depth.

In April 1956, while the *Seawolf* was getting ready for initial criticality, Rickover testified on his training program before the Joint Congressional Committee on Atomic Energy. He described the program he had instituted at the Bettis Laboratory, where Westinghouse recruited professors from nearby University of Pittsburgh and the Carnegie Institute of Technology to supplement the teaching staff recruited companywide from Westinghouse scientists and engineers. Similar programs were set up by GE at the Knolls Atomic Power Laboratory and by Combustion Engineering, Inc. at the new prototype facility being built near Windsor, Connecticut. Nearly all the costs of these programs were borne by the companies, not by the government.

These were not casual lecture series or seminars, explained Rickover. They were carefully designed curricula. There were heavy homework assignments, written examinations, and grades. Most of the courses were given after working hours and on Saturdays. The Bettis reactor engineering program, for example, was a twenty-three-week program consisting of 362 hours of instruction in the following seven courses:

Introduction to the nuclear reactor
Reactor plant technology
Dynamics and control of reactor plants
Heat transfer and fluid flow
Metallurgy
Materials application and development
Stress and vibration analysis

All of these courses stressed fundamentals and were highly analytical, involving the latest mathematical techniques.

Bettis also gave special courses on nuclear design principles, magnetic amplifier theory, statistical design of experiments, physical metallurgy, radiation shielding, and reactor physics. The GE and Combustion Engineering programs were comparable in their depth and scope. In addition, the companies offered joint fellowship programs to encourage their people to go on for master's and doctoral programs at cooperating universities in the vicinity.

In addition to the programs at the three Naval Reactors laboratories, Rickover set up similar training programs at the shipyards involved, or about to get involved, in nuclear shipbuilding. And Duquesne Light Company, in Pittsburgh, had expressed an interest in nuclear power and sent people to Bettis for training. After Duquesne was awarded the contract to operate the first civilian nuclear power station at Shippingport, Pennsylvania, the company set up a training program of its own. Of course, Naval Reactors had a training program for its own people and for others in BuShips who were involved with nuclear power. And Rickover had provided impetus and a great deal of detailed assistance in setting up the training programs at Oak Ridge and at MIT and the special curriculum for medical personnel assigned to the program. He had already started publishing a series of publicly available technical reference books on zirconium, hafnium, reactor physics (three volumes), reactor shielding, and the like.

For the general technical community, Rickover undertook two more significant efforts in addition to the technical reference books just mentioned. In connection with the international "Atoms for Peace" conferences in Geneva in 1955 and 1958, he encouraged his people to work with their counterparts in the Naval Reactors laboratories to prepare technical papers, as a vehicle for declassifying and promulgating the newly developed technology of naval reactors. The showpiece of this series was a full volume entitled *The Shippingport Pressurized Water Reactor*, which was made part of the official U.S. presentation set given to each delegation at the 1958 conference.

The other project for presenting the data and design rationale of the Naval Reactors program involved a long technical paper published in the *Transactions of the Society of Naval Architects and Marine Engineers* 62 (1957): 714–36, which was authored by Rickover, Dunford, Shaw, me, and Willis C. Barnes. Barnes, a particularly bright and imaginative engineer, came to NR from the Naval Academy and MIT in 1954. For ten critical years he was one of the people Rickover depended on most heavily for long-range technical ideas and evaluations.

I still find it incredible that most of this activity was going on with just one nuclear ship operating (see table p. 296).

Getting into the Inner Circle

One of the younger engineers in Naval Reactors came in to see me. He had been looking back over his career and trying to peer into the fog of the future, and he had a serious question. "How do you get into the Inner Circle? You know, whenever there's something really important to go over, a policy matter to discuss, or whatever, there's a certain small group of people Rick asks to come in and talk about it. You're one of that group; I'm not. And I'm convinced I never will be, but I'm not sure why. What do I have to do to get into that select group?"

I looked at him carefully, thinking of several possible approaches to an answer. Then I said, "You know the answer to that, don't you? You don't really need to hear it from me. Right?"

The young man was a little taken aback. He thought a minute and then said slowly, "Yeah, I suppose I do. You guys are here sometimes when I'm someplace else. Maybe on a Scout picnic, or with a church group. Is that it?"

"It's not so much a question of total hours worked. It's just a matter of priorities. You're not willing to pay the price. I'm not saying that's

Projects Begun during The Miracle Decade

DATE	TRAINING	CONSTRUCTION	OPERATIONAL	KEY EVENTS
1949	Bettis Lab (Westinghouse)			
1950	Knolls Atomic Lab (GE)	*Nautilus* Prototype		President OKs sub project
1951	Electric Boat Co.			
1952		*Seawolf* Prototype *Nautilus* 14 Jun.		
1953	Portsmouth NSY	*Seawolf* 15 Sep. Shippingport 6 Sep.	*Nautilus* Prototype	
1954	Mare Island NSY Duquesne P&L Co.		*Nautilus* 30 Sep.	
1955	Newport News SY	*Skate* 21 Jul.	*Seawolf* Prototype	
1956	Bethlehem SY Ingalls SY Combustion Engineering Co.	*Swordfish* 25 Jan. *Sargo* 21 Feb. Carrier Prototype 1&2 *Skipjack* 29 May *Triton* 29 May *Seadragon* 20 Jun. *Triton* Prototype		
1957		*Halibut* 11 Apr. *George Washington* 1 Nov. *Long Beach* 2 Dec. *Tullibee* Prototype	*Seawolf* 30 Mar. *Skate* 23 Dec. Shippingport 18 Dec.	
1958	New York SY	*Sculpin* 3 Feb. *Enterprise* 4 Feb. *Shark* 24 Feb. *Snook* 7 Apr.	*Swordfish* 15 Sep. *Sargo* 1 Oct. Carrier Prototype 1 *Triton* Prototype	*Nautilus* transpolar *Skate* surfaces at Pole

1959	Tullibee 26 May Patrick Henry 26 May Thresher 28 May Theodore Roosevelt 28 May Scorpion 20 Aug. Robert E. Lee 25 Aug. Abraham Lincoln 1 Nov.	Skipjack 15 Apr. Triton 10 Nov. Seadragon 5 Dec. George Washington 30 Dec.	Arctic operations Long Beach launched
1960	Scamp 23 Jan. Bainbridge 15 May Permit 16 Jul. Ethan Allen 14 Sep. Barb 9 Nov. Tinosa 24 Nov. Samuel Houston 28 Dec. Plunger 2 Mar. Pollack 14 Mar. Thomas Edison 15 Mar. John Marshall 4 Apr. Dace 6 Jun. Haddo 9 Sep. Jack 16 Sep. Destroyer Prototype	Tullibee Prototype Carrier Prototype 2 Halibut 4 Jan. Patrick Henry 9 Apr. Scorpion 29 Jul. Robert E. Lee 16 Sep. Tullibee 9 Nov.	Triton round the world Polaris on patrol Enterprise launched
1960–1962	Pearl Harbor, Puget Sound, Norfolk & Charleston NSYs getting ready		

EXTENDING THE EFFECT: EDUCATION

The extent of Rickover's lasting effect on the American educational system is a matter of controversy. Some critics try to dismiss it as inconsequential, but the record shows that he was seriously considered at one time for the position of U.S. commissioner of education. Others argue that his position was merely a more eloquent restatement of the traditional back-to-basics plea. In any case, there is no question that he was heard and understood by a very large audience, and the questions he raised and the documentation with which he supported his arguments had an impact on the thinking of a great many people. His words seem no less relevant today.

---

good or bad. We all make a choice, and we live with the consequences. After it's all over, maybe we can compare notes in that Great Conference Room Up Yonder, and maybe then we can decide who made the better choice."

"But there are guys here who put in even longer hours than you do, and they're not in. So working hard is not the whole story."

"That's true. It's a lot of things, most of which you've got. But you haven't made the full commitment, and I don't think you will."

"I guess you're right. There are some things I'm not willing to push aside for the program."

"Hey, I've seen guys starting to go off on a trip when they should have been home with a sick wife, and Rick insisted that they go home. It's not just blind allegiance. It's . . . well, look around and decide for yourself."

"I know what you mean, I guess. Anyway, thanks for the talk."

THE PRICE OF SUCCESS

As our civilian nuclear power station at Shippingport approached the start-up date, a number of questions arose that we had not had to face before. The rigorous training and grueling examinations we gave Navy operators were unprecedented, but military personnel have always understood that sometimes circumstances require extraordinary mea-

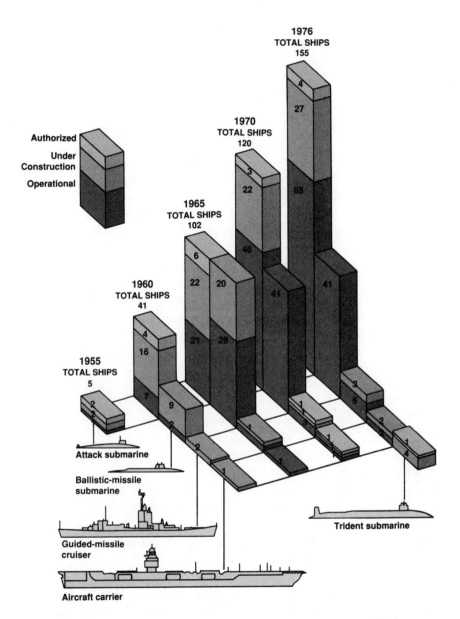

By the mid-1960s the nuclear fleet was beginning to grow rapidly in numbers and diversity. (*Fortune* magazine)

sures, and we had been able to get away with it. The civilian electric utility business, however, had a history and a tradition all its own. In addition, this was a time when the national labor unions were battling for control of large blocks of potential members, and new industries, as precedent-setters, were particular targets. So the AEC had a top official responsible for labor relations, several steps above Rickover in the organization, who made it clear to us that we were not to create any labor problems.

Tension started to build up as the date for the first crew quiz came near. One of the reactor plant operators was a union shop steward, and other key members of the union were also on the operating and maintenance crews to be quizzed. We had been warned that union representatives might insist on monitoring the quiz or even taping it, to object to questions that struck them as unfair and to look for any signs that might be interpreted as "union busting." I approached the day with considerable trepidation. The Admiral was standing by his phone, and I was to call him if there was any action that threatened to impede the free exercise of our quiz. He was prepared to call off the quiz, which would effectively prevent start-up of the plant.

I agreed to have a witness from plant management and one from the union, who could observe but not comment or interfere. We proceeded without incident, but the shop steward was clearly not prepared. At the end of the quiz I asked him, "Do you believe, on the basis of this quiz, that you are prepared to be an operator in this plant?"

He replied, "No, sir. I didn't do very well, did I?"

"Do you consider that our questions were reasonable ones?"

"Yes, sir."

"Were they clear? Did you understand what we were getting at?"

"Yes, sir. No problem there."

"Did you feel any undue pressure, or bias, or intimidation?"

"No. You were real friendly."

"Well, Ron, I can't pass you on today's quiz. But there's no reason you couldn't try again when you're ready. Fair enough?"

"Yes, sir. Fair enough."

Without looking at the union observer, I turned and left the compartment. I had been given all the right answers, in the presence of witnesses. I took a deep breath, excused myself for a moment, and telephoned the good news to the Admiral.

The Admiral and the Union Official

Not long after that, the Admiral called me into his office. "Rockwell, I've just had a call from a high union official who wants to talk with me about Shippingport. He implied that he wanted to talk about radiation and safety. Any idea what that's all about?"

"No, sir, Admiral. I've told you everything I know."

"Well, stay here. He called from the front desk and wants to come up. I want a witness. I don't know what he's going to charge me with. Dixie, bring him up."

During the minute or so it took for the official to appear, Rickover was silent. He was apparently scanning in his mind through possible stances he might take with this unknown opponent. I soon found out.

Looking back now, it all went so fast that it's hard to reconstruct. The visitor began with some pleasantries and some compliments. He was clearly awestruck and somewhat ill at ease. He mentioned ever so casually, "There is one area where I may be able to help you, Admiral."

"Oh?"

"Yes, sir. You know, a number of the men are afraid of radiation exposure, and . . ."

He didn't get to finish the sentence. The Admiral had moved in after the word *radiation*. "Who tells you that? Are you saying I am not properly protecting the men from radiation? That I'm endangering their lives? Is that what you're saying?"

"Oh, no, sir. I'm sure you're doing the right thing. But you know how the workers are, sir. They naturally worry over whether management really has their interests at heart. And so they worry."

"Who is worrying? Who is saying I'm not protecting them? Dixie, get Jim Terrill on the phone. Do you know Dr. Terrill of the United States Public Health Service? He's the man responsible for assuring that the public health is protected against radiation. Have you ever talked with him?"

"Well, yes, sir. I know about Dr. Terrill. He's well known in the public health and safety field, where radiation protection is involved."

"You're damn right he is. Have you ever talked with him about this problem? Have you?"

"Well, yes. I believe we did mention this to him one time. He . . ."

The light on the Admiral's phone blinked and he picked it up. "Jim? This is Rickover. Fine, thanks. Jim, there's some son of a bitch here who says you're not doing your job. He says that we're irradiating people at Shippingport, and that he's told you about it and you haven't done anything. Here, I'll let you talk with him. I'll get off the line and you can talk with him in private."

He handed the phone to the union official, who was now sweating profusely. The official gave his name to Dr. Terrill, then had to repeat it and explain who he was. All he could say was "Well, no, sir. No, of course not. Yes, sir. I understand. Well, I'm pleased to hear that, sir. Yes, sir, I'll tell him."

He hung up, and Rickover just looked at him. "He said to tell you, Admiral, that he considers you're doing a splendid job, and that I shouldn't worry."

At this point most men would have gloated and rubbed the victim's face in the dirt before throwing him out. But Rickover became completely conciliatory. "Now aren't you glad you checked? I appreciate your concern for your people, and now you know that I share your concern, and I'm acting on that concern. I think we should commemorate this meeting in some way." He started looking around, and he spotted the magnificent new embossed leather briefcase his visitor was carrying, resplendent with a gold and crimson union seal. "Why don't we exchange some symbol of our respective offices? Dixie, bring me my official United States Atomic Energy Commission briefcase, the one I carry with me to all official meetings. Would you like to exchange with me?"

The union official mumbled that he would be honored, and the Admiral noted his beautiful silk tie. Taking off his own well-worn bargain-basement tie and handing it to the visitor, he said, "There are few things more personal than a tie. That's the one piece of clothing where a man is permitted to show his personality and character. Would you exchange with me, in honor of this occasion?"

It was an offer that couldn't be refused. The official was removing his tie with a dazed expression when Dixie came in with the Admiral's "briefcase," a government-issue cardboard accordian file. Dixie played right along with the game. "Admiral, this has all of your important official papers in it. What do you want me to do with them?"

With a martyred expression the Admiral said, "You'll just have to put them in something else. I am giving the carrying case to this gentleman as part of a symbolic exchange, in token of our new understanding. Will you escort him out, please." Turning to me after they had left, he said in a matter-of-fact tone, "I don't think he'll give us any trouble."

The Smaller/Lighter/Cheaper Lobby

Panoff first picked it up on the rumor circuit. A group at General Electric, physically and organizationally separate from the Knolls Atomic Power Laboratory, was quietly working on the design of a nuclear power plant that was intended to be smaller, lighter, and cheaper than Rickover's "outmoded" pressurized-water plants. They were talking about a destroyer plant, staying clear of the submarine people, whom they considered Rickover captives. It had started in the summer of 1955. Francis K. McCune was general manager of GE's new Atomic Products Division, charged with the responsibility for developing a commercial nuclear power market independently of the government. But the Knolls Laboratory was also under McCune, and Rickover was still trying to get GE to put more engineers from within the company at Knolls, and to give the Navy work more priority with top GE management.

There were a number of incentives behind McCune's project: technical, political, and psychological. Technically, there were those who believed that higher-temperature nuclear cycles, such as those with a liquid-metal or high-temperature-gas coolant, would ultimately prove superior to the pressurized-water plants. Politically, there was a desire in some parts of GE and the Navy to break free of the tight control of technical and procurement processes that Rickover had established, and to return to the more relaxed, "normal" mode of operation that characterized almost all other government procurement. GE, with an eye toward a future commercial nuclear power market, was concerned with the precedent being set by Rickover in the realm of government/industry relations. Psychologically, there was Rickover the person. It was argued that no one person should unilaterally determine the direction and character of a field as broad and vital as nuclear power. And there were people who would do anything to get around him, just for the sheer satisfaction of doing so.

McCune suggested to Admiral Albert G. Mumma, who was chief of the Bureau of Ships, that GE could team up with the naval architect firm of Gibbs and Cox and with the Bath Iron Works commercial shipyard, to study advanced nuclear power plant concepts for use in Navy destroyers. Moreover, he implied, this could be done in commercially built facilities, so that a government contract would not even be required.

Frank McCune was handsome and articulate, the perfect picture of a successful American executive. William Francis Gibbs was a prominent ship designer whose colorful personality was known to every shipbuilder and ship operator in the hemisphere. And Bath had been building destroyers in Maine since World War I. It was a formidable team, and one with ready access not only to Mumma but also to Chief of Naval Operations Robert B. Carney, and to his successor Arleigh Burke, and to the secretaries of the Navy and defense, present and recently past.

Rickover and his people attacked the proposal for having no technical basis. They argued that GE was selling "smaller/lighter/cheaper" as a product, but was not developing a technical basis for showing that the plants would indeed have these unarguably desirable traits. In fact, GE was putting little effort into the reactor plant, and was giving presentations featuring artist's renderings of sleek destroyers cutting through the stormy seas on their way to battle enemy forces.

In April 1956 the control issue surfaced. GE proposed to pay for one-fourth of the cost of the study by the three companies if GE were given "complete freedom to select the personnel to perform the study and to be solely responsible for direction of the study." At a time when Rickover was charging that GE was trying to transfer its best engineers to nongovernment work, another Navy project competing within the company against Knolls would be completely contrary to the direction in which Rickover was trying to push the company. Over Rickover's vigorous objections, Mumma authorized the three-company study.

At one point the team's preferred coolant was molten lithium metal, a substance even more reactive with air and water than molten sodium. It would run at a temperature too hot to be held in stainless steel, so all of the massive piping and equipment would have to be made of titanium. At operating temperature, the titanium piping and pressure vessels would react with air, so the whole system would have to be encased in an outer shell, which would have to maintain a slight pressure of helium. If the helium were to leak out, the system would be in danger of failing catastrophically. And the helium molecule, being composed of a single atom, is literally the most difficult of all gases to contain.

Panoff discovered that the team was to make a presentation to the chief of naval operations and his people, and although we were not invited, Panoff and I decided to attend. We made nuisances of ourselves by raising questions as to how some of the technical problems just mentioned were to be handled, and as the answers grew more and more complex, we asked, "What reason is there to believe that such a system would be smaller, lighter, or cheaper—let alone all three—than the existing systems using ordinary water?" We were denounced by the operations people as closed-minded wet blankets, but by July 1958, when the team had completed its study, the coolant of choice had become high-temperature gas.

Harold Etherington's group had looked at high-temperature gas for naval reactor application, first at Oak Ridge and then at Argonne, and the Allis-Chalmers Manufacturing Company investigated the matter further in 1950. It had been studied again by Westinghouse in its survey of possible cycles for the aircraft carrier propulsion plant. Each time, the studies concluded that the large size of the equipment required to handle the gas coolant, and the high temperature and pressure necessary to bring the size into a competitive range, made the system considerably less attractive than water-cooled systems. But it wasn't until late in 1958 that this smaller/lighter/cheaper project was finally killed—for the moment. This was only one in a series of attempts, and other such projects continued to arise from its ashes from time to time.

Dinner with Edward Teller

I was deep in a crew quiz at Mare Island when I got a call from Rickover. "I'm coming in tonight and we're having dinner at Teller's. He wants to talk about something; I'm not sure what. Rent a car and pick me up at the airport. Wait a minute. Here, let me give you Teller's address." And he did. But he didn't stop there. Teller had given him instructions on how to get to his house from the airport, and Rickover wanted to pass this information on to me. I didn't want it.

"Admiral, I can imagine only one thing worse than trying to follow instructions from Teller on how to get around in San Francisco traffic, and that's trying to follow instructions from Teller relayed by you."

"Rockwell, do you know anything about San Francisco? Do you know your way around there?"

"No, sir, I sure don't. That's why I'm going to get a map from the rental agency and figure out for myself how to get to the address you gave me. Believe me, it'll be tough enough that way, getting through rush-hour traffic in a strange car in a strange city. Don't make it any worse."

THE WORD ENGINEER AWARD

One day I received a call from Rickover's office and hurried up there to find him holding an impressive scroll, and Dixie grinning widely.

"What is it, Admiral?" I asked. "And why do I feel I'm about to be mousetrapped?"

"Read it to him," ordered the Admiral.

Assuming the most serious face she could muster, Dixie read aloud:

> Whereas you have so ably demonstrated outstanding talents in the field of the written word, and whereas such demonstration has been above and beyond the call of duty, therefore, pursuant to the authority vested in me by the Most Exalted Order of Word Engineers, Theodore Rockwell is awarded, on Ground Hog Day, this scroll and pin as Word Engineer of 1958. Signed, HG Rickover, Highest Potentate.

The document was quite impressive, with a round silver foil seal from a Woodward and Lothrop gift wrapping, and two red-white-and-blue ribbons cut from an airmail envelope. I was not quite sure how to respond to this. "What have I done to deserve this unexpected honor, Admiral? And what's it going to cost me before I'm through?"

"Why, it's given in recognition of your splendid service in helping with congressional testimony, safeguards reports, and the like," said the Admiral, with an expression of great sincerity. "I assume you'll frame it and cherish it forever."

"Why now?" I asked, still suspicious.

"Don't you have considerable work ahead of you, drafting radiation protection standards, procedures, and so on? This is just to encourage you in that endeavor."

I went out clutching the thing, feeling silly but somehow glad to have it. I grinned as I recalled the effort I had put in on a report of hearings before the House Appropriations Committee, where considerable rewrite had been necessary. I was at a subsequent hearing when an argument broke out among the congressmen, who were accusing each other of "altering the *Congressional Record.*" The committee chairman, the venerable Clarence Cannon, was shocked at the very idea, but he was asked, "Have you never altered the record yourself, sir?"

I held my breath, because I had personally rewritten for the *Record* large sections of the chairman's opening remarks, to clarify and focus them. But the question did not faze Cannon, who said forthrightly, "Not substantively, sir, not substantively."

"Rockwell, I'm just trying to make it easy for you. He gave me directions."

"Admiral, you don't drive, and I'll bet he doesn't either. I'll handle it."

Rickover finally relented, and I picked him up that evening and drove to Teller's house. There was a modicum of backseat driving, which I ignored, and we arrived in ample time. Teller greeted us at the door, and before we could get our coats off, he stated the purpose of the visit. "Rick, you've got to build smaller submarines."

I bristled. This was a subject we had debated often, and I was ready for it. But Rickover's response was calm and relaxed. "Why, Edward? The oceans are very big."

"We will need lots of them, Rick. Lots of them."

"We can build lots of them, Edward."

"No, they are too expensive."

"Ah, you don't mean they should be smaller. You mean they should be cheaper."

"Isn't it the same thing?"

"Not at all. You used to be able to buy a big Ingersoll pocket watch for a dollar. I suppose it's a bit more now. But a tiny lady's wristwatch is very expensive. Even without diamonds on it. No, smaller doesn't mean cheaper. Not at all."

It was clear that Teller had been impressed by the General Electric/ Gibbs and Cox "smaller/lighter/cheaper" lobby. The argument continued a little longer, with me chiming in occasionally, and then it died out when Mrs. Teller and their daughter joined us. The daughter was obviously very bright and was taking physics in high school. I asked how she liked the course. She enjoyed the subject, she said, but the textbook was not very good. She was writing one that she was confident would be better.

OPERATION AT SEA

> *Of course, the professional person's insistence that he cannot accept lay control over the methods he uses to perform his tasks cannot be twisted into an excuse for incompetence or for blunder . . . [A] patient's relatives obviously cannot be permitted to lean over the surgeon's shoulder and direct where and how he is to make his incision. He must be completely independent of lay direction in the* performance of *the operation. However, he will most certainly be judged by the* results *of the operation. If too many of his patients die, the public will render judgment on the surgeon and he will soon have much spare time on his hands.*

H.G.R.

The crux of the power struggle between Rickover and the operational Navy, once the selection and training of line officers had been reluctantly accepted, became the control over operation of nuclear ships in ports. Rickover's critics argued that the whole subject was really just a ploy to increase Rickover's personal power. And in a sense, it was. He believed that only he and his people were sufficiently knowledgeable and responsive to the safeguards aspects of operating a nuclear power plant in populous areas, and this was probably true. His critics claimed that it was essential to national security that the Navy be permitted to roam the world unrestricted, and that if the Navy insisted on this right, it could probably get a "waiver" from the AEC. This was probably also true; the Advisory Committee on Reactor Safeguards didn't like being in the squeeze, and it might well have accepted a "military necessity" clause that would have, in effect, excused the committee members from exercising their judgment whenever the Navy accepted responsibility for the consequences.

Getting Control

Whatever the motivation, Rickover was unwilling to accept the "military necessity" argument. He had rejected that approach when he set radiation standards for the crews, and he rejected it here, for the same reasons. He was convinced that with a little extra effort—a lot of effort, by anyone else's measure—the Navy could treat the safety of operating nuclear propulsion plants as rigorously as any application for civilian reactors. Controls were structured and agreed to by the AEC and the Reactor Safeguards Committee to control operation of nuclear-powered ships. These controls directly involved Rickover's headquarters organization and applied equally whether the ships were operating in U.S. waters or elsewhere. Consistency in world-wide operation was built in.

The Navy tried various stratagems to change this situation. At one point, Committee Chairman C. Rogers McCullough and I received formal invitations to discuss the situation with the chief of naval operations over lunch. We arrived at the elegant CNO meeting room in the Pentagon to find that the lunch did indeed involve only the three of us. The U.S. and Navy flags stood proudly before the draped window, and there seemed to be gold everywhere: gleaming from the admiral's cuffs and epaulets and sparkling from the embossed formal dinnerware, faultlessly served by the traditional "Philippine messboy." I whispered to McCullough, "If there's a nuclear attack here, they'll be well shielded from the gamma rays." The CNO stated his position and concerns, and McCullough responded noncommittally. Afterward, McCullough said to me, "We're going to stick to our guns."

Thereafter, Rickover solidified his position with the Safeguards Committee and with the AEC by encouraging them to state their position explicitly with regard to the operation of nuclear ships in populous regions. With regard to operation of the *Nautilus*, the committee wrote on 21 April 1955,

> The conclusions and recommendations are based in part on consideration of the high degree of training which has been given the present operators and the extent of technical review of design and operation presently being conducted. The Committee feels that maintenance of high standards in both of these regards is essential to continued safe operation.

Reviewing operational directives by the Navy intended to codify training and operating procedures for nuclear-powered ships, the committee wrote on 5 March 1958,

> The Committee endorses the present Navy practice to consult with and to be guided by the Naval Reactors Branch regarding reactor safety and operational procedures for nuclear-powered ships. It considers this practice to be important and urges its continuance.

On 5 August 1958 the committee commented as follows on the growing operational activity of the nuclear Navy:

> The Committee reiterates that the prime assurance of safety during the building, operating, and repairing nuclear ships at various locations depends upon the proper prior evaluation of potential hazards. This must be done for each new situation and at present, on a case-by-case basis, by persons having a detailed knowledge of the factors influencing reactor safety. This requires that the training of officers and crews of nuclear ships must continue to emphasize knowledge of reactors and reactor safety. It also means that the experience and technical judgment of the Naval Reactors Branch must be utilized to the maximum extent in evaluating such operations. The problem assumes increasing importance as the number of nuclear-powered ships increases.

The Challenge by Teller

In 1960, after this process had been in effect for some time, Rickover got a surprise in the mail. Edward Teller had written an article for a nationally read Sunday-supplement magazine, in which he suggested that it might be safer if nuclear ships were refueled at sea, away from populous ports. The article had been submitted to the AEC for security clearance, and Rickover was asked to comment. He immediately called Teller. After explaining that he had been asked to comment on the article, he said, "Edward, you haven't discussed our program with us for a long time. You've never ridden one of our new submarines. How would you like to ride the *Patrick Henry*, a Polaris missile ship? We'll let you man the helm for a bit, and we'll get a picture of you there. You can publish it. It'll give your article a lot more authority. But I would like to have the Safeguards Committee along too, and we can discuss your suggestion to refuel at sea. I don't think that's a good idea. I don't think it enhances public safety. And I'd like to explain to you why I feel this way. You can then discuss it with your friends on the Safeguards Committee. We'll give you complete privacy for the discussion. And then let's see how it all comes out. Would you like to do that?"

Of course, it was an offer Teller couldn't refuse. Rickover then had to scramble to persuade the Navy to release the ship for this purpose, just as she was hurrying to start her first Polaris patrol. And then he had to get all thirteen members of the Safeguards Committee to be present on that date. Somehow, he pulled it all off.

I got to the shipyard the day before the meeting and went over the fire drills, collision drills, and other preparations the crew had made to be ready for the committee. I suggested they tighten up security of access to the ship. "These guys are security-conscious, and I don't want to give any impression of flabbiness there." (I sure didn't want a repeat of what had happened when we had the congressmen on the *George Washington*. The Electric Boat Company guards had been rebriefed and checked, and when the ship's captain came down to the boat with the first group, the guard stepped forward and asked for the IDs. But the captain, Commander James Osborn, undid all the preparations with one stroke when he pushed the guard aside and roared, "This is my ship. Step aside!")

Rickover was discomfited because the Safeguards Committee members were obviously more intrigued by the missile systems (which were new to them) than by the reactor plant (which they were quite familiar with). One member asked the missile officer, "What's the mean time-to-failure of the missile system components?"

"About ten years," replied the missile officer proudly. "We expect that the average component in this system should work faultlessly for ten years before experiencing any kind of failure."

"And about how many components are there in the system?"

"About 10 million," replied the officer.

"Well, let's see," said the safety scientist. "There are about 10 million seconds in a year. So that means you should expect some sort of component failure every ten seconds!"

"Gee, that doesn't sound right," said the missile officer. "These things are supposed to be pretty reliable."

"They're waiting for us in the wardroom," growled Rickover, glaring at the missile officer. "I think they are about ready to start. We'd better go ahead."

The Safeguards Committee listened intently behind closed doors while Teller ran through his calculations for a hypothetical worst-case accident. The results he got implied a very serious problem. The committee had previously agreed with my calculations, which led to the conclusion that even under the same unrealistically pessimistic assumptions, the ship would not create an intolerable public hazard. But the committee was now unable to find any fault with Teller's figures.

I was called for, and I went through my own calculations again. Teller said, "You've used engineering units. Let's do it again with physicist's units." I struggled with the unfamiliar terminology but arrived at about the same answer as I had before. Then Teller said, "I can't see where you went wrong, but let's just follow through my approach. I still don't find any flaw with it."

So we started through it, and I had to keep stopping Teller to say, "Edward, you left out a $2\pi/3$ term. Let's put that in." Or, "Don't forget that only half the sphere is active; there's no radiation source for the half that would be under ground. So we have to divide by 2."

Each time, Teller was quite aware that he had dropped the term, but he argued that he was just trying to get a rough number. However, since nearly all the dropped terms worked in the same direction, the final number did in fact come out about as I had suggested. Teller, to his great credit, emerged from the meeting room and said cheerfully, "Rick, I didn't think they could do it, but they did. They convinced me I was wrong." He accepted the revised answer and, after hearing about the problems of trying to refuel on the open sea with no ship's power available, agreed that the dockside refueling procedure was the proper one. He wrote a letter to the AEC, dated 18 August 1960, that included this assessment:

> My trip on the *Patrick Henry* has convinced me that the care that has been exercised in the design, building, and testing of naval nuclear power plants, together with the intelligence and extremely high state of training of the Navy crew, has greatly minimized the risk, but has not eliminated it.
>
> The safety record of these nuclear-powered ships is impressive. I know that this is due in large measure to the safety criteria established by Admiral Rickover in his close working with the Reactor Safeguards Committee. I also know of the pressure he has been under to relax these standards in design and training. In light of the risks that are unavoidably involved, it is of concern to me, and I am sure to the members of the Reactor Safeguards Committee, that such pressures do exist.

Admiral Rickover and his staff have an excellent insight into the entire reactor safety field. Undoubtedly their naval plants are setting the pace in the field of reactor safety. With so many nuclear submarines contemplated, the Navy is fortunate to have such a qualified group to advise them; their advice should be respected . . .

My conclusion, however, that such risks are acceptable, is based on present design standards, maintaining the present care in building these power plants and testing them, and maintaining careful selection and training of their operating crews. My conclusion would change if the standards were relaxed.

"We Fought a War over That!"

Most people didn't really understand Rickover's thinking, so they were always being surprised by what they considered to be inconsistencies in his actions. Most Navy operations people were convinced that he did not attach very high importance to the Navy's need to have freedom of operation, or he would not have taken the position he did on controlling ship operations. So they were unprepared for his reaction to the first visit to a British port.

As the ship approached port, a cheery message was received, welcoming her to England and asking permission to come aboard for a spot of tea in the wardroom and a briefing on some of the local customs. "That's a friendly gesture," thought the ship's captain, and he invited the visitor aboard. The same procedure was applied to the next U.S. visitor, and it was all very warm and friendly. Until Rickover found out about it.

"You damned fools," he roared, "don't you see what you've done? You've established the precedent that we can't bring a nuclear warship into a British port without first admitting a boarding party. We fought a war over that! What do you think the War of 1812 was all about? Precisely that issue. And now you guys have just given it all away."

In vain the captains argued that it was all very harmless and very friendly. Nobody had tried to inspect the reactor or quiz the crew. Rickover brushed all that aside. "They've taken the first and biggest step in that direction. They've established the right to board our warships. The first guy who refuses now is going to cause a scene. You guys never think in historical terms. Dammit, you've got to keep the big picture in mind, all the time."

In a similar vein, the Navy had wisely developed a standard answer to the question "Do you have any nuclear weapons aboard?" The only permissible answer was (verbatim) "It is U.S. policy neither to confirm nor deny the presence or absence of nuclear weapons on a U.S. warship." But when the captain of the first submarine tender to put into Holy Loch, Scotland, was asked the question, he was delighted to be able to say, "Nope, nary a one." This, of course, was fine for that particular moment, but it created an unnecessary problem the next time around.

To avoid this sort of problem, Rickover arranged for me and Sir Solly Zuckerman, chief scientist for the British Defence Establishment, to go into the British Embassy one Sunday night and work out privately between us a one-page definition of safety assurances for nuclear-powered warships. This statement of assurances by the United States would be accepted by the British as the basis for letting our warships use our repair base at Holy Loch in the United Kingdom and to visit British ports. In turn, the United States would accept visits by U.K. nuclear-powered warships in this country on the basis of receiving essentially identical safety assurances from the British government. This made clear that there would be no right of inspection.

The feelings engendered by walking into the secret depths of the embassy through one set of locked doors after another, à la Maxwell Smart, drove home to me the realization that I was legally no longer on American soil or under U.S. law. But the venture was a success, and we were able to forestall an effort just getting under way in the U.S. Defense Department to establish a vast international Court of Nuclear Ship Operation at The Hague, to adjudicate each port entry as a matter of international law. This project was based on the premise that a large international nuclear merchant marine would soon be in operation, but the nuclear merchant marine never materialized, and the little one-page bilateral agreement format worked just fine.

THE LOSS OF THE THRESHER

No management system can substitute for hard work. A manager who does not work hard or devote extra effort cannot expect his people to do so. He must set the example. The manager may not be the smartest or most knowledgeable person, but if he dedicates himself to the job and devotes the required effort, his people will follow his lead.

H.G.R.

After a series of stunning public triumphs, it was bound to come: the first public problem or setback in the naval nuclear propulsion program. And it was a serious one. The USS *Thresher*, first of a new class of attack submarines, was lost at sea with all hands. The *Thresher*'s characteristics included greater quietness, higher submerged speed, and far greater depth of operation. These characteristics called for significant untried innovations in the ship, yet the Navy planned to have several of the ships under construction before the first one had been tested at sea, a plan that made Rickover and his people very nervous.

To achieve quietness in a submarine, the sources of noise must be acoustically isolated from the hull, so that the sound waves will not be transmitted into the ocean to be detected by enemy listening devices. This meant that machinery in the *Thresher* was to be mounted on resilient mountings, and high-pressure piping had to be connected to the machinery through flexible pipe couplings. Rickover was not at all convinced that this would be practical, and he was disturbed to find an unknown, but potentially major, increase in the probability of casualty in the engine room. In addition, Admiral Albert G. Mumma, chief of BuShips, had selected the Portsmouth Naval Shipyard, rather than Electric Boat, as the lead shipyard, meaning that Portsmouth would be responsible for developing this first-of-a-class ship. Portsmouth had built lots of submarines, but it had not been the lead shipyard for any of the first nuclear ships. Mumma's decision would therefore broaden the nation's nuclear submarine design base, but it would load yet another uncertainty onto the *Thresher*.

Since the nuclear reactor already developed for the first high-speed attack submarine, the *Skipjack*, was to be used in the *Thresher*, the cognizance of Naval Reactors for the *Thresher* was limited to the reactor systems; the bulk of the engine room was the responsibility of other sections of BuShips. Although the engine-room changes were officially none of their business, Rickover, Panoff, and Howard Marks, head of Rickover's submarine propulsion plant engineering section, finally persuaded Admiral Mumma to study further some of the questions they had raised.

The ability to operate at greater depth depended on widespread use of a new high-strength steel called HY-80, meaning "high yield, 80,000 pounds per square inch." This steel had proved highly effective in the laboratory, but its large-scale use in the field was still limited, and welding was known to be a problem. The *Thresher* was to have her entire hull and frame made of HY-80. The wisdom of this decision was reexamined by a special board set up by the CNO, which reported that HY-80 could be welded safely, so long as the special procedures were followed carefully. But at one shipyard after another, reports of welding problems began to come in. These welds had passed inspection, and further investigation revealed two ominous facts: in nearly all cases, the yard's handling of the quality control and inspection practices was slipshod, and, even more threatening, some of the welds had indeed been satisfactory at the time of inspection and then failed weeks, or even months, later. Repairs were found to be extremely difficult and unreliable. Some welds had to be repaired as many as six times.

Concluding that it was important to get the ship to sea quickly in view of the large number of submarines depending on the same technology, BuShips pushed ahead the already tight schedule for initial sea trials. The shipyard commander announced the new date to his people with the words "The Portsmouth Naval Shipyard has been given one of the biggest challenges it has ever faced. It is a greater challenge than any other shipyard has."

BuShips sent out a civilian engineer to check the HY-80 hull welds at Electric Boat and at Portsmouth. He concluded that both the work itself and the quality control records at Electric Boat were good, but those at Portsmouth were unacceptable. When the laboratory at Portsmouth developed a radiograph that showed a weld to be defective, it was often not possible to determine which weld was involved. Four weeks after he filed his report, the *Thresher* was launched.

Even more worrisome than the HY-80 problem was the question of integrity of the seawater piping joints. The seawater piping constituted a part of the envelope that kept out the ocean. A watertight hull was no protection if a large seawater pipe were to fail under deep submergence. It would take immediate action by a well-trained crew, plus a bit of luck, to close off such a leak and save the ship. But seawater was the ultimate cooling source for the ship. Air conditioning, bearing and lube oil temperatures, and even the propulsion plant itself depended critically on the continuous flow of cooling water from the sea. At great depths, blowing air into the ballast tanks was a slow and dangerous procedure, and a submarine counted on her propulsion plant and her diving planes to drive her quickly and safely to the surface. But the propulsion plant could not operate if her seawater valves had been closed.

The hull plates were welded, and welding was a problem. But welds can be radiographed, and a poor weld detected and corrected. The piping, on the other hand, was not welded but brazed. Welding melts the metal to be joined, along with similar metal in the welding rod, and a properly welded joint is a continuous metallic structure, stronger than the adjacent parts. Brazing, on the other hand, is a process that flows a lower-melting metal (in this case, a silver-copper alloy) into the crack between the pipe and its fitting, without melting the pipe or fitting. There was no reliable way to check the integrity of a brazed joint, and even a perfect brazed joint was not as strong as a welded one. Although brazing also requires highly skilled workers, it is cheaper than welding and can be used to join dissimilar metals, which welding cannot.

All the shipyards were having troubles with brazed joints, and there had been some near-tragedies at sea. During her test dive, the *Thresher* sprung a small seawater leak and, while repairing it, discovered another failed joint. Although BuShips had reached no final answer to the problem, Rickover decided to weld all joints in the few systems for which he was responsible and all joints in other systems as they came through his reactor compartment. He applied this requirement to all nuclear submarines, those operational as well as those under construction or design. BuShips deplored the double standard but continued to rely on brazed joints. Through all this, the propulsion plant continued to work well, and the *Thresher*'s captain reported after extensive sea trials, "The propulsion plant functioned beautifully throughout the trials and has been a joy to operate."

On 11 July 1962, after a year and a quarter of rigorous sea trials, shock tests, and acoustic testing, the *Thresher* returned to Portsmouth for nine months of overhaul and repair work. After completion of this work, she went to make her test dives in eighty-four hundred feet of water, which gave her more than enough depth to maneuver in. During the diving tests, her escort vessel for the test received the routine message by underwater phone: "Proceeding to test depth." The next message was a calm voice announcing, "Experiencing minor difficulties. Have positive up angle. Attempting to blow."

That was the last intelligible message. There were one or two more, unintelligible, and then silence. Attempts to exchange "Gertrude checks" were unsuccessful. (Gertrude checks are simple messages, one or two words, repeated on the underwater telephone to confirm communication.) Hand grenades tossed over the side in groups o. three, the traditional signal for a submarine to surface, produced no response. Finally, the escort ship radioed that the *Thresher* was overdue and presumed missing at sea, with 129 souls aboard.

The *Thresher*'s Wake

The *Thresher*'s loss had wide impact. Admiral Rickover dropped everything to hand-write 129 personal letters to survivors of the ship's crew. Typically, he would not accept the Navy's official survivor list. "Those lists are always screwed up," he announced. "I've seen condolences and insurance money sent to former wives, while the current wife and children are unintentionally ignored. I'm not going to do that. It's no consolation to the person who was ignored that you got most of the other names right."

He insisted on having one of his senior people check the list, including first names and street names that seemed to be spelled wrong. He found several mistakes, and then he had it rechecked by someone else. Years later, he heard that there had still been a mistake or two, and people said, "You'd think he'd at least have taken the trouble to do it right."

I had developed considerable data showing that the *Thresher*'s nuclear plant, lying at the bottom of the sea, posed no public hazard, and I presented this information on request to officials in the Navy, the Defense Department, and the Atomic Energy Commission. Indeed, even when the ship was found, no significant radioactivity was detectable on the sea bottom where her remains were scattered, and this has continued to be the case.

A Court of Inquiry was quickly established and, after forty-five days of testimony from 121 persons, issued its conclusions: 166 findings of fact, 55 paragraphs of opinions, and 20 recommendations. The most probable scenario, the court concluded, was that the casualty began with a seawater leak in the engine room, possibly from a brazed joint, and the leak sprayed salt water across electrical equipment and shut down the reactor. Blowing the tanks at that depth was apparently not effective, and the ship never resurfaced. The court admitted that the conclusions were tentative, but they were supported by a computer program based on acoustical data picked up on the Navy's submarine monitoring system, which heard sounds interpreted as pumps slowing down, attempts to blow ballast tanks, and, finally, the hull imploding.

There seemed to be some people who were anxious to pin the loss of the ship on a failure of the reactor plant, perhaps to discredit Rickover's widespread reputation for quality. But the Admiral and his people did not find the preferred scenario convincing. Rickover, Panoff, and Leighton went over the computer analyses and discussed them with the acoustic and computer experts who had developed them. They learned that the "most probable scenario" had in fact never been run; it had been interpolated from other scenarios and then adjusted to make the data consistent. It was an honest effort, but it implied more certainty than was warranted. Panoff got the computer people to actually run the "most probable scenario" and found that the ship did not sink under the conditions postulated! This did not reveal what had in fact happened to the ship, but it indicated that one should not credit the various speculations with great weight, despite the implied validity of all the high-precision computer analysis.

Rickover was anxious to have the Navy and American industry learn from the tragedy that excellence must be achieved at all cost, and that the price for not doing so was apt to be disastrous. He had specific recommendations toward that end, which he had long ago implemented in his own program but which he was now reviewing and upgrading where appropriate. He put a great deal of effort into preparing his testimony, hoping that a greater good might result from this sad event. But the Navy was not convinced that it was necessary to pay such a price. BuShips was still letting shipyards unilaterally issue waivers to their specifications and was unwilling to relinquish brazed joints.

The Navy made a number of important changes in design and procedure on the basis of lessons learned from the *Thresher*, but many of these came slowly. One of the very next initial sea trials on a new nuclear submarine came with Rickover in the hospital, and Panoff was put in charge of the tests for BuShips. He and I were not very happy that of the roughly thirty thousand brazed joints on the ship's seawater systems, three thousand were spot-checked and three hundred found defective to some degree. These three hundred were repaired, but one could conclude that about twenty-seven hundred other defective joints had not even been located. In that condition we put to sea for a two-day check-out of the propulsion plant and the watertight integrity of the ship. Fortunately, all went well.

Perhaps the most far-reaching change was the establishment of the "SubSafe" program, to determine what changes had to be made on each submarine before she could be certified for full-submergence operation. Until then, the ship was limited in operating depth and maneuvers. A SubSafe Board was established to oversee the implementation of this program. It was originally conceived that this program would expire after the initial reviews were completed, but it was later decided that continued surveillance was needed, and the program settled into an essentially permanent mode of operation.

"Stay Out of It! That's None of Your Business"

The *Thresher* incident illustrates the bind Rickover was constantly put in. On the one hand, he was continually accused of trying to run the whole Navy, of being unwilling to stay within his own area of responsibility. On the other hand, when the "rest of the Navy" (sometimes called by his critics the "real Navy") failed to heed his warning on something like brazed joints, the consequences could impinge on the operability of the ship and raise questions as to the safety and reliability of nuclear power.

Sometimes he could figure out how to take a nonconfrontational approach and still win. A humorous example was the matter of designating ships as nuclear with an *N* in their number: SSN would stand for "submersible ship, nuclear," CVAN would denote "carrier vessel (aircraft), nuclear," and so on. Thus, the *Nautilus* would be SSN-571 rather than merely SS-571. But the naval powers-that-be scoffed at the idea of indicating the nature of the power plant that lurked in the bowels of the ship. "Who cares?" they argued. They finally settled for putting in an *N* in parentheses, thus: SS(N)-571. Rickover went along with that, but after a while he quietly put out the word to his people: "Drop the parentheses in all your memos and reports. The other people rotate; we endure. Before long, the parentheses will be gone." And he was right.

Milton Shaw, who was in charge of surface ship power plant systems and arrangements, repeatedly found himself in the middle of these conflicts. Shaw had wanted to work on nuclear-powered submarines ever since he read Jules Verne. After serving as an engineering officer on an LSM, a military landing ship, in the Pacific, he returned to graduate school to study physics and advanced math. He kept trying to find someone in the Navy who was working on nuclear propulsion, and in 1949 he heard about Rickover's program. He told Rickover that he wanted to work for him; he was thoroughly interviewed, and Rickover offered him a job. At the time, he was working on advanced propulsion concepts at the Navy's Engineering Experiment Station (EES) near Annapolis, Maryland, and he was told by his bosses that the program he was working on had the highest priority in the Navy, whereas Rickover's had none. The Navy would not release him for this transfer. Finally, in May 1950, he broke loose and called Rickover, who said, "I don't want you. You're too anxious."

"But Captain," he protested, "you already said you wanted me."

"I've changed my mind," he was told.

He finally persuaded the Captain to see him, and after another interview, in which he agreed to take a cut in salary to prove his sincerity, he was hired.

From the beginning there were many parts of the Navy that had some basis for influencing the design of any new ship. "Each new nuclear ship was looked upon by some people in the Navy as an opportunity to prove out their own pet idea," said Shaw. "Generally, these were first-of-a-kind developmental ideas that had never been proved out for shipboard use. I'd often hear about them, and I'd tell the Admiral. He would usually scream, 'Shaw, you stay out of it! It's none of your business.' But I'd keep my contacts active and keep fighting him on the serious ones, because I didn't want to let them wreck any of our first-ever nuclear-powered ships."

The first eye-opener was consideration by BuShips of a developmental hydraulic coupling for the main propulsion shafts of the *Nautilus.* Shaw had actually tested this very coupling system at EES a year before and found it unreliable. Under certain simulated operating conditions, the after part of the shaft and propeller could drop off into the ocean! But somehow the reports of these tests had not stopped BuShips from pushing to use this system on the first nuclear-powered ship.

Counterrotating propellers on concentric shafts was another such idea, one that BuShips engineers wanted to try out on the *Seawolf.* That was also outside Rickover's cognizance, none of his business. But if the propellers didn't work, the ship would be dead in the water. Or worse, a faulty shaft seal might flood the ship. That might have killed nuclear power, as well as the crew. Luckily, Rickover was able to talk the BuShips chief, Admiral Mumma, into vetoing that idea, which was later tried on the USS *Jack*. Today the *Jack* is retired, and no other major ships have this feature.

"The carrier prototype at Idaho was another good example," said Shaw. "I was Rickover's project officer. Other sections of BuShips were responsible for the steam plant; we in NR were just supposed to feed them steam from the reactor plant. But when the plant was started up, a continuous series of failures developed in most of the 'proven,' or conventional, components outside NR's cognizance, and a number of changes had to be made to the steam plant." The catapults were an even tougher problem. Catapults are mammoth devices that hurl aircraft off the ship. Modern high-speed fighter planes cannot get up sufficient speed to take off from an aircraft carrier deck, despite its thousand-foot length and four-acre deck area. So giant slingshots are used to get them up to speed, which requires a great deal of energy delivered in a short time. These catapults, of course, were not mocked up on the prototype plant at Idaho, and they were clearly "none of our business."

The British had developed steam piston catapults that were thoroughly proven, but our Navy was developing an "internal combustion catapult," which was in effect a gigantic automobile piston in which fuel would be exploded. As a backup, BuShips was looking at a huge compressed-air system. Part of the justification given by the bureau for undertaking these alternative developments was the belief that the reactor plant could not supply the quantity and quality of steam needed to operate steam catapults. Shaw objected strenuously to the argument that the reactor plant could not deliver the necessary steam, and he had grave doubts about the feasibility of the alternative systems. He kept complaining to Rickover that we were going to have a carrier that couldn't launch aircraft, and this could kill nuclear power for all surface ships. Rickover, having just negotiated a cognizance treaty, kept telling Shaw to stay out of it.

Shaw made a visit to the catapult development facilities at Lakehurst, New Jersey, and after talking with the engineering personnel there, he came away more convinced than ever. Shortly thereafter, the test system was wrecked by an explosion, and the Navy finally turned to the compressed-air system. Shaw meanwhile had calculations and tests made,

RICKOVER AS TEAM PLAYER

The most memorable interactions with Rickover, the ones that were burned deep into your psyche, were those in which you and everyone else in the room were in violent disagreement with him, and he insisted on doing it his way, and he turned out to be right. These demonstrations of his awesome technical intuition, and his incredible nerve and confidence, are the basis for much of the Rickover legend. They certainly make the best stories. But this sort of interaction was much more the exception than the rule. Who would have stayed with him otherwise?

I should note parenthetically that part of the basis for his remarkable record of being right on technical issues was his dogged determination to make *any* decision right by overwhelming it with hard work, backup approaches, safety margins, flexibility on other factors involved, and sheer intentionality. But of course, Nature does not often yield to bullheadedness; she generally gets her own way in such contests. You can win a few that way, but not many.

Most of the time in technical discussions, Rickover acted as *primus inter pares*—first among equals. He would be insistent, sometimes nastily so, shouting, "How do you know? Where are the data? Why haven't I heard about this before?" He was determined to find out whether you knew what you were talking about and how strongly you were convinced of it. And you couldn't slink away and return later to say, "I tried to tell you, Admiral, but you wouldn't listen." That didn't work. He would just say, "You should have kept arguing."

None of us would have put up with this badgering from anyone else. He wasn't pulling rank; he really wanted to get to the same truth we were after. None of us doubted that. He had plenty of ego, but no interest at all in proving that he was right. He always said, "The only thing I've done is to surround myself with people who are smarter than I am. I'm counting on you guys to keep me out of trouble." With a few exceptions, we all knew we were not as smart as he was, but we did know more than he did about certain things—each of us in his own area—and he was not threatened by that situation. In fact, as he said, he was counting on it, and that was empowering. We found it exciting to be surrounded by exceptionally bright and creative people who could always get an openminded hearing for their ideas. In that sense, Naval Reactors was almost like an idealized university setting.

with a great deal of dedicated and competent help from the Westing-house-Bettis people, to ensure that the reactor plant could deliver the large quantities of steam needed for a steam catapult. It wasn't until after the ship was launched that the Bureau of Naval Weapons (formed from the old Bureau of Aeronautics and the Bureau of Ordnance) finally agreed to use steam catapults. Fortunately, Rickover had already per-suaded BuShips to provide enough room in the ship for the steam launching equipment, and Shaw, with Rickover's blessing, had seen to it that the prototype was equipped to demonstrate the ability of the plant to deliver the necessary quantity and quality of steam while pow-ering the ship up to flank speed ahead and full speed astern. He gave a convincing demonstration to the key people, and steam catapults have been used with great success on all aircraft carriers.

Although Rickover was reluctant to initiate fights with the rest of the Navy, once involved in one he was always determined to win it. One time he was pressing a point with the chief of BuShips, a point that Shaw was convinced didn't matter much, one way or the other. They had just won the major points, and Shaw couldn't understand why Rickover insisted on winning the little one too. After the meeting, Shaw told him, "Admiral, sometimes we ought to let them win one." The Admiral stopped dead in his tracks and delivered Shaw a long and blistering lecture:

"Shaw, you still don't get it, do you? You keep urging me to get into fights I'd rather avoid. But when you get me into one, by God I'm going to win it. Each time you win a fight, you're that much stronger. People are more leery of taking you on. And each time you lose one, people start thinking, *He isn't invincible. He can be beaten. Maybe I've been too scared of him.* No, sir. I'm never going to give an inch on any fight I get into. People know that, and that's why I'm generally able to win them. You'd better learn that principle."

ONE MORE TRY FOR PERMANENCE

> *Anti-intellectualism has long been our besetting sin. With us, hostility to superior intelligence masquerades as belief in the equality of man and puts forth the false claim that it is undemocratic to recognize and nurture superior intelligence.*
>
> H.G.R.

From 1958, when Congress persuaded the Navy to give Rickover a third star, making him a vice admiral, until 1962, when he turned sixty-two years old, the Admiral's tenure was comparatively secure; he served at the pleasure of the secretary of the Navy. But under the law, the secretary did not have authority to hold an officer in active status beyond age sixty-two. President John F. Kennedy came in with a last-minute rescue at that point, and he authorized Rickover's period of service to be extended for two more years. So in August 1963 Rickover and his staff were staring at a deadline of January 1964, at which point he would presumably have to retire.

Determined once again not to stand idly by, Mandil, Panoff, and I, along with Leighton, who was then Rickover's project officer for surface ships, got in touch with John T. Conway, the able executive director of the Joint Congressional Committee on Atomic Energy, and asked if we could discuss the situation with members of the committee and seek their advice. Conway said, "Sure. In fact, I'll have them request you to testify on the subject. They'll want to have your input." We weren't quite sure how to prepare for the hearing, or what materials to take over with us. I recalled a time when Rickover showed up for a hearing without the massive notes, files, and visual materials a congressional witness usually brings with him. One of the members asked him, "Did you prepare for this hearing?" Rickover replied, "Of course, Senator. I shaved and put on a clean shirt." So we decided to follow his example.

On 15 August 1963 the Legislative Subcommittee of the Joint Committee met with us for an hour and forty minutes in the committee's meeting room (S-407) in the Capitol. Subcommittee Chairman Representative Chet Holifield, Full Committee Chairman Senator John O. Pastore, and a good number of members were present, as were Executive Director Conway, Assistant Director Edward J. Bauser, Staff Counsel Jack R. Newman, and professional staff member George F. Murphy, Jr.

A verbatim record was kept, and a complete report was printed by the Government Printing Office. But it was never published or distributed.

The report began thus:

> With the imminent retirement of Vice Admiral H. G. Rickover in January 1964, the Legislative Subcommittee of the Joint Congressional Committee on Atomic Energy has been considering the necessity for any legislation or other action to: (1) insure the continued service of Admiral Rickover as head of the joint AEC-Navy nuclear propulsion program and, (2) provide for the future continuity of technical management and retention of the joint agency concept which has proved so successful in carrying out this program.
>
> To obtain a greater understanding of the problems in this matter, the Legislative Subcommittee requested senior members of Admiral Rickover's staff to testify . . . The committee members were impressed by the genuine concern these people expressed that unilateral action on the part of the Navy could lead to this vital program being assimilated into the routine business of the Navy with resultant technical degradation of the entire AEC-Navy nuclear propulsion program. This committee is well aware of the history of continuous conflict between the traditional Navy approach to technical programs and that taken by Admiral Rickover and his organization.

The report noted for the record that Rickover's staff people had already had a similar discussion with the AEC and later with Secretary of the Navy Paul H. Nitze.

After the chairman's opening remarks, Panoff tried to summarize our concerns:

> We all believe, as the Admiral testified to you last month in connection with the loss of the USS *Thresher*, that many of the Navy's problems result from the transience of its technical management. We believe one of the most important features of Admiral Rickover's organization is that there has been relatively permanent technical management. So our first concern is that permanent technical management continue.

Leighton quantified this point:

> To give an example, in the 17 years you have been talking to Admiral Rickover in regard to naval nuclear propulsion, one man only, there has been an average of 10 different shipyard commanders in each of the 6 shipyards; 15 different planning officers in each shipyard; and 12 different production officers in each shipyard.

Panoff continued:

> Equally important to the effectiveness of the organization is its two-hatted nature—which has existed because this committee has backed it. This means we have the ability to operate as one technical group both in the Navy and in the AEC.
>
> Our major concerns are whether the naval reactors program will continue to operate under a permanent type of technical management and as a fully two-hatted organization after the Admiral reaches mandatory retirement age next January.
>
> The Secretary of the Navy did say the Admiral could stay on as a retired officer after next January. But that has an element of uncertainty . . . It was [AEC Chairman] Seaborg's proposal that the Admiral stay on as a civilian. We understood that was going forward . . . Later on that was changed.

Senator Anderson asked, "Isn't that what you would like?" And Panoff answered, "Yes, sir. We believe that for him to stay on as a civilian would give him and the organization much more permanence than if he were merely called back as a retired officer."

But this was a point the committee had a hard time getting. Senator Anderson said, "If you have a reason for wanting him to serve as a civilian, we want to have it made very clear to us." And Panoff tried to explain it: "First of all, as a retired officer he is there at the pleasure of the Secretary of the Navy, so in a sense his tenure is tied to that of Mr. Korth. Not knowing for sure how long Mr. Korth is going to be there, we have no idea how long Admiral Rickover's tenure is going to be." (In fact, Paul Nitze replaced Secretary Fred Korth before the report of this meeting could be printed.)

Representative Holifield said, "In other words, this is a personal arrangement rather than a formal arrangement." Panoff agreed and gave examples of such arrangements that had not survived after the person making the promise left. All seemed well so far.

But the committee members never accepted the idea that Rickover could carry out his functions as a civilian. Representative Price said that this matter had been discussed in great detail with the Navy, and the Navy had been very clear that the job required an officer. Senator Pastore said, "There is no way you can make Rickover a civilian and then endow him with all the prerogatives of the Navy."

I tried to clarify the issue:

It is important to understand how this works. The Chief of Naval Personnel provides Admiral Rickover with a list of people whom the Bureau of Naval Personnel have determined are fit and suitable for duty on nuclear powered ships, from the military standpoint. That determination is made before the names come to Admiral Rickover.

At that point, Admiral Rickover, who is identified in Navy instructions not by name, nor as an admiral, nor as Assistant Chief of the Bureau of Ships, but as Manager of Naval Reactors, AEC, interviews officers selected from that list. We civilians also interview these people. We are judging only their suitability to be operators and managers of reactor facilities which are going to be operated in populous regions.

And then the discussion fell off the track again:

SENATOR ANDERSON: What would happen if he were to go there as a civilian?

MR. ROCKWELL: Just exactly the same thing.

SENATOR ANDERSON: That is what we are arguing about. What is the difference?

MR. ROCKWELL: I had understood the Chairman to say he would have to be an officer to do this.

CHAIRMAN PASTORE: I am just saying that the prerogative that comes to him to do this is because he is an admiral.

MR. LEIGHTON: No, sir. I don't believe that is so.

REPRESENTATIVE HOLIFIELD: They say no.

CHAIRMAN PASTORE: That doesn't make it so. The Secretary of the Navy says it isn't so.

REPRESENTATIVE HOLIFIELD: I don't know whether it is so or not.

Finally, Chairman Pastore asked, "You are suggesting here—and I think Rickover is of the mind—that he would like to be separated from the Navy. He would like to come exclusively under the AEC. Am I right?"

Panoff tried again:

> No, sir. We would like to see Admiral Rickover continue to have the same responsibility and authority he now has, both in the Navy and in the AEC. We would like to see him hired as a civilian by the AEC and put on non-reimbursable loan to the Bureau of Ships, in the same type of arrangement we are in. We have heard no legal or substantive objection to this . . . Advising on the selection of crews for nuclear ships he does as Manager of Naval Reactors, AEC. As far as trials of ships are concerned, he is a technical advisor; he does not exercise oper-

---

EXTENDING THE EFFECT: THE NONNUCLEAR NAVY

Rickover's impact on what some call the "real Navy"—the parts beyond his official cognizance—is still clearly apparent. Although he declined to participate directly in the SubSafe program, noting that it involved matters almost entirely outside his responsibility, that program was modeled on his own procedures, and he cooperated with it. It is still an important program. His practice of training nonengineering administrative officers in the technical basics of their ships has been applied across the board. And the quality of a number of other aspects of technical work in the Navy still shows his mark. But it would be a mistake to conclude that the transformation has been complete. The Navy tried, and then quickly abandoned, a position of chief engineer of the Navy. The once-proud engineering duty corps has deteriorated, and now even the chief of the Naval Sea Systems Command (the former BuShips) is not an engineering duty officer. Rickover's insistence that highly technical programs be run by technically qualified personnel has not yet been achieved—not in the Navy, nor in the country at large.

ational control of the ship. When he was in the hospital, I did it as a civilian. So there is nothing intrinsic in his present job that requires him to be an officer.

Pastore said, "If you have a civilian, then the whole organization is not under the aegis of the Navy."

To which Leighton replied, "No, sir. The Navy doesn't lose it. If Admiral Rickover is given the job as a civilian, then [in the post-Rickover future] the Commission and the Navy have the choice of picking whom they want, either civilian or officer. If, on the other hand, you establish the precedent that it must be an officer—that even Mr. Rickover can't fill it—then no civilian ever can. Then there is only one person who can make the choice. That is the secretary of the Navy, and he has to choose from the officer corps."

After nearly two hours the hearing was adjourned. The members were polite and sincerely sympathetic, but we were convinced that we had not made our point. "They think we're just trying to get a crack at the throne for ourselves," I said. "I'm not even sure that Rick himself isn't having second thoughts about it. I think he likes being an Admiral, in spite of what he says. And deep down, hidden from himself even, he may not give a damn what happens after he's gone. *Après moi, le déluge*."

"To hell with it," said Panoff. "I'm getting tired of fighting it."

The issue was finally settled—for the moment—when Navy Secretary Nitze ordered Rickover to be kept on active duty on the retired list for another two years. But somehow we felt we had crossed a watershed. It was not that we wanted Rickover's job. It was just that there did not seem to be any basis for continuity of the program, even after all those productive years.

Part VI

Extending the Rickover Effect
(1964–1986)

VI.

As subordinates develop, work should be constantly added so that no one can finish his job. This serves as a prod and a challenge. It brings out their capabilities and frees the manager to assume added responsibilities. As members of the organization become capable of assuming new and more difficult duties, they develop pride in doing the job well. This attitude soon permeates the entire organization.

H.G.R.

Extending the Rickover Effect
1964–1986

SOMETIME DURING the mid-1960s, the Rickover Effect began to operate in two new modes. Before that time, Rickover's influence had been exerted primarily through the organization he had assembled, and it impacted mostly his own program. But now his personal influence and reputation had grown to the point where he could directly impact other activities outside his own sphere of cognizance (such as the non-nuclear Navy and the national educational system), and his people had begun to leave his program and exert their own effect (shaped by the lessons they had learned with him) on other programs. The recovery effort after the 1979 incident at the commercial nuclear power plant at Three Mile Island, near Harrisburg, Pennsylvania, provided a striking example of this latter effect. Rickover alumni at all levels in the utility company that operated the stricken plant, and others who worked for the Nuclear Regulatory Commission, for the Department of Energy, and for the various outside organizations brought in to help, all demonstrated the unique importance of the special experience and training they had received in the Rickover program.

LEAVING NAVAL REACTORS

*Attention to detail does not require a manager to do every-
thing himself. No one can work more than twenty-four
hours each day. Therefore, to multiply his efforts, he must
create an environment where his subordinates can work to
their maximum ability. Some management experts advocate
strict limits to the number of people reporting to a common
superior—generally five to seven. But if one has capable
people who require but a few moments of his time during
the day, there is no reason to set such arbitrary constraints.
Some forty key people report frequently and directly to me.
This enables me to keep up with what is going on and
makes it possible for them to get fast action. The latter
aspect is particularly important. Capable people will not
work for long where they cannot get prompt decisions and
actions from their superior.*

H.G.R.

One day in the spring of 1964, as Bob Panoff and I were ducking down
to the snack bar for a quick carry-out lunch, Panoff said, "Walk with
me around the reflecting pool. We both need the exercise." He obviously
had something on his mind, so I went along. The long, tree-lined path
around the pool that stretched from Seventeenth Street to the stately
Lincoln Memorial was a favorite spot for lunchtime walks.

"I have less authority—a shorter leash—today than I had ten years
ago," began Panoff. "I've learned a lot in this program, and I give the
Old Man credit for teaching me. But he doesn't use that increased
knowledge and experience by giving me more responsibility. Just the
opposite. He's checking into details he never used to question me on.
And who knows what the future of this place is, anyway?"

"The future is clear," I said. "The Old Man will hang on by one
means or another, and keep running things for years. And then someday
he'll be gone. But I'm not sure I want to hang around and see it. I'm
having the same problem you are."

"Well, there's an alternative. How would you like to start an engineering firm with Harry Mandil and me? I've talked with Harry, and
he's interested. Let's see if we can accomplish anything without Rickover
standing behind us. See if we can apply all the good stuff about Naval
Reactors with a minimum of frantic fire drills and personal hysterics.

No pinks of drafts. Do it in our own image, but using everything we learned from him. Maybe we'll fall on our face and end up having to shine shoes. But I'd like to try. Are you game?"

I was a little taken aback. People had asked me, from time to time, if I was interested in this or that opportunity, but I'd brushed them aside. I had once been offered a professorship at a top university, with a chair of engineering and public policy that I could define in my own way, but I hadn't really considered it seriously. However, I couldn't brush off Panoff, and I didn't want to.

"Gee, Bob, you just threw this at me. Let me sleep on it. What kind of an outfit do you have in mind? What do we do?"

"I'd like to do the same sort of high-class engineering we do now. No management consulting crap or lobbying for contractors. Just good engineering. After all, how many people in the country have had the kind of experience we've had, designing, building, starting up, operating, maintaining, refueling nuclear power plants? That should be a marketable skill, no?"

"I guess so. Do we start looking for possible clients? I'd feel funny doing that. Or do we walk away from a salaried job, with no contracts and no basis for knowing how hard it'll be to get contracts, and then start looking?"

"I don't think it would be ethical to lift a finger on this thing until after we're out the door. And that may be a while. I think we should give Rick all the notice he wants. So we may go quite a while with no income."

I was a little surprised to find that the idea of leaving Naval Reactors didn't shock me. I was forty-two; Bob and Harry were a year or two older. I had never consciously thought about it, had subconsciously thought of myself as being there forever, but now I realized I had been getting restless, and the idea looked attractive. I didn't wait to sleep on it. "I guess I'm with you," I said.

Setting Up MPR Associates, Inc.

We told Rickover our tentative plans and were surprised that his reaction seemed so low-key. "I can't complain. You guys have been here fifteen to twenty years. You've done a good job. You're nearly the age I was when I got into this business. You want to get out on your own. How can I object to that? But I want you to promise me two things: Don't raid my people, and don't sell yourselves out as experts on how to get around Rickover. In other words, stay out of my business. There's plenty of other work to do in the world."

We assured him that we fully intended to respect both of those requests. We would not hire anyone working at Naval Reactors, even if an NR person approached us first. And we would not do any work that involved his area of responsibility. This was no burden; we had decided without even thinking about it that these were two conditions we would voluntarily impose on ourselves. We asked how much notice he would like, and he suggested three to four months. He asked us what contracts we had lined up, and we told him we had none and that we would not attempt to get any business until we had left government employment. Much later, we learned that he was considerably more upset by our leaving than he had indicated to us. He tried to convince us separately to stay. I believe he never really became reconciled to our departure.

And so on 4 August 1964 we found ourselves unemployed, with no definite plans. We met with a lawyer and drew up a corporate charter for "MPR Associates, Inc." We interviewed and hired a secretary suggested by a friend, and told her to go out and buy a coffee pot. Then, by previous agreement, we went our separate ways for a one-month vacation at the beach with our families, the longest vacation any of us had ever had.

"How Do You Run a Business?"

We had worked all our lives at salaried positions, with bosses, assigned tasks, deadlines, and facilities supplied. Now we found ourselves in an empty rented office, with a telephone, a few desks, tables, chairs, and a bookcase. We didn't even have a file cabinet, and we sure didn't have any files. There were numerous technical documents we would have liked to have had from our previous job, but we had decided to bring absolutely nothing with us.

"What do we do now?" I asked, a little nervously.

"Well, for starters," said Panoff, "a number of people saw that article in *Nucleonics Week* about us leaving NR and asked us to come talk with them about helping on their commercial work. Completely outside Rick's sphere."

"Right. And I checked on that government call. They would like us to evaluate some classified stuff. We could do a good job on that, and they're anxious to have us. But I told them to go to hell."

"Why would you do a thing like that?" asked Mandil.

"In addition to all the security checks, which I didn't mind—we've already had about every security check in the books—in addition to that, they insisted they would have to give us a lie detector test. After all the clearances I've had, I'm not about to let some technician on a quirky machine decide I'm no longer a loyal American at this stage in my life."

"I'll buy that."

And, amazingly, we never had to put out an ad or an unsolicited proposal. Just by answering telephone calls for help, we quickly built up a business and found ourselves scrambling to find personnel. We discovered that starting a business is like mixing a martini or having a baby: it's a process on which people just can't help kibitzing. We'd been told all sorts of tales about "what you have to do to survive in business." But despite the advice, we had decided, without even talking about it, that ethics and professionalism would come first. In fact, the criterion we adopted was that if Rickover were to pay us a surprise visit at any point in the years ahead and ask what we were doing, we would be proud to tell him, and he would have to be proud of us, whether he admitted it or not.

We soon had a chance to put our idealism to the test. Mandil got a call from a company investigating a new type of nuclear power plant. The caller was offering a juicy contract to MPR to review the concept and write up an evaluation report. We had heard a little about the project, and we were not enthusiastic about what we'd heard. So Mandil asked, "I understand you people are on a pretty tight schedule. Are you prepared to set that back if we convince you that the approach you're on is not a good one?"

The reply was ambiguous. "I'm confident that once you get into our design, when our people have shown you the unique advantages of this approach, um . . . yes, I am sure you'll be quite excited about it, as we are."

Mandil pursued the question. "I'm certainly open to that possibility. We would like to see some big breakthroughs in the field, just as you would. But I really have to know: Would you be willing to stop short and redirect the effort, if we could convince your people that this is not the promising track you now think it is? In other words, do you really want our technical evaluation? Or do you just want applause?"

The caller repeated his point about how we would be pleased with the design once we had studied it, and Mandil ended the conversation by saying, "I'm sorry, but you're telling me that you don't want a technical evaluation; you want an endorsement. That's not what we do. I'm sorry." And he hung up and told Panoff and me what he had done.

We both agreed with him, and we all sat around a while, feeling very noble. We had put principle ahead of profit, and we would find out whether a business can survive doing that. We soon found, and the next twenty-five years confirmed it, that when word gets around that you have a high-class outfit, the customers come to you. We discovered that there is a great demand for honesty, and the more we put integrity and professionalism first, the more we prospered. We were surprised to learn this, but we certainly didn't complain about it. We realized that this principle might not apply to all types of businesses, but we were glad that it apparently applied to ours.

At first all of our work was with private commercial firms, but at one point we were asked by the Navy to help with the SubSafe program that had been initiated as a follow-up to the loss of the *Thresher*. We were delighted to be asked, but the contract seemed to take an inordinately long time to come through. When it did, the contract officer confided in us, "Your old boss really fought me on this one. Told me it wasn't proper to give it to you guys. I told him it was none of his business. He hadn't participated in the SubSafe program, it wouldn't involve his part of the ship. He was mad as hell, but he couldn't stop me."

"The old bastard!" I said. "Why would he do a thing like that? We've really leaned over backwards to stay out of his area. We haven't touched any of his people, even when they came to us. Why would he want to hurt us?"

"He may just not want to see us succeed," said Panoff. "It might give some of his other people ideas. He doesn't want them to know there could be Life After Rickover. You know, I ran into him in the airport the other night. It was a friendly discussion, but he said it was probably just as well we left. We were holding the younger people back."

We found that life was very different "on the outside," as government workers say. First of all, we had learned in NR that extensive technical files, history, and reference material were essential to do a good job. We had none of these. But we found a way to reverse that situation. We discovered that our clients usually had great difficulty in locating the drawings and specifications they needed for any particular task. So we systematically dug out what we needed from their files and, with their blessing, made copies for our own files. In the course of our work we added to these, and soon people from all over were calling us with questions, since "you people apparently have the only complete and organized files on these plants." In this way we were able to organize our own work, and to provide a continuing service to the clients in a variety of other areas for which we weren't even under contract. We began setting up quality control and quality assurance programs for nuclear power plants, and then for coal, oil, and hydroelectric plants. In all these areas, we found our clients coming to us because of the completeness and accessibility of our file material, as well as for our engineering skills.

Panoff kept marveling at the joy of not having an endless stream of "fire drills." "When I think of the weeks on end I spent putting out fires the Old Man had started because some field guy had failed to report some two-bit problem! He kept doing that sort of thing to keep everybody in a state of panic, to keep them putting ten times as much effort into each item as any reasonable person would. Yeah, it got results, but it was so wasteful of human talent. I get exhausted just remembering it. We may regret not doing it, but I think we can apply the good stuff we learned, without all the emotional excess."

We were very conscious of applying what we considered the "good things" we had learned from Rickover. We did not keep pinks of drafts—indeed, with photocopying, there was no need for carbon copies of any color—but we did insist on reviewing and approving every outgoing report or technical letter. The young engineers objected vigorously to this process of "word engineering." But they were told, "When you've done 90 percent of the work on a project, you'd better have 50 percent of the money left in the budget." And the employees protested, "You know what I mean. Why do we have to spend all this time rewriting?"

But the fact was that until the meaning was crystal-clear, the job wasn't done, as far as M, P, or R was concerned. And we often found that when the meaning was clear, it was no longer true. "Is that what you're trying to say? Is that your conclusion?" one of us would ask. "Yeah, yeah. That's it," the engineer would say, glad to be finally at the end of the process.

"This conclusion is clear and important, but it isn't supported by your data. If that's what you want to tell the client, you'd better go back and do a better job of supporting it."

As Rickover had taught, and our own experience in his program had confirmed, we believed that management should serve as preacher and exemplar, insisting that standards never be lowered for expedience, laziness, or any other reason. And the more scrupulously we practiced this principle, the more our business thrived.

Another surprise was that, for the most part, past enmities were forgotten. Shortly after we had set up shop, we cringed as we saw a former BuShips chief approaching us on the sidewalk. We had had some rough arguments with him under Rickover, so we were amazed when he greeted us heartily and wished us well in our new endeavor. "If there's ever anything I can do to help you fellows, don't hesitate to call on me. I'm delighted with what you're doing."

We thought long and hard about that. "Maybe he's just glad we're not still with Rickover, causing him trouble," I said.

"That can't be it; he's retired," replied Panoff. "I think it's just the old American Dream: everybody admires and envies the guy who starts his own business. It's almost a civic duty to wish him well."

"Well, whatever it is, I'm all for it."

Even people we had opposed bitterly on various issues came to us for help. As MPR we once worked for a machinery manufacturer, investigating the cause of an expensive machine failure. We concluded, and convincingly demonstrated, that the utility had contributed to the problem by not operating the equipment correctly. It had cost the utility a lot of money. Years later we got a call from the same utility, asking for our help on another problem. "We had some battles in the old days. But I'll have to admit, you guys generally knew what you were talking about, and you were always honest and up-front. I've got a tough problem here, and I need the best help I can find."

Panoff issued the usual caveat: "We'll call it as we see it, and we would come up with the same answer whether we worked for you or for the machinery manufacturer. Are you willing to take us on on that basis? We may conclude you guys are wrong again. Can you live with that?" And, surprisingly, the answer was yes. "Sooner or later, the truth will out. My people keep telling me what they think I want to hear. I've got to know if I'm in trouble. You guys will tell me that. And you'll also have the best ideas for a technical fix. I think we'll be glad we called you."

MPR also applied the Rickover lessons in recruiting and training personnel. We started by rounding up some experienced engineers we

could count on. We found a few of our former Naval Reactors colleagues, superb engineers who had left the program for other endeavors:
Bill Schmidt, John Dyer, Sterling Weems, Herb Estrada, Julian Nichols,
Bob Weiner, and later Ray Zogran, Dwight Harrision, Noman Cole,
and Doug Chapin. Then we started interviewing engineering students
about to graduate near the top of their class from good engineering
schools. We used the procedures we had developed at NR. First, we
got resumes from a few top engineering schools and reviewed them
carefully. Typically, we selected about thirty out of a graduating class
of three hundred. We wrote letters to each of the thirty, describing the
company, why it was interested in them, and why we thought they
might be interested in MPR as a career. About half of these would show
up for a campus interview, and this was as many as one could talk with
in a day. If there were more, we would stay a second day.

The on-campus interviews would yield one, two, or three candidates
for further interviews at MPR. Or sometimes none. Their records would
be reviewed by the three engineers selected to interview each of them.
The interviewers would write up their conclusions and recommendations and discuss them with the three of us and with the engineer who
originally selected them from the campus. Finally, there was the interview with the three of us. Sometimes this led to still another interview.
We would say to one of the interviewers, "You concluded this guy was
pretty sharp in mechanical matters, but he fell on his face with us in
that area. Let's have someone else quiz him on that stuff and get back
to us."

The yield from the office interviews was about one in five, but all
these yields varied from day to day, and a lot of effort was devoted to
trying to understand why. Some days many of the candidates looked
good; other days they were all turkeys. Typically, from the original
three hundred resumes came fifteen campus interviews, two or three
office interviews, and less than one final selection. As at NR, we knew
we were turning away some good people, and occasionally we hired
one who disappointed us in performance. But on the whole we assembled an exceptional crew. And we then set about creating an intensive
and continuing training program, which, as at NR, took a great deal
of time and effort, but was indispensable to the performance to which
we were committed.

The three of us—Mandil, Panoff, and I—were determined to run
MPR as equals. We concluded that this would work only if we practiced

"minority rule"; that is, anytime one of us objected strongly to a course proposed by the other two, they would not override him. This, of course, was a very different situation from life in Naval Reactors, but it led to a familiar Rickover practice. In an effort to reach full consensus, we constantly went out of our way to seek out differing viewpoints and divergent data. In other words, we generally put in ten times as much effort to reach a decision as any normal person would consider reasonable. And in doing this, we were on familiar ground, and we were confident from our experience that we were doing the right thing.

RICKOVER AS HISTORIAN

> *Act as if you were going to live forever and cast your plans way ahead. You must feel responsible without time limitations, and the consideration of whether you may or may not be around to see the results should never enter your thoughts.*

> H.G.R.

Rickover had always had a strong interest in history. From early youth he had liked to read history, and he always saw and evaluated important events in a broad historical context. In this he was competently aided and encouraged by his first wife, Ruth. When he first began to realize the relevance of the weaknesses in the American educational system to the problems he encountered in training people for nuclear power, Ruth helped him with research for the books on education he wrote and published.

As each new submarine put to sea for the first time, Rickover wrote a letter while aboard, telling of the ship and her place in the growing nuclear fleet. This too ultimately grew into a historical project. He described that development as follows:

> Ever since the first nuclear submarine—the USS *Nautilus*—went to sea in January 1955, I have been responsible for directing the initial sea trials of each of our nuclear ships so as to make sure that their nuclear propulsion plants functioned properly and that the officers and men had been well trained. Because many members of Congress had given strong support in getting the *Nautilus* built, I decided that it would be no more than proper for me to

send each of them a letter reporting what the ship had done. I remember writing some 80 letters in long-hand during that first voyage. Soon I expanded the list of recipients to include all members of Congress and appropriate officials in the executive branch.

When it came time to test our first Polaris submarine, the USS *George Washington* in 1960, I thought it would be appropriate to include in my letter a brief biography of the man for whom the ship was named, and I continued this practice for each of the 40 Polaris submarines which followed. These letters were well received, and most of them were printed in the *Congressional Record*. Frequently I was urged to publish them in book form. This I agreed to do and Congress, in 1968, passed a resolution authorizing the printing of this book.

The book he was referring to was a beautifully bound volume called *Eminent Americans: Namesakes of the Polaris Submarine Fleet*, published by the Congress as House Document no. 92-345 but copyrighted by Admiral Rickover.

It had been traditional to name submarines after fish and other undersea life, but with the missile ships, great capital ships displacing over nine thousand tons—larger than many cruisers—each carrying sixteen nuclear-tipped long-range missiles, it was decided to name them after well-known figures in American history. The distinguished patriots chosen for this purpose were remarkably diverse, ranging from George Washington, Thomas Jefferson, and Patrick Henry to Daniel Boone, Will Rogers, Simón Bolívar, George Washington Carver, Tecumseh, the Shawnee chief, and Kamehameha, the Hawaiian king. Rickover noted in his preface to the book, "The careers of the men for whom the Polaris submarines are named span the full range of American history from the time of the Revolution to the present century. The preparation of these essays therefore required me to explore many aspects of our national history."

He soon found that he had undertaken quite a chore: "Because these letters had been written aboard ship, they had been necessarily limited to two or three pages. For the purposes of a book, I wanted to expand the original brief sketches of these figures into more complete essays. During the past 4 years I have devoted virtually all of my spare time to this task. Had it not been for the devoted efforts of my dear wife, who did most of the research for these essays, I could not possibly have completed this task."

Rickover described his long-term fascination with history and added, "This broader interest in the history of the United States led me to the conclusion that I should try to reflect in these biographical essays some of those historical themes which seem to me to have particular relevance for the kinds of problems our Nation faces today . . . I therefore decided to use the careers of the men for whom the Polaris submarines were named as the focus for essays which would be broad enough to include some of the significant events which occurred during their lifetimes."

The result was a unique history text, both authentic and readable, which was popular among a wide variety of readers. Sadly, Ruth Rickover died just before the book was completed, and the Admiral dedicated it to her, as "at once the most human and intelligent person I ever knew, the greatest influence on my life and work." And he closed his dedication with words of Tibullus, leaving the translation as an exercise for the reader: *"Tu mihi curarum requies, tu nocte vel atra lumen, et in solis tu mihi turba locis"* ("You are my refuge from care, my light in darkest night, and in my loneliness a place of activity").

His wife's death was a severe blow to the Admiral. Although he always kept his personal feelings to himself, we could not help but feel his pain. So we were surprised but pleased when, some years later, he married Eleonore Bednowicz, a commander in the Navy Nurse Corps since 1954. She had taken care of the Admiral when he was in the hospital with his first heart attack in 1961, and he had kept in touch with her all through the subsequent years.

Rickover's final foray into historical publishing was quite a different effort. Partly as a result of the time he spent in Panama and in the Philippines, he came to look at the Spanish–American War as a turning point in American history. So in 1974 he was quite impressed with a story by John M. Taylor in the *Washington Star-News* entitled "Returning to the Riddle of the Explosion that Sunk the *Maine*." Taylor noted that the question of whether the *Maine* was sunk by an enemy mine or by an accidental explosion had never been settled satisfactorily, although the battle cry "Remember the *Maine*!" had fanned the lust for war on the premise that the Spanish were in fact the cause of the tragedy that had cost 266 lives. That much was not new. But Taylor noted that an atmosphere of rushing to a predetermined verdict seemed to prevail throughout the Navy's investigations of the matter, and he reported that although the chief of the Navy's Bureau of Steam Engineering had said that the cause of the disaster was an explosion in one of the ship's ammunition magazines, he was not asked to testify despite his official position of expertise and responsibility within the Navy.

These points intrigued Rickover. He believed that modern knowledge and analytical techniques concerning explosions and structures might be able to shed some light on the nature of the explosion, and a reexamination of how the Court of Inquiry was selected and how it carried out its business might also be illuminating.

He carried out his investigation with characteristic thoroughness. First, he determined to work with the Navy's director of naval history, who made available to him historians and archival material, and who published the report of his investigation in hard cover, with an endorsement in the foreword: "In this work, Admiral H. G. Rickover makes a unique contribution by studying the loss of the *Maine* in the light of modern technical knowledge . . . The result is this volume which presents significant new insights in an important event in American history."

Rickover also obtained material from the Spanish, British, and French naval archives, through their respective naval attachés. For a broader view of the picture, he brought in the president of the Naval War College and a professor of international law. He then commissioned a special study by explosives and structures experts from the Naval Surface Weapons Center and the Naval Ship Research and Development Center, who examined reports, photographs, and drawings from the Court of Inquiry of 1898 and the Board of Inspection investigation of 1911. The report of this technical study was included as an appendix to Admiral Rickover's book. He even brought in the curator of the Division of Naval History at the Smithsonian Institution, an expert on mines and mining techniques of the Spanish-American War period. He then had the book reviewed prior to publication by a number of independent historians and technical specialists.

Rickover's investigation and report present persuasive arguments that there was no evidence to support the conclusion that a mine had destroyed the *Maine*, and that there was considerable evidence pointing to, although not proving beyond doubt, an internal explosion as the cause. The type of bituminous coal carried on ships at the time was often the source of fires resulting from spontaneous combustion. On the *Maine*, only a single thin metal wall separated some of the coal bunkers from munitions magazines, and this was an invitation to an explosion sooner or later. The lesson for us, Rickover concluded, is that "we can no longer approach technical problems with the casualness and confidence held by Americans in 1898. The *Maine* should impress us that technical problems must be examined by competent and qualified people; and that the results of their investigation must be fully and fairly presented to their fellow citizens." He closed with the following somber warning, even more relevant today than when it was written in 1976:

> With the vastness of our government and the difficulty of controlling it, we must make sure that those in "high places" do not, without most careful consideration of the consequences, exert our prestige and might. Such uses of our power may result in serious international actions at great cost in lives and money—injurious to the interests and standing of the United States.

As was the case when he published his views on education, Rickover's words were viewed condescendingly by some of the professionals in the field. The *Naval War College Review* ran such a review, bewailing attempts by amateur historians to add anything to the field. Rickover responded simply:

> I could approach the problem technically, and this I did. I did not "avail" myself of the "opportunity" to make a full historical study of the interplay of administrative, political, personal, human, and technological factors in the loss of the battleship since this was not my intention and, further, there were limitations of time and professional qualifications in these areas. Nor did I write a psycho-history—a morass into which historians too often descend. Dr. Cosmas criticizes me for restricting myself to areas of my knowledge and experience. I would have criticized myself if I had gone beyond them.

Rickover then went on to note that a learned journal "is no better than its reviews," and "there are several publications already covering the same fields . . . at no expense to the government." He therefore suggested that "in these days, when the government is attempting to reduce paperwork, do away with superfluous employees, and save money, eliminating the *Review* would be a noteworthy, precedent-setting action by the War College."

Eminent Americans did not add any original material to scholars' historical data base, but it was good readable history and Rickover hoped it would interest and inspire young people and their teachers. He was disappointed that it did not receive the attention he had anticipated. The *Maine*, on the other hand, was—and is—a real contribution to a hundred-year-old controversy. It continues to be cited in various historical works. This could not have happened if the Admiral had not tackled its writing in the same exhaustive way he undertook all his technical projects—it was a truly novel procedure for the field.

Between the writing of these two books, in December 1973, Rickover was awarded a fourth star and became a full admiral, the highest peacetime rank in the military service.

THE THREE MILE ISLAND INCIDENT

> *It seems to me a clear obligation for all bureaucratic organizations—private as well as public—to do nothing that will diminish individual autonomy. Public bureaucracies need constant watching, but they can be restrained. With private bureaucracies, the obligation cannot be imposed or enforced. But it can be publicly discussed, and public disapproval can be visited on those who violate the obligation. This will not be helpful to the violator's "image" . . .*
>
> *Of course, every corporation is free to manage its affairs as it wishes . . . but there is this point to consider: Corporations have long striven to obtain full citizenship rights as "persons" in the sight of the law. They have largely obtained that objective. The courts for all practical purposes treat them as state or federal citizens. Does achievement of citizenship status then not entail on the part of corporations the obligation to assume as well the civic duties of natural citizens? In law, "right and obligation are correlative."*
>
> H.G.R.

On 28 March 1979, at about 4:00 A.M., an incident began at the second Three Mile Island commercial nuclear power plant (TMI-2), which released some radioactivity into the surroundings. Its sister plant, TMI-1, had been operating commercially for over four years without any significant problems, but it was shut down after the incident and kept down for seven years by the hysteria engendered by the incident in TMI-2. A presidential commission and several other prestigious outside investigatory groups concluded after prolonged study that despite the serious implications of the accident, and the necessity to minimize the possibility of future incidents, there was absolutely no public hazard or health threat resulting from this event—no deaths, no injuries, no potential injuries. But for weeks the media devoted thousands of column inches and unprecedented television time to proclaiming that what had occurred was an unmitigated catastrophe of horrendous proportions. The good, gray *New York Times* ran a column that read like a voodoo curse, conjuring up fearful Jungian archetypes: "A frightening array of biological problems in animals ranging from cats to cows . . . spontaneous abortions, stillbirths, sterility, mutant offspring, blindness, defective bone structure and sudden death . . . Wild birds, game animals and snakes have greatly diminished in numbers . . . One Hershey woman chose to have an abortion and then had herself sterilized rather than rear an infant where 'it will never be clean.' "

Door-to-door surveys proliferated, asking, in effect, "Are you beginning to feel sick yet?" Not surprisingly, these studies showed 14 percent of the people in the area drinking more, 32 percent smoking more, 88 percent using more tranquilizers, 113 percent using more sleeping pills. As late as the June 1991 issue of the *American Journal of Public Health*, a study by researchers from Columbia University and the National Audubon Society reported "a modest post-accident increase in cancer near TMI that is unlikely to be explained by radiation emissions. Such a pattern might reflect the impact of accident stress on cancer progression."

President Carter Asks Rickover's Help

To allay public fears, President Jimmy Carter took his wife to the site, and photographs of the couple in the "disaster area" appeared in papers throughout the world. He also appointed a President's Commission on the Accident at Three Mile Island under Dr. John Kemeny of Dartmouth College, to investigate and draw lessons from the accident. One of the key witnesses to testify before this commission was Dr. John Deutsch, director of energy research and acting assistant secretary for energy technology in the U.S. Department of Energy. Dr. Deutsch told the commission of Rickover's program and the lessons it had for the commercial atomic energy enterprise:

It emphasizes training and education in a way that would be thoroughly astonishing to you if you were not already familiar with it. And I urge you, in the strongest possible terms, to take a look at that program. It is not enough to ask Admiral Rickover to come here and testify in front of you. Mr. Rickover is part of our organization but the Admiral will convey an incredible sense of what he does and how he does it, and the history he brings with it. That will be important to you. I urge you to do it. But I also urge you to step beyond that and actually look and see what is involved in the technical depth of his organization, . . . in the training and education, continuity and certification of operators, exercises, component testing, [and] quality assurance.

So on 23 July 1979 the commission met with Rickover and some of his senior people. Rickover stated his belief that there was much the commercial atomic power industry could learn from the naval program, but he cautioned against looking for some "magical formula" to be applied blindly and effortlessly. That would not work. The answer lay in all the people involved, from top management to lowest technicians, continuously applying great care to everything they do, and doing so with a competence born of technical training that is both broad and deep.

Rickover believed that too much attention was being paid to dealing with low-probability accidents and not enough to preventing accidents. The design should assume that even well-trained operators and maintenance personnel will make mistakes, and the design should be able to tolerate such mistakes. He also warned that the design of commercial plants had too many alarms. They sounded under trivial and even normal circumstances, so that operators soon learned to ignore them. The President's Commission's Report indicated that under normal conditions, at least fifty alarms were activated that operators assumed could be ignored, and after the reactor trip there were over one hundred. Clearly, such a profusion of alarms did not help operators make intelligent decisions.

To get these lessons across to the commercial nuclear industry, Deutsch arranged, at Rickover's urging, for the Admiral to meet with a number of utility executives for a six-hour discussion of his philosophy and its application to their power plants. Rickover was sorely disappointed in the lack of utility follow-up, and he was not optimistic that his message had gotten across. More accurately, he felt that the utility people would probably agree with him in principle, but would not be willing to devote the extraordinary effort to carry it out, year after year. But he felt that he had done what he could. In addition to his efforts with the Kemeny Commission, he had also provided testimony before the Subcommittee on Energy Research and Development of the House Committee on Science and Technology, backing up his presentation with a 111-page written report. But there was to be one more effort.

President Carter, as a young naval officer, had been briefly associated with the Naval Reactors program. In his book *Why Not the Best?* he wrote, "Admiral Rickover had a profound effect on my life—perhaps more than anyone except my own parents." Elsewhere in the book, Carter noted that despite Rickover's awesome responsibilities and his rank of full admiral, he had "twenty-one intermediate authorities between him and the Secretary of Defense. Each of the twenty-one could veto or delay a proposal, but none could give final approval." Carter admired Rickover's ability to operate under these circumstances almost as if he were an unencumbered individual.

Rickover had visited Carter in the White House, and on 27 May 1977 he arranged for the president to ride one of his submarines. But their meeting on 31 May 1979 was an unusual one. The president and his wife and daughter paid a surprise visit to the Admiral at his apartment in Crystal City, overlooking the Washington National Airport. The visit had been secretly arranged by Mrs. Rickover, who had confided in Mrs. Carter that she had never been able to surprise the Admiral. Mrs. Rickover cooked and served the dinner, so the Secret Service people did not have to check the food, and they kept completely out of the way. The conversation was informal and wide-ranging, and the Carters said they had not spent so relaxed an evening in a long, long time.

Although the visit was ostensibly a social call, in the course of the evening Carter asked Rickover to review the report and conclusions of the Kemeny Commission and to report to him his personal views on the matter. Carter had been one of the many submarine officers Rickover had sent to help the Canadians clean up the NRX reactor after its partial meltdown in December 1952. He had donned "anti-C" clothing and done his bit in the contaminated area. So he had a firsthand feeling for the situation at TMI, and he knew that Rickover would take a pragmatic view, that he was neither an alarmist nor a Pollyanna.

On 1 December Rickover submitted his report to the president. He noted that the accident was being used as a justification to spend vast sums on safety research and on devices to prevent or alleviate accidents. He warned that this was not what was needed:

There has been too much emphasis on research and development in nuclear power and not enough on the daily drudgery of seeing that every aspect of nuclear power is in fact properly handled every day by each of the organizations involved. *That* is where the emphasis is needed.

He then took aim at the next easy out discussed in the commission's report:

I am concerned that the overwhelming emphasis the President's Commission placed on reorganizing the NRC [Nuclear Regulatory Commission] may result in inadequate attention being paid to the fundamental changes required in the way industry is handling commercial nuclear power.

Safe design, construction, and operation of nuclear power plants owned and operated by the utilities will not result from expanding the NRC, reorganizing the NRC, or passing more laws. Nor will it be derived from establishing new diverse, non-expert oversight groups. If commercial nuclear power plants are to be operated safely, the organizations that own and operate the plants—the utilities—must know what they are doing and commit themselves to take the steps necessary to achieve nuclear safety. If the utilities do not establish stringent standards, institute rigorous training programs, and police themselves, there is little hope for assured safe operation of commercial nuclear power.

He summarized what he considered deficiencies in the situation prior to the accident, judged against what his experience dictated to be necessary:

There was an apparent lack of attention and devotion of resources to the training of operators. Site managers did not consider themselves responsible for operator training. The training department was undermanned and was staffed by instructors no more qualified educationally than their students. There was no training for engineers or managers at a level higher than that for control room operators, although during the accident the operators turned to their supervisors for guidance.

There was no formally approved training program for steam plant operators although there is a direct interaction between the steam plant and the reactor plant. It was the steam plant operators, in fact, whose actions initiated the events which ultimately led to the accident.

The training for newly-qualifying control room operators was done essentially on a self-study basis. The curriculum did not cover the principles of science and engineering necessary for understanding the operation of the power plant, nor was it reviewed and approved by people qualified to do so. The requalification program, which served as a continuing training program, was shallow and haphazard. It did not continually upgrade knowledge and understanding through reinforcement of principles and procedures. Course content was not reviewed and approved by management, nor did they monitor the conduct of formal instruction.

Rickover then outlined briefly what he considered necessary to assure a reasonable degree of safety in a commercial nuclear power industry. He noted the need to upgrade the technical competence of management and the need for "direct and frequent access to top management." He cited the importance of formal standards, specifications, and procedures. And he gave particular emphasis to the need for strong central technical control, of the sort provided by his own headquarters organization:

> For many years I have recommended that the utilities unite to establish a central technical organization which could provide a more coordinated and expert technical input and control for the commercial nuclear power program than is presently possible for each utility with its limited staff . . . Among the things such an organization could do are:
>
> a. Develop the standards and specifications . . .
> b. Establish staffing requirements . . .
> c. Establish requirements of a standard organization . . .

    d. Establish standards for general operating procedures . . .

    e. Establish criteria for selection of nuclear plant operators . . .

    f. Develop comprehensive training and retraining programs . . .

    g. Provide . . . periodic in-depth audits . . .

    h. Conduct continuous reviews of operating experience . . .

    i Provide direct, in-depth technical assistance to utilities . . .

    j. Have authority to suspend operations . . . or impose other penalties.

Anticipating the objection that his ideas might not be applicable to private utilities, Rickover wrote simply, "Discipline is an essential characteristic of any successful program and of any successful person. The discipline in the naval nuclear program has been successful not because this involves military applications, but because I have insisted upon staffing the program with intelligent, motivated people, whom I hold accountable."

President Carter penciled a note to his staff on the report: "Incorporate key recommendations in our message . . . I have marked important points."

Rickover Alumni Get into the Act

While Rickover was operating on one level at Three Mile Island, his alumni in various organizations were working on another. Design and construction work on the site was being carried out by a division of the huge architect/constructor firm Bechtel Corporation, and there were few Rickover alumni in the company. But in GPU Nuclear Corporation, the subsidiary of General Public Utilities, which owned and operated the plant, there were many. Critical in the early stages of recovery was Robert Arnold, the vice president at company headquarters who was placed in overall charge of the recovery operation. He had been an officer on a nuclear-powered submarine. Under him were John Barton, the senior GPU officer at the site for recovery operations, who had been a test engineer at New York Shipbuilding Corporation for nuclear ships, and Jack Devine, in charge of technical planning at the site, who had been a nuclear submarine officer. Later, Philip R. Clark, who had succeeded Harry Mandil at Naval Reactors, and Ed Kintner, who had headed Rickover's operation at Idaho and then at the Mare Island Naval

Shipyard, came in as president and executive vice president, respectively.

Another Rickover alumnus who played a critical role was Herbert Feinroth, the representative of the Department of Energy to the TMI-2 recovery program. He was concerned with the slow pace of the operation and felt strongly that it was on a wrong path. He came to Harry Mandil with his concerns, and they came up with the idea of setting up a technical advisory group. "No, let's make it a Technical Advisory *and Assistance* Group," suggested Mandil. "That way, they can do more than just talk." And so the TAAG was set up, and the most experienced and respected people in the field were brought in to man it. Not surprisingly, at one time six of the eight members were Rickover alumni. The group was ably headed by William Hamilton, who had been head of the Westinghouse-Bettis naval reactors laboratory for many years. The TAAG group became the real driving force to bring practical nuclear power experience to bear on the difficult problems associated with cleanup of the plant.

Another alumnus was the senior representative of the Nuclear Regulatory Commission, Bernie Snyder, who had worked at NR from 1958 to 1962. And, of course, there was MPR, which had a high concentration of experienced alumni. MPR already had a working relationship with GPU, and shortly after the incident, MPR was asked to send a small team to the site to evaluate the situation and offer assistance. At that time, the media were alarmed at the possibility of a catastrophic explosion of the reactor vessel, since it had been announced that there was a hydrogen bubble over the reactor core and everyone knew that hydrogen was explosive. Jane Fonda's movie *The China Syndrome* had just come out, describing the potential for "devastating an area the size of Pennsylvania," and this was the public image of the situation at TMI. In fact, people were beginning to evacuate the area. But the Rickover alumni knew that reactors in the naval program all operated routinely with hydrogen overpressure, and that this presented no hazard because a hydrogen explosion cannot occur without oxygen also being present. Hydrogen will suppress any trace of oxygen, and an explosion was therefore physically impossible. This word was finally put out, but of course it did not receive the public attention of the original cry of alarm.

The initial work at MPR was under Harry Mandil, who continued to direct it until he retired in 1985. The key man for this project was Noman Cole. Cole had worked in Naval Reactors starting in 1956, in charge of irradiation test work and spent-fuel handling and processing.

He came to MPR in 1967, and by the time of the TMI incident he had accumulated a mass of direct experience in dealing with spent fuel and highly radioactive equipment and systems.

Bechtel had estimated that if personnel were to try to enter the reactor containment building, radiation exposures would be at near-lethal levels, meaning that any cleanup effort would be an almost hopeless task. This gloomy mind-set cast a heavy pall over the program that was a constant impediment to progress. But based on their own experience, Dave Strawson and others at MPR calculated that the Bechtel numbers were a thousandfold too high. Since the Bechtel estimates were "official," and other "radiation experts" had agreed with them, site planning was proceeding on the basis of the high-radiation numbers, which meant that any inspection and cleanup actions would have to be done by specially developed robotic devices, remotely controlled from outside the reactor building.

The next challenge was to vent the radioactive gas from the reactor containment building. The radioactivity was almost entirely due to the short-lived fission product krypton. Since krypton is a completely inert gas, it is not retained in the body. Thus, at the levels encountered here, it did not present a significant hazard. Nonetheless, radioactivity in any form had become an emotionally charged problem, and so various extravagant schemes were proposed, such as freezing the krypton out of the air and retaining it in a cryogenic system, or releasing it into the stratosphere through a long plastic hose held aloft by balloons. Finally, Cole was able to show that the radioactivity from the krypton was less than that being continuously released into the air by natural radon in the heating gas used in the homes in the area—totally unrelated to the reactor or any other human activity. And so the venting was done directly into the air, slowly and under controlled conditions, and radiation measurements confirmed that no hazard was created by so doing.

Cleaning up the spilled water was done with ion exchangers, using the same sort of process as that employed in home water softeners. Here again, alarms were raised that the purification resins used in the process would disintegrate in the radiation field. And again, Naval Reactors experience showed that this would not be a problem, and it was not.

By the end of 1979 some test probes had yielded radiation measurements inside the building that were almost identical to the much lower MPR calculations. But this information was largely ignored, and the perception of the situation created by the early high-radiation figures continued to dominate the thinking and planning for the next year. It was about this time that the TAAG was set up, and the first task it undertook was to look at the question: Is it possible to have persons enter the reactor building and work directly there? Bechtel had estimated that this would not be possible for another two years, but TAAG member Cole suggested that MPR might be able to come up with something.

When the preliminary evaluation looked favorable, Tom Cramer of Electric Boat and Ed Sise of the Newport News shipyard pulled in radiation experts from their companies, who calculated radiation levels at various locations around the reactor plant, based on the few measurements available. Ironically, one of the lowest-radiation zones was directly above the reactor, and Cole developed the idea of a "quick look" inspection. The intent was to get an idea of the approximate condition of the reactor fuel and core structure. This would avoid the need for basing the planning of future operations on unsupported worst-case assumptions. Such assumptions claim to be conservative, but they can lead to outlandish requirements that complicate the work—as they did in this case.

Cole, working with the TAAG people and MPR engineers and draftsmen, developed an ingenious approach. They pulled a one-and-one-half-inch control rod drive shaft out of the reactor vessel and inserted a one-and-one-quarter-inch commercially available television camera down into the hole, to photograph the condition of the reactor core and its pressure vessel walls. To do this required overcoming a number of obstacles that had been said to be insurmountable. But the result was well worth the effort.

First, it proved that radiation exposure from working in the containment building was even lower than had been calculated. Bechtel had estimated that the job would result in personnel exposure of up to 1,600 man–rem (a standard measure of radiation exposure). The TAAG group had estimated 40 man–rem. The actual exposure was about 20.

Second, it showed that the reactor system could be depressurized without creating the air contamination problems predicted by some. It also showed that the water level in the reactor system could be lowered without overheating the core, and that the level could be monitored in this position by clever use of existing plant instrumentation. Both these problems had been considered formidable. Several other potential problems were also evaluated and found less severe than predicted. (For example, it was believed that the forty-ton shielding blocks directly over the reactor would prevent access to the control ports, since the large building crane that normally moves these blocks was not operable. But the TAAG team found that there were narrow spaces between the blocks, one of which opened down onto a central control rod port. It was just large enough for the purpose. Bill Sylvester, Nevin Hoke, and other MPR engineers and draftsmen worked their way through this tricky problem, with the help of drawings, calculations, and mock-ups.) This inspection was completed in about six months—not years, as originally projected. It showed dramatically that the top five feet of the core was gone!

TAAG and MPR designed and carried out a subsequent inspection, down to the bottom of the core, which showed that nearly half the reactor core had melted to some extent, and that ten to twenty tons of molten core material had slumped to the bottom of the reactor vessel. Since the half that had melted contained most of the fission products, this is about the worst accident that could happen to a water-cooled reactor. This is what some people have suggested could lead to the "China Syndrome," in which the core would melt through the reactor vessel and into the earth, supposedly "all the way to China." But the TMI reactor vessel's integrity was little affected by the molten mass, which quickly refroze.

Rickover's reactors had always been defueled by removing the reactor vessel head and working directly with long-handled tools from above. No robotic devices were necessary. But the recovery operation was proceeding on the premise that such an approach would not work at TMI. The proposed method for removing the damaged fuel required that the structure be ground up underwater, using a remotely controlled robotic clamshell crusher and a shredder. The highly radioactive slurry of water, fuel particles, and fission products would be pumped into a shielded tank for shipment. This scheme would have required flooding the reactor refueling cavity with 350,000 to 400,000 gallons of water, which would be vulnerable to high-level contamination from the core. All the machinery would have had to work underwater, unattended. With fifty-seven feet of water above the bottom of the reactor vessel, the use of long-handled tools as a backup would not be feasible.

Kintner realized the folly of this concept and had the courage to stop it. He asked TAAG member Cole if defueling with long-handled manual tools—an approach similar to the one used on naval plants—might be possible at TMI. After a hurried preliminary study, Cole concluded that it was feasible, and he proceeded to submit a formal detailed proposal. There were many problems unique to TMI, but these were overcome, and the refueling was successfully carried out. The core has now been completely removed. The experience of refueling naval reactors, operating fuel irradiation tests, and cleaning up the damaged Canadian NRX reactor were what sustained the confidence of the Rickover alumni in fighting against the prevailing opinions of those without this experience.

In 1990, as a final inspection, MPR was given thirty days to cut samples for metallurgical examination from the bottom wall of the reactor vessel and from various internal structures. Using a specially designed electrical discharge machining device and forty-foot-long tools, they removed thirty-one metal specimens, some of which were six and a half inches long, and three inches wide, with a two-and-a-half-inch-deep triangular cross-section. Upon examination, these tests showed that the vessel's integrity had not been impaired.

Based on what was learned from all this work, MPR published a number of recommendations to make such work easier if it ever had to be done again on another plant.

Rickover Returns to Three Mile Island

In the summer of 1983, after the undamaged TMI-1 plant, which was *not* involved in the accident, had been shut down for over four years, the utility officials called Mandil to say that they felt the condition of the plant and the state of training of the operators were excellent, but they did not seem to be making any progress in getting permission to restart the plant. "That plant has had as good a record as any in the country," complained the official. "And we've reexamined and improved everything we can get our hands on. But we don't seem to be able to persuade anyone to examine us and pronounce us ready to go. We are thinking of hiring Admiral Rickover, if he is willing, to make such an evaluation, using whatever additional personnel he wishes. What do you think of that? Does that make sense?"

Mandil replied that Rickover was noted for his unpredictability and his uncontrollability, and the utility might find itself with a tiger by the tail. "But who is there with as much competence and credibility to do the job?" was the reply. There was no answer to that one, and so the utility called him in. Rickover brought in three of his former leading people to assist him, Robert V. Laney, James M. Dunford, and Jack C.

AN OPPORTUNITY MISSED

Rickover's letter to President Carter, and his subsequent report to the utility, make clear the kind of nuclear power industry Rickover would have tried to bring about had he been in a position to do so. And despite the extraordinary effort he made, in his reports on TMI, and in the tours and discussions he gave to utility people after the accident to describe the changes he believed were necessary, he came away convinced that his impact had been minimal. It is intriguing to consider what might have been.

In mid-1955, only a few months after the *Nautilus* first signaled, "Under way on nuclear power," AEC Commissioner Thomas E. Murray recommended that Rickover be put in charge of all of the agency's power reactor programs, both civilian and military. President Eisenhower had presented his "Atoms for Peace" vision and was anxious to have something solid to back it up. The civilian reactor program, which was to have led the way for the more difficult military programs, had never really gotten started. Murray believed that Rickover's demonstrated ability to create a dynamic program from scratch, with a commitment to engineering excellence, was just what the civilian program needed.

AEC Chairman Lewis Strauss was strongly opposed to the idea and asked for time to explore other possibilities. He was known to be an ardent advocate for carrying out the free-enterprise charter of the new 1954 Atomic Energy Act, and he might have seen a strong military leader as an obstacle to that goal. For whatever reason, he spent a great deal of time and effort trying to locate a suitable alternative to Rickover. Finally, with the situation still at an impasse, the commissioners met in executive session to settle the matter. Mr. Murray returned to his office after the meeting and told Jack Crawford, whom Rickover had made available as Murray's assistant, "They voted him down."

"What did they give as a reason?" asked Crawford.

"Strauss announced that Rickover was opposed by one of the two leading electrical manufacturers in the nation," said Murray.

Crawford suggested the company he considered most likely to be the opponent, and Murray nodded agreement.

Whether or not Rickover could have achieved the kind of nuclear power industry he described in his letter to Carter and his report to the utility is, of course, now a moot question. But it is a fact that Rickover oversaw the construction, operation, maintenance, and refueling of many more power reactors than were built by all other reactor builders in the country combined. He selected and trained sailors to operate and maintain them, and he supplied many of these trained operators to the commercial reactor industry, which could always pay them more. He developed engineering codes, standards, and designs on which nearly all the world's reactors are based. And he never had a Chernobyl or a Three Mile Island accident.

Grigg, and insisted on a major fee for the work. He then told the utility that he would not accept any money for himself, and asked that the money be given directly to the Rickover Foundation, which the Admiral had set up to encourage bright science and math students. After extensive investigation, Rickover turned in his report. Its basic conclusion was that the utility "had the management competence and integrity to safely operate TMI-1." A year later, start-up approval had still not been given by the Nuclear Regulatory Commission (which had taken over from the old AEC), and the utility called Rickover back to make a further evaluation. He reported that the process of deciding whether to restart the plant "has already taken too long . . . I strongly recommend that GPU Nuclear Corp. be authorized to operate TMI-1 without further delay." The plant was finally permitted to return to full power in 1986, after having been shut down for seven years, and in 1989 it chalked up a record as the most reliable nuclear plant in the world, out of several hundred competing internationally for that title.

Rickover's report to President Carter had outlined what a national central nuclear utility oversight organization had to do in order to achieve the sort of assurance of safety and reliability he had created in the naval program. Now, in their report to the utility, the Rickover team outlined principles of operation that each nuclear utility management had to understand and follow, if the process was to work. These were stated in the form of management objectives:

1. Require rising standards of adequacy.
2. Be technically self-sufficient.
3. Face facts.
4. Respect even small amounts of radiation.
5. Require adherence to the concept of total responsibility.
6. Develop the capacity to learn from experience.

Again, Rickover had tried to spell out the hard, tedious day-to-day work and attention required to run any large and complex system—not just nuclear. GPU made the report public, so that other utilities could learn from its bitter experience.

THE RICKOVER HALL OF ENGINEERING

> *Progress—like freedom—is desired by nearly all men, but not all understand that both come at a cost. Whenever society advances—be it in culture and education or science and technology—there is a rise in the requirements man must meet to function successfully. The price of progress is acceptance of these more exacting standards of performance and relinquishment of familiar habits and conventions rendered obsolete because they no longer meet the new standards. To move but one rung up the ladder of civilization, man must surpass himself. The simple life comes "naturally," the civilized life compels effort . . . That is the never-ending challenge.*
>
> H.G.R.

Rickover received many honors during his career, honors bestowed by Navy secretaries, by presidents, by the Congress, and by a worshipful press and an admiring public. But one honor that received only modest public notice was perhaps most dear to him. The U.S. Naval Academy, which had accorded him so little respect and recognition when he was a plebe, built a grand Hall of Engineering and named it in his honor. With over three hundred thousand square feet of classroom and faculty office space within its reinforced concrete and structural steel hull, its exterior was finished with granite and precast concrete. It boasted of having the "latest features required for teaching modern naval engineering and design."

On Friday, 29 March 1974, an inscription ceremony was held, attended by the secretary of the Navy and the superintendent of the academy. Rickover etched the initials *H.G.* onto a main support column of the building, using an arc-welding torch, as President Truman had marked the hull plate of the submarine *Nautilus* nearly twenty-two years previously. Then he gave the torch to his wife, who inscribed the final *R*. On this occasion, as on several others, the Admiral had insisted that an official invitation be tendered to his wife, and he took special pride in breaking the ice for wives for events to which they had never before been invited.

On 19 June 1981, at an unveiling ceremony, a bronze bust of the Admiral, in his usual civilian shirt-sleeves, was dedicated. Admiral James

D. Watkins, the chief of naval operations and a Rickover alumnus, was guest speaker. Mrs. Rickover unveiled the bust and made a few gracious remarks. (The Admiral had headed off on another sea trial, and when Mrs. Rickover asked if he wanted her to convey any remarks, he replied simply, "No.") The bust was the work of the internationally famous sculptor Paul Wegner, and was cast in the foundry that he and his brothers Mike, Steven, and Stewart own and operate with their father, William. William Wegner, a Naval Academy graduate, was a key figure on Rickover's staff from 1956 through 1979.

RICKOVER GETS FIRED

> *Unpleasant facts are unwelcome and no one builds statues to critics. But today we are not quite as impatient of a critic as the ancient Locrians. These people gave freedom of speech to all citizens. At public meetings anyone could stand up and argue for changes in law or custom, on one condition. A rope was placed around his neck before he began to speak and, if what he said did not meet with public approval, he was forthwith hanged. That, no doubt, prevented disturbing the even tenor of familiar customs and ways of life.*
>
> *I have encountered some in the Navy who look with nostalgia on this ancient custom.*
>
> H.G.R.

Early in November 1981 Rickover returned home from sea trials of the attack submarine USS *Boston*. The trials had gone well, and he was in good spirits. Mrs. Rickover asked if he had heard the news, and he asked, "What news?" She told him she had just heard on the radio that President Reagan had decided to retire him. Over the years, the Admiral had heard a lot of rumors about his future, and he had learned not to put too much stock in them. On more than one occasion Reagan had been asked by reporters whether he considered Rickover too old to continue his important job, and Reagan had always brushed such questions aside, sometimes referring to other notables who had made major contributions in their eighties or nineties.

But this time, Rickover was summoned to the office of Secretary of Defense Caspar Weinberger and told that the president had decided not to renew his appointment. Weinberger and Navy Secretary John

Lehman made nice little speeches about Rickover's contributions, but when they turned to him for a response, Rickover just got up and walked out of the room. There was no more to be said. His career was over.

Shortly after his meeting with Weinberger, Rickover received another significant telephone call, this time from the chief of the Justice Department's Fraud Section, telling him that the department was closing out its criminal investigation of General Dynamics. Rickover had been pressing the government to file criminal charges against some shipbuilders, because of what he considered illegal cost overruns. The caller agreed that there were indications of fraud, but she concluded that a winning case could not be made. Rickover wrote a protest letter to the U.S. attorney general, but it didn't change anything. The government had closed its books on what the *Washington Post* called "the largest criminal investigation directed against a major U.S. defense contractor in recent history."

On 8 January 1982 Rickover was called to the Oval Office for a farewell meeting with the president. He saw Weinberger and Lehman standing at President Reagan's side, and he asked to talk with the president alone. After the secretaries had made their embarrassed exit, Rickover said bluntly that Weinberger and Lehman were not serving the president well; they were unwilling to investigate nearly a billion dollars in overrun costs at General Dynamics, costs that were criminally fraudulent. The only reason they wanted him out of the way, Rickover said, was that he would not go along with the deal. Reagan was taken aback, mumbled some words about being against fraud, congratulated Rickover on his lifetime of achievements, and escorted him to the door.

Adding insult to injury, rumors were picked up by Panoff and me from more than one source that General Dynamics officials were bragging around Washington that they had "gotten Rickover." Later, when Rickover's friends arranged a postretirement party for him, attended by all three living U.S. ex-presidents and an international galaxy of other notables, they requested a military band for the occasion. The Pentagon brusquely turned down the request. The once-invincible Admiral was now history.

Rickover "in Retirement"

About a year after Rickover's retirement, Panoff, Mandil, and I agreed that we should visit him in his "retirement quarters." We had not seen much of him since we left to form MPR, and we wanted to see how he was faring. Panoff called him at his office and suggested we join him for lunch. "We'll bring some fruit and sandwiches, Admiral. Unless you'd rather go out."

"Naw, the fruit and sandwiches sound fine. I'll see you about noon."

Rickover was officially retired, but he maintained an office in the old Washington Navy Yard, off M Street Southwest, on the Potomac riverfront. The Navy provided him with an aide, a secretary, and a small, old, sparsely furnished office. We had not seen it before this visit, and we were quick to notice that the decor was in keeping with that of his previous quarters. The building itself was a decrepit, frequently painted cinderblock construction, typical of many old government buildings. The Admiral sat in his worn Kennedy-style rocker, which showed its age and heavy usage and sported a tired green cushion. A standard, battle-scarred G.I. metal desk and metal bookcases completed the furnishings. Behind Rickover were framed photographs of Navy Secretary Lehman and his predecessor Edward Hidalgo, the two who had engineered the General Dynamics deal. "Two biggest goddamned fools who ever ran the Navy," he told a *Washington Post* reporter, who wrote that to emphasize the point, he later added a third picture, of Benedict Arnold.

We started the conversation on a light vein, leaving it up to the Admiral to get into more substantive issues if he wished. He seemed warm but somewhat guarded. He mentioned that his work at this office was directed toward overturning the cost-overrun settlements that had been worked out between the Navy and the three largest American shipyards six years earlier, which he was convinced were fraudulent claims. We had heard that his war with the shipyards had become bitter, and that his old ally, hardworking Joe Pierce, trying to be loyal both to Rickover and to the shipyard, had finally been denounced by both sides and had been sacrificed to the fray, retiring from the yard in defeat. Rickover had not given up on fighting the overrun claims. His eyes still burned and his voice still rang with indignation. The encroaching signs of old age could not quench the image of the Rickover we had known so well and so long.

In due course we took our leave and agreed to get together again in the near future, which we did, a number of times. We were quick to remark after we left that the Navy had provided Rickover with remarkably sensitive and intelligent aides, people who seemed determined that their charge be treated with the respect and consideration they clearly believed he deserved. We were glad about that.

Launching the USS *Hyman G. Rickover*

Navy Secretary Lehman had reportedly promised Rickover that he would name a nuclear-powered aircraft carrier after him. But as soon as Rickover was safely booted from power, Lehman reneged and issued a public announcement that a submarine was to be named in his honor. Now, on 27 August 1983, with Rickover safely retired, the Navy and General Dynamics were ready to honor him by launching a nuclear-powered attack submarine of the Los Angeles class, the USS *Hyman G. Rickover* (SSN-709). The occasion brought out the biggest reunion of Rickover alumni in memory, and this alone was enough to give the whole day a warmth and nostalgia that would last for some time. The group from Washington, including spouses, was big enough to justify a chartered plane, and we made a reunion party out of the trip each way.

John Francis O'Grady was there, a big, handsome fellow who enjoyed playing the role of the classic Irishman. He had expedited many crucial items back onto schedule for Rickover, beginning with Rickover's tour of duty at Okinawa and continuing through many critical years at Naval Reactors. At the launching he rounded up people he considered the "charter team," and he had a photographer ready to record the assemblage for posterity. "Where's the Admiral, John? This whole thing is no good without him," someone shouted. "You all just wait there, I'll get him," responded O'Grady.

"He's talking to a senator and a lot of other big shots. How're ya going to get him over here?" he was asked.

"Have ye fergottin yer talkin' to John Francis O'Grady of the Philadelphia O'Gradys?" he replied in his best Irish brogue. And in a moment he was back, with the Admiral meekly in tow.

"How did you do that?" the group wanted to know.

"I told him I had all his original gang lined up, and he shouldn't keep them waiting just to talk to those people," replied John. He signaled the photographer, and some days later he mailed to each of us a perfect group portrait, which all of us treasure to this day.

The formal launching program was simple, consisting of a brief welcome by Fritz Tovar, general manager of Electric Boat, and the usual words of fulsome praise for everyone concerned by General Dynamics Chairman David S. Lewis. After an excellent speech by CNO Watkins, the ship was blessed by the chaplain and christened by Mrs. Rickover. This ended the formal program, and everyone went in for a sumptuous sit-down dinner. There were some further pleasantries, and the submarine skipper and his wife were introduced, as well as a number of General Dynamics officials and government dignitaries.

Mrs. Rickover was then introduced, and she began about as follows: "My husband asked if I expected to say a few words, and I replied that I might. He asked if I would like him to help me, and I replied that I didn't think that would be necessary. Later, he asked if I would like him to review my remarks, and again I said I didn't think that would be necessary. So he is now as concerned about what I might say as many of you may have been at times when he was about to speak."

And with a loving, good-natured grin in the Admiral's direction, she then made a few gracious remarks. The old-timers were particularly touched when she said that she wished the first, late, Mrs. Rickover could have been there. Having stood by him during the early years, she deserved to see this glorious culmination of all those difficult, unsung days and nights. I remembered the reports that the Navy had promised Ruth Rickover that she would sponsor the twin-reactor submarine *Triton*, at that time the biggest, most powerful submarine in the world, and then had reneged on that promise; that memory made Eleonore Rickover's remark all the more poignant.

Up to this point, praise and congratulations had ruled the day. Then Rickover was given his chance. His talk was not long, but to people who knew what lay behind it, the words were memorable. After a few kind comments about the sponsor, his wife, he delivered his message: "I will now say a few words that should have been said many years ago. We have become accustomed to giving praise to organizations and not to people. Consider today's events: the speakers always give credit to the corporation—in this case General Dynamics. But I will tell the real story why Electric Boat is the leading submarine builder in the United States."

He then told how he had tried to get the Portsmouth Naval Shipyard to build the first nuclear submarine. He said the "reluctant dragon" who ran the yard was unwilling to do it, so he called O. P. Robinson, manager of Electric Boat, who immediately responded yes. Rickover continued:

Mr. Robinson demonstrated an attitude of hearty cooperation and not of dignified acquiescence—as has been the experience at the beginning of some honeymoons. This relationship between the Navy and Electric Boat continued to be outstanding even after it was taken over by General Dynamics Corporation—except for one recent set of events: the local manager attempted to impose his will on the United States Navy. But, that official is no longer at Electric Boat.

I trust that the lesson from this event will be long remembered and will remain deeply imbedded in the brains of General Dynamic officials in St. Louis.

Fair and honest dealing with the United States Government is the best policy for the individual citizen, as is the fulfillment of legal obligations on the part of corporations doing business with the United States Government.

I believe that this relationship will continue to be mutually beneficial from now on, if Electric Boat acts as a responsible supplier and not as a contractor trying to dominate the customer.

In large corporations, it is customary to assign credit to the senior officials and blame to the lower ranks when something goes wrong. In the case of the Portsmouth Naval Shipyard, due to the lack of vision and courage by the shipyard's naval management, Electric Boat became the leading submarine yard in the United States.

Bear in mind, all effort in the world is done by and through *people*, not organizations. So, whenever you read the full-page shipbuilders' advertisements, just remember how the job really got done. Also remember that the actions of some shipyard officials have not been in the best interests of the customer or even of their own yard.

With that, he sat down. And it was a while before the conversation of the crowd resumed its previous cheery pace.

"Wow!" said I. "How does he keep it up? And why?"

"I guess we'll never understand how," said Panoff. "But the *why* was pretty well summed up in Jim Watkins's opening words this morning." Watkins had begun his talk with the following little story, which Rickover liked to cite:

On this special day, I would like to share with you a story of an ancient philosopher who came to a city, determined to save its inhabitants from sin and wickedness. Night and day the philosopher walked the streets and haunted marketplaces. He preached against greed and envy; against falsehood and indifference. At first, people listened and smiled. Later, they turned away; for he no longer amused them. Finally, a child asked: "Why do you go on? Do you not see it is hopeless?"

The philosopher answered, "In the beginning, I thought I would change men. If I still shout, it is to prevent men from changing me."

"He Accepted Gifts from a Contractor"

On 18 July 1984, two and a half years after Rickover was replaced, the *Washington Post* ran a front-page story charging that Admiral Rickover had accepted personal gifts from Electric Boat. The charge was based on a file turned over to the reporter, Patrick Tyler, by P. Takis Veliotis, former head of Electric Boat. Veliotis had been indicted for receiving kickbacks in a former job, and he had fled to Greece to avoid prosecution. His motives for releasing the material on Rickover were unclear and probably mixed. Tyler was investigating rumors that the massive cost overruns for which Electric Boat was trying to get government reimbursement were fraudulent, and Veliotis was very much in the center of that picture. Veliotis may have been trying to get back at Rickover for the relentless questioning of the validity of the cost overruns, questioning that got Veliotis in trouble with his superiors. Or he may have been trying to discredit his superiors, who in his opinion were trying to make him the fall guy in the overrun scandal.

Tyler described confronting Rickover with this information:

I was surprised when Rickover looked me straight in the eye and told me he took gifts from the shipbuilders a number of times over the years. "Trinkets," he called them. He said he didn't remember the ones Veliotis had so carefully documented. Then, in his school-teacher way, he asked: "Did anyone ever suggest that I stopped taking them [the defense contractors] on? Did anyone ever suggest that I did not try to get the best deal I could for the government? What did they hope to gain by giving me the gifts?"

"They thought you could hurt them and maybe they thought you would go easier on them," I said.

"Well, I could hurt them. But did I ever stop taking them on? That's the question you ought to be asking."

"No, Admiral," I replied.

After the fifth or sixth time he had made the point that he had never stopped taking the shipbuilders on for the alleged fraud in their cost overrun claims, I summoned the courage to say, "With all due respect, Admiral, that isn't the point."

"I know it isn't," he said in an instant, and for a moment I thought he was repentant for the sake of the tens of thousands of young men and women whose minds were shaped and whose commitment to public service and uncompromising integrity sprang from the example and high standards set by Hyman G. Rickover. But the instant passed and he was off again on the shipbuilders.

Navy Secretary Lehman tallied up the list of gifts with ill-disguised glee and released the information to the press. There were numerous tie-clips in the shape of a nuclear submarine, which Rickover had passed out by the dozens to congressmen and workers in the program. They were great morale-boosters. Everybody in the program had them, including me. There were some desktop plaques with the words of a Breton fisherman's prayer on them: "O, God, Thy sea is so great and my boat is so small." Rickover gave one to each submarine skipper as he assumed command. He had also given one to Kennedy, one to Nixon, and one to Carter. And there was a variety of ship models and engine-room models that Rickover and his people used for training and for telling people about the program.

Of course, handing out fancy launching gifts and souvenirs has been common practice in the shipbuilding business for as long as there have been ships. And I have seen scores of similar models and tie-clips and ladies' pins handed out by aircraft manufacturers, but I have never seen the practice played up as a scandal in the newspapers. However, Veliotis's list contained a $695 pair of earrings and a $400 jade pendant, which had been disguised on Electric Boat's books as retirement watches and were not associated with any launching. This had a different flavor.

We had occasionally argued with Rickover about his willingness to accept favors from contractors. One time Panoff went to pay his hotel bill at a shipyard and asked if Rickover was about to pay his. "Let the damn shipyard pay," he replied. "They're making plenty of money off of us."

"That's stupid, Admiral. Pay the damn bill," said Panoff. But Rickover didn't move, so Panoff went and paid both bills. He told Rickover what he had done and the Admiral reimbursed him, but not without some grousing. Panoff didn't see any point in putting oneself in the position of accepting favors from a contractor. But Rickover knew that no one could accuse him of going soft on contractors, so he figured he'd make them pay whenever he could.

The secretary of the Navy had the last word. He entered a letter of reprimand into Rickover's personnel file. Tyler commented in the *Washington Post* as follows: "Lehman, whose gift to the shipbuilders was the most profitable contracts in navy shipbuilding history during the Reagan administration, and who showed a conspicuous disinterest in new evidence suggesting that the Treasury had been raided in the 1978 claims settlements, should have disqualified himself from sitting in judgment of Rickover."

The *Nautilus* Comes Home to Stay

On Saturday, 6 July 1985, the *Nautilus* came back home to Groton for the last time. As the world's first nuclear submarine, she had served the fleet well for nearly twenty-six years. She then went to the Mare Island Naval Shipyard off San Francisco, and there she was decommissioned and officially declared a National Historic Landmark. Her nuclear reactor and her weapons were removed, and she was towed through the Panama Canal, back to the place of her birth, to become the centerpiece of the USS Nautilus Memorial Submarine Force Library and Museum.

Led through the heavy fog by the tall ship *Providence*, a full-scale reproduction of John Paul Jones's famous fighting ship, the *Nautilus* was towed by three Navy tugboats up Connecticut's Thames River and nudged into Pier 33 at the U.S. Submarine Base, while thousands cheered from both sides of the river. Cannon from nearby Fort Griswold boomed their welcome. Thousands of balloons were released simultaneously in Groton and New London. And some three hundred pleasure craft tooted their whistles and waved hearty greetings. Boom boxes in the crowd blared forth the country song by former Groton resident Tom Cox, which pleaded, "Bring the *Nautilus* home to Groton." That song played a part in the decade-long fight to win for Groton the honor of being the *Nautilus*'s final home.

For a while it looked as if the Naval Academy at Annapolis, Maryland, would win that honor, and then San Francisco and the Navy Yard at Washington, D.C., put in their bid. But the question was settled when Ella T. Grasso, then governor of Connecticut, agreed to guarantee $5 million in loans and grants for a museum. At that point President Carter signed an executive order that sent the submarine—Connecticut's official state ship—back home.

"Welcome home, *Nautilus*," said former governor John N. Dempsey, chairman of the committee that was raising money for the Nautilus Museum. "Thank God, at last you're home."

Governor William A. O'Neill, on the platform with other dignitaries, including many former *Nautilus* crew members, said, "*Nautilus* represents much more than a triumph of technology. *Nautilus* really represents a triumph of the spirit of Connecticut and the realization of the dreams of her citizens." Rear Admiral J. D. Williams, commander of Submarine Group Two, summed it up with these words: "The *Nautilus* is more than just a tourist attraction. She serves as a reminder of our future."

But Admiral Rickover was not able to participate in these festivities; two days before, on the fourth of July, he had suffered a stroke.

RICKOVER AT HOME

After the launching of the USS *Rickover*, we didn't see the Admiral for a while, partly because we were very busy at MPR, and partly because we had heard that he was grumbling about us to other people. We weren't quite sure what his problem was, but he seemed to be down on us for some reason. We had checked once with Mrs. Rickover, and she suggested that it was not then a good time to visit. Apparently the Admiral was in a bitter mood, and she feared that our visit might just aggravate the situation. "He seems to be churning over a lot of remembered wrongs, and you three seem to figure in some of them."

We were surprised at this. He had never given any indication of it directly, although we had picked up an occasional rumor that he had expressed annoyance with us, as a sort of trial balloon for whomever he was talking with. If the listener challenged the point, the Admiral would retreat from it. So we waited, and one day Mrs. Rickover called and said she thought he would be glad to see us any time now.

It was April 1986. Bob Panoff had died of a brain tumor two years previously, and Harry Mandil and I arranged to drop by the Rickovers' after work. They lived in "The Representative," a recently built luxury apartment building looking over the Arlington rooftops to the city of Washington. When the Naval Reactors office was in Crystal City, the Rickovers had lived at the Buchanan House apartments, and the Admiral would wave to Mrs. Rickover from the sidewalk as he headed off each morning to his nearby office. But after his retirement, Mrs. Rickover had suggested that they move, because she noticed that looking out of their apartment at his old office building seemed to depress him. Their new apartment was spacious and tastefully furnished, but not extravagant. She projected the warmth of a dedicated nurse and the firm strength of a career naval officer as she said, "Thank you for coming. He is looking forward to seeing you."

"We didn't want to be a burden," I said. "I know you must have hordes of visitors."

"Well, yes, we do. But you people from NR are very special. You who were with him in the early days, and stuck with him through the formative years, he often talks of you."

The Admiral was propped up in a chair, looking wan and weak. But his mind proved to be remarkably sharp, and his spirit was strong. Mrs. Rickover told me later that his memory had become vague, which might have accounted for his change in attitude about perceived wrongs in the past. She also said that he had been depressed and felt abandoned. "They've all forgotten me," he would say. So she had taken to keeping a logbook with the names of all the visitors, and she would show him how many people had come to see him. Each time, he seemed surprised at this, and his wife's constant reassurance that he was not forgotten was an important factor in maintaining his spirits.

People still at Naval Reactors continued to send him articles, speeches, and information on subjects he was interested in, and they went to visit him. They inevitably felt they should update him on what was going on in the program, but he would put them at ease by saying he didn't want to talk about that. He said once you are no longer in charge, that's it, and you shouldn't try to hold on to the job. So they would talk about the people, and it was particularly gratifying to him that the headquarters people had stayed on after he left. There were rumors that many of them would leave after his retirement, but those rumors were generated by people who did not understand the level of commitment of these people to the responsibilities they had undertaken.

On Rickover's eighty-sixth (and last) birthday, several of the key people at NR, who had worked for him for decades, brought him a birthday cake in the shape of a pink tissue memo copy, just like those he had scrutinized by the thousands all those years. It showed that the "pink" was "on hold," which meant that it could not be released without being personally cleared by him. And that is what the group had come to do. On it was scrawled in large letters the familiar Rickover notation: "N/B," standing for the Latin words for "Note well," which he often used to draw particular attention to a point he considered important.

But when Mandil and I were there, he couldn't help asking, "How is the program going? What do you hear? They don't tell me anything anymore."

I replied in all honesty, "I'm really not in touch with the program anymore, Admiral. I'm sure it's different from when you were running it. But I understand they're doing OK."

Rickover had come alive now and added, "I hear they don't work weekends anymore. Did you hear about that? They're not working weekends. I'll bet they knocked that off as soon as they were sure I was out of earshot."

We smiled at that, and Mandil said, "I have no comment on that, Admiral." But knowing the caliber and character of the people still in Naval Reactors, we couldn't really believe they had slacked off much. They weren't that kind of people, or they wouldn't be there.

The conversation went on along those lines for a few more minutes, light banter, in which the Admiral demonstrated that he still controlled a facile mind and a quick wit. But he was obviously weak, and we didn't want to tire him further. So we took our leave, and agreed to get back and see him again.

"They Tell Me I'm Dying"

Later I went back to see the Admiral again. This time he was in the bedroom.

"How's he doing?" I asked Mrs. Rickover.

"He's very weak. He's had a severe case of septicemia, and it's really weakened him. They've put a tube through his abdomen into his bladder, and he has trouble speaking and eating, but his mind is still keen. Why don't we go on in?"

She led me into the bedroom. Rickover was flat on his back and did not raise his head or move his body at all. Mrs. Rickover said, in a slightly louder voice, to bring him out of his reverie, "I've brought Mr. Rockwell to see you."

"Hello, Admiral. Are you in pain?"

I was shocked at how much effort it obviously cost him to reply, very softly and with slurred speech, "No-o-o. But I'm not as active as I'd like to be."

Here was a man, dying, who could move only a few muscles in his face, and he still came back fast with a wisecrack! I had to laugh. Then, with some bravado I said, "Oh, that won't last, Admiral. It would take more than that to keep you down for long."

"They tell me I'm dying," he said suddenly. There was an awkward silence for a moment, and then he went on. "I guess you're supposed to be embarrassed and I'm supposed to be scared. Hell, it's no big deal! I've already done it once. There's nothing to it."

He coughed, and paused to get his breath. Mrs. Rickover picked up the conversation. "He's referring to the time he was coming back from a trip on that overnight red-eye flight. You may remember it. He walked to his office from the airport, as he often did, and got to his office about 6:30 A.M. There was no one there, of course, and he stopped just inside his office to get his breath. You know how fast he walks! But he had a sudden stroke or heart attack, and he fell to the floor and hit his head on the desk. We don't know how long he lay there, but the doctors figured it must have been several minutes. They believe he was clinically dead. Then his aide showed up and immediately sized up the situation. They had trained him in CPR and emergency first aid, knowing that Admiral had had previous heart attacks." (She liked to refer to him as "Admiral," without a *the*.) "The aide listened for a heartbeat and found none. So he started pounding on Admiral's chest, trying to restart his heart, when his secretary came in. The aide yelled at her to start mouth-to-mouth resuscitation, which she did. Finally, he gave up pounding on his chest and called for emergency first aid. And somehow he came through it all unscathed. He's a tough one to beat."

Rickover had been listening to all this, and now he chimed in on his own behalf. "Yeah, I died. There was nothing to it. No hellfire, no angels. Just nothing. I don't know why everybody's so scared of it. It's no big deal."

I laughed again, despite the grimness of the topic. "I never doubted that you could pull it off competently when the time comes, Admiral. Take care of yourself, I don't want to wear you out."

Rickover managed to reclaim a bit of his old commanding demeanor. "The whole damn crowd of you couldn't wear me out, Rockwell! I'm not licked yet."

Humphrey's Retirement Party

Bill Humphrey had been in the Naval Reactors program since August 1954. If you counted his time in the Rickover course at MIT and elsewhere, he liked to say that he had actually been in the program longer than anyone else, including the Admiral himself. So he had a goodly crowd of the old-timers at his retirement party at the Bethesda Officers' Club on 10 May 1986. I was enjoying seeing again many people I had worked closely with but hadn't seen in years.

Suddenly, everyone was looking at the entrance to the ballroom, and when I looked I saw, to my amazement, Admiral Rickover being pushed into the room in a wheelchair. I couldn't believe my eyes! The man who had appeared to be inches from death's door only a few days before was sitting up, eyes twinkling, a smile on his face. People flocked around him, anxious to see him and exchange a few words, but also determined not to overtire him. My wife thanked him again for bringing her, years before, a bird-of-paradise flower in his lap all the way from Hawaii, and for sending her twelve-year-old son as his official representative to the International Naval Review, which the Admiral had called the Parade of the Dinosaurs. He said he remembered it well, but he probably did not.

Humphrey asked if he wanted to say a few words over the microphone, since it was clear that everyone was not going to be able to talk with him individually. He agreed to do so, and they wheeled him to the mike. Humphrey was so excited that he fumbled interminably with the mike, and when the Admiral finally got it he said, "I was going to tell people how competent you are, Humphrey. But I can't now, without looking like a damn fool." But of course, he did go on to say some nice things, along with some wisecracks and some recollections of the old days, and there was hardly a dry eye in the house.

After he had bantered for more than two hours with all comers, he and Mrs. Rickover left, with trails of good wishes following them. As always seemed to be the case after he left a room, all the conversation for some time was about him. He hadn't lost it.

ASSESSING THE RICKOVER EFFECT

After Rickover's retirement, his alumni still gathered from time to time in different-sized groups, at various places, and when they did, they invariably started talking about Rickover. The clearest evidence, they all agreed, of the impact that he had had on all of them was the fact that he continued to be a central topic of conversation among them even after he had retired, and after they had all embarked on busy and important lives of their own. Having served with Rickover was analogous, in some ways, to having served in an elite combat group; those who had shared the experience felt a kinship with each other, and a special quality that distinguished them from everyone else.

LOU RODDIS was one of the first of the old-timers to leave the group. A few months after the *Nautilus* first put to sea, he left to join the staff of the Atomic Energy Commission and became deputy director of the Reactor Development Division—in effect, Rickover's boss. In 1958 he retired from government service to accept a position as president of Pennsylvania Electric Company, becoming chairman in 1967. He was made director of nuclear power activities of General Public Utilities, and then president of Consolidated Edison in New York. He became prominent in the atomic power field, was made president of the industry's international trade association, and was awarded numerous honors.

The contrast between the strict and controlled training, construction, operation, and maintenance program he was so intimately familiar with and the more tradition-bound, union-dominated, laissez-faire world of the utility industry shocked him. Utilities typically managed by general fiat, and they delegated their technical decisions to their architect-engineer contractors. Roddis tried to change the situation, but it became clear that it was more than one man could do alone. So he had asked MPR Associates to help him apply the lessons they had learned together over the Rickover years.

Mandil and Panoff both came. The problem at hand was a metallurgical one, involving the reactor vessel nozzles at the Oyster Creek plant in New Jersey. But the conversation soon turned to broader issues.

"I've tried to instill in these guys some of the things we learned from the Old Man over the years," said Roddis, "but it's completely alien to their way of thinking and the way they've all been brought up to do business. When something screws up, I try to find out who violated what specific procedure, and I find that the procedures are rather vague on this particular point. And a lot of others too, it turns out. For example, the relays in a plant might not be quite the same as the ones in the procedures manuals. Some joker in Purchasing finds another manufacturer who'll give him a better price. It may be an acceptable relay, but we now have a mismatch between the hardware and the manual. I find there's nothing to prevent Purchasing from making that sort of decision, so long as the substituted material meets all the specs. So then you look at the specs, and they're not quite everything you'd like either. Every thread you pull on just unravels the sweater further. Hey, put it in perspective. The situation here is much better than your average power plant. But it's not like the nuclear Navy."

"But you've got a number of former nuclear submarine sailors here," said Mandil. "Can't they help keep things on the track? At least they should know what you're talking about."

"Sure. If we lead properly, they'll follow. But they won't initiate basic changes to the whole system. You can't expect them to. That's where I need help from you guys. You know as well as I do that Rick didn't create all the procedures and systems and hardware by himself. *We* did it, and we did it in our own image, to a great extent. What he did was to create an environment in which the stuff we did was possible. More than that, he made what we did inevitable. First, by hiring the kind of people he did, by how he trained them, and by setting standards. Then what we all created was a natural consequence. We've got to figure out how to do that here. Then these guys will do their part."

JIM WATKINS left Naval Reactors to assume command of the attack submarine *Snook*, and then became executive officer of the first nuclear-powered cruiser, the *Long Beach*. He became chief of naval personnel, then chief of naval operations. He had hoped to get some overdue rest after that, but President Reagan asked him to take over a special task force on AIDS, which was embroiled in vicious infighting and resignations. The press was astonished at such an unlikely appointment, but then there was universal praise when the task force issued its final report. Watkins found himself on the cover of the *Saturday Evening Post* and the *Washington Post*'s Sunday Magazine, and he was prominently featured on talk shows. Shortly after that he was made secretary of energy.

Mandil and I saw him from time to time. We immediately fell into telling Rickover stories, of course. Watkins had found that part of the solution to his problems at the Department of Energy lay in getting some Rickover alumni to help him. "You can tell them, 'Look into this mess, and tell me what we should do.' You don't have to define *look into*, or *mess*, or what options of action are permissible, possible, or adequate. And you know they're not going to tell you what they think you want to hear, or try to protect the people they're reporting on, or second-guess your motives. And they will be technically competent and will understand what they're investigating. It's incredible how hard it is to find people like that. You must have found that at MPR too, haven't you?"

We agreed that, like Rickover, we found most of our time at MPR taken up by recruiting and training. We are always sacrificing present gains for the long-term benefit. But we have lots of experience telling us that this is the only way to go, if you want quality. And we believe we are inculcating these ideas into a few others, slowly but surely.

HENRY STONE reported a different sort of impact from his Rickover days. He was a General Electric employee and started out in the radiation shielding group at the Knolls Laboratory. He steadily worked his way up to the management level. GE had a particular approach to grooming managers. Whenever they thought they had a winner, they put him through a kind of Maoist brainwashing program, pinned a silver elm tree on him, and pronounced him a GE executive. (I say *him* because in those days nearly all executives were male.) The typical new GE executive came out with a sort of hard, impenetrable sheen on him that was instantly recognizable. We used to say, "You can always tell a GE man, but you can't tell him much." GE had some very sharp people— Harry Stevens, Ken Kesselring—but they all had that GE brand on the forehead. But Stone was not a typical GE official. GE was never quite able to do it to Henry. He had lived through *Kristallnacht* as a child, and he had a quiet strength that belied his self-effacing manner. GE was surprised when Rickover, strongly urged on by Mandil, Panoff, and others, suggested Stone as manager of the Knolls Laboratory. No one doubted his fierce loyalty to GE, but Rickover's people also felt he was "one of us," in that we could talk as one engineer to another.

Stone made an excellent manager, and when GE wanted to give him a prominent position in its emerging commercial atomic power program, Rickover and his people knew they would miss him, but they didn't want to hold him back. He learned a lot in his new position too. Years later he and I got together at some meeting, and Stone related how his Rickover experience had proved to be an asset in an unexpected way. He was trying to open up the Japanese market for GE, and he had met with a cold reception there. The Japanese utility executive said they were being constantly besieged by American salesmen: "Such people can offer us nothing. We do not need American salesmen."

Stone pleaded that he was there not as a salesman but as an experienced nuclear engineer. "What have you done?" asked the executive, and he did not seem impressed by Stone's recitation of his work in GE's commercial power program. Then Stone spotted a copy of the *Reactor Shielding Design Manual* on the desk, one of the series of technical reference books the Naval Reactors program had published. Stone had been a major contributor to that book, which was still in print after more than thirty years. He picked up the book and pointed out his own name among the contributors. "And the guy's whole manner changed," grinned Stone, as he related the story. " 'So you are really a technical person,' said the Japanese executive. 'Perhaps we should talk after all.' "

My own children also felt the second-generational Rickover Effect, each in his or her own way. My eldest, BOB, I have already mentioned. Next in line, son TEED, grew up on the leading edge of the hippy generation. He recalls reading, in those days, Paul Goodman's *Growing Up Absurd*, which claimed to speak for his generation. Goodman lamented that their generation was never given any values, either to accept or to react against, and Teed's response was "This guy isn't speaking for me! I haven't figured out yet which of my parents' values I will accept and which I will rebel against, but I sure have a clear idea of what their values are." And he attributes his feelings on this in large measure to Rickover's attitude toward the importance of maintaining high standards of excellence, and keeping those values clearly in sight at all times, an attitude he had absorbed from the many Rickover stories I brought home.

Number three son, LARRY, missed knowing a grandfather, since both of his grandfathers had died while he was still young. He told me recently that he always thought of Admiral Rickover in that niche. He didn't see him often, but the Admiral always called him by name, and often had a little gadget or a story for him. In his teens Larry took a lowly job as an orderly in a Hebrew home for the aged, and when he left there, he wrote a note (unbeknownst to me) saying that he had taken the job to help fill that void. The administrators were always after him to do some meaningless chore, but he knew what was important: he always found time, even on his own time, to listen to the old men, to ask them questions, and to do little favors for them, things no one else seemed to have time to do. He told me he was emboldened in this by my stories of how Rickover would take time to size up what was really needed and do it, and not to waste any more time than necessary on the bureaucratic nonsense of his bosses.

My daughter, JUANITA, was only six when I left Naval Reactors, and she was too young to have had much personal input from the Admiral. Today she is artistic director of Company One, an Equity Theater Company in Hartford, Connecticut, and she faces many of the kinds of problems Rickover first faced in trying to create legitimacy, authority, and support where little is given voluntarily. She notes that I usually preface my advice to her with words such as "One thing I learned from Rickover is . . ." She finds that she even passes along some of these stories, in connection with training others. So she feels that she too is a direct beneficiary of the Rickover Effect.

ED KINTNER had a different perspective. He had been with Rickover since 1950, and he had been Mark I project officer at Idaho and nuclear power superintendent at Mare Island Naval Shipyard. "The Rickover anecdotes are fine, as far as they go," he said. "But they give a confusing and contradictory picture of the man."

"He was a confusing and contradictory person," I replied.

But Kintner pressed his point. "He had certain basic principles that he lived by and taught. Absolute technical honesty was one; he never tried to compromise with Nature. An incredible strength of will and intentionality was another; he just *made* things happen because he wouldn't permit any other outcome. The priority he gave to selection and training of personnel was another basic tenet. And there was the breadth of his knowledge and understanding, which he never considered a diversion, but a prerequisite to wise decisions on the job. His intense sense of personal responsibility was another factor. And—surprisingly—his humility. Humility before Nature and even with his colleagues. I've never known any other official of his rank to treat me and others so fully as equals when it came to discussing what should be done about a technical problem."

BILL WEGNER had a problem with that. Wegner had been with him twenty-three years, ending up as his deputy. "You can't sum up Rickover in a few neat phrases. He was a very complex person. Each of us saw him through a narrow slit. We got to know him well in that context, but none of us saw the whole person. If you tried to put all the individual portraits together, you'd get a contradictory mishmash."

"That's beside the point," said Kintner. "I grant you that to an outside observer, many of the things he did seemed inconsistent. But anyone who worked closely with him for a long period would agree that his ability to get things done, in a way that still astonishes people, was the result of several basic characteristics he had, the ones I've just named, which he preached and practiced consistently right from the start of the program. These characteristics led to an environment in which all of us could be remarkably effective. The creation of a zirconium industry and a hafnium industry and the development of all the technology that led to a fully operational *Nautilus* in a few short years— it was a miracle, pure and simple. And we need to know what made that miracle possible. And I don't think we should let psychological or political aspects confuse us or deflect us from learning those lessons."

DAVE LEIGHTON said, "I think I knew him personally as well as anyone in the program. Through my father, who was class of 1909 at the Naval Academy, and my uncle, class of 1913, I met many of the people Rickover knew in years past. So I don't share the impression many people have that Rickover thought all other naval officers were fools. He had many friends in the Navy whom he admired and enjoyed.

"He said many times that a man should be judged by his works, and I agree with that. Those who worked closely with him truly understood the depth and breadth of his personal contributions to the development of nuclear power. The superb performance of our nuclear fleet is a living testimonial to his engineering and management genius."

JIM WATKINS stated what he believed to be the bottom line. "We've all been talking about the personal impact Rickover had on us and on people we know. That's important, but one could argue that it's subjective and ephemeral. But he left behind two very solid legacies that can be seen by anyone. First, the entire Navy—not just the nuclear part—has now formally adopted his approach to engineering. A hands-on training facility was set up, first in Idaho and now at Newport, Rhode Island, for skippers, squadron commanders, and even flag officers dealing with major combat vessels—destroyers and larger. The training program and the proficiency inspection system were modeled directly after Rickover's. It isn't perfect, but the framework is there, the goals and procedures are spelled out in official documents, so there's a clearly visible standard to work against.

"The other example of a dream made physical is an executive order, which Bill Wegner and I drafted in concert with several of the NR people, which incorporates all the responsibilities Rickover embraced. This executive order was signed by the president, effective when Rickover left office in 1982, and a law passed in 1986 requires congressional approval to change it. So you have not only Rickover's impact on individuals, but a codification of the Rickover approach, which gives structure and substance to the philosophy and should help maintain the Admiral's approach as the normal mode of operation within the Navy and the Department of Energy.

"As a consequence, there was no gap in nuclear power leadership or standards of technical excellence when the Admiral stepped down. This was his long-sought dream—that those he selected, educated, and trained would one day carry on after he left. And they have."

But JACK CRAWFORD wanted to end on a cautionary note. "The Rickover Effect has been felt throughout most of the Navy, and much of civilian industry, as you've noted. But I find it strange and ironic that it has almost disappeared in the very area where you would most expect it and where it is most needed: the Navy's engineering duty officers. This is the historically elite corps that the Navy has counted on to develop, design, build, and service its technologically sophisticated fleet.

"Many officers were concerned that extended duty in the Naval Reactors program would hurt their chances of promotion in competition with officers who rotated among various types of billets in the traditional naval pattern. To offset this fear, Rickover was able to get the chief of naval personnel to issue a fleetwide directive stating that duty in the Naval Reactors program would be considered a positive, rather than a negative, factor in career evaluation. Reassured by this directive, many outstanding EDs (engineering duty officers) were attracted to NR. But around 1960 the EDs began to see a different picture. The previous year a selection board had reached below the selection zone and recommended six commanders for early promotion to captain, none of whom had nuclear engineering training or experience. Three of their classmates serving in NR, with graduate education in nuclear engineering and ten years' experience in the naval nuclear program, were effectively bypassed. Yes, I know they were not legally 'passed over,' since they were not in the promotion zone, but actions by subsequent selection boards proved this action to be what it appeared to be: a signal that service in the nuclear program was a detriment to promotion.

"The effect of this is what you would expect. ED volunteers for the nuclear program dropped precipitously, and those already in the program began to leave the Navy for high-paying civilian jobs, for which they were eagerly sought. Only two EDs from the program made flag rank, Bill Barnes and Jim Webber, and they did so only by getting out and undertaking several years of ordinary, nonnuclear duty. I might also add Bob Moore, who was in the program for less than a year. Officers other than EDs in the program were well recognized and rewarded: the line officers rose to the topmost ranks, as did Supply Corps and Civil Engineer Corps officers.

"This situation mirrors what is happening in American society at large. Industrial enterprises that were started by engineers such as George Westinghouse, Henry Ford, Glenn Martin, and George Eastman are now run by lawyers and accountants. These 'bean counters' have taken their engineering companies out of the technical specialties they created, such as gas turbines and electrical appliances, and put them in the business of selling records and running Caribbean hotels and car rental operations. Our space program is run by fiscal specialists and 'management experts,' and we lionize the astronauts while nameless engineers, deep in the organization, write unread warnings about technical trivia such as O-rings.

"The EDs who came into the nuclear program in its infancy brought with them graduate-level education in marine engineering and naval architecture, plus master's degrees in nuclear engineering, plus years of experience on the waterfront actually designing, building, and repairing ships. This is all gone. Today the program is not getting people with such backgrounds. This is a repudiation of everything Rickover stood for. This is where we need to relearn and reapply the lessons of the Rickover Effect."

To seek out and accept responsibility; to persevere; to be committed to excellence; to be creative and courageous; to be unrelenting in the pursuit of intellectual development; to maintain high standards of ethics and morality; and to bring these basic principles of existence to bear through active participation in life—these are some of my ideas on the goals which must be met to achieve meaning and purpose in life.

H.G.R.

Epilogue

RICKOVER DEPARTS

Some time after the Humphrey party, I returned to the Rickover apartment, again feeling that this might be my last visit with the Admiral. Mrs. Rickover looked tired, but she was as cordial as ever. "It's good to see you again. Come on in."

"How is he?" I asked. "And how are you, by the way? I know this has been rough on you, even though you're a nurse."

"Well, I do have an outside nurse come in part-time now, as you know. I've had some back problems, and some other things, but it's mostly exhaustion, I think. I've lost a lot of weight. But let me tell you about my husband. He's having great trouble swallowing anything, and the doctors want him to go back into the hospital, so that they can feed him intravenously, and give him oxygen, and fit him up with tubes and hoses, and he just won't do that. He's not taking food anymore. He's determined to die right here, in his own home, in dignity and with friends. I'm not going to deny him that."

"I can certainly support that position, Eleonore."

We went into the bedroom. Rickover was still completely immobile; his voice was weak but insistent. His wife said, "Here's Mr. Rockwell again."

Rickover reacted as if he'd been saving up the question: "How the hell are you supposed to know what God wants you to do with your

385

life, eh? Maybe I blew it completely. Maybe I was supposed to be a cello player." (At the time, I thought he was just picking a ridiculous example, to make his point. But later, Mrs. Rickover told me that he had said more than once that he always regretted never having learned to play the violin!)

I didn't have a quick answer for that one, but I started to reply. "Well, Admiral . . ."

"You're going to have to answer that kind of question yourself, Rockwell. And maybe sooner than you think. I'll guarantee it will seem sooner, whenever it comes. What about it? How am I supposed to know?"

I didn't stop to think. I just spoke from the heart. "Admiral, all any of us can do is play the hand we're dealt. You've certainly played yours with vigor, skill, and integrity. And startling originality. People praise you for the hardware you developed, but the thing that amazes me the most is your complete originality. Nothing like your organizational approach ever existed before. People have tried to copy your approach, but they don't really understand it, and they're not willing to pay the price it takes to make such an operation work."

"What about all that stuff in the papers about me accepting gifts from the shipbuilder? Do people think I'm a crook? Is that how my life is to be judged in the end? You know, the last word in my personnel jacket, the first piece of paper you see when you open it up, is a reprimand from the secretary of the Navy."

"Admiral, I have no idea what the man in the street thinks, but . . ."

"They said I accepted $60,000 in personal gifts. You know what the biggest part of that was? It was the detailed models of the engine rooms they made, which we used in our office for training and for showing congressmen what we were doing. And you know, they also included the cost of hundreds of times they picked me up at the train station in the company car. They listed it as a gift, every time they picked me up. You remember all the times you and I took that damn overnight train to Boston and had to get off at 5:49 A.M. at New London. I could have taken a taxi and charged it to the government, but I figured the Boat Company was already paying for their car and no one else was using it at that time of day. But they kept a detailed record through the years, and then the bastards used it to make me out a crook. Well, they sure can't claim I let up on them. The reason they got me kicked out of the Navy was so they could collect all those unjustified overcharges I had been fighting them on. You notice the Navy called off the criminal investigation as soon as I was out of the way." He fell back exhausted.

All I could say was "Admiral, your record will speak for itself."

"Aw, I know you guys understand it, but who else gives a damn?"

"Well," I said, "the last two chiefs of naval operations were graduates of your program, and it's a near certainty the next one will be too. You picked them, you trained them, and you made them fit to be the top officer in the Navy. For years everyone's assumed that aviators should run the Navy. The flyboys, and everyone else, took it for granted. You changed all that. Who would ever have predicted that submariners would be selected for CNO?"

"Oh, you know all that stuff is transient; it doesn't mean a thing. Where's the enduring value? What does it all add up to?"

I presented my last argument. "Admiral, you told us many times that if all of the hardware were to disappear without a trace, and even the memory of it faded away, you'd be content to live with the impact of the program on the people. I call it the Rickover Effect. A reborn recognition of the need for excellence, quality, professionalism, and integrity. We've put thousands and thousands of officers and enlisted men through that program. In addition, there's the vast industrial empire we've built up to make this hardware. The impact of our program on those people has even spilled over onto some of their commercial products. And these are the welding standards, boiler and pressure-vessel codes, university and research institution programs—the whole industrial world has felt the impact of your program. That's a pretty impressive heritage to leave behind. Can't you settle for that?"

I never knew whether the argument satisfied the Admiral, or whether he just gave up. He said weakly, "I guess I can settle for that. The impact on the people."

Those were the last words I ever heard him say.

On 8 July 1986 Admiral Rickover's body gave up the long struggle to hold on to life. On 12 July I received a phone call from the office of the chief of naval operations, informing me that a private memorial service was to be held the next day at the Washington Cathedral and that I was invited to attend. I assured the caller that I would be there, and I was surprised the next day to find twelve hundred other persons attending, including former president and Mrs. Jimmy Carter, Secretary of State George Schultz, Senator Strom Thurmond, most of the members of the House Armed Services Committee, and Navy Secretary John Lehman, along with countless other dignitaries. Virtually all of the Naval Reactors staff were there, along with Admiral Kinnaird R. McKee, who had succeeded Admiral Rickover as director, and many former NR personnel who had flown in on short notice from all over the country.

When the uniquely stirring Navy Hymn was played and all present joined in singing it, I felt the upwelling of tears and a cathartic sense of grief, joy, and release that the sound of that great hymn always evokes, filled as it is with memories of other Navy funerals and memorial services. After the traditional verse describing sailors at peril on the restless wave came the submariners' prayer:

> Lord God, our power evermore, whose arm doth reach the
> ocean floor,
> Dive with our men beneath the sea; traverse the depths
> protectively.
> Oh hear us when we pray, and keep them safe from peril in
> the deep.

Admiral Watkins and others praised Rickover and what he stood for, but I couldn't forget that the Admiral had been feared and hated by many important people. Former CNO Elmo Zumwalt had been quoted as saying that the Navy had three enemies: the Air Force, the Soviet Union, and Hyman Rickover. I decided that Max Lerner, the noted social philosopher, had sized this situation up best when he wrote of such people,

> The real hate and fear are not of *him*, but of their own weakness
> and bewilderment in the face of new forces they cannot under-
> stand. Rickover is of the breed of men in our time who dare
> confront them.

THE RICKOIDS

> *I believe it is the duty of each of us to act as if the fate of the world depended on him. Admittedly, one man by himself cannot do the job. However, one man can make a difference . . . We must live for the future of the human race, and not for our own comfort or success.*
>
> H.G.R.

I got a different perspective on the Rickover Effect when I accepted an invitation to attend the exhibition of finalists of the National Science Talent Search, at the National Academy of Sciences Building in Washington. I was particularly impressed with one exhibit, a complex one involving the role of free ionic radicals in environmental degradation. I got talking with the lad, who finally blurted out, "Did I just see you talking to Dr. Glenn Seaborg? He's one of the judges for this show, you know. Do you know him? Gosh, he got the Nobel Prize for discovering plutonium and a lot of other stuff. I'd sure like to meet him. He's a real hero of mine."

I replied, "Sure, I'll introduce you to him. He was chairman of the U.S. Atomic Energy Commission when I worked for Admiral Rickover, and he was one of the few people who really tried to help us do the job. He understood it more than a lot of the regular bureaucrats."

"You knew Admiral Rickover? Honest? You knew him *personally*? I mean, like, you saw him every day? Wow!"

"Yeah, I saw him all right. Every day, and most nights too. Tell me, how did you learn to do all the stuff you've got in your project? All that complicated stuff about the interaction of various free radicals in the environment. You sure didn't learn that in high school."

"No, I'm a Rickoid."

"A what?"

"A Rickover Fellow. We call ourselves Rickoids. You know about the foundation that Admiral Rickover set up? This foundation gets the brightest high school science students in the country and gives them a summer they'll never forget. We all got together with some really good science teachers. They worked us like crazy, but what a program! It made regular school seem like mostly sitting around, which it is, I guess. I saw a videotape of Admiral Rickover. Gosh, I wish I could've met him."

I knew a little something about the foundation. It had accumulated enough money, mostly through the Admiral's speeches, to set up the first Rickover Science Institute (RSI) for six weeks in the summer of 1984. It provided intensive classroom instruction and internships in scientific research for sixty high school students from the United States and abroad who had demonstrated excellence in mathematics and the other sciences. The Admiral hoped that other groups would follow his example, so that many more students could be helped in this way.

At the end of 1984 RSI, Rickover gave an inspiring address to the youngsters, which the foundation fortunately taped. At the graduation ceremony of the second RSI in August 1985, the Admiral was still suffering from the effects of his stroke on the fourth of July that year. The 1984 tape was run, and the Admiral, with his wife beside him, talked with each of the students. When he saw the tape and then talked with the students, he brightened and reacted with real enthusiasm. It was an inspiring moment for all, and the students loved it.

By 5 February 1986, when he was no longer able to run it and control its actions, the Admiral resigned from the foundation and asked that his name no longer be associated with it. The foundation's counsel, David M. Rubenstein, replied on 3 May 1986, "The name of the Rickover Foundation has been changed to the Center for Excellence in Education . . . From this point forward, your name will not be associated in any way with the Center or any of the Center's activities."

But the youngsters are still inspired by the tape of the Admiral's address, and they still call themselves Rickoids. Even after his death, the strength of Rickover's personality and character continues to come through to inspire yet another generation of budding scientists and engineers.

Index

APPENDIX: The First Fifteen Years

Table 1: Naval Reactors Technical Personnel

Table 2: Naval Reactors Administrative and Fiscal Personnel

Table 3: Naval Reactors Civil Engineer Corps Personnel

Table 4: Alphabetical Crosslist

THE FIRST FIFTEEN YEARS

Key to Tables 1 through 3

The information in these tables was compiled by Donald E. Fry of Naval Reactors from incomplete records, phone calls and direct correspondence. It is the best available, but it is incomplete and may contain some errors. In some cases, even the person named could not recall some of the data. Any additional information or corrections sent to the author at 3403 Woolsey Drive, Chevy Chase, MD 20815, would be welcome.

"Special Training" Column:

OR47	=	Oak Ridge School of Reactor Technology, Class of 1947
ARG	=	Argonne National Laboratory
OR	=	Employee of Oak Ridge National Laboratory
ESEC	=	Electrical Section, BuShips (given special nuclear study program at NR)
MIT50	=	MIT Naval Nuclear Engineering Graduate Program, Class of 1950
R ED	=	Reserve Engineering Duty Officer
LDO	=	Limited Duty Officer
SC	=	Supply Corps Officer
CEC	=	Civil Engineer Corps Officer
WVE	=	WAVE Officer
Y MAR	=	Shipyard Engineer, Mare Island Naval Shipyard
Y PTH	=	Shipyard Engineer, Portsmouth Naval Shipyard
Y BNY	=	Shipyard Engineer, Brooklyn Naval Shipyard
Y PUG	=	Shipyard Engineer, Puget Sound Naval Shipyard
SIGC	=	Came from Army Signal Corps
MEDC	=	Medical Corps Officer
MEDS	=	Medical Service Corps Officer

"From NR" Column:

L	=	Left
R	=	Retired
D	=	Died while at Naval Reactors
No entry	=	still at Naval Reactors

"Months at NR" is as of 1 January 1993

TABLE 1: NAVAL REACTORS TECHNICAL PERSONNEL 1946–1961

NO	NAME	TO NR		FR NR	AT NR	MO SPECIAL TRNING	BA/BS	COLLEGE	MA/MS	COLLEGE	PHD/OTH	COLLEGE
1	RICKOVER, H.G.	6 46	R	1 82	402	OR47	NAV SCI	USNA22	E E	COLUMBIA29		
2	DUNFORD, JAS.M.	6 46	R	1 61	136	OR47	NAV SCI	USNA39	NAV C/E	MIT44		
3	LIBBEY, MILES A.	6 46	L	50	17	OR47	NAV SCI	USNA40	NAV C/E	MIT45		
4	RODDIS, LOU H.	6 46	L	4 55	81	OR47	NAV SCI	USNA39	NAV C/E	MIT44		
5	DICK, RAY H.	6 46	D	1 53	54	OR47	MET E	OHIO STATE42				
6	EMERSON, GEO.B.	6 46	L	55	77	OR47	M E?	WORCESTER				
7	BLIZARD, EVERITT P.	6 46	L	11 46	5	OR47	CHEM	WESLEYAN37	PHYS	COLUMBIA38		
8	AMOROSI, ALFRED	6 46	L	11 46	5	OR47	M E	CORNELL34	CHEM	CARNEGIE42		
9	ROTH, ELI B.	5 48	L	2 54	69	ARG	NAV SCI	USNA39	NAV E	NAVY PG SCH49		
10	NAYMARK, SHERM.	6 48	L	2 54	68	ARG	NAV SCI	USNA41	NAV C/E	MIT46		
11	KYGER, JACK A.	6 48	L	11 54	77	OR	CHEM	YALE35			P CHEM	MIT40
12	LANEY, ROBT. V.	8 48	L	8 59	132	XX	NAV SCI	USNA39	NAV C/E	MIT44		
13	TURNBAUGH, MARSH.E.	8 48	R	9 59	133	ARG	NAV SCI	USNA39	NAV C/E	MIT45		
14	WILSON, WM. H.	10 48	L	7 60	141	OR	MET E	PURDUE47				
15	GEIGER, LAWTON D.	12 48	R	6 73	294	ARG	AE E	GA TECH39				
16	RADKOWSKY, ALVIN	12 48	R	6 72	282	ARG	E E	CITY COLL NY35	PHYS	GWU41	PHYS	CATHOLIC47
17	WILKINSON, E.P.	12 48	L	3 50	15	ARG		SAN DIEGO STATE				
18	GRANT, PAUL	49	L	50	12	ARG						
19	KELLEY, ARCH. P.	2 49	L	11 55	81	XX	NAV SCI	USNA41	N PHYS	MIT46		
20	LASPADA, J.A.	2 49	L	11 52	45	XX	NAV SCI	USNA41	NAV C/E	MIT46		
21	GRAY, JOHN EDMUND	3 49	L	9 50	18	XX	CH E	RHODE ISLAND43				
22	BARKER, J.A.	6 49	L	8 56	86	ARG	NAV SCI	USNA42	NAV E	NAVY PG SCH		
23	MANDIL, I.HARRY	11 49	L	8 64	177	OR50	E E	U of LONDON39	E E	MIT41	SCIENCE	THIEL60
24	ROCKWELL, TED	11 49	L	8 64	177	OR	CH E	PRINCETON43	CH E	PRINCETON45	SCIENCE	TRI STATE60
25	FINKELSTEIN, PHIL	11 49	L	11 50	12	OR50	M E	NYU32	M E	SYRACUSE35		
26	RODIN, MAX	12 49	L	8 50	9	ARG	M E	NOTRE DAME34	M E	PURDUE36		

TABLE 1: NAVAL REACTORS TECHNICAL PERSONNEL 1946–1961

NO	NAME	TO NR	R/L	FR NR	AT NR	MO SPECIAL TRNING	BA/BS	COLLEGE	MAMS	COLLEGE	PHD/OTH	COLLEGE
27	MARKS, HOWARD K.	1 50	R	6 72	269	OR50	M E	STANFORD35		NORTHWESTERN		
28	CONDON, JOS. F.	2 50	L	6 59	112	OR50	E E	NORTHWESTERN2	E E	COLUMBIA38	CH E	NYU41
31	KERZE, FRANK	5 50	L	55	55	OR	CH E	CASE29	SCIENCE			
32	PANOFF, ROBT	5 50	L	8 64	171	ESEC	E E	UNION COLL42				
33	SHAW, MILTON	6 50	L	9 61	135	OR51	M E	TENNESSEE44	M E	PENN STATE47		
35	DEBOLT, H.E.(TOM)	7 50	L	9 55	62	WEST	E E	CARNEGIE47	E E	CARNEGIE48	E E	CARNEGIE49
37	CRAWFORD, JACK W.	8 50	R	8 63	156	MIT50	NAV SCI	USNA42	NAV C/E	MIT46	N PHYS	MIT50
38	KINTNER, ED. E.	8 50	L	11 66	177	MIT50	NAV SCI	USNA42	NAV C/E	MIT46	N PHYS	MIT50
39	DIGNAN, PAUL ELMER	51	R	52	12	LDO	NONE	LDO				
40	O'GRADY, JOHN F.	51	L	53	27	XX	NONE	TEMPLE				
41	SCHNEIDER, OSCAR	51	L	54	36	MEDC.						
42	WELCH, GERALD H.	51	L	52	12	WEST						
44	CLARK, ART H.	1 51	L	1 53	24	DET E	M E	MICHIGAN34	E E	MICHIGAN34?		
45	HARTWELL, ROBT.	1 51	L	1 53	24	DET E	M E	MICHIGAN39	MBA	MICHIGAN40		
46	ILTIS, TED J.	1 51	L	10 65	177	GE	CH E	WISCONSIN50				
47	JACOBSON, JEROME	2 51	L	8 54	42	GE	M E	ILLINOIS50	M E	MARYLAND53*		
48	HOWELL, JERRY DEAN	3 51	L	53	21	WEST	M E	ARIZONA?				
49	FAUROT, G. WES	3 51	L	8 62	137	ESEC	E E	WASHINGTON39				
50	RESNICK, BERNIE T.	4 51	L	1 59	93	OR50	M E	NORTHEASTERN43				
51	FRANCIS, ART E.	8 51	R	11 79	339	MIT51	M E	STEVENS42	NAV C/E	MIT48	N PHYS	MIT51
52	HINCHEY, J.J.	8 51	L	12 68	208	MIT51	NAV SCI	USNA42	NAV C/E	MIT48	N PHYS	MIT51
53	MOORE, R.L.	8 51	L	6 52	10	MIT51	NAV SCI	USNA30	NAV E	CAL BERKELEY39	NONE	MIT51
56	BROOKS, DANIEL PHILLIP	11 51	L	10 52	11	XX	NAV SCI	USNA44	NUC PHY	CAL BERKELEY50		
57	MANIERO, DANIEL A.	52	L	53	12	OR53	M E	CARNEGIE				
58	PURDY, DAVID C.	52	L	12 55	48	OR53	MAR E	WEBB				
59	SHOR, S.W.W.	2 52	L	4 58	74	XX	NAV SCI	USNA43	NAV C/E	MIT49		

TABLE 1: NAVAL REACTORS TECHNICAL PERSONNEL 1946–1961

NO	NAME	TO NR		FR NR	AT NR	MO SPECIAL TRNING	BA/BS	COLLEGE	MAMS	COLLEGE	PHD/OTH	COLLEGE
61	MEALIA, JOHN E.	4 52		93	491	OR52	M E	NJIT51	PHYS	CINCINNATI51		
62	MINOGUE, ROBT. B.	4 52	L	12 56	56	OR52	PHY/MAT	THOMAS MORE49				
64	FLOOD, THOS. P.	6 52	L	3 64	141	OR53	PHYS	FORDHAM52				
66	SULLIVAN, R.P.	6 52	L	6 57	60	OR53	PHYS	FORDHAM52				
67	GRIGG, JACK C.	7 52	R	12 78	317	ESEC	E E	TEXAS TECH41				
68	ROETHEL, D.A.H.	7 52	L	8 57	61	OR53	CHEM	MARQUETTE50	RADCHEM	MARQUETTE52		
69	GLENN, STUART VER.	8 52	R	8 59	84	LDO	NONE	NONE				
70	BAUSER, ED. J.	8 52	L	8 58	72	MIT52	M E	MINNESOTA41	NAV E	NAVY PG SCH45	N PHYS	MIT52
71	HEINTZ, JOHN	8 52	L	8 53	12	MIT52	NAV SCI	USNA44	NAV C/E	MIT49	N PHYS	MIT52
72	NELSON, N. ROLAND	8 52	L	10 57	62	MIT52	NAV SCI	USNA38	NAV C/E	MIT43	N PHYS	MIT52
73	SWEEK, R.F.	8 52	L	10 55	38	MIT52	NAV SCI	USNA42	NAV C/E	MIT45	N PHYS	MIT52
75	CLENDINNING, W.R.	53	L	5 57	53	OR54	MATH	N TEX STATE52				
76	MARCH, RICHARD J	1 53	R	8 84	379	OR52	M E	CLARKSON50		NORTHWESTERN51?		
77	MURPHY, JOS. A.	1 53	L	7 72	234	OR54	PHYS	FORDHAM53				
84	HAUSSLER, W.M.	6 53	L	12 57	54	XX	CH E	ROCHESTER47	CH E	ROCHESTER49	PHYS	
85	KAY, ROBERT	6 53	L	12 56	42	XX	M E	CITY COLL NY42	NONE	NAVY PG SCH	N PHYS	MIT52
86	FRALEY, RAY. F.	6 53	L	6 59	72	OR54	MAR ENG	SUNY MARITIME52				
88	FLYNN, T.A.	7 53	L	6 57	47	OR54	PHYS	FORDHAM52	PHYS	FORDHAM53		
89	COCHRAN, J.C.	8 53	L	10 55	26	MIT53	NAV SCI	USNA40	NAV C/E	MIT	N PHYS	MIT53
90	DICKINSON, R.W.	8 53	L	4 56	32	MIT53	NAV SCI	CAL BERKELEY41		NAVY PG SCH48	N PHYS	MIT53
91	HAWKINS, R.A.	8 53	L	3 55	19	MIT53	NAV SCI	USNA44	NAV C/E	MIT49	NUC E	MIT53
92	LEIGHTON, DAV. T.	8 53	R	2 80	318	OR53	NAV SCI	USNA46	E E	MIT48	NUC E	MIT53
93	BRODSKY, ROBT. S.	9 53	R	8 79	311	OR53	PHYS	MIT52				
94	SCOTT, RICH. G.	9 53	L	8 65	143	OR55	M E	GWU51				
95	MICHELS, JOHN. F.	10 53	R	4 89	426	OR55	M E	PENN53				
96	LLOYD, REBECCAH A.	11 53	L	1 57	38	WVE	RECREA	N CAROLINA50	PERS ADM	NYU53		

TABLE 1: NAVAL REACTORS TECHNICAL PERSONNEL 1946-1961

NO	NAME	TO NR		FR NR	MO AT NR	SPECIAL TRNING	BA/BS	COLLEGE	MAMS	COLLEGE	PHD/OTH COLLEGE
97	NIXON, S. REED	12 53	L	55	12	OR54	E E	CAL TECH46	PHYS	BYU47	
99	KELLY, HENRY R.	54	L	57	36	SIGC					
100	SKOW, R.K.	54	L	7 57	43	MSC					
101	ROOF, R.R.	1 54	L	7 62	102	OR54	E E	MICHIGAN52			
104	ZIMMER, JOS. P.	6 54		93	465	OR55	MATH	FORDHAM54			
105	BARNES, W.C.	6 54	L	6 64	120	XX	NAV SCI	USNA45	NAV C/E+N	MIT52	
106	CASE, EDSON G.	6 54	L	4 57	34	XX	NAV SCI	USNA47	NAV C/E+N	MIT52	
107	COTTER, MAURICE J.	6 54	L	3 57	33	OR55	MATH	FORDHAM54			
108	NINE, H.D.	6 54	L	1 58	43	OR56	PHYS	MICHIGAN53	PHYS	MICHIGAN54	
109	THOMAS, CHUCK R.	6 54	R	7 85	373	OR55	M E	KANSAS54			
110	CLARK, PHIL. R.	7 54	R	8 79	301	OR54	C E	BROOKL TECH51			
111	ROGERS, GENE L.	7 54	R	5 87	394	OR55	E E	KANSAS54			
112	BASSETT, O.E.(SAM)	8 54	L	10 57	38	MIT54	NAV SCI	USNA46	E E	MIT49	NUC E MIT54
113	BROOKS, DAVE M.	8 54	L	9 58	49	MIT54	NAV SCI	USNA44	NAV C/E	MIT	NUC E MIT54
114	CALLAHAN, F.J.	8 54	L	1 58	41	MIT54	NAV SCI	USNA46	NAV C/E	MIT	NUC E MIT54
115	FALCI, FRANK P.	8 54	L	5 61	81	OR56	NA/ME	WEBB54			
116	HILL, ROBERT F.	8 54	L	8 57	36	OR55	CH E	PURDUE53	CH E	PURDUE54	
117	HUMPHREY, WM. S.	8 54	R	5 86	381	MIT54	E E	USNA43	CH E	CORNELL48	NUC E MIT54
119	SCHWENDTNER, A.H.	8 54	L	3 56	19	XX	NA/ME	WEBB54			
120	SIGNORELLI, J.A.	8 54	L	12 63	112	OR56	NA/ME	WEBB54			
122	HAYES, PAUL W.	9 54	R	4 88	403	OR56	NA/ME	WEBB54			
123	CALVERT, JAS. FRANCIS.	55	L	1 57	25	PCO	NAV SCI	USNA43	BIO PHY	CAL BERKELEY50	
124	ANDERSON, WM. ROBT.	55	L	57	24	PCO	NAV SCI	USNA43			
125	DUNLAVY, VERN. A.	55	L	56	12	YMAR					
126	KENNEY, M.C.	55	L	55	0	B 5					
128	FLYNN, CHARLIE W	1 55	R	8 77	271	XX	M E	CARNEGIE39	M E	CORNELL47	

TABLE 1: NAVAL REACTORS TECHNICAL PERSONNEL 1946-1961

NO	NAME	TO NR		FR NR	MO AT NR	SPECIAL TRNING	BA/BS	COLLEGE	MAMS	COLLEGE	PHD/OTH	COLLEGE
129	BARON, RAY. G.	1 55	L	7 56	18	YPTH	M E	NEW HAMPSH40				
130	HAMMOND, HERB.C.	1 55	L	7 56	18	YPTH	M E	NORTHEASTERN40				
131	HARRIS, W.N.	1 55	L	1 58	36	B 5	M E	CAL TECH49	M E	CAL TECH50		
132	ROBINSON, ROD. A.	1 55	L	7 56	18	YPTH	E E	NEW HAMPSH50	E E	NEW HAMPSH60		
134	BROSIUS, R.B.	4 55	L	4 56	12	YMAR		KANSAS				
138	BURR, A.A.	5 55	L	1 63	92	OR56	NAME	WEBB55				
139	COUCHMAN, DON. L.	6 55	L	5 60	59	XX	M E	CAL BERKELEY52				
140	HARRISON, DWGHT.H.	6 55	L	8 62	86	B 5	M E	KANSAS55				
141	JOHNSON, LYNN E.	6 55	L	6 58	36	B 5	M E	OREGON STATE54	M E	OREGON STATE55		
142	KENNEDY, R.S.	6 55	L	8 57	26	B 5	E E	KANSAS55				
143	MERRIGAN, LAWR. J.	6 55	R	11 91	437	OR56	C E	KANSAS55				
144	MILES, MURRAY E.	6 55	R	8 79	290	B 5	NONE		ENGR PHY	CORNELL53		
145	SULLIVAN, J.J.	6 55	L	6 58	36	B 5	PHYS	NOTRE DAME55				
146	FORSSELL, R. MARK	6 55	R	8 88	398	OR57	M E	WEBB55				
147	KOCH, URIAH H.	6 55	L	8 59	50	OR57	NAME	WEBB55				
149	BLOCK, ALAN J.	7 55	DROP	56	12	XX	MET	MIT52?				
150	QUIGLEY, HANK C.	7 55	L	7 58	36	XX	CH E	MIT50				
151	METZGER, ROBT. P.	7 55	R	2 80	295	B 9	NAV SCI	USNA48A	NAV C/E	MIT55		
152	WAGNER, ED. J.	7 55	L	7 70	180	XX	M E	CARNEGIE53				
154	BOOTH, MERSON	8 55	L	6 57	22	MIT55	NAV SCI	USNA47	NAV C/E	MIT53	NUC E	MIT55
155	LAMARTIN, FRED. H.	8 55	L	3 63	91	MIT55	NAV SCI	USNA45	NAV C/E	MIT49	NUC E	MIT55
156	LEVINE, SAUL	8 55	L	7 58	35	MIT55	NAV SCI	USNA46	NAV C/E	MIT	NUC E	MIT55
157	WHITEHEAD, ANDY D.	8 55	R	1 80	293	MIT55		BROWN44	NAV C/E	MIT48	NUC E	MIT55
159	GILLILAND, FRANK	9 55	R	5 81	308	MIT57	NAV E	VIRGINIA46(V-12)	NAV C/E	MIT52	NUC E	MIT57
161	RADKOWSKY, LARRY	9 55	R	3 90	414	OR57	NAV SCI	USNA51	E E	COLUMBIA55		MIT57
163	GAMBELLO, ANTH. V.	11 55	L	60	49	YBNY						

TABLE 1: NAVAL REACTORS TECHNICAL PERSONNEL 1946–1961

NO	NAME	TO NR	FR NR		MO AT NR	SPECIAL TRNING	BA/BS	COLLEGE	MAMS	COLLEGE	PHD/OTH	COLLEGE
164	LAMBERT, JOS. L.	11 55	L	1 58	26	YPUG	E E	IDAHO39				
165	NORMANN, JAMES R.	11 55	L	1 58	35	YBNY						
166	SPILLER, WM. C.	11 55	L	1 58	26	YPUG	E E	WASHINGTON36				
167	STOLZENBERG, MLT.D.	11 55	L	7 61	68	YBNY	MAR E	MER MAR ACAD51				
168	SWENSON, KARL E.	11 55	R	12 74	229	ARG	M E	NEW HAMPSH39				
169	STANDERFER, FRNK.R.	12 55	L	12 59	41	OR57	CH E	WASHINGTON55				
171	PERMAN, BERN	56	L	1 58	293	Y ?						
172	RICINAK, MICH. DON.	56	L	58	24	XX						
173	NELSON, OSC B "OB"	56	R	11 59	47	XX						
175	PUGH, R.C.	2 56	L	3 58	25	XX	MET E	OHIO STATE52				
176	KRAM, P.	2 56	L	3 60	49	B 7	M E	NYU52				
177	DINUNNO, JOS.J.	2 56	L	11 59	45	OR57	E E	PENN STATE42	E E	MARYLAND54		
179	FORSSELL, ALAN G.	3 56		93	444	OR57	NA/ME	WEBB53				
180	HEMMER, WM. C.	3 56	R	10 77	259	ESEC	E E	ST LOUIS UNIV49				
181	COLE, NOMAN M.	3 56	L	1 66	118	B 6	M E	FLORIDA55				
182	GRIDER, A. DOUG.	3 56	R	11 89	404	B 7	E E	FLORIDA54				
183	JUDD, P.V.	3 56	L	6 66	123	B 6	E E	PENN STATE54				
185	DELAPAZ, ARMANDO	5 56	L	5 61	60	B 6	CH E	TULANE55	CH E	TULANE56		
186	ROBNETT, J.D. IV	5 56	L	5 60	48	B 7	M E	STEVENS51				
187	SHIELDS, JEREM. D.	5 56	DROP	56	6	XX						
188	ARROWSMITH, PET. D.	6 56	L	9 63	87	OR58	CH E	KANSAS56				
189	SCHMOKER, DAN. N.	6 56		93	441	B 6	PHYS	OKLAHOMA56				
190	ZIEBOLD, T.O.	6 56	L	6 60	48	B 6	CH E	YALE56				
191	CLAYTOR, RICK A.	7 56	R	8 73	205	B 7	NAV SCI	USNA49	NA/ME	WEBB56		
192	CARPENTER, J.W.	8 56	L	5 61	57	MIT56	NAV SCI	USNA49	NAV C/E	MIT54	NUC E	MIT56
193	DYER, J.C.	8 56	L	10 64	98	MIT56	NAV SCI	USNA48A	NUC E	MIT56		

TABLE 1: NAVAL REACTORS TECHNICAL PERSONNEL 1946-1961

NO	NAME	TO NR	FR NR			AT NR	MO SPECIAL TRNING	BA/BS	COLLEGE	MA/MS	COLLEGE	PHD/OTH	COLLEGE
194	LEUTZ, L.H.	8 56	L	5	60	45	MIT56				MIT56		
195	MATHESON, J.C.	8 56	L	9	65	109	MIT56	NAV SCI	USNA45	NA/ME	MIT52	NUC E	MIT56
196	WEGNER, WM	8 56	R	8	79	276	MIT56	NAV SCI	USNA48B	NA/ME	WEBB53	NUC E	MIT56
197	WILKINSON, R.F.	8 56	L	1	67	125	MIT56	NAV ENG	VA TECH45(V-12)	NAV C/E	MIT51	NUC E	MIT56
198	YOUNG, WM. H.	8 56	L	5	71	177	B 7	NA/ME	WEBB56	ENG	GWU61*		
199	BODE, H.J. jr	10 56	L	9	60	47	B 8	M E	SWARTHMORE55				
200	MEDEIROS, MAN. S.	10 56	L	10	77	252	B 8	E E	BRDFRD DRFEE56				
201	McKINLEY, JOHN C.	10 56	L	10	60	48	B 7	M E	COLORADO A&M55				
203	DRISCOLL, MIKE J.	1 57	L	8	60	43	OR58	CH E	CARNEGIE55				
204	FOERSTER, PAUL A.	2 57	L	10	60	44	OR58	CH E	TEXAS57				
205	KOSIBA, RICH. E.	2 57	L	1	70	155	B 7	NAV SCI	USNA48A	NAV C/E	MIT53		
206	HEILER, F.J.	3 57	L	10	60	43	B 7	NONE	GWU		MARYLAND		
207	KENNEDY, J.E.	3 57	L	9	59	30	B 9	M E	PRINCETON56				
208	RAKER, SAM. K.	3 57			93	432	B 8	E E	YALE55				
209	VOSE, F.H.E.	3 57	L	1	63	70	B 7	NAV SCI	USNA47	NAV C/E	MIT53		
212	FLEMING, J.H.	5 57	L	4	61	47	B 9	E E	STANFORD55	E E	STANFORD57		
213	JILG, E.T.	5 57	L	6	61	49	B 8	M E	STANFORD56	M E	STANFORD57		
214	KOOYMAN, W.J.	5 57	L	6	61	49	B 8	CH E	NORTHWESTERN57				
215	LANG, E.M.jr	5 57	L	6	61	49	B 9	M E	U SO CAL56	M E	U SO CAL57		
218	CAVE, JAS. W.	6 57	R	11	90	401	B 9	E E	PURDUE57				
219	COLE, G. FRANK III	6 57	L	4	72	178	B 9	E E	VANDERBILT57				
220	DAUGHERTY, J.D.	6 57	L		61	42	B10	E E	IOWA STATE57		PURDUE		
221	DOWLING, ROBT. J.	6 57	L	2	69	140	B 9	PHYS	RPI57	PHYS	GEORGETOWN62		
222	DURNAN, DENNIS. D.	6 57			93	429	B 9	CH E	WASHINGTON57	ENG	GWU63*		
223	FEINROTH, HERBERT	6 57	L	1	72	175	B10	CH E	PENN57				
224	FISHER, G.D.	6 57	L	6	61	48	B 8	CH E	TEXAS57				

TABLE 1: NAVAL REACTORS TECHNICAL PERSONNEL 1946–1961

NO	NAME	TO NR		FR NR	MO AT NR	SPECIAL TRNING	BA/BS	COLLEGE	MAMS	COLLEGE	PHD/OTH	COLLEGE
225	GRIFFIN, R.F.	6 57	L	6 61	48	B10	CH E	STANFORD57				
226	HANESSIAN, SOUREN J.	6 57		93	429	B 8	M E	CORNELL57				
227	HENDRICKSON, THOS.A.	6 57	L	1 72	175	B 8	PHYS	HARVARD57	PHYS	GEORGETOWN62		
228	KELLER, K.H.	6 57	L	5 61	47	B 8	CHEM	COLUMBIA56	CH E	COLUMBIA57		
229	LIVINGSTON, W.C.	6 57	L	5 61	47	B 9	CH E	GA TECH57				
230	MUGGLIN, M.G.	6 57	L	6 61	48	B10	E E	RPI57				
231	SCHEETZ, KARL G.	6 57		93	429	B 9	M E	VILLANOVA57				
232	SCOTT, L.J.	6 57	L	6 61	48	B 9	CH E	CORNELL57				
233	STAEHLE, R.W.	6 57	L	6 61	48	B10	MET E	OHIO STATE57	MET E	OHIO STATE57		
234	THOMAS, GEO. ADEN	6 57	L	10 59	28	B 8	MATH/EE	OKLAHOMA57				
235	VAUGHAN, JAS. W.	6 57	L	4 84	322	B 9	E E	DUKE57				
236	WEINER, ROBT. M.	6 57	L	5 65	95	B 9	CH E	NOTRE DAME57				
238	FICK, T.R.	8 57	L	8 63	72	MIT57	NAV SCI	USNA44	NAV C/E	MIT52	NUC E	MIT57
239	HALEY, J.V.	8 57	L	5 62	57	MIT57	NAV SCI	USNA49	NAV C/E	MIT54	NUC E	MIT57
240	LAKEY, K.G.	8 57	L	7 61	47	MIT57	NAV SCI	USNA47	NAV C/E	MIT51	NUC E	MIT57
241	LESAGE, LEO G.	8 57	L	9 61	49	B10	PHYS	KANSAS57				
242	RISSER, J. BRUCE	8 57	R	2 86	342	MIT57	NAV SCI	USNA49(V-12)	NAV C/E	WEBB54	NUC E	MIT57
246	WILLIAMS, JOHN G.	11 57	L	11 59	24	XX	NAV SC1	USNA47				
249	BUTEAU, B.L.	1 58	L	9 66	104	B 9	NAV SCI	USNA50	NAV C/E	MIT55		
250	MOKSKI, D.J.	1 58	L	1 62	48	B10	M E	SUNY BUFFALO54				
251	BLATCHFORD, J.D.	2 58	L	1 62	47	B10	M E	PENN STATE58				
252	KONKLIN, J.E.	2 58	L	1 62	47	B10	ENG PHY	OKLAHOMA58				
253	WILLE, DON. JAY	2 58	L	6 62	52	B10	M E	MICHIGAN58				
260	BELSER, T.M. jr	6 58	L	6 62	48	B13	CH E	GA TECH58				
261	BRANDEL,J.P.	6 58	L	12 60	30	B11	M E	AUBURN57				
262	BROWNELL, R.B.	6 58	L	6 62	48	B12	E E	DUKE58				

TABLE 1: NAVAL REACTORS TECHNICAL PERSONNEL 1946–1961

NO	NAME	TO NR		FR NR	AT NR	MO SPECIAL TRNING	BA/BS	COLLEGE	MA/MS	COLLEGE	PHD/OTH	COLLEGE
263	BROWNING, ROBT. E.	6 58	L	4 79	250	B12	CH E	NORTHWESTERN58				
264	ENGEL, WALT. P.	6 58		93	417	B11	PHYS	HOLY CROSS58	PHYS	GEORGETOWN68*		
265	ERICKSON, B.T.	6 58	L	6 62	48	B12	M E	TUFTS58				
266	GRAFTON, R.B.	6 58	L	7 62	49	B11	M E	BROWN58				
267	HEMMINGHAUS, R.R.	6 58	L	6 62	48	B11	CH E	AUBURN58				
268	HEWITT, W.M.	6 58		93	417	B11	M E	YALE58				
269	KELLER, A.J.	6 58		93	417	B12	NONE		E E	STANFORD58		
270	MORRISON, W.M.	6 58	R	9 67	111	B 9	NAV SCI	USNA48A	NAV C/E	MIT52		
271	ROSSI, C.E.	6 58	L	6 62	48	B12	ENG PHY	HARVARD58				
272	SPRIGG, M.W.	6 58	L	6 62	48	B12	CH E	LOUISVILLE58				
273	STEELE, R.H.	6 58		93	417	B11	MET E	CORNELL58				
274	TEVEBAUGH, C.R.	6 58	L	6 62	48	B11	CH E	CORNELL58				
275	TRAYLOR, R.C.	6 58	L	8 62	50	B11	M E	GA TECH58				
277	D'APPOLITO, J.A.	7 58	L	7 62	48	B11	E E	RPI58				
278	HUSTED, J.M.	7 58	L	6 62	47	B11	E E	VILLANOVA58				
279	SCOTT, D.G.	7 58		93	416	B12	NONE		E E	STANFORD58		
280	SHAW, S.H.	7 58	L	8 62	49	B11	M E	ROCHESTER58				
281	SNYDER, B.J.	7 58	L	6 62	47	B12	M E	CORNELL58	M E	CORNELL58		
282	TODREAS, N.E.	7 58	L	6 62	47	B12	M E	CORNELL58	M E	CORNELL58		
283	PADGETT, CLARENCE W.	8 58	L	8 59	12	XX	PHYS	BEREA53				
284	JONES, H.L.	8 58	L	7 62	47	B12	PHY/MAT	TEXAS58				
285	MARTIN, W.L. III	8 58	L	11 69	135	MIT58	NAV SCI	USNA49	NAV C/E	MIT54	NUC E	MIT58
286	WHITE, A.T.	8 58	R	8 74	192	MIT58	NAV SCI	USNA46	E E	MIT48	NUC E	MIT58
287	WOODS, J.B.jr	8 58	D	5 62	45	B11	CH E	MISSISSIPPI56	NUC PHY	OXFORD58		
289	BASS, R.W.	1 59	R	7 79	246	B10	NAV SCI	USNA48A	NAV C/E	MIT53		
290	HAYMAN, R.B.	1 59	L	12 63	59	B10	M E	COLUMBIA50	M E	COLUMBIA51	NA/ME	MIT56

TABLE 1: NAVAL REACTORS TECHNICAL PERSONNEL 1946–1961

NO	NAME	TO NR	FR NR	MO AT NR	SPECIAL TRNING	BA/BS	COLLEGE	MAMS COLLEGE	PHD/OTH COLLEGE
291	HINDS, J.A.	1 59	L 12 62	47	B13	PRE-ENG	POMONA COLL58		
292	VAN WOUDENBERG, S.G.	1 59	L 8 62	43	B13	E E	WASHINGTON58		
293	HILL, A.J.	2 59	L 2 63	48	B13	M E	TEXAS59		
294	HOLLOWAY, C.A.	2 59	L 2 63	48	B13	E E	CAL BERKELEY59		
295	LEE, B.A.	2 59	L 8 65	78	MIT57	NAV SCI	USNA50	NAV C/E+N MIT57	
296	WOLL, S.A.	2 59	L 2 63	48	B12	CH E	WISCONSIN59		
298	BECKLEAN, W.R.	4 59	L 8 66	88	B13	E E	YALE58		
299	ANCKONIE, A.	6 59	L 7 63	49	B14	GEN ENG	MICHIGAN59		
300	BARONDES, E.D.	6 59	L 2 67	92	B11	NAV SCI	USNA48A	NAV C/E MIT52	
301	BORLICK, R.L.	6 59	DROP 60	6	XX	E E	ILL INST TECH59		
302	BROLIN, E.C.	6 59	L 9 74	183	B14	C E	TUFTS59		
303	HOLMES, J.F.	6 59	L 6 63	48	B14	E E	WASHINGTON59		
304	MALONEY, J.M.	6 59	93	405	B15	CH E	NOTRE DAME59		
305	NELSON, G.A.	6 59	L 6 62	36	B13	E E	RPI59		
306	ROBERTS, P.J.	6 59	L 6 63	48	B13	PHYS	GA TECH59		
307	SAVAGE, R.L.	6 59	L 6 63	48	B15	E E	AUBURN59		
308	SCHMIDT, W.R.	6 59	L 5 63	47	B13	M E	RICE59		
309	TENKHOF, P.A.	6 59	L 6 63	48	B14	E E	U SO CAL59		
310	TRIMBACH, C.G.	6 59	L 9 67	99	B14	M E	CAL BERKELEY59		
311	VAN NORT, P.S.	6 59	L 1 68	103	B13	NAV SCI	USNA59		
312	WARD, S.R.	6 59	L 7 63	49	B13	E E	MICHIGAN59		
317	CAMBELL, WM.ED.	8 59	L 7 64	59	MIT57	NAV SCI	USNA51	NAV C/E+N MIT57	
318	GARDNER, R.	8 59	L 6 67	94	MIT57	NAV SCI	USNA51	NAV C/E+N MIT57	
319	GORMAN, J.A.	8 59	L 7 65	71	B14	C E	CORNELL58		
320	HERKNER, R.T.	8 59	L 4 62	32	MIT59	NAV SCI	USNA53	NAV C/E MIT59	
321	HERMAN, J.M.	8 59	L 8 64	60	B14	M E	AUBURN59		

TABLE 1: NAVAL REACTORS TECHNICAL PERSONNEL 1946-1961

NO	NAME	TO NR		FR NR	AT NR	MO SPECIAL TRNING	BA/BS	COLLEGE	MA/MS	COLLEGE	PHD/OTH	COLLEGE
322	PANCIERA, V.W.	8 59	L	8 64	60	MIT57	NAV SCI	USNA51	NAV C/E+N	MIT57		
323	PEARSON, J.F.	8 59	R	8 70	132	MIT59	NAV SCI	USNA52	NAV C/E+N	MIT59		
324	WALTERS, T.J.	8 59	R	10 70	134	MIT59	NAV SCI	USNA49	NAV C/E	MIT56	NUC E	MIT59
325	WEBBER, J.H.	8 59	L	8 64	60	MIT59	NAV SCI	USNA49	NAV C/E	MIT55	NUC E	MIT59
326	KROL, J.A.	9 59	L	9 63	48	B14	CHEM	TUFTS58	CHEM	TUFTS59		
327	HALL, A.E.	1 60	L	1 64	48	B14	MET E	WASHINGTON59				
328	NEWHOUSE, A.R.	2 60	L	5 92	387	B15	E E	CORNELL60				
329	SIMMONS, GERRY M	2 60	DROP	61	10	XX	CH E	KANSAS60				
330	JORDAN, M.H.	4 60	L	3 64	47	B16	CH E	YALE57	CH E	PRINCETON58		
331	LINDEMAN, C.F.	5 60	L	5 64	48	B16	M E	IOWA STATE60				
332	SIERER, PAYSON D.	5 60	L	6 66	73	MIT58	NAV SCI	USNA52	NAV C/E+N	MIT58		
333	CARLSON, F.P.	6 60	L	7 64	49	B16	E E	WASHINGTON60	E E	MARYLAND64		
334	KEISTER, J.C.	6 60	L	6 64	48	B15	ENG PHY	CORNELL60				
335	KEY, P.L.	6 60	L	7 64	49	B17	M E	RICE60	M E	GWU64*		
336	KOH, B.	6 60	L	9 64	51	B16	M E	COLUMBIA60				
337	NICHOLS, J.C.	6 60	L	7 64	49	B15	CH E	RICE60				
338	OLDFATHER, D.O.	6 60	L	6 64	48	B14	E E	OREGON STATE60				
339	PATERSON, R.W.	6 60	L	7 64	49	B16	M E	PRINCETON60				
340	RIEHM, C.E. Jr	6 60	L	8 64	50	B15	E E	NOTRE DAME60				
341	SCOVILLE, F.W.	6 60	L	6 64	48	B15	E E	RPI60				
342	WILBUR, P.J.	6 60	L	8 64	50	B16	M E	UTAH60				
343	ALRICK, R.D.	7 60	L	6 64	47	B16	E E	WASHINGTON60				
344	COLLINGHAM, R.E.	7 60	L	8 64	49	B15	M E	WASHINGTON59	M E	WASHINGTON60		
345	LEIMONAS, S.	7 60	L	5 68	94	B16	PHYS	TUFTS60				
346	POMREHN, H.P.	7 60	L	6 64	47	B16	M E	U SO CAL60				
347	TRIMBLE, D.C.	7 60	L	6 64	47	B16	E E	TUFTS60				

TABLE 1: NAVAL REACTORS TECHNICAL PERSONNEL 1946-1961

NO	NAME	TO NR			FR NR		AT NR	MO SPECIAL TRNING	BA/BS	COLLEGE	MA/MS	COLLEGE	PHD/OTH COLLEGE
348	WALTERS, R.M.	7	60	L	6	64	47	B15	ENG	USNA60			
349	HEARN, J.J.	8	60	L	7	64	47	B16	E E	VILLANOVA59			
351	OATES, K.L.	9	60	R	9	92	384	B15	CH E	OHIO STATE60	CH E	OHIO STATE60	
356	DOHERTY, D.P.	2	61			93	385	B17	GEN E	ILLINOIS61	NUC E	MARYLAND71	
357	SCHOOLEY, L.C.	2	61	L	8	65	54	B17	E E	KANSAS61			
358	STOLLMEYER, M.A.	2	61	L	1	65	47	B17	E E	PENN STATE59	E E	MICHIGAN61	
359	DENEUI, R.J.	3	61	L	6	65	51	B18	PHY/CHE	DUBUQUE59	PHY/CHEM	IOWA STATE61	
362	HOUSE, EDWARD C.	5	61	L	5	69	96	MIT59	ENG PHY	KANSAS53	NA/ME	MIT59	
363	ALLYN, E.G.	6	61	L	6	66	60	B20	E E	ROCHESTER61			
364	BURGET, J.E.	6	61	L	12	70	114	B17	ENG PHY	CORNELL61			
365	CHESSICK, A.W.	6	61	L	2	67	68	B17	ENG SCI	NOTRE DAME61			
366	JOHNSON, R.W.	6	61	L	6	76	180	B17	E E	UTAH61			
367	MAGEE, G.T.	6	61	L	6	65	48	B18	CH E	MISSOURI61			
368	MAGEE, J.E.	6	61	L	6	65	48	B18	CH E	MISSOURI61			
369	MILLER, C.A.	6	61	L	8	65	50	B18	CH E	RICE61			
370	PINNOW, D.A.	6	61	L	6	65	48	B18	ENG PHY	CORNELL61			
371	PREZBINDOWSKI, D.L.	6	61	DROP		63	20	B17	ENG SCI	PURDUE61			
372	WHITNEY, J.W.	6	61	L	8	69	98	B17	CH E	NOTRE DAME61			
373	WHITSETT, J.B.	6	61	L	7	76	181	B18	E E	DUKE61			
374	BARKER, B.C.	7	61	L	10	67	75	B19	E E	TEXAS61			
375	KARP, S.S.	7	61	L	9	63	26	B18	E E	TUFTS61			
376	LEDGETT, R.A.	7	61	R	6	86	299	B18	E E	STANFORD61			
377	SCHLANGER, L.M.	7	61	L	6	66	59	B19	CH E	ROCHESTER61			
378	EASLEY, C.E.	8	61	L	8	66	60	B18	CH E	PURDUE61			
379	GREGG, M.C.	8	61	L	8	66	60	B18	PHYS	YALE61			
380	HUBERMAN, B.N.	8	61	L	6	66	58	B18	E E	COLUMBIA60	E E	UNIV LONDON61	

TABLE 1: NAVAL REACTORS TECHNICAL PERSONNEL 1946–1961

NO	NAME	TO NR		FR NR	MO AT NR	SPECIAL TRNING	BA/BS	COLLEGE	MA/MS	COLLEGE	PHD/OTH	COLLEGE
381	TATUM, L.I.	8	61	93	379	B17	E E	OKLAHOMA61				
384	PINKERTON, ROY T.	10	61	L	6 64	32	MIT59	N PHYS	TEXAS50	NA/ME	MIT59	

TABLE 2: NAVAL REACTORS ADMINISTRATIVE & FISCAL PERSONNEL 1946–1961

NO	NAME	TO NR	FR NR	AT NR	MO SPECIAL TRNING	BA/BS	COLLEGE	MAMS	COLLEGE	PHD/OTH	COLLEGE
30	THOMPSON, LUCILE S.	3 50	L 1 54	46	WVE	JOUR/SCI	STANDFORD44				
43	EVANS, WILLIAM H.	51	L 55	48	ADMIN						
54	SMALL, WILLIE (KLEIN)	10 51	L 6 55	44	WVE	ELEM ED	WSTCHSTER ST51				
55	PANOFF, KAY (BECK)	10 51	L 10 53	24	WVE	MATH	ST JOSEPH50				
60	WEYANT, ETH. ADEL.	3 52	L 9 55	42	WVE	BIOL/CHE	DUKE36				
78	RICHARDSON, WM. C.	4 53	L 1 60	81	SC	NAV SCI	USNA42				
79	LASCARA, VINCE. A.	4 53	L 7 64	135	SC	ECON/ACC	WM & MARY42	MBA	STANFORD51		
80	HASHAGEN, RALPH L.	4 53	L 4 56	36	SC	M E	TEXAS38	BUS ADM	HARVARD45	MBA	STANFORD51
81	KAUFMAN, SID	5 53	R 1 85	380	CIV	ACCOUN	COLORADO49				
82	POLATTY, MARG.M.	5 53	L 10 55	29	WVE	ECON	WM & MARY42				
83	SCROGGINS, JEAN	5 53	R 2 82	345	CIV	NONE	BOB JONES UNIV				
87	CASE, GEORGE O.	6 53	L 6 58	60	SC	NAV SCI	NOTRE DAME45				
98	LEONE, THERESA	12 53	R 12 69	192	WVE	NONE	NONE				
102	FISHER, ROBT. D.	1 54	L 12 58	59	SC	NAV SCI	NORTHWESTERN46				
103	LEWIS. RAY. O.	4 54	L 10 60	78	SC	NAV SCI	MARQUETTE45				
127	MCCORD, LAPS D.	55	L 59		ADMIN						
133	MURPHY, GEO. A.	2 55	L 1 61	71	SC	ECON	VILLANOVA48				
135	BELLAS, MARY CATH.	4 55	L 5 58	37	WVE	POLY SCI	FLORIDA STATE42				
136	CHANCE, CARL	4 55	L 7 60	63	SC	NONE	V-12				
137	RENFRO, ED. E.	4 55	L 8 61	76	SC	NONE		MBA	HARVARD47		
148	JOHNSON, HERB. L.	6 55	L 5 60	59	SC	ACCOUN	U SO CAL43	MBA	STANFORD52		
153	WRIGHT, JOHN E.	7 55	L 7 60	60	SC						
162	HIGGINS, SALLY P. (HARBAUGH)	10 55	L 3 58	29	WVE	HISTORY	WSLEYAN(GA)53				
170	WALTHER, FRED. W.	12 55	L 6 60	54	SC	BUS ADM	CAL BERKELEY44	MBA	HARVARD47		
178	STEWART, ROBT W.	2 56	L 2 61	60	SC	ECON	MISSOURI STATE	MBA	HARVARD		
184	PORTER, ROBT C.	4 56	L 4 60	48	SC	NAV SCI	USNA45				

TABLE 2: NAVAL REACTORS ADMINISTRATIVE & FISCAL PERSONNEL 1946-1961

NO	NAME	TO NR	FR NR	MO AT NR	SPECIAL TRNING	BA/BS	COLLEGE	MA/MS	COLLEGE	PHD/OTH	COLLEGE
202	HARBAUGH, NORM. R.	12 56	L 6 61	54	SC	BUS ED	COLUMBIA50	ED ADM	STANFORD51	MBA	HARVARD55
210	LANING, GEO. H.	3 57	L 1 62	58	SC	NAV SCI	USNA47				
211	MERCADANTE, JAS.A.	3 57	L 3 62	60	SC	NONE	NONE				
216	CLEMENT, EARL G.	5 57	L 6 62	61	SC	ECON	OHIO STATE37	ECON	COLUMBIA38	MBA	HARVARD47
217	FOSTER, PAUL L.	5 57	L 8 60	39	SC	BUS ADM	NORTHWESTERN50				
243	MCCORMICK, RBT. J.	9 57	L 3 63	66	SC	BUS ADM	S CAROLINA53	MBA	HARVARD56		
244	ZOOK, JOAN ELIZ.	10 57	L 5 61	43	WVE	MATH	ALLEGHENY COLL49				
245	HENN, CARL L.	10 57	L 9 62	59	SC	BUS ADM	NORTHWESTERN44	MBA	HARVARD47		
247	WOODFIN, KEN. L.	11 57	L 8 65	93	SC	BUS ADM	SMU46	MBA	STANFORD55		
255	DILORENZO, JULIA J.	3 58	L 1 61	34	WVE	ROM LANG	BOSTON UNIV55				
256	BASHE, KATHL. ANN (HENSELER)	3 58	L 12 60	33	WVE	EDUCATIO	MARION COLL54				
257	FOREHAND, JOS. L.	5 58	L 6 64	73	SC	ECON	MERCER48	MBA	MICHIGAN51		
258	HENSELER, RICH. C.	5 58	L 11 62	54	SC	NAV SCI	USNA55				
259	JERAULD, WM. E.	5 58	L 6 63	61	SC	NAV SCI	USNA55				
276	SHEPARD, JOHN. C.	6 58	L 6 63	60	SC	ENGR	MINNESOTA46	MBA	STANFORD56		
288	BECKLER, S.	59	R 72		ADMIN						
313	GREER, MEL C.	6 59	L 8 72	158	SC	ACCOUN	ARIZONA STATE52				
314	POWELL, WM. M.	6 59	L 8 64	62	SC		COLORADO55				
315	SULLIVAN, PATR. D.	6 59	L 7 63	49	SC	MATH/EDU	MIAMI(OHIO)55				
316	TAYLOR, ROBT. R.	6 59	L 8 64	62	SC	BUS	MIAMI(OHIO)55				
350	RYAN, WM. J.	8 60	L 5 65	57	SC	NAV SCI	USNA52				
352	GHOSTLEY, GARY D.	9 60	L 11 63	38	SC	ECON	MINNEAPOLIS51		NAVY PG SCH		
353	VIRDEN, FRANK S.	9 60	L 1 62	16	SC	POLY SCI	DUKE55				
354	SARBAUGH, RACH. J.	12 60	R 5 75	173	WVE	ENGL/SPN	N CAROLINA52	EDUC	N CAROLINA56		
355	DUPES, YVNNE M.	1 61	L 6 64	41	WVE	ZOOL	MCCALLISTER53	MED TEC	MCCALLISTER54		
360	SMITH, F.D.	3 61	L 6 64	39	SC	NAV SCI	USNA56				

TABLE 2: NAVAL REACTORS ADMINISTRATIVE & FISCAL PERSONNEL 1946–1961

NO	NAME	TO NR		FR NR		AT NR	MO SPECIAL TRNING	BA/BS	COLLEGE	MA/MS	COLLEGE	PHD/OTH	COLLEGE
361	WHITE, JAS.A.	4	61	L 6	66	62	SC	NAV SCI	USNA56				
382	HURT, R.O.	8	61	L 8	66	60	SC	ECON	GRINNELL50	MBA	MICHIGAN51		
383	KUHLMANN, D.H.	8	61	L 5	66	57	SC	NAV SCI	USNA53				
385	JOHNSON, M.J.	11	61	L 5	66	54	SC	BUS ADM	BEREA53				

TABLE 3: CIVIL ENGINEER CORPS OFFICERS IN NR PROGRAM

NO	NAME	TO NR		FR NR		MO AT N	SPECIAL TRNING	BA/BS	COLLEGE	MA/M	COLLEGE	PHD/OTH	COLLEGE
29	McGARAGHAN, J. J.	2	50	1	54	47	CEC	C E	CAL BERKELEY34				
34	BOOTHE, PERRY M.	7	50	7	54	48	CEC	C E	CAL TECH31	C E	CAL TECH32		
36	SCHAFER, CARL J.	7	50	7	55	60	CEC	C E	CLARKSON31				
63	DIBERTO, EDWARD T.	6	52	4	57	58	CEC	C E	TUFTS43				
65	MALLORY, C.W.	6	52	11	58	77	CEC	M E	COLORADO46	C E	RPI50(BS)		
74	BARKER, J.H.jr	12	52	4	58	64	CEC	NAV SCI	USNA36	C E	RPI41/42	BIORDIOL	CAL BERKELEY52
118	ISELIN, DONALD G.	8	54	7	58	47	CEC	NAV SCI	USNA46	C E	RPI48(MS)		
121	STURMAN, W.H.	8	54	3	58	43	CEC	C E	N MEX STATE48	C E	ILLINOIS54		
158	GALBRAITH, FRANK W	9	55	L	58	27	CEC	M E		C E	RPI(BS)	C E	ILLINOIS55
160	LOCKE, HARRY A.	9	55	6	59	45	CEC	C E	OKLAHOMA46	C E	ILLINOIS55		
174	GREGORY, GEO. W.	1	56	11	60	58	CEC	E E	WORCESTER44	C E	RPI54(BS)		
237	LOEFFLER, HAL H jr	7	57	12	59	29	CEC	NAV SCI	USNA44	C E	RPI48		
248	ERICKSON, J.A.		58	L	61	36	CEC	C E	SYRACUSE58	C E	MICHIGAN		
254	ANDERSON, GORD. A.	3	58	6	64	75	CEC	NAV SCI	USNA48B	C E	RPI52(BS)	ENG MGT	RPI61(MS)
297	WYNNE, WM. E.	3	59	6	66	87	CEC	NAV SCI	USNA49	C E	RPI51(BS)		

ALPHABETICAL CROSSLISTING — ALL NR PERSONNEL

NO	NAME	NO	NAME	NO	NAME	NO	NAME	NO	NAME
363	ALLYN, E.G.	114	CALLAHAN, F.J.	222	DURNAN, DENNIS D.	379	GREGG, M.C.	117	HUMPHREY, WM. S.
343	ALRICK, R.D.	123	CALVERT, JIM F.	193	DYER, J.C.	174	GREGORY, GEO. W.	382	HURT, R.O.
8	AMOROSI, ALFRED	317	CAMBELL, WM.ED.	277	D'APPOLITO, J.A.	182	GRIDER, A. DOUG.	278	HUSTED, J.M.
299	ANCKONIE, A.	333	CARLSON, F.P.	378	EASLEY, C.E.	225	GRIFFIN, R.F.	46	ILTIS, TED J.
124	ANDERSON, BILL R.	192	CARPENTER, J.W.	6	EMERSON, GEO.B.	67	GRIGG, JACK C.	118	ISELIN, DONALD G.
254	ANDERSON, GORDON	106	CASE, EDSON G.	264	ENGEL, WALT. P.	239	HALEY, J.V.	47	JACOBSON, JEROME
188	ARROWSMITH, PET. D.	87	CASE, GEORGE O.	265	ERICKSON, B.T.	327	HALL, A.E.	259	JERAULD, WM. E.
374	BARKER, B.C.	218	CAVE, JAS. W.	248	ERICKSON, J.A.	130	HAMMOND, HERB.C.	213	JILG, E.T.
22	BARKER, J.A.	136	CHANCE, CARL	43	EVANS, WILLIAM H.	226	HANESSIAN, S.J.	148	JOHNSON, HERB. L.
74	BARKER, J.H.jr	365	CHESSICK, A.W.	115	FALCI, FRANK P.	202	HARBAUGH, NORM	141	JOHNSON, LYNN E.
105	BARNES, W.C.	44	CLARK, ART H.	49	FAUROT, G. WES	131	HARRIS, W.N.	385	JOHNSON, M.J.
129	BARON, RAY. G.	110	CLARK, PHIL. R.	223	FEINROTH, HERBERT	140	HARRISON, DWIGHT	366	JOHNSON, R.W.
300	BARONDES, E.D.	191	CLAYTOR, RICK A.	238	FICK, T.R.	45	HARTWELL, ROBT.	284	JONES, H.L.
256	BASHE, K.A. (HENSELER)	216	CLEMENT, EARL G.	25	FINKELSTEIN, PHIL	80	HASHAGEN, RALPH	330	JORDAN, M.H.
289	BASS, R.W.	75	CLENDINNING, W.R.	224	FISHER, G.D.	84	HAUSSLER, W.M.	183	JUDD, P.V.
112	BASSETT, O.E.(SAM)	89	COCHRAN, J.C.	102	FISHER, ROBT. D.	91	HAWKINS, R.A.	375	KARP, S.S.
70	BAUSER, ED. J.	219	COLE, G. FRANK III	212	FLEMING, J.H.	122	HAYES, PAUL W.	81	KAUFMAN, SID
298	BECKLEAN, W.R.	181	COLE, NOMAN M.	64	FLOOD, THOS. P.	290	HAYMAN, R.B.	85	KAY, ROBERT
288	BECKLER, S.	344	COLLINGHAM, R.E.	128	FLYNN, CHARLIE W	349	HEARN, J.J.	334	KEISTER, J.C.
135	BELLAS, MARY CATH.	28	CONDON, JOS. F.	88	FLYNN, T.A.	206	HEILER, F.J.	269	KELLER, A.J.
260	BELSER, T.M. jr	107	COTTER, MAURICE J.	204	FOERSTER, PAUL A.	71	HEINTZ, JOHN	228	KELLER, K.H.
251	BLATCHFORD, J.D.	139	COUCHMAN, DON. L.	257	FOREHAND, JOS. L.	180	HEMMER, WM. C.	19	KELLEY, ARCH. P.
7	BLIZARD, EVERITT P.	37	CRAWFORD, JACK W.	179	FORSSELL, ALAN G.	267	HEMMINGHAUS,R.R.	99	KELLY, HENRY R.
149	BLOCK, ALAN J.	220	DAUGHERTY, J.D.	146	FORSSELL, R. MARK	227	HENDRICKSON, TOM	207	KENNEDY, J.E.
199	BODE, H.J. jr	35	DEBOLT, H.E.(TOM)	217	FOSTER, PAUL L.	245	HENN, CARL L.	142	KENNEDY, R.S.
154	BOOTH, MERSON	185	DELAPAZ, ARMANDO	86	FRALEY, RAY. F.	258	HENSELER, RICH. C.	126	KENNEY, M.C.
34	BOOTHE, PERRY M.	359	DENEUI, R.J.	51	FRANCIS, ART E.	320	HERKNER, R.T.	31	KERZE, FRANK
301	BORLICK, R.L.	63	DIBERTO, EDWARD T.	158	GALBRAITH, FRANK W.	321	HERMAN, J.M.	335	KEY, P.L.
261	BRANDEL, J.P.	5	DICK, RAY H.	163	GAMBELLO, ANTH. V.	268	HEWITT, W.M.	38	KINTNER, ED. E.
93	BRODSKY, ROBT. S.	90	DICKINSON, R.W.	318	GARDNER, R.	162	HIGGINS, S.P.	147	KOCH, URIAH H.
302	BROLIN, E.C.	39	DIGNAN, PAUL ELMER	15	GEIGER, LAWTON D.	293	HILL, A.J.	336	KOH, B.
56	BROOKS, DANIEL P.	255	DILORENZO, JULIA J.	352	GHOSTLEY, GARY D.	116	HILL, ROBERT F.	252	KONKLIN, J.E.
113	BROOKS, DAVE M.	177	DINUNNO, JOS.J.	159	GILLILAND, FRANK	52	HINCHEY, J.J.	214	KOOYMAN, W.J.
134	BROSIUS, R.B.	356	DOHERTY, D.P.	69	GLENN, STUART VER.	291	HINDS, J.A.	205	KOSIBA, RICH. E.
262	BROWNELL, R.B.	221	DOWLING, ROBT. J.	319	GORMAN, J.A.	294	HOLLOWAY, C.A.	176	KRAM, P.
263	BROWNING, ROBT. E.	203	DRISCOLL, MIKE J.	266	GRAFTON, R.B.	303	HOLMES, J.F.	326	KROL, J.A.
364	BURGET, J.E.	2	DUNFORD, JAS.M.	18	GRANT, PAUL	362	HOUSE, EDWARD C.	383	KUHLMANN, D.H.
138	BURR, A.A.	125	DUNLAVY, VERN. A.	21	GRAY, JOHN E.	48	HOWELL, JERRY	11	KYGER, JACK A.
249	BUTEAU, B.L.	355	DUPES, YVNNE M.	313	GREER, MEL C.	380	HUBERMAN, B.N.	240	LAKEY, K.G.

NO	NAME	NO	NAME	NO	NAME	NO	NAME	NO	NAME
155	LAMARTIN, FRED. H.	143	MERRIGAN, LAWR. J.	58	PURDY, DAVID C.	33	SHAW, MILTON	292	VAN WOUDENBERG, S.G.
164	LAMBERT, JOS. L.	151	METZGER, ROBT. P.	150	QUIGLEY, HANK C.	280	SHAW, S.H.	235	VAUGHAN, JAS. W.
12	LANEY, ROBT. V.	95	MICHELS, JOHN. F.	16	RADKOWSKY, ALVIN	276	SHEPARD, JOHN. C.	353	VIRDEN, FRANK S.
215	LANG, E.M.jr	144	MILES, MURRAY E.	160	RADKOWSKY, LARRY	187	SHIELDS, JEREM. D.	209	VOSE, F.H.E.
210	LANING, GEO. H.	369	MILLER, C.A.	209	RAKER, SAM. K.	59	SHOR, S.W.W.	152	WAGNER, ED. J.
79	LASCARA, VINCE. A.	62	MINOGUE, ROBT. B.	135	RENFRO, ED. E.	332	SIERER, PAYSON D.	348	WALTERS, R.M.
20	LASPADA, J.A.	250	MOKSKI, D.J.	49	RESNICK, BERNIE T.	120	SIGNORELLI, J.A.	324	WALTERS, T.J.
376	LEDGETT, R.A.	53	MOORE, R.L.	78	RICHARDSON, WM. C.	329	SIMMONS, GERRY M	170	WALTHER, FRED. W.
295	LEE, B.A.	270	MORRISON, W.M.	171	RICINAK, MICH. DON.	100	SKOW, R.K.	312	WARD, S.R.
92	LEIGHTON, DAV. T.	230	MUGGLIN, M.G.	1	RICKOVER, H.G.	54	SMALL, WILLIE (KLEIN)	325	WEBBER, J.H.
345	LEIMONAS, S.	133	MURPHY, GEO. A.	339	RIEHM, C.E. jr	360	SMITH, F.D.	196	WEGNER, WM
98	LEONE, THERESA	77	MURPHY, JOS. A.	241	RISSER, J. BRUCE	281	SNYDER, B.J.	236	WEINER, ROBT. M.
241	LESAGE, LEO G.	10	NAYMARK, SHERM.	309	ROBERTS, P.J.	166	SPILLER, WM. C.	42	WELCH, GERALD H.
194	LEUTZ, L.H.	305	NELSON, G.A.	131	ROBINSON, ROD. A.	272	SPRIGG, M.W.	60	WEYANT, ETH. ADEL.
156	LEVINE, SAUL	72	NELSON, N. ROLAND	185	ROBNETT, J.D. IV	233	STAEHLE, R.W.	286	WHITE, A.T.
103	LEWIS, RAY. O.	173	NELSON, OSC B "OB"	24	ROCKWELL, TED	169	STANDERFER, FRNK.R.	361	WHITE, JAS.A.
3	LIBBEY, MILES A.	328	NEWHOUSE, A.R.	4	RODDIS, LOU H.	273	STEELE, R.H.	157	WHITEHEAD, ANDY D.
331	LINDEMAN, C.F.	337	NICHOLS, J.C.	26	RODIN, MAX	178	STEWART, ROBT W.	372	WHITNEY, J.W.
229	LIVINGSTON, W.C.	108	NINE, H.D.	68	ROETHEL, D.A.H.	358	STOLLMEYER, M.A.	373	WHITSETT, J.B.
96	LLOYD, REBECCAH A.	97	NIXON, S. REED	108	ROGERS, GENE L.	167	STOLZENBERG, MLT.D.	342	WILBUR, P.J.
160	LOCKE, HARRY A.	165	NORMANN, JAMES R.	100	ROOF, R.R.	121	STURMAN, W.H.	17	WILKINSON, E.P.
237	LOEFFLER, HAL H jr	351	OATES, K.L.	271	ROSSI, C.E.	145	SULLIVAN, J.J.	197	WILKINSON, R.F.
367	MAGEE, G.T.	338	OLDFATHER, D.O.	9	ROTH, ELI B.	315	SULLIVAN, PATR. D.	253	WILLE, DON. JAY
368	MAGEE, J.E.	40	O'GRADY, JOHN F.	348	RYAN, WM. J.	66	SULLIVAN, R.P.	246	WILLIAMS, JOHN G.
65	MALLORY, C.W.	283	PADGETT, CLARENCE	353	SARBAUGH, RACH. J.	73	SWEEK, R.F.	14	WILSON, WM. H.
304	MALONEY, J.M.	322	PANCIERA, V.W.	310	SAVAGE, R.L.	168	SWENSON, KARL E.	296	WOLL, S.A.
23	MANDIL, I.HARRY	55	PANOFF, KAY (BECK)	36	SCHAFER, CARL J.	381	TATUM, L.I.	247	WOODFIN, KEN. L.
57	MANIERO, DANIEL A.	32	PANOFF, ROBT	231	SCHEETZ, KARL G.	316	TAYLOR, ROBT. R.	287	WOODS, J.B.jr
76	MARCH, RICHARD J	338	PATERSON, R.W.	377	SCHLANGER, L.M.	309	TENKHOF, P.A.	153	WRIGHT, JOHN E.
27	MARKS, HOWARD. K.	322	PEARSON, J.F.	308	SCHMIDT, W.R.	274	TEVEBAUGH, C.R.	297	WYNNE, WM. E.
285	MARTIN, W.L. III	170	PERMAN, BERN	189	SCHMOKER, DAN. N.	109	THOMAS, CHUCK R.	198	YOUNG, WM. H.
195	MATHESON, J.C.	383	PINKERTON, ROY T.	41	SCHNEIDER, OSCAR	234	THOMAS, GEO. ADEN	190	ZIEBOLD, T.O.
127	MCCORD, LAPS D.	369	PINNOW, D.A.	357	SCHOOLEY, L.C.	30	THOMPSON, LUCILE S.	104	ZIMMER, JOS. P.
243	MCCORMICK, RBT. J.	82	POLATTY, MARG.M.	119	SCHWENDTNER, A.H.	282	TODREAS, N.E.	244	ZOOK, JOAN ELIZ.
29	McGARAGHAN, J. J.	345	POMREHN, H.P.	279	SCOTT, D.G.	275	TRAYLOR, R.C.		
201	McKINLEY, JOHN C.	183	PORTER, ROBT C.	232	SCOTT, L.J.	310	TRIMBACH, C.G.		
61	MEALIA, JOHN E.	94	POWELL, WM. M.	94	SCOTT, RICH. G.	347	TRIMBLE, D.C.		
200	MEDEIROS, MAN. S.	299	PREZBINDOWSKI, D.L.	341	SCOVILLE, F.W.	13	TURNBAUGH, MARSH.E.		
211	MERCADANTE, JAS.A.	174	PUGH, R.C.	83	SCROGGINS, JEAN	311	VAN NORT, P.S.		

About the Author

Theodore Rockwell has been involved in nuclear power for nearly half a century. After completing his master's degree in chemical engineering at Princeton, he worked in a Process Improvement Task Force at the war-time atomic bomb project at Oak Ridge, Tennessee. After the war he transferred to the Oak Ridge National Laboratory and became head of the Radiation Shield Engineering Group. In 1949 then-Captain H. G. Rickover hired him to work in the Naval Nuclear Propulsion Program, where he became director of the Nuclear Technology Divisions, which handled problems posed by reactor coolants. In late 1954 he was made technical director, responsible to Admiral Rickover for helping to develop criteria, procedures, and facilities for safe operation of nuclear-powered naval vessels and the first commercial central station nuclear power plant. In 1964 he and two colleagues set up the engineering firm MPR Associates, Inc. He is now an engineer in private practice.

Mr. Rockwell has received numerous awards and has written extensively. He is co-author of *Arms Control Agreements* (Johns Hopkins Press, 1968), which was used in connection with U.S.-USSR talks at the White House; articles include "Frontier Life Among the Atom Splitters" (*Saturday Evening Post*, Dec. 8, 1945), "Bred for Fury" (*True*, July 1946), and "Heresy, Excommunication and Other Weeds in the Garden of Science" (*New Realities*, Dec. 1981).

The **Naval Institute Press** is the book-publishing arm of the U.S. Naval Institute, a private, nonprofit society for sea service professionals and others who share an interest in naval and maritime affairs. Established in 1873 at the U.S. Naval Academy in Annapolis, Maryland, where its offices remain, today the Naval Institute has more than 100,000 members worldwide.

Members of the Naval Institute receive the influential monthly magazine *Proceedings* and discounts on fine nautical prints, ship and aircraft photos, and subscriptions to the quarterly *Naval History* magazine. They also have access to the transcripts of the Institute's Oral History Program and get discounted admission to any of the Institute-sponsored seminars offered around the country.

The Naval Institute's book-publishing program, begun in 1898 with basic guides to naval practices, has broadened its scope in recent years to include books of more general interest. Now the Naval Institute Press publishes more than sixty titles each year, ranging from how-to books on boating and navigation to battle histories, biographies, ship and aircraft guides, and novels. Institute members receive discounts on the Press's nearly 400 books in print.

Full-time students are eligible for special half-price membership rates. Life memberships are also available.

For a free catalog describing Naval Institute Press books currently available, and for further information about U.S. Naval Institute membership, please write to:

Membership & Communications Department
U.S. Naval Institute
118 Maryland Avenue
Annapolis, Maryland 21402-5035

Or call, toll-free, (800) 233-USNI.

KEY DATES

The leftmost columns list: EISENHOWER (President); THOMAS, GATES, FRANKE (SecNav); CARNEY, BURKE (Chief, NavOps); LEGGETT, MUMMA, JAMES (Chief, BuShips); STRAUSS, McCONE (Chm, AEC/ERDA/DoE).

30 Dec	The *Nautilus* reaches initial criticality.
17 Jan **1955**	The *Nautilus* puts to sea for first time.
26 Apr	Rickover picks uranium oxide in zirconium tubing for Shippingport fuel.
May	The *Nautilus* cruises New London to San Juan, 1,300 miles in 84 hours.
Jun	The *Seawolf* prototype simulates a 2,000 mile continuous high-power run.
21 Jul	The *Seawolf* launched.
21 Jul	*Skate* keel laid.
Jul	The *Seawolf* prototype springs a steam generator leak.
Sep	**1st Atoms for Peace Conference, Geneva.**
Oct	Defense Department requests AEC develop high-speed submarine plant.
25 Jun **1956**	The *Seawolf* reaches initial criticality.
26 Oct	**International Atomic Energy Agency (IAEA) established.**
Dec	Navy drops Jupiter missile project, starts Polaris Project.
Feb **1957**	The *Seawolf* initial sea trials.
Mar	Basic parameters of Polaris submarine set.
Apr	The *Nautilus* refueled—first core had traveled 62,562 miles.
Jun	CNO Burke approves Polaris submarine ships characteristics.
Aug	**USSR launches intercontinental ballistic missile (ICBM).**
Sep	Advisory Comm. on Reactor Safeguards incorporated into law.
4 Oct	**USSR launches sputnik.**
27 Oct	The *Skate* initial sea trials.
2 Dec	Shippingport Atomic Power Station reaches initial criticality.
18 Dec	First commercial electricity from Shippingport.
23 Dec	The *Skate* commissioned.
12 Aug **1958**	The *Nautilus* completes Hawaii/Pole/England trip.
Aug	Congress votes medal for Rickover. Navy makes him a vice admiral.
6 Oct	The *Seawolf* completes 60-day submerged run, 13,761 miles.
12 Dec	The *Seawolf* starts conversion to PWR—71,611 miles on sodium plant.
Mar **1959**	Rickover publishes "Education and Freedom."
8 Mar	The *Skipjack* initial sea trials.
17 Mar	The *Skate* surfaces at the North Pole.
28 May	The *Nautilus* first overhaul, second refueling, Portsmouth Naval Shipyard.
9 Jun	First Polaris sub launched.
24 Jul	Rickover tours USSR.
18 Aug	Rickover publishes "Report on Russia."
Aug	McCone considers transferring AEC's safety responsibilities to Navy.
30 Dec	First Polaris sub commissioned.